Radical Feminism

Radical Feminism

edited by

Anne Koedt · Ellen Levine · Anita Rapone

NYT

QUADRANGLE/
The New York Times Book Co.

Library of Congress Catalog Card Number: 72-91380
International Standard Book Number: 0-8129-6220-6
Fourth paperback printing, April 1976

Contents

Preface

The contemporary feminist movement began in the late 1960's and has grown enormously in the six years of its existence both in the numbers of women who have participated in feminist activities and in the nature and scope of its analytic writings. In its most general formulation the goal of the radical feminist movement is the complete elimination of the sex role system. The articles in this collection, although each covers a specific aspect of sexism, all reflect this basic feminist goal.

The book is divided into five sections. The first, *Liberating History*, briefly sketches the history of the feminist struggle from its radical beginnings in the 19th century when women weren't even allowed to speak in public. Although this anthology is primarily concerned with the analysis and activities of the current movement, the awareness that women's history needs "liberating" makes such a section currently relevant.

Sexism is a political system and basic to an understanding of how it works is the recognition of women as a political class. In contrast to conventionally accepted views of women, feminism argues that an individual woman's "problems" are not in fact idiosyncratic, but rather are a product of sexist ideology and institutions. Section two, *Women's Experience*, reflects this understanding of the political nature of what has always been deemed personal.

Section three, *Theory and Analysis,* is composed of articles that examine in more broadly analytic terms the areas of feminist concern. Fundamental subjects such as abortion, marriage, housework, rape, law, socialization, sex, psychology, and religion, are examined. It is important to note that since sexism is so basic and pervasive an ideology, feminists are continuously extending their critique into areas hitherto unrecognized as "political." This process of an evolving critique has in part been possible because, unlike some other political movements, feminism has not been burdened by an early, narrowly defined theoretical structure. Rather, there has been a much more organic relationship between analysis and activity: theory evolves from and contributes to the growth of the movement.

Section four, *Building a Movement,* covers such intramovement concerns as the consciousness raising process, internal group structure, and the feminist debate with the Left. It also includes several major manifestos.

The last section, *The Arts,* reflects the growing feminist interest in this area. Male prejudice against female writers, the portrayal of women in movies, the function of diaries, and the writings of several contemporary women authors are discussed.

The purpose in selecting and organizing this anthology was to present primary source material not so much about as from the radical feminist movement. Although such a collection of writings by definition constitutes a kind of overview of the growth of the movement, the articles are more a product than an explanation of that political process.

Many of the articles included in *Radical Feminism* previously appeared in the first three issues of *Notes,* a yearly journal of writings from the feminist movement. We would like to thank all of the authors in this anthology for their permissions to reprint their articles.

New York City   A.K., E.L., A.R.
June, 1972

Radical Feminism

Liberating History

The First Feminists

by Judith Hole and Ellen Levine

Judith Hole and Ellen Levine are the authors of Rebirth of Feminism, *a study of the resurgence of feminism in the United States. The book is a history and analysis of the origins, organizational development, philosophy, issues, and activities of the new women's movement. The following excerpt, the introductory chapter, is a brief discussion of the first feminist movement in America in the nineteenth and early twentieth centuries. It is not meant to be a detailed description of the earlier movement, but rather to serve as an indication that the contemporary women's movement has a much ignored historical predecessor.*

The contemporary women's movement is not the first such movement in American history to offer a wide-ranging feminist critique of society. In fact, much of what seems "radical" in contemporary feminist analysis parallels the critique made by the feminists of the nineteenth century. Both the early and the contemporary feminists have engaged in a fundamental reexamination of the role of women in all spheres of life, and of the relationships of men and women in all social, political, economic and cultural institutions. Both have defined women as an oppressed group and have traced the origin of women's subjugation to male-defined and male-dominated social institutions and value systems.

When the early feminist movement emerged in the nineteenth century, the "woman issue" was extensively debated in the national press, in political gatherings, and from church pulpits. The women's groups, their platforms, and their leaders, although not always well received or understood, were extremely well known. Until recently, however, that early feminist movement has been only cursorily discussed in American history textbooks, and then only in terms of the drive for suffrage. Even a brief reading of early feminist writings and of the few histories that have dealt specifically with the woman's movement (as it was called then) reveals that the drive for suffrage became the single focus of the movement only after several decades of a more multi-issued campaign for women's equality.

The woman's movement emerged during the 1800's. It was a time of geographic expansion, industrial development, growth of social reform movements, and a general intellectual ferment with a philosophical emphasis on individual freedom, the "rights of man," and universal education. In fact, some of the earliest efforts to extend opportunities to women were made in the field of education. In 1833, Oberlin became the first college to open its doors to both men and women. Although female education at Oberlin was regarded as necessary to ensure the development of good and proper wives and mothers, the open admission policy paved the way for the founding of other schools, some devoted entirely to women's education.[1] Much of the ground-breaking work in education was done by Emma Willard, who had campaigned vigorously for educational facilities for women beginning in the early 1820's. Frances Wright, one of the first women orators, was also a strong advocate of education for women. She viewed women as an oppressed group and argued that, "Until women assume the place in society which good sense and good feeling alike assign to them, human improvement must advance but feebly."[2] Central to her discussion of the inequalities between the sexes was a particular concern with the need for equal educational training for women.

It was in the abolition movement of the 1830's, however, that the woman's rights movement as such had its political origins. When women began working in earnest for the abolition of slavery, they quickly learned that they could not function as political equals with their male abolitionist friends. Not only were they barred from membership in some organizations, but they had to wage an uphill battle for the right simply to speak in public. Sarah and Angelina Grimké, daughters of a South Carolina slaveholding family, were among the first to fight this battle. Early in their lives the sisters left

South Carolina, moved north, and began to speak out publicly on the abolition issue. Within a short time they drew the wrath of different sectors of society. A Pastoral letter from the Council of the Congregationalist Ministers of Massachusetts typified the attack:

> The appropriate duties and influence of woman are clearly stated in the New Testament. . . . The power of woman is her dependence, flowing from the consciousness of that weakness which God has given her for her protection. . . . When she assumes the place and tone of man as a public reformer . . . she yields the power which God has given her . . . and her character becomes unnatural.[3]

The brutal and unceasing attacks (sometimes physical) on the women convinced the Grimkés that the issues of freedom for slaves and freedom for women were inextricably linked. The women began to speak about both issues, but because of the objections from male abolitionists who were afraid that discussions of woman's rights would "muddy the waters," they often spoke about the "woman question" as a separate issue. (In fact, Lucy Stone, an early feminist and abolitionist, lectured on abolition on Saturdays and Sundays and on women's rights during the week.)

In an 1837 letter to the President of the Boston Female Anti-Slavery Society—by that time many female anti-slavery societies had been established in response to the exclusionary policy of the male abolitionist groups—Sarah Grimké addressed herself directly to the question of woman's status:

> All history attests that man has subjugated woman to his will, used her as a means to promote his selfish gratification, to minister to his sensual pleasure, to be instrumental in promoting his comfort; but never has he desired to elevate her to that rank she was created to fill. He has done all he could to debase and enslave her mind; and now he looks triumphantly on the ruin he has wrought, and says, the being he has thus deeply injured is his inferior. . . . But I ask no favors for my sex. . . . All I ask of our brethren is, that they will take their feet from off our necks and permit us to stand upright on that ground which God designed us to occupy.[4]

The Grimkés challenged both the assumption of the "natural superiority of man" and the social institutions predicated on that assumption. For example, in her "Letters on the Equality of the Sexes," Sarah Grimké argued against both religious dogma and the institution of marriage. Two brief examples are indicative:

... Adam's ready acquiescence with his wife's proposal, does not savor much of that superiority *in strength of mind,* which is arrogated by man.[5]

... man has exercised the most unlimited and brutal power over woman, in the peculiar character of husband—a word in most countries synonymous with tyrant.... Woman, instead of being elevated by her union with man, which might be expected from an alliance with a superior being, is in reality lowered. She generally loses her individuality, her independent character, her moral being. She becomes absorbed into him, and henceforth is looked at, and acts through the medium of her husband.[6]

They attacked as well the manifestations of "male superiority" in the employment market. In a letter "On the Condition of Women in the United States" Sarah Grimké wrote of:

... the disproportionate value set on the time and labor of men and of women. A man who is engaged in teaching, can always, I believe, command a higher price for tuition than a woman—even when he teaches the same branches, and is not in any respect superior to the woman.... [Or] for example, in tailoring, a man has twice, or three times as much for making a waistcoat or pantaloons as a woman, although the work done by each may be equally good.[7]

The abolition movement continued to expand, and in 1840 a World Anti-Slavery Convention was held in London. The American delegation included a group of women, among them Lucretia Mott and Elizabeth Cady Stanton. In Volume I of the *History of Woman Suffrage,* written and edited by Stanton, Susan B. Anthony, and Matilda Joslyn Gage, the authors note that the mere presence of women delegates produced an "excitement and vehemence of protest and denunciation [that] could not have been greater, if the news had come that the French were about to invade England."[8] The women were relegated to the galleries and prohibited from participating in any of the proceedings. That society at large frowned upon women participating in political activities was one thing; that the leading male radicals, those most concerned with social inequalities, should also discriminate against women was quite another. The events at the world conference reinforced the women's growing awareness that the battle for the abolition of Negro slavery could never be won without a battle for the abolition of woman's slavery:

As Lucretia Mott and Elizabeth Cady Stanton wended their way arm in arm down Great Queen Street that night, reviewing the exciting scenes of the day, they agreed to hold a woman's rights convention on their return to America, as the men to whom they had just listened had manifested their great need of some education on that question.[9]

Mott and Stanton returned to America and continued their abolitionist work as well as pressing for state legislative reforms on woman's property and family rights. Although the women had discussed the idea of calling a public meeting on woman's rights, the possibility did not materialize until eight years after the London Convention. On July 14, 1848, they placed a small notice in the *Seneca* (New York) *County Courier* announcing a "Woman's Rights Convention." Five days later, on July 19 and 20, some three hundred interested women and men, coming from as far as fifty miles, crowded into the small Wesleyan Chapel (now a gas station) and approved a Declaration of Sentiments (modeled on the Declaration of Independence) and twelve Resolutions. The delineation of issues in the Declaration bears a startling resemblance to contemporary feminist writings. Some excerpts are illustrative:[10]

> We hold these truths to be self-evident: that all men and women are created equal; that they are endowed by their Creator with certain inalienable rights; that among these are life, liberty, and the pursuit of happiness. . . .
> The history of mankind is a history of repeated injuries and usurpations on the part of man toward woman, having in direct object the establishment of an absolute tyranny over her. To prove this, let facts be submitted to a candid world. . . .
> He has compelled her to submit to laws, in the formation of which she has no voice. . . .
> He has made her, if married, in the eye of the law, civilly dead.
> He has monopolized nearly all the profitable employments, and from those she is permitted to follow, she receives but a scanty remuneration. He closes against her all the avenues to wealth and distinction which he considers most honorable to himself. As a teacher of theology, medicine, or law, she is not known.
> He allows her in church, as well as State, but a subordinate position, claiming Apostolic authority for her exclusion from the ministry, and, with some exceptions, from any public participation in the affairs of the Church.
> He has created a false public sentiment by giving to the world a different code of morals for men and women, by which moral delinquencies which exclude women from society, are not only tolerated, but deemed of little account in man.
> He has usurped the prerogative of Jehovah himself, claiming it as

his right to assign for her a sphere of action, when that belongs
to her conscience and to her God.

He has endeavored, in every way that he could, to destroy her confidence in her own powers, to lessen her self-respect, and to
make her willing to lead a dependent and abject life.

Included in the list of twelve resolutions was one which read: "*Resolved*, That it is the duty of the women of this country to secure to
themselves their sacred right to the elective franchise."

Although the Seneca Falls Convention is considered the official
beginning of the woman's suffrage movement, it is important to re-
iterate that the goal of the early woman's rights movement was not
limited to the demand for suffrage. In fact, the suffrage resolution
was included only after lengthy debate, and was the only resolution
not accepted unanimously. Those participants at the Convention
who actively opposed the inclusion of the suffrage resolution:

> ... feared a demand for the right to vote would defeat others they
> deemed more rational, and make the whole movement ridiculous.
> But Mrs. Stanton and Frederick Douglass seeing that the power to
> choose rulers and make laws, was the right by which all others
> could be secured, persistently advocated the resolution. . . .[11]

Far more important to most of the women at the Convention was
their desire to gain control of their property and earnings, guardian-
ship of their children, rights to divorce, etc. Notwithstanding the
disagreements at the Convention, the Seneca Falls meeting was of
great historical significance. As Flexner has noted:

> [The women] themselves were fully aware of the nature of the
> step they were taking; today's debt to them has been inadequately
> acknowledged. . . . Beginning in 1848 it was possible for women
> who rebelled against the circumstances of their lives, to know that
> they were not alone—although often the news reached them only
> through a vitriolic sermon or an abusive newspaper editorial. But
> a movement had been launched which they could either join, or
> ignore, that would leave its imprint on the lives of their daughters
> and of women throughout the world.[12]

From 1848 until the beginning of the Civil War, Woman's Rights
Conventions were held nearly every year in different cities in the
East and Midwest. The 1850 Convention in Salem, Ohio:

> ... had one peculiar characteristic. It was officered entirely by
> women; not a man was allowed to sit on the platform, to speak,

or vote. *Never did men so suffer.* They implored just to say a word; but no; the President was inflexible—no man should be heard. If one meekly arose to make a suggestion he was at once ruled out of order. For the first time in the world's history, men learned how it felt to sit in silence when questions in which they were interested were under discussion.[13]

As the woman's movement gained in strength, attacks upon it became more vitriolic. In newspaper editorials and church sermons anti-feminists argued vociferously that the public arena was not the proper place for women. In response to such criticism, Stanton wrote in an article in the Rochester, New York *National Reformer:*

> If God has assigned a sphere to man and one to woman, we claim the right to judge ourselves of His design in reference to *us,* and we accord to man the same privilege. . . . We have all seen a man making a jackass of himself in the pulpit, at the bar, or in our legislative halls. . . . Now, is it to be wondered at that woman has some doubts about the present position assigned her being the true one, when her every-day experience shows her that man makes such fatal mistakes in regard to himself?[14]

It was abundantly clear to the women that they could not rely on the pulpit or the "establishment" press for either factual or sympathetic reportage; nor could they use the press as a means to disseminate their ideas. As a result they depended on the abolitionist papers of the day, and in addition founded a number of independent women's journals including *The Lily, The Una, Woman's Advocate, Pittsburgh Visiter* [*sic*], etc.

One of the many issues with which the women activists were concerned was dress reform. Some began to wear the "bloomer" costume (a misnomer since Amelia Bloomer, although an advocate of the loose-fitting dress, was neither its originator nor the first to wear it) in protest against the tight-fitting and singularly uncomfortable cinched-waisted stays and layers of petticoats. However, as Flexner has noted, "The attempt at dress reform, although badly needed, was not only unsuccessful, but boomeranged and had to be abandoned."[15] Women's rights advocates became known as "bloomers" and the movement for equal rights as well as the individual women were subjected to increasing ridicule. Elizabeth Cady Stanton, one of the earliest to wear the more comfortable outfit, was one of the first to suggest its rejection. In a letter to Susan B. Anthony she wrote:

We put the dress on for greater freedom, but what is physical freedom compared with mental bondage? . . . It is not wise, Susan, to use up so much energy and feeling that way. You can put them to better use. I speak from experience.[16]

When the Civil War began in 1861, woman's rights advocates were urged to abandon their cause and support the war effort. Although Anthony and Stanton continued arguing that any battle for freedom must include woman's freedom, the woman's movement activities essentially stopped for the duration of the war. After the war and the ratification of the Thirteenth Amendment abolishing slavery (for which the women activists had campaigned vigorously), the abolitionists began to press for passage of a Fourteenth Amendment to secure the rights, privileges, and immunities of citizens (the new freedmen) under the law. In the second section of the proposed Amendment, however, the word "male" appeared, introducing a sex distinction into the Constitution for the first time. Shocked and enraged by the introduction of the word "male," the women activists mounted an extensive campaign to eliminate it. They were dismayed to find that no one, neither the Republican administration nor their old abolitionist allies, had any intention of "complicating" the campaign for Negroes' rights by advocating women's rights as well. Over and over again the women were told, "This is the Negroes' hour." The authors of *History of Woman Suffrage* analyzed the women's situation:

> During the six years they held their own claims in abeyance to the slaves of the South, and labored to inspire the people with enthusiasm for the great measures of the Republican party, they were highly honored as "wise, loyal, and clear-sighted." But again when the slaves were emancipated and they asked that women should be recognized in the reconstruction as citizens of the Republic, equal before the law, all these transcendent virtues vanished like dew before the morning sun. And thus it ever is so long as woman labors to second man's endeavors and exalt *his sex* above her own, her virtues pass unquestioned; but when she dares to demand rights and privileges for herself, her motives, manners, dress, personal appearance, character, are subjects for ridicule and detraction.[17]

The women met with the same response when they campaigned to get the word "sex" added to the proposed Fifteenth Amendment which would prohibit the denial of suffrage on account of race.[18]

As a result of these setbacks, the woman's movement assumed as its first priority the drive for woman's suffrage. It must be noted, however, that while nearly all the women activists agreed on the need for suffrage, in 1869 the movement split over ideological and tactical questions into two major factions. In May of that year, Susan B. Anthony and Elizabeth Cady Stanton organized the National Woman Suffrage Association. Six months later, Lucy Stone and others organized the American Woman Suffrage Association. The American, in an attempt to make the idea of woman's suffrage "respectable," limited its activities to that issue, and refused to address itself to any of the more "controversial" subjects such as marriage or the church. The National, on the other hand, embraced the broad cause of woman's rights of which the vote was seen primarily as a *means* of achieving those rights. During this time Anthony and Stanton founded *The Revolution,* which became one of the best known of the independent women's newspapers. The weekly journal began in January, 1868, and took as its motto, "Men, their rights and nothing more; women, their rights and nothing less." In addition to discussion of suffrage, *The Revolution* examined the institutions of marriage, the law, organized religion, etc. Moreover, the newspaper touched on "such incendiary topics as the double standard and prostitution."[19] Flexner describes the paper:

> [It] made a contribution to the women's cause out of all proportion to either its size, brief lifespan, or modest circulation. . . . Here was news not to be found elsewhere—of the organization of women typesetters, tailoresses, and laundry workers, of the first women's clubs, of pioneers in the professions, of women abroad. But *The Revolution* did more than just carry news, or set a new standard of professionalism for papers edited by and for women. It gave their movement a forum, focus, and direction. It pointed, it led, and it fought, with vigor and vehemence.[20]

The two suffrage organizations coexisted for over twenty years and used some of the same tactics in their campaigns for suffrage: lecture tours, lobbying activities, petition campaigns, etc. The American, however, focused exclusively on state-by-state action, while the National in addition pushed for a woman suffrage amendment to the Constitution. Susan B. Anthony and others also attempted to gain the vote through court decisions. The Supreme Court, however, held in 1875[21] that suffrage was not necessarily one of the privileges and immunities of citizens protected by the Fourteenth

Amendment. Thus, although women were *citizens* it was nonetheless permissible, according to the Court, to constitutionally limit the right to vote to males.

During this same period, a strong temperance movement had also emerged. Large numbers of women, including some suffragists, became actively involved in the temperance cause. It is important to note that one of the main reasons women became involved in pressing for laws restricting the sale and consumption of alcohol was that their legal status as married women offered them no protection against either physical abuse or abandonment by a drunken husband. It might be added that the reason separate women's temperance organizations were formed was that women were not permitted to participate in the men's groups. In spite of the fact that temperance was in "women's interests," the growth of the women's temperance movement solidified the liquor and brewing industries' opposition to woman suffrage. As a result, suffrage leaders became convinced of the necessity of keeping the two issues separate.

As the campaign for woman suffrage grew, more and more sympathizers were attracted to the conservative and "respectable" American Association which, as noted above, deliberately limited its work to the single issue of suffrage. After two decades "respectability" won out, and the broad-ranging issues of the earlier movement had been largely subsumed by suffrage. (Even the Stanton-Anthony forces had somewhat redefined their goals and were focusing primarily on suffrage.) By 1890, when the American and the National merged to become the National American Woman Suffrage Association, the woman's movement had, in fact, been transformed into the single-issue suffrage movement. Moreover, although Elizabeth Cady Stanton, NAWSA's first president, was succeeded two years later by Susan B. Anthony, the first women activists, with their catholic range of concerns, were slowly being replaced by a second group far more limited in their political analysis. It should be noted that Stanton herself, after her two-year term as president of the new organization, withdrew from active work in the suffrage campaign. Although one of the earliest feminist leaders to understand the need for woman suffrage, by this time Stanton believed that the main obstacle to woman's equality was the church and organized religion.

During the entire development of the woman's movement, perhaps the argument most often used by anti-feminists was that the subjugation of women was divinely ordained as written in the Bible. Stanton attacked the argument head-on. She and a group of twenty-three women, including three ordained ministers, produced *The Woman's Bible*[22], which presented a systematic feminist critique of woman's role and image in the Bible. Some Biblical chapters were presented as proof that the Scripture itself was the source of woman's subjugation; others to show that, if reinterpreted, men and women were indeed equals in the Bible, not superior and inferior beings. "We have made a fetich [*sic*] of the Bible long enough. The time has come to read it as we do all other books, accepting the good and rejecting the evil it teaches."[23] Dismissing the "rib story" as a "petty surgical operation," Stanton argued further that the entire structure of the Bible was predicated on the notion of Eve's (woman's) corruption:

> Take the snake, the fruit-tree and the woman from the tableau, and we have no fall, nor frowning Judge, no Inferno, no everlasting punishment;—hence no need of a Savior. Thus the bottom falls out of the whole Christian theology. Here is the reason why in all the Biblical researches and higher criticisms, the scholars never touch the position of women.[24]

Not surprisingly, *The Woman's Bible* was considered scandalous and sacrilegious by most. The Suffrage Association members themselves, with the exception of Anthony and a few others, publicly disavowed Stanton and her work. They feared that the image of the already controversial suffrage movement would be irreparably damaged if the public were to associate it with Stanton's radical tract.

Shortly after the turn of the century, the second generation of woman suffragists came of age and new leaders replaced the old. Carrie Chapman Catt is perhaps the best known; she succeeded Anthony as president of the National American Woman Suffrage Association, which by then had become a large and somewhat unwieldy organization. Although limited gains were achieved (a number of western states had enfranchised women), no major progress was made in the campaign for suffrage until Alice Paul, a young and extremely militant suffragist, became active in the movement. In April, 1913, she formed a small radical group known as the Congressional Union (later reorganized as the Woman's Party) to work exclusively on a campaign for a *federal* woman's suffrage Amendment using any tactics necessary, no matter how unorthodox. Her group organized parades, mass demonstrations, hunger strikes, and its members were on several occasions arrested and jailed.[25] Although many suffragists rejected both the militant style and tactics of the Congressional Union, they nonetheless did consider Paul and her followers in large part responsible for "shocking" the languishing movement into actively pressuring for the federal Amendment. The woman suffrage Amendment (known as the "Anthony Amendment"), introduced into every session of Congress from 1878 on, was finally ratified on August 26, 1920.

Nearly three-quarters of a century had passed since the demand for woman suffrage had first been made at the Seneca Falls Convention. By 1920, so much energy had been expended in achieving the right to vote that the woman's movement virtually collapsed from exhaustion. To achieve the vote alone, as Carrie Chapman Catt had computed, took:

> ... fifty-two years of pauseless campaign ... fifty-six campaigns of referenda to male voters; 480 campaigns to get Legislatures to submit suffrage amendments to votes; 47 campaigns to get State constitutional conventions to write woman suffrage into state constitutions; 277 campaigns to get State party conventions to include woman suffrage planks; 30 campaigns to get presidential party conventions to adopt woman suffrage planks in party platforms, and 19 campaigns with 19 successive Congresses.[26]

With the passage of the Nineteenth Amendment the majority of women activists as well as the public at large assumed that having gained the vote woman's complete equality had been virtually obtained.

It must be remembered, however, that for most of the period that the woman's movement existed, suffrage had not been seen as an all-inclusive goal, but as a means of achieving equality—suffrage was only one element in the wide-ranging feminist critique questioning the fundamental organization of society. Historians, however, have for the most part ignored this radical critique and focused exclusively on the suffrage campaign. By virtue of this omission they have, to all intents and purposes, denied the political significance of the early feminist analysis. Moreover, the summary treatment by historians of the nineteenth- and twentieth-century drive for woman's suffrage has made that campaign almost a footnote to the abolitionist movement and the campaign for Negro suffrage. In addition, the traditional textbook image of the early feminists—if not wild-eyed women waving placards for the vote, then wild-eyed women swinging axes at saloon doors—has further demeaned the importance of their philosophical analysis.

The woman's movement virtually died in 1920 and, with the exception of a few organizations, feminism was to lie dormant for forty years.

Footnotes

[1] Mount Holyoke opened in 1837; Vassar, 1865; Smith and Wellesley, 1875; Radcliffe, 1879; Bryn Mawr, 1885.

[2] Quoted in Eleanor Flexner, *Century of Struggle: The Woman's Rights Movement in the United States* (Cambridge, Mass.: The Belknap Press of Harvard University Press, 1959), p. 27.

[3] *History of Woman Suffrage* (republished by Arno Press and *The New York Times*, New York, 1969), Vol. I, p. 81. Hereafter cited as *HWS*. Volumes I–III were edited by Elizabeth Cady Stanton, Susan B. Anthony, and Matilda Joslyn Gage. The first two volumes were published in 1881, the third in 1886. Volume IV was edited by Susan B. Anthony and Ida Husted Harper and was published in 1902. Volumes V and VI were edited by Ida Husted Harper and published in 1922.

[4] Sarah M. Grimké, *Letters on the Equality of the Sexes and the Condition of Woman* (Boston: Issac Kanapp, 1838, reprinted by Source Book Press, New York, 1970), p. 10ff.

[5] *Ibid.*, pp. 9–10.

[6] *Ibid.*, pp. 85–86.

[7] *Ibid.*, p. 51.

[8] *HWS*, p. 54.

[9] *Ibid.*, p. 61.

[10] *Ibid.*, pp. 70–73.

[11] *HWS*, p. 73.

[12] Flexner, p. 77.

[13] *HWS*, p. 110.

[14] *Ibid.*, p. 806.

[15] Flexner, p. 83.

[16] *Ibid.*, p. 84.

[17] *HWS*, Vol. II, p. 51.

[18] The Thirteenth Amendment was ratified in 1865; the Fourteenth in 1868; the Fifteenth in 1870.

[19] Flexner, p. 151.

[20] *Loc. cit.*

[21] *Minor v. Happersett*, 21 Wall. 162, 22 L. Ed. 627 (1875).

22 (New York: European Publishing Company, 1895 and 1898, Two Parts.)

23 *Ibid.*, Part II, pp. 7–8.

24 Stanton, letter to the editor of *The Critic* (New York), March 28, 1896, quoted in Aileen S. Kraditor, *The Ideas of the Woman Suffrage Movement, 1890–1920* (New York: Columbia University Press, 1965), n. 11, p. 86.

25 A total of 218 women from 26 states were arrested during the first session of the Sixty-fifth Congress (1917). Ninety-seven went to prison.

26 Carrie Chapman Catt and Nettie Rogers Shuler, *Woman Suffrage and Politics* (New York, 1923), p. 107. Quoted in Flexner, p. 173.

Account of the Proceedings on the Trial of Susan B. Anthony on the Charge of Illegal Voting at the Presidential Election in November, 1872

JUDGE HUNT: (Ordering the defendant to stand up), Has the prisoner anything to say why sentence shall not be pronounced?

MISS ANTHONY: Yes, your honor, I have many things to say; for in your ordered verdict of guilty, you have trampled under foot every vital principle of our government. My natural rights, my civil rights, my political rights, my judicial rights, are all alike ignored. Robbed of the fundamental privilege of citizenship, I am degraded from the status of a citizen to that of a subject; and not only myself individually, but all of my sex, are, by your honor's verdict, doomed to political subjection under this, so-called, form of government.

JUDGE HUNT: The Court cannot listen to a rehearsal of arguments the prisoner's counsel has already consumed three hours in presenting.

MISS ANTHONY: May it please your honor, I am not arguing the question, but simply stating the reasons why sentence cannot, in justice, be pronounced against me. Your denial of my citizen's right to vote, is the denial of my right of consent as one of the governed, the denial of my right of representation as one of the taxed, the

Rochester, N.Y. Daily Democrat and Chronicle Book Print, 3 West Main St. 1874. This article appeared in *Notes From the Third Year*.

denial of my right to a trial by a jury of my peers as an offender against law, therefore, the denial of my sacred rights to life, liberty, property and—

JUDGE HUNT: The Court cannot allow the prisoner to go on.

MISS ANTHONY: But your honor will not deny me this one and only poor privilege of protest against this high-handed outrage upon my citizen's rights. May it please the Court to remember that since the day of my arrest last November, this is the first time that either myself or any person of my disfranchised class has been allowed a word of defense before judge or jury—

JUDGE HUNT: The prisoner must sit down—the Court cannot allow it.

MISS ANTHONY: All of my prosecutors, from the 8th ward corner grocery politician, who entered the complaint, to the United States Marshal, Commissioner, District Attorney, District Judge, your honor on the bench, not one is my peer, but each and all are my political sovereigns; and had your honor submitted my case to the jury, as was clearly your duty, even then I should have had just cause of protest, for not one of those men was my peer; but, native or foreign born, white or black, rich or poor, educated or ignorant, awake or asleep, sober or drunk, each and every man of them was my political superior; hence, in no sense, my peer. Even, under such circumstances, a commoner of England, tried before a jury of Lords, would have far less cause to complain than should I, a woman, tried before a jury of men. Even my counsel, the Hon. Henry R. Selden, who has argued my cause so ably, so earnestly, so unanswerably before your honor, is my political sovereign. Precisely as no disfranchised person is entitled to sit upon a jury, and no woman is entitled to the franchise, so, none but a regularly admitted lawyer is allowed to practice in the courts, and no woman can gain admission to the bar—hence, jury, judge, counsel, must all be of the superior class.

JUDGE HUNT: The Court must insist—the prisoner has been tried according to the established forms of law.

MISS ANTHONY: Yes, your honor, but by forms of law all made by men, interpreted by men, administered by men, in favor of men, and against women; and hence, your honor's ordered verdict of guilty, against a United States citizen for the exercise of *"that citizen's right to vote,"* simply because that citizen was a woman and not a man. But, yesterday, the same man-made forms of law, declared it a crime punishable with $1,000 fine and six months' imprisonment, for you, or me, or any of us, to give a cup of cold water, a crust of bread, or a night's shelter to a panting fugitive as he was tracking his way to Canada. And every man or woman in whose veins coursed a drop of human sympathy violated that wicked law, reckless of consequences, and was justified in so doing. As then, the slaves who got their freedom must take it over, or under, or through the unjust forms of law, precisely so, now, must women, to get their right to a voice in this government, take it; and I have taken mine, and mean to take it at every possible opportunity.

JUDGE HUNT: The Court orders the prisoner to sit down. It will not allow another word.

MISS ANTHONY: When I was brought before your honor for trial, I hoped for a broad and liberal interpretation of the Constitution and its recent amendments, that should declare all United States citizens under its protecting aegis—that should declare equality of rights the national guarantee to all persons born or naturalized in the United States. But failing to get this justice—failing, even, to get a trial by a jury *not* of my peers—I ask not leniency at your hands—but rather the full rigors of the law.

JUDGE HUNT: The Court must insist—

(Here the prisoner sat down.)

JUDGE HUNT: The prisoner will stand up.

(Here Miss Anthony arose again.)

The sentence of the Court is that you pay a fine of one hundred dollars and the costs of the prosecution.

MISS ANTHONY: May it please your honor, I shall never pay a dollar of your unjust penalty. All the stock in trade I possess is a $10,-000 debt, incurred by publishing my paper—*The Revolution*—four years ago, the sole object of which was to educate all women to do precisely as I have done, rebel against your man-made, unjust, unconstitutional forms of law, that tax, fine, imprison and hang women, while they deny them the right of representation in the government; and I shall work on with might and main to pay every dollar of that honest debt, but not a penny shall go to this unjust claim. And I shall earnestly and persistently continue to urge all women to the practical recognition of the old revolutionary maxim, that "Resistance to tyranny is obedience to God."

JUDGE HUNT: Madam, the Court will not order you committed until the fine is paid.

Women's
Experience

Woman and Her Mind: The Story of Everyday Life

by Meredith Tax

This article is the first half of a longer article published by the New England Free Press, 791 Tremont St., Boston, Massachusetts, under the title Woman and Her Mind. The other two parts of the article deal with psychological aspects of consumerism, and of work as it is defined for women, including sex as work. Meredith Tax was a founding member of Bread and Roses, a socialist women's liberation organization in Boston, many of whose members contributed to the conception and writing of this article. She is now completing work on her book The Rising of the Women, a history of women in the labor movement from 1890 to 1920, to be published by McGraw-Hill.

In our society, where competitive individualism and the cash nexus are the dominant values, men are raised to see the world as a series of "challenges." They are taught to view everyone as a competitor for money, prestige, women, and the rest; and to be constantly on guard. American men arc brought up, moreover, to see these challenges in sexual terms, as if each involved their "masculinity," and to meet each embryonic threat with the maximum aggressive response.

They are taught that to be masculine is to be physically and verbally aggressive, hyper-active sexually, authoritarian in manner, and capable of abstract thought. Being observant of the ordinary details of daily life is not considered part of being masculine. Men are taught to chart the stars in their courses, but not to notice when someone in the room has been crying. Or, if they are forced to

This article first appeared in *Notes From the Second Year* and is here reprinted with the permission of the author.

notice, to regard it as a threat and act aggressively or condescendingly or helplessly. Sensitivity to other people's needs is considered, in our society, to be feminine. So is vulnerability to other people. The ideal American male, in terms of the dominant values of our society, is a competitive machine, competent, achieving, hard-driving, and soulless, with a *sexual* life, but no *personal* life. Fortunately, most men can't live up to this ideal; but the strain of trying is considerable.

Further, men are relatively unaware of their social environment because they don't have to be. It's not their job. They don't have to notice the comparative cost and beauty of various costumes. They don't have to be tuned in to the nuances of social behavior so that they can please those whom it is essential to please. They don't have to listen for footsteps behind them in the street at night (though they have to more than they used to). The passing scene presents no social opportunities to them which must be seized or forever lost. Men are taught to be active, to go and seek what they need; not to look pretty and wait for it to come into their vicinity. Men don't observe each passing cloud over human relations as if their whole future depended on it.

There's a reason for that: it doesn't. Women are hyper-aware of their surroundings. They have to be. Walk down a city street without being tuned in and you're in real danger; our society is one in which men rape, mug, and murder women whom they don't even know every day. You'd better keep track of what car is slowing down, and of who is walking up behind you.

You must be constantly on the watch for other reasons. Without this radar, how can you be sure of taking advantage of your opportunities? The role you have been given is a passive one; you can't go out and promote what you want, but must think fast and grab it as it flies past. You must be prepared to return the right kind of smile to passing Prince Charmings. And since your role also includes being a mediator between the men in your life and their acquaintances, you must also be perpetually on guard to smooth out a fight, be conciliatory or forgiving or cute, and keep unpleasant things from happening.

The self-consciousness and consciousness of others that is trained into women is necessary, but it is also extreme and oppressive. There's a lot to be said for being conscious of other people's behavior and needs; and even the self-effacing emotional service-station aspect of many women's behavior is preferable to the unconsciousness bred into men. But the price is high. Since our awareness of others is considered our duty, our job, the price we pay when things go wrong is guilt, self-hatred. And things always go wrong. We respond with apologies; we continue to apologize long after the event is forgotten—and even if it had no causal relation to anything we did to begin with. If the rain spoils someone's picnic, we apologize. We apologize for taking up space in a room, for living. How willingly we would suffer to prevent someone else a moment's discomfort! This is one of the hardest habits to break. And it's a vicious circle—our self-hating desire to preserve men from the consciousness of the pain they are causing enables them to remain unaware that they are causing it, and thus to remain less human than they could be. If we could only break out of this circle, stop apologizing and effacing ourselves, and live less tortuously! But of course there are reasons why this doesn't happen easily. Men and women are brought up to be like pieces of a jigsaw puzzle, with pieces carved out of their selves so they can fit into one another in the neurotic dependence most of us call love. If you make yourself whole, where are you going to find a jigsaw puzzle to fit into?

But those pieces that have been taken out of our heads! The self-consciousness we are filled with! It is so painful, so physical. We are taught to feel that our only asset is our physical presence, that that is all other people notice about us. The most minute blemish on a total person—a pimple, excess weight, a funny nose, larger than average breasts—can ruin a day, or years, with the agonies of constant awareness of it. The whole world is looking only at that pimple! These agonies are adolescent and excessive, if considered from a detached viewpoint. It is precisely in adolescence that we become conscious of how immensely we are impinged on by the world, how easily it can destroy us, how much we must have on the ball to survive. It is as we grow older that we desensitize ourselves and block out these agonies of consciousness in order to function. But we pay the price of false consciousness.

We make ourselves viable by blocking out the everyday realization of how we have been emotionally deformed by our socialization, and how convenient this deformation is for men, employers, advertisers, and anyone else who wishes to use us. What damage has been done to us as girls—what a sowing of self-doubt and self-hate that is never completely harvested, always springing up again. How we have been denied the opportunity to *choose*—a self, a man, a career, a life-style—until we become unable to make choices of the most trivial kind. Our inability to choose is part of American folklore: the woman in cartoons who sits dithering in a shoestore for hours, unable to decide between two pairs of pumps. When you have been told all of your life that the right pair of shoes, or the right hair-do, can determine your whole destiny, it is difficult to make such decisions casually, especially if the only sphere in which you have the scope to make decisions at all is this limited one.

To realize this is just to live with the everyday knowledge that one has lost an arm. But to block out this realization is to pay the price of false consciousness. It is to think that you are miserable because you have a pimple, rather than because you have been taught to think of yourself, and always been treated, as an object for sale, and your market value (thus your only value) has been temporarily impaired by the pimple.

We have to face the fact that pieces have been cut out of us to make us fit into this society. We have to try to imagine what we could have been if we hadn't been taught from birth that we are stupid, unable to analyze anything, "intuitive," passive, physically weak, hysterical, overemotional, dependent by nature, incapable of defending ourselves against any attack, fit only to be the housekeeper, sex object, and emotional service center for some man, or men, and children. And that only if we're lucky—otherwise we must act out a commercial mockery of even these roles as someone's secretary!

We didn't get this way by heredity or by accident. We have been *molded* into these deformed postures, *pushed* into these service jobs, *made* to apologize for existing, *taught* to be unable to do anything requiring any strength at all, like opening doors or bottles. We have been told to be stupid, to be silly. We have had our mental and emotional feet bound for thousands of years. And the fact that some of the pieces that have been cut out of us are ones we can never replace or reconstruct—an ego, self-confidence, an ability to make choices—is the most difficult of all to deal with.

All of the women I know who have done things, jumped hurdles, and stepped even a pace outside of the charmed circle of the bourgeois family, have had to face the damage that has been done to them, and struggle with the rules they have internalized. To some of us, this process has taken the form of a "nervous breakdown"; for others, a long period of sheer personal horror; to others, a more drawn-out process of repeatedly sinking under despair, and rising again. I think that for some of my generation, caught in the kind of double binds we have all been caught in, it is impossible to achieve revolutionary consciousness without some sort of confrontation with the self. Politically, this is both a weakness and a strength. It is an asset to come to political understanding through personal pain: it makes possible a gut understanding of how society works as a system dependent on the personal suffering and deprivation of each of us. Such understanding is a help in building a revolutionary movement. Only by realizing what we might have been, can we imagine how different women in a post-revolutionary society might be able to be. But knowing that we cannot achieve this ourselves, that no matter how we struggle we are still in some part of ourselves "damaged goods" (to use the appropriate capitalist terminology), that we can see what has gone wrong within ourselves, and still be unable to put it permanently right—this is very painful and discouraging. But it is necessary: it is this realization that makes it evident that there really are no individual solutions to woman's oppression, no way that one can float free of our society and its conditioning. The pain of it is what makes us search so urgently for new forms of social organization that can help us, and others, change and transcend our limitations. This pain is what makes us realize, in our everyday lives, that *social* change is absolutely necessary. As Lucy Stone put it almost a century ago:

> In education, in marriage, in everything, disappointment is the lot of women. It shall be the business of my life to deepen this disappointment in every woman's heart until she bows down to it no longer.

The things that mess us up are so built into the structure of society that only the most radical of social changes—one far more radical in its attack on the basic institutions of this society that traps us, and far more drastic in the changes it effects on human consciousness, than previous revolutions—has a chance of doing the job, of freeing us and freeing those who will be born out of our lives.

Female Schizophrenia

A young woman is walking down a city street. She is excruciat-ingly aware of her appearance and of the reaction to it (imagined or real) of every person she meets. She walks through a group of construction workers who are eating lunch in a line along the pave-ment. Her stomach tightens with terror and revulsion; her face becomes contorted into a grimace of self-control and fake unaware-ness; her walk and carriage become stiff and dehumanized. No matter what they say to her, it will be unbearable. She knows that they will not physically assault her or hurt her. They will only do so metaphorically. What they will do is *impinge* on her. They will demand that her thoughts be focussed on them. They will use her body with their eyes. They will evaluate her market price. They will comment on her defects, or compare them to those of other passers-by. They will make her a participant in their fantasies with-out asking if she is willing. They will make her feel ridiculous, or grotesquely sexual, or hideously ugly. Above all, they will make her feel like a *thing*.

You can say what you like about class and race. Those differences are real. But in this everyday scenario, any man on earth, no matter what his color or class is, has the power to make any woman who is exposed to him hate herself and her body. Any man has this power as *man*, the dominant sex, to dehumanize woman, even to herself.

No woman can have an autonomous self unaffected by such en-counters. Either she remains sensitive and vulnerable to this pain; or she shuts it out, by saying, "It's only my *body* they are talking about. It doesn't affect *me*. They know nothing about *me*." What-ever the process, the solution is a split between mind and body, be-tween one self and another. One may hate the body and consider the mind the real "self." One may glorify the body, as a means of satisfying one's desires by becoming an instrument to satisfy the desires of others; in this case the body becomes a thing, and the mind a puppeteer to manipulate it.

Both of these solutions (and most of us get sucked into one or the other) can be called *schizophrenic*. R. D. Laing defines schizo-phrenia as a social process in *The Politics of Experience:*

> ... *no* schizophrenic has been studied whose disturbed patterns of communication has not been shown to be a reflection of, and reac-

tion to, the disturbed and disturbing pattern characterizing his or
her family of origin. . . . When one person comes to be regarded
as schizophrenic, it seems that *without exception* the experiences
and behavior that gets labelled schizophrenic is a *special strategy
that a person invents in order to live in an unlivable situation.*

In *The Divided Self,* Laing describes the experience of schizo-
phrenia, the contradictory kind of self-consciousness that extends to
one's very existence, that is, who is literally not sure he exists:

> 1. Being aware of himself and knowing that other people are
> aware of him are a means of assuring himself that he exists, and
> also that they exist. . . . The need to gain a conviction of his own
> aliveness and the realness of things is, therefore, the basic issue in
> his existence. His way of seeking to gain such conviction is by
> feeling himself to be an object in the real world; but, since *his*
> world is unreal, he must be an object in the world of someone
> else, for objects to other people seem to be real. . . .
> 2. In a world full of danger, to be a potentially seeable object is
> to be constantly exposed to danger. Self-consciousness, then, may
> be the apprehensive awareness of oneself as potentially exposed to
> danger by the simple fact of being visible to others. The obvious
> defense against such a danger is to make oneself invisible in one
> way or another. (Penguin edition, pp. 108–109.)

Let us translate this into the terms of everyday life; go into the
mind of a woman who is confined to her house, who goes out only
to shop, to visit other women, or to chauffeur her kids, and whose
only work, or function, is to take care of a man and some children.
For her the contradiction will present itself this way:

"I am nothing when I am by myself. In myself, I am nothing. I
only know that I exist because I am needed by someone who is real,
my husband, and by my children. My husband goes out into the
real world. Other people recognize him as real, and take him into
account. He affects other people and events. He does things and
changes things and they are different afterwards. I stay in my imag-
inary world in this house, doing jobs that I largely invent, and that
no-one cares about but myself. I do not change things. The work I
do changes nothing; what I cook disappears, what I clean one day
must be cleaned again the next. I seem to be involved in some sort
of mysterious process rather than actions that have results.

"The only time that I think I might be real in myself is when I
hear myself screaming or having hysterics. But it is at these times
that I am in the most danger—of being told that I am wrong, or

that I'm really not like what I'm acting like, or that he hates me. If he stops loving me, I'm sunk; I won't have any purpose in life, or be sure I exist any more. I must efface myself in order to avoid this, and not make any demands on him, or do anything that might offend him. I feel dead now, but if he stops loving me I am really dead, because I am nothing by myself. I have to be noticed to know I exist.

"But, if I efface myself, how can I be noticed?"

It is a basic contradiction.

Laing explores it further. His language is extreme, since he is describing extreme states; but they are only heightened versions of what most of us go through at some point in our lives, or every day.

> As a death ray, consciousness has two main properties: its power to petrify (to turn to stone; to turn oneself or the other into things); and its power to penetrate. Thus, if it is in these terms that the gaze of others is experienced, there is a constant dread and resentment at being turned into someone else's thing, of being penetrated by him, and a sense of being in someone else's power and control. Freedom then consists in being inaccessible.

To turn people into stone is the ultimate way of objectifying them. To be able to penetrate them is to be able to see through them; the slang is an accurate description of that feeling: "I can see right through you" means "You don't fool me; I see what you're really like."

We often experience these states as projections from our own minds onto someone else's. It is that someone who turns us into stone, makes us objects, oxen sick-tongued and slow of motion. We are petrified with fear of someone else's power; someone else can see through us, can see what we are really like under our fragile veneer of normality. The person who sees through us has power over us.

In the walking-down-the-street scenario, our heroine can experience verbal assault in four different ways:

1) She can turn the construction workers to stone: "Look at them—what a mechanical response—they are like puppets. I don't have to listen to them. I can black them right out. I can petrify them with a look. How dare they speak to me!"

2) She can see right through them: "How ridiculous they are, to think they can attract me by behaving so obnoxiously. They are

pathetic and gross. Probably no one loves them. They can't fool me. I know what they are really like, even if they're trying to act big." She may exchange a look with them, nod graciously, or ignore them.

3) Inversely, she can experience these states as projections onto the group of men:

i.) "Look at them staring at me! I'm petrified! What will they do? I can't move fast enough to get away! My hands and feet are so cold. I feel as if I'm moving through ice water. I will turn into a block of ice if I don't get away."

ii.) "I feel as if I'm naked—so ashamed. They are laughing at me. They are pretending to think I'm pretty, just so they can make fun of me. They know what I'm really like, that this dress and makeup are just a fake to hide my ineptness, terror, and ugliness. I feel like I'm being broken into little bits." She will walk miserably by like a dead thing.

These states of mind are heightened, metaphoric reflections of the real conditions of a woman's life in our society. For a woman is either an object (turned to stone), belonging to some man and getting her money, status, friends, and very identity from her association with him—or else she is nowhere, disappeared, teetering on the edge of a void with no work to do and no felt identity at all.

From the earliest age a girl is deprived of a sense of herself (ego), the sense of having an identity separate from other people's evaluations of her. She is also deprived of a sense of her own competence, of her ability to do and understand things. She is told she must be pretty and sweet; she must be loveable; she mustn't make messes or play rough; she must perform services for Mommy and Daddy and be useful. How different this is from the way boys are socialized—they know they will be loved even if they make messes, stay out late without phoning, get dirty, and act like brats. That's what boys are supposed to do: have strong, competitive egos. Whereas girls are taught to see themselves as *objects* rather than subjects (if only by being continually told what they look like, and how important it is to have other people like them). They are taught to be charming, yet passive. They are taught to fail at most activities, so as not to be threatening or "unfeminine." They are taught to be of "service" to others, not to themselves, so that when they grow up they can be a wife and mother like their Mommy.

Women are stupefied, made *stupid,* by the roles they are pushed into. Books on educational psychology always remark the junior high and high school years as ones in which the boys "catch up" to the girls, and begin to surpass them scholastically and on IQ tests. It's no accident that these years are the ones of increased social pressure upon girls to take up their post-pubescent feminine roles and learn to live with them. It's not that the boys are growing smarter; the girls are becoming stupefied! Their IQ's—which, it is now recognized, are largely determined by social pressure and by the subject's expectations and sense of his own worth—continue to decline.

But this training in stupidity starts long before puberty. It starts before the small girl has enough ego to resist it. A teacher's training course at Boston University, that a friend of mine is taking, started with a snappy lecture on how children learn to read. The lecturer was a progressive educator; he believed in teaching people differently, according to the educational method most appropriate to *them*. "Little boys learn by taking things apart; they like to know how things work. The way to teach them to read is to show them an object, like a toy truck, and teach them the names of its different parts. They learn best through tactile and mechanical tools, so that's how to teach them language. Little girls learn best by rote. They learn faster than boys for this reason. All you have to do is show them flashcards." My friend was enraged: "But don't you see that that's how girls *get* this way," she said; "that's why we're unable to *think!*" The teacher admitted that the question might ultimately be one of socialization rather than nature, but "After all, you have to teach them the way they learn best, no matter what the cause is. And it makes your job easier—they're easier to teach." Less demanding. And so the cycle is perpetuated.

This remorseless stifling of a girl's intelligence and ego, this socialization into a life of service, this continued undermining of any possibility of independent achievement outside of the prescribed realm, all constitute a condition one could describe as *female schizophrenia*. Most women suffer from some form of it at some point in their lives. And most of them think of it as a "personal problem" rather than a social disease. That's part of the way they're trapped. For this condition is too widespread and too structurally based to be merely "personal" in origin. Our society could be described as one which drives women crazy.

Many women are so systematically deprived of an ego that they must constantly refer to a mirror, to their physical presence, to reassure themselves that they are actually there, still in one piece. Women's lives are a series of small dramas in which they play shifting defensive roles. The necessity to do so is real, for they are under economic necessity, and often physical constraint as well, to faithfully play the parts of sister, daughter, wife, mother and lover. Many women see that these are a collection of roles, but the face behind the shifting masks is a mystery even to themselves. The only constant in their lives is misery and a never-ending unsureness of themselves. A woman must, in order to make it as a woman, reflect the desires and preconceptions of every man who has power over her. Otherwise she is out of a job, out of her parents' house, out of a marriage, with no available slot left to fill. Women have to *play* at being themselves—that is, their *nice* selves, the selves made to order on standard patterns. "Just be yourself, dear," we are told as we go off to the prom. And we wonder, "What does that mean? What am I expected to do?"

The greatest women writers, in all ages, have recorded the effects of such expectations upon their mind. Charlotte Brontë, a nineteenth-century feminist as well as a great novelist of feminine roles, wrote in *Shirley:*

> Their sisters have no earthly employment but household work and sewing, no earthly pleasure but an unprofitable visiting, and no hope, in all their life to come, of anything better. This stagnant state of things makes them decline in health. They are never well, and their minds and views shrink to wondrous narrowness. The great wish, the sole aim of every one of them, is to be married, but the majority will never marry; they will die as they now live. They scheme, they plot, they dress to ensnare husbands. The gentlemen turn them into ridicule; they don't want them; they hold them very cheap. They say—I have heard them say it with sneering laughs many a time—the matrimonial market is overstocked. Fathers say likewise, and are angry with their daughters when they observe their manoeuvres—they order them to stay at home. What do they expect them to do at home? If you ask, they would answer, sew and cook. They expect them to do this, and this only, contentedly, regularly, uncomplainingly, all their lives long, as if they had no germ of faculties for anything else—a doctrine as reasonable to hold as it would be that the fathers have no faculties but for eating what their daughters cook or for wearing what they

sew. Could men live so themselves? Would they not be very weary? And when there came no relief to their weariness, but only reproaches at its slightest manifestation, would not their weariness ferment in time to frenzy?

A contemporary novelist, Anaïs Nin, writes of such things at length in her diaries. The following excerpts are from her *Diary, 1931– 1934* (Harcourt, Brace & World, and the Swallow Press, 1966):

> They all want to sanctify me, to turn me into an effigy, a myth. They want to idealize me and pray to me, use me for consolation, comfort. Curse my image, the image of me which faces me every day with the same over-fineness, over-delicacy, the pride, the vulnerability which makes people want to preserve me, treat me with care. Curse my eyes which are sad, and deep, and my hands which are delicate, and my walk which is a glide, my voice which is a whisper, all that can be used for a poem, and too fragile to be raped, violated, used. I am near death from solitude, near dissolution.
>
> I have always been tormented by the image of multiplicity of selves. Some days I call it a richness, and other days I see it as a disease, a proliferation as dangerous as cancer. My first concept of people about me was that all of them were coordinated into a whole, whereas I was made up of a multitude of selves, of fragments.
>
> There were always, in me, two women at least, one woman desperate and bewildered, who felt she was drowning, and another who only wanted to bring beauty, grace, and aliveness to people, and who would leap into a scene, as upon a stage, conceal her true emotions because they were weaknesses, helplessness, despair, and present to the world only a smile, an eagerness, curiosity, enthusiasm, interest.

From the day she learns to understand signals, all a woman hears is a series of contradictory instructions and conflicting descriptions of the way she is to look and behave. She must be sexy and a virgin at once. She must be appreciative, yet challenging. She must be strong, yet weak. Vulnerable, yet able to protect herself. Smart enough to get a man, but not smart enough to threaten him, or, rather, smart enough to conceal her intelligence and act manipulatively. Desired by all, but interested only in one. Sophisticated, yet naive at heart. And so on down the line.

She is in the position of the little boy Laing talks about in *The Self and Others*, whom a policeman saw run around the block ten times. The cop asked him what he was doing. The boy said, "I'm running away from home, but my father won't let me cross the street."

These contradictory injunctions are, of course, most acute in the realm of sexual behavior. For the first part of their lives, until they leave for college (if they do), most girls are still inculcated with an absolute Puritanism that no longer accurately reflects either the social norms nor the necessities of the economic structure. When a girl becomes "independent," this older, repressive ideology is replaced by the new, improved, trendy, but equally manipulative, equally mystified, and equally destructive ideology of the "new morality," in which women are defined as sex objects *even to themselves*. One of the definitive statements of this ideology can be found in *Cosmopolitan*, June, 1969. It is an article by a female gynecologist, Barbara Bross, entitled "How To Love Like a Real Woman." Dr. Bross states:

> Sexual abstinence in a normally constituted person is always pathogenic. [Translation: that means "getting sick."] We have been given sex organs to use them. If we don't use them, they decay and cause irreparable damage to body and mind. This is blunt, firm, indisputable, and true. . . .
>
> Woman is man's intermediary between himself and nature. He considers her as part of nature, though he will never say so, but that is what he feels. Her periods echo the rhythm of nature. Her ability to give birth makes her part of nature. She is the mother. She is the earth. She *senses* where he can only *think* or *act*. Woman *is*, man *does*. That is the strength and weakness of *both* sexes.

Getting
Angry

by Susi Kaplow

In 1970 Susi Kaplow was part of the nucleus of the now expanded women's liberation group in Paris. When she returned to New York in the fall of 1970 she joined New York Radical Feminists. She organized four consciousness-raising groups and was on the organizing committee for the Speak-out on Rape held in New York City, January, 1971.

Two scenarios. An angry man: someone has infringed on his rights, gone against his interests, or harmed a loved one. Or perhaps his anger is social—against racism or militarism. He holds his anger in check (on the screen we can see the muscles of his face tighten, his fists clench) and then, at the strategic moment, he lets it go. We see him yelling, shouting his angry phrases with sureness and confidence—or pushing a fist into his opponent's stomach with equal conviction. In either event, the anger is resolved; our hero has vented it and is content with success or accepts what he knows to be unmerited deféat.

Dissolve to scene two. An angry woman: angry at her man for cheating on her or (more likely) at the other woman. If we're in the good old days, she stomps up to her man and begins to scream wildly, he holds her down with his pinky, her anger melts in his embrace. After the fade-out, we find a puzzled heroine wondering how she could have been angry at such a good man. Or she marches over to the local saloon, hurls a few choice epithets at her rival, and then the hair-pulling begins. This ludicrous scene is always broken up by the amused and slightly scandalized gentlemen on the sidelines. In modern dress the same episode would be played differently. Discovering her husband's or lover's infidelity, the woman would smolder inwardly until the anger had burned down to a bitter resentment or become such a pressurized force that it could only come out in a rage so uncontrollable that the man (and the audience) can dismiss it as irrational. "I can't talk to you when you're like this." Hell hath no fury like a woman scorned.

For a woman in our society is denied the forthright expression of her healthy anger. Her attempts at physical confrontation seem ridiculous; "ladies" do a slow burn, letting out their anger indirectly in catty little phrases, often directed against a third party, especially children. A woman has learned to hold back her anger: It's unseemly, aesthetically displeasing, and against the sweet, pliant feminine image to be angry. And the woman fears her own anger: She, the great conciliator, the steadier of rocked boats, moves, out of her fear, to quiet not only others' anger but also her own. Small wonder that when the vacuum-sealed lid bursts off, the angry woman seems either like a freaked-out nut or a bitch on wheels. Her frenzy is intensified by the shakiness of her commitment to her own anger. What if she's really wrong? What if the other person is right? —Or worse (and this is the greatest fear) hits back with "You're crazy, I don't know what you're so mad about."

Why can't women allow themselves the outlet of their contained anger? Why do those around them find an angry woman so frightening that they must demoralize and deflate her into a degraded, inauthentic calm? Healthy anger says "I'm a person. I have certain human rights which you can't deny. I have a right to be treated with fairness and compassion, I have a right to live my life as I see fit, I have a right to get what I can for myself without hurting you. And if you deprive me of my rights, I'm not going to thank you, I'm going to say 'fuck off' and fight you if I have to." A person's anger puts him or her on center stage. It claims attention for itself and demands to be taken seriously, or else. (Or else I won't talk to you, I won't work with you or be friendly toward you, or else, ultimately, our association is over.)

Expressing anger means risking. Risking that the other person will be angry in return, risking that he or she will misunderstand the anger or refuse to deal with it, risking that the anger itself is misplaced or misinformed. So you need strength to say you're angry

—both the courage of your convictions and the ability to accept that your anger may be unwarranted without feeling crushed into nothingness. You must not have your total worth as a person riding on the worth of each individual case of anger.

Thus anger is self-confident, willing to fight for itself even at the jeopardy of the status quo, capable of taking a risk and, if necessary, of accepting defeat without total demise. Above all, anger is assertive. The traditional woman is the polar opposite of this description. Lacking confidence in herself and in her own perceptions, she backs away from a fight or, following the rules of chivalry, lets someone else do battle for her. Strong emotions disturb her for the disruption they bring to things-as-they-are. So shaky is her self-image that every criticism is seen as an indictment of her person. She is a living, walking apology for her own existence—what could be more foreign to self-assertion?

Although the reality has changed somewhat, most women will recognize themselves somewhere in this description. And society clings to this model as its ideal and calls an angry woman unfeminine. Because anger takes the woman out of her earth mother role as bastion of peace and calm, out of her familial role as peacemaker, out of her political role as preserver of the status quo, out of her economic role as cheap labor, out of her social role as second-class citizen. It takes her out of roles altogether and makes her a person.

It is no accident, then, that the emotion which accompanies the first steps toward liberation is, for most women, anger. Whatever sense of self-worth you have been able to emerge with after twenty or thirty years of having your mind messed with, gives you the vague feeling that your situation is not what it should be and sends you looking tentatively at the world around you for explanations. Realizations are, at first, halting, and then begin to hit you like a relentless sledge hammer, driving the anger deeper and deeper into your consciousness with every blow.

Your fury focuses on the select group of individuals who have done you the most damage. You are furious at your parents for having wanted a boy instead; at your mother (and this fury is mixed with compassion) for having let herself be stifled and having failed to show you another model of female behavior; at your father for having gotten a cheap bolster to his ego at your and your mother's expense.

You are furious at those who groom you to play your shabby role. At the teachers who demanded less of you because you were a girl. At the doctors who told you birth control was the woman's responsibility, gave you a Hobson's choice of dangerous and ineffectual devices, then refused you an abortion when these failed to work. At the psychiatrist who called you frigid because you didn't have vaginal orgasms and who told you you were neurotic for wanting more than the unpaid, unappreciated role of maid, wet nurse, and occasional lay. At employers who paid you less and kept you in lousy jobs. At the message from the media which you never understood before: "You've come a long way, baby"—down the dead-end, pre-fab street we designed for you.

Furious, above all, at men. For the grocer who has always called you "honey" you now have a stiff, curt "don't call me honey." For the men on the street who visit their daily indignities on your body, you have a "fuck off," or, if you're brave, a knee in the right place. For your male friends (and these get fewer and fewer) who are "all for women's lib" you reserve a cynical eye and a ready put-down. And for your man (if he's still around), a lot of hostile, angry questions. Is he different from other men? How? And when he fails to prove himself, your rage explodes readily from just beneath the surface.

This is an uncomfortable period to live through. You are raw with an anger that seems to have a mind and will of its own. Your friends, most of whom disagree with you, find you strident and difficult. And you become all the more so because of your fear that they are right, that you're crazy after all. You yourself get tired of this anger—it's exhausting to be furious all the time—which won't even let you watch a movie or have a conversation in peace.

But from your fury, you are gaining strength. The exercise of your anger gives you a sense of self and of self-worth. And the more this sense increases, the angrier you become. The two elements run in a dialectic whirlwind, smashing idols and myths all around them. You see, too, that you can get angry and it doesn't kill people, they don't kill you, the world doesn't fall apart.

Then this anger, burning white hot against the outside world, suddenly veers around and turns its flame toward you. Sure, they fucked you up and over, sure, they oppressed you, sure they continue to degrade and use you. But—why did you let it happen? Why do you continue to let it happen? All of a sudden you are up against the part you played in your own oppression. You were the indispensable accomplice to the crime. You internalized your own inferiority, the pressing necessity to be beautiful and seductive, the belief that men are more important than women, the conviction that marriage is the ultimate goal. Seeing this, you are violent against yourself for every time you were afraid to try something for fear of failing, for all the hours lost on make-up and shopping, for every woman you missed because there was a man in the room, for getting *yourself* stuck as a housewife or in a job you hate because "marriage is your career."

This phase of anger turned inward is terrifying. You are alone with your own failed responsibilities toward yourself, however much you can still blame others. It is this phase that some women find unbearable and flee from, returning to the first phase of anger or dropping out altogether. Because this inturned anger demands action—change—and won't let go until its demands begin to be satisfied. You can fall back on your inability to control others and their behavior toward you. But you can't comfortably claim powerlessness over your own conduct. Nor can you, at least for long, go on being furious at others (the forty-five year old who still blames mommy, flounders) if you don't even try to get yourself together.

This inturned anger is a constructive or rather reconstructive catalyst. For what you can do under its impetus is to restructure yourself, putting new images, patterns, and expectations in place of the old, no longer viable ones. As you use your anger, you also tame it. Anger becomes a tool which you can control, not only to help you make personal changes but to deal with the world outside as well. You can mobilize your anger to warn those around you that you're not having any more bullshit, to underscore your seriousness, to dare to drive your point home.

Through the exercise of your anger, as you see its efficacy and thus your own, you gain strength. And the growing feeling that you control your anger and not vice versa adds to this strength. As you gain this control, become surer of yourself, less afraid of being told you're crazy, your anger is less enraged and, in a sense, calmer. So it becomes discriminating. You reserve it for those individuals and groups who are messing with your mind—be they men or other women.

This progression of anger finds its ultimate meaning as an experience shared with other women. All striving to understand their collective situation, women in a group can help each other through the first, painful phase of outward-directed anger. Through consciousness-raising each woman can (at least ideally) find sufficient confirmation of her perceptions to be reassured of her own sanity—and can find growing strength to do without such confirmation when necessary.

In the second phase of inturned anger, women can support one another in their attempts at self-definition and change, change which others will try to forestall. And, at the same time, they can start to move together to create new social forms and structures in which individual changes can come to fruition. Controlled, directed, but nonetheless passionate, anger moves from the personal to the political and becomes a force for shaping our new destiny.

Woman
in the Middle

by Florence Rush

Florence Rush came into the women's movement last October as a member of OWL (Older Women's Liberation) and soon after began to write on subjects pertaining to women. She now belongs to an independent consciousness-raising group and is a member of the New York Radical Feminists and the Westchester Women's Liberation Coalition.

The woman in the middle is between forty and fifty-five years of age and at the point in her life when her aging parents are becoming increasingly dependent and her children, past eighteen, should be increasingly independent, but are not. Her parents may become helpless, ill, and although her children may be in college or living away from home, they come back for holidays, also become ill, get into trouble and mother is needed. The woman in the middle is caught between two generations. She has about ten or maybe fifteen good years left and if she does not use them for herself, she will never have another opportunity.

Contrary to popular opinion, many women look forward to this period in life when, free at last, they can be concerned with only themselves. Some women plan to go back to school, take a job, study music, travel, or just enjoy some well-earned leisure. There may be those who break down from lack of household chores, absence of children, or the feeling of not being wanted, but that is only because these women have had no alternative way to live beyond child care and housework. If a woman has skills, job opportunity, lives in a world that does not discriminate against women, particularly older women, and is not programmed to believe in her own uselessness, loss of dependent children will never be a problem. The woman in the middle is depressed not because she is going through her menopause or her children have left home, but because wherever she turns, she is prevented from fulfilling herself as a human being. She is not even allowed to control the few years of her life between the end of child rearing and old age.

For the woman who tries to salvage those years, there may be a strange feeling after the last child leaves home, but not for long. It is easy to become accustomed to the lack of chores and obligations, but this happy state, if reached at all, does not last. In this age of interminable child dependency, children, long after maturity, continue to look to their parents for help.

We live in a society that does not assume responsibility for the most elementary human needs and provides inadequate public service for the poor, sick, aged, and young. The old, sick, and poor individual is at the mercy of a community with so little concern for human life that it allows old people to die alone every day from neglect and starvation. Similarly, young people with few legal rights are subject to abuse, exploitation, and forced destructive relationships with parents and guardians. Children and the aged have no protection beyond the family. Because society has failed to make provision, it is, as always, the wife, mother, or daughter who must cope with and find solutions for the needs of the family members. She may do a good job, a bad job, or overwhelmed, may even walk away from the job, but no matter which way it goes, the responsibility for the care of the dependent person belongs to the woman.

My training as a female to fill this role started it an early age. I was the baby daughter, cute, and, I'm told, always had a lot of feeling for other people. At age four, when I saw my mother scrubbing the kitchen floor, I said, "Mommy, why do you work so hard for everyone?" My mother remembered the words well and told them to me very often. She was grateful to have a daughter who could really feel for her. She often commented that a boy is wonderful but a girl really cares.

At age eight I was awakened in the middle of the night by my father's angry shouts and my mother slamming down the window so the neighbors wouldn't hear. Soon I became aware that my parents' quarrels were part of our normal family life. When I asked my mother why she and father hated each other so much, she told me not to be silly, they really loved each other, but, since I was her only daughter and showed interest, and, since she had to have someone to talk to, and since I was a big girl (age ten), she thought it was time I knew what kind of a man my father really was.

When my father learned that my mother confided in me, he demanded equal time and they both complained to me about each other. I was later surprised to learn that my brother, ten years my senior, was totally unaware and unaffected by my parents' actively hateful relationship. They never involved him because he was, after all, a man.

Later, after I married and my children were finally grown and in the process of leaving home, my father had two massive heart attacks. I was drawn into a nightmare of nurses, doctors, and hospitals, while my mother, crying and helpless, also needed attention. I asked my brother to help and he gladly agreed but since he had no preparation for this kind of work, the instruction and supervision required more effort than the job itself, so I did everything. I was soberly informed by family and friends that I had this neurotic attachment to my father which would not allow me to have anyone else care for him. My father got better and enjoyed one good year when we learned he had terminal cancer. Doctors agreed that he had nine months to live but he survived for two years, and I was needed more than ever. I became very efficient at dealing with hospital personnel, became an expert at sick benefits and insurance, and even learned how to read X-rays.

Anyway, my father died and left all his money to my brother. I didn't get a penny but fortunately my mother had enough money to manage. At my father's funeral, my mother's widowed state was much discussed but was not of great concern because she had a daughter to care for her. Later, I saw her regularly. I took her shopping, for doctor's appointments, kept her finances in order and responded, in addition, to frequent emergencies—she fell, was cheated by Macy's, or a neighbor insulted her. After a year, it struck me that half my life was spent with my mother. I figured out that my mother, now eighty, in good health and with a family history of longevity, would probably live till ninety and, if I owed her for the rest of her life, I would not finish paying my dues until I was fifty-five.

During this period, I noticed that my husband was never plagued by similar problems. His mother lived with and was supported by an unmarried sister. When, at my suggestion, my husband sent a check to help with the burden of support, his mother returned the money. She would take help from her daughter but not from her son. I once asked a young woman who was active in the women's liberation movement and wise in the ways of sexism, why men responded so differently from women to human needs and suffering, and she told me to examine how differently the sexes are raised by their parents. I compared the attitudes of my parents to myself and my brother, and then my husband's parents' attitudes to him and his sister. Males are trained to do different jobs, have different responsibilities, and are programmed to feel different feelings than females.

At the other end of the spectrum, I had to cope with my grown children and these problems were no less disturbing or complicated. For eighteen years I had raised my children practically alone because this is regarded as woman's work and my husband had little to do with the job. I nursed them when they were ill, ran to school when called, helped with homework, made costumes for Halloween, prepared birthday parties, supervised their sex education, worried about stammering, thumbsucking and other neurotic symptoms, in addition to doing the usual cooking and cleaning.

Before I married, I had been trained and worked as a social worker, so when Bob, my oldest son, went off to college, and Anne, my daughter, was in high school, and Bill, my youngest son, was in junior high, I decided to go back to work. I found an agency that would employ me after my long years of absence. Although initially nervous, I soon found the change of scene, the challenge of the job, and the weekly pay check the most rewarding experience in eighteen years. Even though extremely busy, I managed children, husband, home, and job. Six weeks after Bob left for school, he returned in a succession of holidays, usually with guests, that made my head spin and kept me hopping. I never realized that Thanksgiving, Christmas, and intersession were so close. I looked forward eagerly to the free time between intersession and Easter when, soon after intersession, Bob called from school to tell us that he had seriously injured his knee. His father fetched him home and this represented the total sum of his parental obligation.

Bob had to be put in traction for about six weeks. Hospitalization was impossible because of the length of time involved, so there was no question but that I would take care of him at home. I carried trays, turned TV channels, entertained visitors, got books from the library, and because he was a young, healthy man who became bored and irritable from being confined, I also received a large amount of abuse. My supervisor kept wanting to know when I'd come back to work and finally I suggested she find someone to take my place. After seven weeks, Bob went back to school and I was without a job.

It took me six months to find other employment. After a year and a half on my second job, the agency offered to send me back to school, at their expense, to get my master's degree. It would mean giving up income for a year but I would receive, in return, after a year, a supervisory position and a substantial increase in salary. While completing my school application, Bill's school counselor informed me that my youngest child was failing miserably in junior high. He had never been a good student and since third grade I ran regularly to school conferences, supervised his studies and forced him to do hated homework. Nothing helped. The counselor offered no solution to the present problem, thought the difficulty might stem from the home, put it to me to figure something out, and of course I did.

I found a very expensive private school fully staffed with hand-picked educators and psychiatric experts dedicated to help the underachiever. I gave up my school plans in order to earn the money necessary to pay for Bill's private school. Almost every penny I earned went for tuition, psychiatric treatment, carfare, lunches, etc. The school, steeped in psychiatric principles, maintained that students who could not function academically usually suffered from disturbed parental relationships. Since Bill's father had little to do with raising his son, it was naturally I who was the controlling and domineering parent unable to let her son grow up. With years of experience and authority in all matters pertaining to education, and in order to obtain each student's confidence, the school established the rule that parents were not permitted to communicate with any staff member. Since the mother was usually the greatest threat to the child, the school director emphasized for my benefit that I would not be given any information regarding my son's progress. I was not permitted a phone conversation with a teacher and I was warned against trying to wheedle information from my son. I was advised to trust the school and relax control. No one seemed to notice that since I had previously given so much time and energy to Bill and his school problems, what they suggested was like a welcomed vacation. I gladly obeyed.

One year later, I received a phone call from the school psychiatrist who did not bother to disguise his annoyance and impatience with me. He questioned my lack of interest in my son, wondered why I never contacted the school or asked for a progress report. Before I could protest, I was informed that my son was not only failing everything, but was also using hard drugs. When I broke down in tears and confusion, I was told I had good reason to cry because my son was seriously emotionally ill and needed to be hospitalized.

Later, when I confronted Bill, he swore he did not use drugs, was having the same problems in private school as in public school, and never spoke of this before because he was advised to consult only with staff and never to discuss anything with his parents. I didn't believe him. I dragged him to doctors, put him through physical and psychological tests until one kind psychologist held me down long enough to convince me that Bill was not on drugs, was not sick, and there was no reason to have him hospitalized. When the panic passed, I gained my senses and took Bill out of school. Very soon after, he got himself a job in a hospital working on a brain research program, ran a computer, experimented with cats, loved his work, and is now getting along just fine.

When my daughter Anne graduated from college, she embarked on a career to conquer the world, and I was her assistant. She went on a diet, lost fifteen pounds, went shopping, got great clothes, got her hair done at Sassoon, got an exciting job, and, thus armed, moved out of my home to the world, life, and adventure.

To her horror and mine, she discovered that there were millions out there like herself. Her work, which consisted of an enormous amount of detailed and boring writing, was credited to her boss, and with all her clothes and fantastic figure, no one cared if she lived or died. Married women would not associate with a single girl and a single woman would not be seen with another single woman who was looking for friends. Men, generally in great demand, did not find it necessary to be even passingly polite, and their style was one of utter contempt, particularly toward a woman eager for a relationship. Anne, far away from the security and community of friends at college, had no one but me and this forced dependency resulted in hostility and fear. Unable to cope with the outside rejection and isolation, Anne moved back home, let her frustration out on me, and we fought constantly.

Finally she left her job and experimented with different life styles. She moved to a farm and came home; she went to the coast and came home; she found a commune and came home and nearly exhausted me with her activity and anxiety. Anne's father never got too involved because he did not wish to interfere in problems between mother and daughter. Finally, Anne became aware of her desperate behavior, stopped, found a better and more independent way to live, and we were again good friends.

It is hard, if not impossible, to estimate the cost to a human being in terms of time, energy, pain, and guilt as a result of the above relationships. The woman in the middle is the target of all negative emotions stemming from each family member's failure and frustration, and the damage can never be measured. When things go wrong, and they always do, she bears the burden, the responsibility and the blame.

If she is to save herself, the woman in the middle must learn to reject the myths regarding her family ties and responsibilities. She must no longer accept as natural her designated role as servant to all. She must question and challenge the privilege that excludes men from responsibilities and involvement with other human beings. She must reject the passivity of husbands, fathers, and brothers who sit by while wives, daughters, and sisters struggle alone with the devastating hardships involved in caring for the dependent. She must reject the lies and advices of the patronizing professionals and experts who, because of their own incompetence and inadequacy, have mystified reality and have shifted the blame for their failure to find social, economic, psychological, and educational remedies onto the mother, wife, and woman.

I am told that the women's liberation movement is for young women, but older women are looking to be liberated from their particular oppression, as well as the oppression common to all women. The only reason I am writing this paper instead of sitting with my poor old mother or sweating over a large family dinner for children and relatives is because my right to my own life has been supported by my sisters in the movement. Being fifty is not so bad if you are not torn by guilt, brutal obligation, and socially induced feelings of low self-esteem. Sooner or later, the woman in the middle is you and me, and together we must find a way not to be crushed.

The Bitch Manifesto

by Joreen

Joreen is a Chicago free-lance writer and photographer who organized the first independent women's liberation group in the nation in Chicago, 1967, and founded and edited the now defunct first national newsletter, Voice of the Women's Liberation Movement.

> ... man is defined as a human being and woman is defined as a female. Whenever she tries to behave as a human being she is accused of trying to emulate the male. ...
>
> —Simone de Beauvoir

BITCH is an organization which does not yet exist. The name is not an acronym.

BITCH is composed of Bitches. There are many definitions of a bitch. The most complimentary definition is a female dog. Those definitions of bitches who are also *homo sapiens* are rarely as objective. They vary from person to person and depend strongly on how much of a bitch the definer considers herself. However, everyone agrees that a bitch is always female, dog or otherwise.

It is also generally agreed that Bitch is aggressive, and therefore unfeminine (ahem). She may be sexy, in which case she becomes a Bitch Goddess, a special case which will not concern us here. But she is never a "true woman."

Bitches have some or all of the following characteristics:

1) *Personality*. Bitches are aggressive, assertive, domineering, overbearing, strong-minded, spiteful, hostile, direct, blunt, candid, obnoxious, thick-skinned, hard-headed, vicious, dogmatic, com-

petent, competitive, pushy, loud-mouthed, independent, stubborn, demanding, manipulative, egoistic, driven, achieving, overwhelming, threatening, scary, ambitious, tough, brassy, masculine, boisterous, and turbulent. Among other things. A Bitch occupies a lot of psychological space. You always know she is around. A Bitch takes shit from no one. You may not like her, but you cannot ignore her.

2) *Physical*. Bitches are big, tall, strong, large, loud, brash, harsh, awkward, clumsy, sprawling, strident, ugly. Bitches move their bodies freely rather than restrain, refine and confine their motions in the proper feminine manner. They clomp up stairs, stride when they walk and don't worry about where they put their legs when they sit. They have loud voices and often use them. Bitches are not pretty.

3) *Orientation*. Bitches seek their identity strictly through themselves and what they do. They are subjects, not objects. They may have a relationship with a person or organization, but they never *marry* anyone or anything: man, mansion, or movement. Thus Bitches prefer to plan their own lives rather than live from day to day, action to action, or person to person. They are independent cusses and believe they are capable of doing anything they damn well want to. If something gets in their way, well, that's why they become Bitches. If they are professionally inclined, they will seek careers and have no fear of competing with anyone. If not professionally inclined, they still seek self-expression and self-actualization. Whatever they do, they want an active role and are frequently perceived as domineering. Often they do dominate other people when roles are not available to them which more creatively sublimate their energies and utilize their capabilities. More often they are accused of domineering when doing what would be considered natural by a man.

A true Bitch is self-determined, but the term "bitch" is usually applied with less discrimination. It is a popular derogation to put down uppity women that was created by man and adopted by women. Like the term "nigger," "bitch" serves the social function of isolating and discrediting a class of people who do not conform to the socially accepted patterns of behavior.

Bitch does not use this word in the negative sense. A woman should be proud to declare she is a Bitch, because Bitch is Beautiful. It should be an act of affirmation by self and not negation by others. Not everyone can qualify as a Bitch. One does not have to have all of the above three qualities, but should be well possessed of at least two of them to be considered a Bitch. If a woman qualifies in all three, at least partially, she is a Bitch's Bitch. Only Superbitches qualify totally in all three categories and there are very few of those. Most don't last long in this society.

The most prominent characteristic of all Bitches is that they rudely violate conceptions of proper sex role behavior. They violate them in different ways, but they all violate them. Their attitudes towards themselves and other people, their goal orientations, their personal style, their appearence and way of handling their bodies, all jar people and make them feel uneasy. Sometimes it's conscious and sometimes it's not but people generally feel uncomfortable around Bitches. They consider them aberrations. They find their style disturbing. So they create a dumping ground for all whom they deplore as bitchy and call them frustrated women. Frustrated they may be, but the cause is social, not sexual.

What is disturbing about a Bitch is that she is androgynous. She incorporates within herself qualities traditionally defined as "masculine" as well as "feminine." A Bitch is blunt, direct, arrogant, at times egoistic. She has no liking for the indirect, subtle, mysterious ways of the "eternal feminine." She disdains the vicarious life deemed natural to women because she wants to live a life of her own.

Our society has defined humanity as male, and female as something other than male. In this way, females could be human only by living vicariously through a male. To be able to live, a woman has to agree to serve, honor and obey a man and what she gets in exchange is at best a shadow life. Bitches refuse to serve, honor or obey anyone. They demand to be fully functioning human beings, not just shadows. They want to be both female and human. This makes them social contradictions. The mere existence of Bitches negates the idea that a woman's reality must come through her relationship to a man and defies the belief that women are perpetual children who must always be under the guidance of another.

Therefore, if taken seriously, a Bitch is a threat to the social structures which enslave women and the social values which justify keeping them in their place. She is living testimony that woman's oppression does not have to be, and as such raises doubts about the validity of the whole social system. Because she is a threat she is not taken seriously. Instead, she is dismissed as a deviant. Men create a special category for her in which she is accounted at least partially human, but not really a woman. To the extent to which they relate to her as a human being, they refuse to relate to her as a sexual being. Women are even more threatened by her because they cannot forget she is a woman. They are afraid they will identify with her too closely. She has a freedom and an independence which they envy; she challenges them to forsake the security of their chains. Neither men nor women can face the reality of a Bitch because to do so would force them to face the corrupt reality of themselves. She is dangerous. So they dismiss her as a freak.

This is the root of her own oppression as a woman. Bitches are not only oppressed as women, they are oppressed for not being like women. Because she has insisted on being human before being feminine, on being true to herself before kowtowing to social pressures, a Bitch grows up an outsider. Even as girls, Bitches violated the limits of accepted sex role behavior. They did not identify with other women and few were lucky enough to have an adult Bitch serve as a role model. They had to make their own way and the pitfalls this uncharted course posed contributed to both their uncertainty and their independence.

Bitches are good examples of how women can be strong enough to survive even the rigid, punitive socialization of our society. As young girls it never quite penetrated their consciousness that women were supposed to be inferior to men in any but the mother/helpmate role. They asserted themselves as children and never really internalized the slave style of wheedling and cajolery which is called feminine. Some Bitches were oblivious to the usual social pressures and some stubbornly resisted them. Some developed a superficial feminine style and some remained tomboys long past the time when such behavior is tolerated. All Bitches refused, in mind and spirit, to conform to the idea that there were limits on what they could be and do. They placed no bounds on their aspirations or their conduct.

For this resistance they were roundly condemned. They were put down, snubbed, sneered at, talked about, laughed at and ostracised. Our society made women into slaves and then condemned them for acting like slaves. Those who refused to act like slaves they disparaged for not being true women.

It was all done very subtly. Few people were so direct as to say that they did not like Bitches because they did not play the sex role game. In fact, few were sure why they did not like Bitches. They did not realize that their violation of the reality structure endangered the structure. Somehow, from early childhood on, some girls didn't fit in and were good objects to make fun of. But few people consciously recognized the root of their dislike. The issue was never confronted. If it was talked about at all, it was done with snide remarks behind the young girl's back. Bitches were made to feel that there was something wrong with them; something personally wrong.

Teenage girls are particularly vicious in the scapegoat game. This is the time of life when women are told they must compete the hardest for the spoils (i.e., men) which society allows. They must assert their femininity or see it denied. They are very unsure of themselves and adopt the rigidity that goes with uncertainty. They are hard on their competitors and even harder on those who decline to compete. Those of their peers who do not share their concerns and practice the arts of charming men are excluded from most social groupings. If she didn't know it before, a Bitch learns during these years that she is different.

As she gets older she learns more about why she is different. As Bitches begin to take jobs, or participate in organizations, they are rarely content to sit quietly and do what they are told. A Bitch has a mind of her own and wants to use it. She wants to rise high, be creative, assume responsibility. She knows she is capable and wants to use her capabilities. This, not pleasing the men she works for, is her primary goal.

When she meets the hard brick wall of sex prejudice she is not compliant. She will knock herself out batting her head against the wall because she will not accept her defined role as an auxiliary. Occasionally she crashes her way through. Or she uses her ingenuity to find a loophole, or creates one. Or she is ten times better than anyone else competing with her. She also accepts less than her due. Like other women her ambitions have often been dulled for she has not totally escaped the badge of inferiority placed upon the "weaker sex." She will often espouse contentment with being the power behind the throne—provided that she does have real power—while rationalizing that she really does not want the recognition that comes with also having the throne. Because she has been put down most of her life, both for being a woman and for not being a true woman, a Bitch will not always recognize that what she has achieved is not attainable by the typical woman. A highly competent Bitch often deprecates herself by refusing to recognize her own superiority. She is wont to say that she is average or less; if she can do it, anyone can.

As adults, Bitches may have learned the feminine role, at least the outward style, but they are rarely comfortable in it. This is particularly true of those women who are physical Bitches. They want to free their bodies as well as their minds and deplore the effort they must waste confining their physical motions or dressing the role in order not to turn people off. Too, because they violate sex role expectations physically, they are not as free to violate them psychologically or intellectually. A few deviations from the norm can be tolerated but too many are too threatening. It's bad enough not to think like a woman, sound like a woman or do the kinds of things women are supposed to do. To also not look like a woman, move like a woman, or act like a woman is to go way beyond the pale. Ours is a rigid society with narrow limits placed on the extent of human diversity. Women in particular are defined by their physical characteristics. Bitches who do not violate these limits are freer to violate others. Bitches who do violate them in style or size can be somewhat envious of those who do not have to so severely restrain the expansiveness of their personalities and behavior. Often these Bitches are tortured more because their deviancy is always evident. But they do have a compensation in that large Bitches have a good deal less difficulty being taken seriously than small women. One of the sources of their suffering as women is also a source of their strength.

This trial by fire which most Bitches go through while growing up either makes them or breaks them. They are strung tautly between the two poles of being true to their own nature of being accepted as a social being. This makes them very sensitive people, but it is a sensitivity the rest of the world is unaware of. For on the outside they have frequently grown a thick defensive callus which can make them seem hard and bitter at times. This is particularly true of those Bitches who have been forced to become isolates in order to avoid being remade and destroyed by their peers. Those who are fortunate enough to have grown up with some similar companions, understanding parents, a good role model or two and a very strong will, can avoid some of the worse aspects of being a Bitch. Having endured less psychological punishment for being what they were they can accept their differentness with the ease that comes from self-confidence.

Those who had to make their way entirely on their own have an uncertain path. Some finally realize that their pain comes not just because they do not conform but because they do not want to conform. With this comes the recognition that there is nothing particularly wrong with *them*—they just don't fit into this kind of society. Many eventually learn to insulate themselves from the harsh social environment. However, this too has its price. Unless they are cautious and conscious, the confidence gained in this painful manner—with no support from their sisters—is more often a kind of arrogance. Bitches can become so hard and calloused that the last vestiges of humanity become buried deep within and almost destroyed.

Not all Bitches make it. Instead of calluses, they develop open sores. Instead of confidence they develop an unhealthy sensitivity to rejection. Seemingly tough on the outside, on the inside they are a bloody pulp, raw from the lifelong verbal whipping they have had to endure. These are Bitches who have gone Bad. They often go around with a chip on their shoulders and use their strength for unproductive retaliation when someone accepts their dare to knock it off. These Bitches can be very obnoxious because they never really trust people. They have not learned to use their strength constructively.

Bitches who have been mutilated as human beings often turn their fury on other people—particularly other women. This is one example of how women are trained to keep themselves and other women in their place. Bitches are no less guilty than non-Bitches of self-hatred and group-hatred and those who have gone Bad suffer the worst of both these afflictions. All Bitches are scapegoats and those who have not survived the psychological gauntlet are the butt of everyone's disdain. As a group, Bitches are treated by other women much as women in general are treated by society—all right in their place, good to exploit and gossip about, but otherwise to be ignored or put down. They are threats to the traditional woman's position and they are also an outgroup to which she can feel superior. Most women feel both better than and jealous of Bitches. While comforting themselves that they are not like these aggressive, masculine freaks, they have a sneaking suspicion that perhaps men, the most important thing in their lives, do find the freer, more assertive, independent Bitch preferable as a woman.

Bitches, likewise, don't care too much for other women. They grow up disliking other women. They can't relate to them, they don't identify with them, they have nothing in common with them. Other women have been the norm into which they have not fit. They reject those who have rejected them. This is one of the reasons Bitches who are successful in hurdling the obstacles society places before women scorn these women who are not. They tend to feel those who can take it will make it. Most women have been the direct agents of much of the shit Bitches have had to endure and few of either group has had the political consciousness to realize why this is. Bitches have been oppressed by other women as much if not more than by men and their hatred for them is usually greater.

Bitches are also uncomfortable around other women because frequently women are less their psychological peers than are men. Bitches don't particularly like passive people. They are always slightly afraid they will crush the fragile things. Women are trained to be passive and have learned to act that way even when they are not. A Bitch is not very passive and is not comfortable acting that role. But she usually does not like to be domineering either—whether this is from natural distaste at dominating others or fear of seeming too masculine. Thus a Bitch can relax and be her natural nonpassive self without worrying about macerating someone only in the company of those who are as strong as she. This is more frequently in the company of men than of women but those Bitches who have not succumbed totally to self-hatred are most comfortable of all only in the company of fellow Bitches. These are her true peers and the only ones with whom she does not have to play some sort of role. Only with other Bitches can a Bitch be truly free.

These moments come rarely. Most of the time Bitches must remain psychologically isolated. Women and men are so threatened by them and react so adversely that Bitches guard their true selves carefully. They are suspicious of those few whom they think they might be able to trust because so often it turns out to be a sham.

But in this loneliness there is a strength and from their isolation and their bitterness come contributions that other women do not make. Bitches are among the most unsung of the unsung heroes of this society. They are the pioneers, the vanguard, the spearhead. Whether they want to be or not this is the role they serve just by their very being. Many would not choose to be the groundbreakers for the mass of women for whom they have no sisterly feelings but they cannot avoid it. Those who violate the limits, extend them; or cause the system to break.

Bitches were the first women to go to college, the first to break through the Invisible Bar of the professions, the first social revolutionaries, the first labor leaders, the first to organize other women. Because they were not passive beings and acted on their resentment at being kept down, they dared to do what other women would not. They took the flak and the shit that society dishes out to those who would change it and opened up portions of the world to women that they would otherwise not have known. They have lived on the fringes. And alone or with the support of their sisters they have changed the world we live in.

By definition Bitches are marginal beings in this society. They have no proper place and wouldn't stay in it if they did. They are women but not true women. They are human but they are not male. Some don't even know they are women because they cannot relate to other women. They may play the feminine game at times, but they know it is a game they are playing. Their major psychological oppression is not a belief that they are inferior but a belief that they are not. Thus, all their lives they have been told they were freaks. More polite terms were used, of course, but the message got through. Like most women they were taught to hate themselves as well as all women. In different ways and for different reasons perhaps, but the effect was similar. Internalization of a derogatory self-concept always results in a good deal of bitterness and resentment. This anger is usually either turned in on the self—making one an unpleasant person—or on other women—reinforcing the social clichés about them. Only with political consciousness is it directed at the source—the social system.

The bulk of this Manifesto has been about Bitches. The remainder will be about BITCH. The organization does not yet exist and perhaps it never can. Bitches are so damned independent and they have learned so well not to trust other women that it will be difficult for them to learn to even trust each other. This is what BITCH must teach them to do. Bitches have to learn to accept themselves as Bitches and to give their sisters the support they need to be creative Bitches. Bitches must learn to be proud of their strength and proud of themselves. They must move away from the isolation which has been their protection and help their younger sisters avoid its perils. They must recognize that women are often less tolerant of other women than are men because they have been taught to view all women as their enemies. And Bitches must form together in a movement to deal with their problems in a political manner. They must organize for their own liberation as all women must organize for theirs. We must be strong, we must be militant, we must be dangerous. We must realize that Bitch is Beautiful and that we have nothing to lose. Nothing whatsover.

This Manifesto was written and revised with the help of several of my sisters, to whom it is dedicated.

Why I Want A Wife

by Judy Syfers

Judy Syfers has been in the women's movement for almost two years and is a member of Sudsofloppen, a small California group. She was one of the organizers of Breakaway, a community liberation school for women's studies and was a co-teacher in an introductory seminar called "A Wide Range Look at Women's Oppression" at Breakaway. She worked on and spoke at the August 26 demonstration last year in San Francisco and is now active in the Women's Abortion Coalition. On the less glamorous side, she says, "I am married, am a housewife, and have two female children; all three of those factors serve to keep my anger alive."

I belong to that classification of people known as wives. I am A Wife. And, not altogether incidentally, I am a mother.

Not too long ago a male friend of mine appeared on the scene from the Midwest fresh from a recent divorce. He had one child, who is, of course, with his ex-wife. He is obviously looking for another wife. As I thought about him while I was ironing one evening, it suddenly occurred to me that I, too, would like to have a wife. Why do I want a wife?

I would like to go back to school so that I can become economically independent, support myself, and, if need be, support those dependent upon me. I want a wife who will work and send me to school. And while I am going to school I want a wife to take care of my children. I want a wife to keep track of the children's doctor and dentist appointments. And to keep track of mine, too. I want a wife to make sure my children eat properly and are kept clean. I want a wife who will wash the children's clothes and keep them mended. I want a wife who is a good nurturant attendant to my children, arranges for their schooling, makes sure that they have an adequate social life with their peers, takes them to the park, the zoo, etc. I want a wife who takes care of the children when they are sick, a wife who arranges to be around when the children need special care, because, of course, I cannot miss classes at school. My wife must arrange to lose time at work and not lose the job. It may mean a small cut in my wife's income from time to time, but I guess I can tolerate that. Needless to say, my wife will arrange and pay for the care of the children while my wife is working.

I want a wife who will take care of *my* physical needs. I want a wife who will keep my house clean. A wife who will pick up after my children, a wife who will pick up after me. I want a wife who will keep my clothes clean, ironed, mended, replaced when need be, and who will see to it that my personal things are kept in their proper place so that I can find what I need the minute I need it. I want a wife who cooks the meals, a wife who is a *good* cook. I want a wife who will plan the menus, do the necessary grocery shopping, prepare the meals, serve them pleasantly, and then do the cleaning up while I do my studying. I want a wife who will care for me when I am sick and sympathize with my pain and loss of time from school. I want a wife to go along when our family takes a vacation so that someone can continue to care for me and my children when I need a rest and a change of scene.

I want a wife who will not bother me with rambling complaints about a wife's duties. But I want a wife who will listen to me when I feel the need to explain a rather difficult point I have come across in my course of studies. And I want a wife who will type my papers for me when I have written them.

I want a wife who will take care of the details of my social life. When my wife and I are invited out by my friends, I want a wife who will take care of the babysitting arrangements. When I meet people at school that I like and want to entertain, I want a wife who will have the house clean, will prepare a special meal, serve it to me and my friends, and not interrupt when I talk about the things that interest me and my friends. I want a wife who will have arranged that the children are fed and ready for bed before my guests arrive so that the children do not bother us. I want a wife who takes care of the needs of my guests so that they feel comfortable, who makes sure that they have an ashtray, that they are passed the hor d'oeuvres, that they are offered a second helping of the food, that their wine glasses are replenished when necessary, that their coffee is served to them as they like it. And I want a wife who knows that sometimes I need a night out by myself.

I want a wife who is sensitive to my sexual needs, a wife who makes love passionately and eagerly when I feel like it, a wife who makes sure that I am satisfied. And, of course, I want a wife who will not demand sexual attention when I am not in the mood for it. I want a wife who assumes the complete responsibility for birth control, because I do not want more children. I want a wife who will remain sexually faithful to me so that I do not have to clutter up my intellectual life with jealousies. And I want a wife who understands that *my* sexual needs may entail more than strict adherence to monogamy. I must, after all, be able to relate to people as fully as possible.

If, by chance, I find another person more suitable as a wife than the wife I already have, I want the liberty to replace my present wife with another one. Naturally, I will expect a fresh, new life; my wife will take the children and be solely responsible for them so that I am left free.

When I am through with school and have acquired a job, I want my wife to quit working and remain at home so that my wife can more fully and completely take care of a wife's duties.

My God, who *wouldn't* want a wife?

Men and Violence

The following is a transcript of a taped consciousness-raising session. It is one of twenty such tapes produced for WBAI-FM Radio in New York City.

The WBAI consciousness-raising group, consisting of seven women, was formed in the fall of 1970. The women met every week —sometimes twice a week and on Sundays—in the WBAI studios to produce a CR tape on a specific topic. The topics included Adolescent Puberty Rituals (How I First Learned About Menstruation), Housework, Masturbation, and Monogamy.

The program was broadcast in two parts on Fridays at noon. The daytime hour was chosen to reach women who, because they have small children and other female responsibilities, are often unable to join a CR group. During Part I of the program a forty-five minute edited version of a tape was played. During Part II women in the audience phoned in and did their own consciousness-raising on the air. The first broadcast of the CR program received more mail than any other first broadcast in WBAI history.

Members of the group are Kate Ellis, Sebern Fisher, Marian Meade, Vivian Neimann, Gloria Schuh, Mary Winslow, and Rosemary Gaffney (who unfortunately was absent the night "Men and Violence" was taped). The program was produced and edited by Nanette Rainone.

SEBERN: I just started a new job with a messenger service, and in the last two days when my son has been on vacation from school, he's been riding in the car with me mainly to save me from tow away zones. He's nine years old. And, as we go around the streets of New York, he points out to me every time a man is looking in my direction, or, which is more obvious to me, when a man is whistling at me. And he has this kind of grin on his face whenever he does it.

Finally today I asked him why he felt so compelled to point it out, and he said that he really didn't know. But it seems that he was getting a grandstand view of male chauvinism and enjoying it, just as he was enjoying the sights of the World Trade Center or the heliport, you know? I came in on that level.

And it became difficult because I was dealing with that issue of the whistling which was out there, and here was my kid who was reflecting it all in my car. So I turned on the radio, which was the only thing to keep them . . . to keep all the sounds out.

GLORIA: What I feel is rage. I mean *I* feel outraged in terms of the street and in terms of my position on the street, in terms of the fact that the streets are owned by men. I just feel that the men stake out the street and each block is owned by different men, and that men travel those blocks with the consent and permission of other men. Women travel those blocks also with the consent and permission of men, but on a different level, in that you are at any time susceptible to those whims in far more of a real way than those men are.

You know, it's becoming a well-known thing that women in the movement hate to be whistled at. They hate to be stopped in the street. I mean, men laugh at it—other women laugh at it. They say that we're too sensitive, that we're too upset, that we get too outraged and that it's really a compliment to be stopped and to be whistled at and to be thought pretty and that we should start worrying when it stops.

But what I find outrageous is the fact that their fantasy can be activated into a reality at any time. And you're the object of it, so that you cannot escape. That's what happened tonight. I mean, we were coming to the studio and Vivian and I had stopped in front of a store, and a man came up to her and asked her for twenty cents. She said "No," and she proceeded to walk into the store. He blocked her way and he shoved her against a plate glass window. And he called her a strange name. And all I could feel was contained rage, because if I hit him, he would've killed me. He was really a violent man. Much larger, much stronger. And I had no effective way of dealing with it.

If it happened again when we walked out of the studio, there would be no way of dealing with it. If you walk up to the police, as I wanted to do, the reality is that *they* probably wouldn't deal with it, because it's much too frequent. So you have to begin to choose your neighborhoods and choose the hours, and choose the circumstances that you can be out.

And that's the rage I feel as a woman. That complete physical powerlessness in a situation. And the only way of dealing with it is to react with some sort of violence, which women don't want to do. I don't want to become a man, in the sense of becoming someone that can beat the crap out of another person. Yet, the only alternative women have on the street is to become a part of the street. To react in the same way men do, which makes them immune in the sense that nobody walks up to a huge man in the street and beats him up, or presumes upon him.

KATE: Or asks him for twenty cents, even.

GLORIA: Well, they might ask, but they'll ask politely. And certainly they're not going to beat someone up over twenty cents. It's really so heavy.

SEBERN: So what are you going to do?

GLORIA: I'm going to start learning to be violent, I guess. I mean I can only contain for so long my pure thoughts about how one power structure shouldn't presume upon another, and how you don't remove violence by being violent. That theory works only until you're ripped off against a wall or raped, or someone you know is killed. And then you begin to see that powerlessness is not the answer to that kind of street situation.

KATE: Because, in fact, it's not simply nonviolence, it's nonviolence combined with powerlessness, which doesn't make any sense at all.

GLORIA: I just remember an incident when I was visiting one night, and a man who was a friend of this family started to talk to me. I was talking about the movement, and I was telling him about myself and who I was and what I was doing. He tried the usual thing about, well, you should wear lighter colors and you'll look better. And I just ignored him. I didn't pick up on any of that.

Toward the end of the evening we were talking about women and men's natural superiority over women, and he kind of looked in my direction. All of a sudden he became very agitated and said, "Well, if I really wanted to right now, I could kill you. I could beat the shit out of you." And I looked at him and I said, "Probably, but that doesn't make you a superior person." And he said, "But I really could. You know, I really could beat you up."

I've noticed a degree of violence that men have in relationship to me. I think maybe that's their second line of action when the first line doesn't really work. You know . . . like when they walk up to you . . .

KATE: A male chauvinist would say that you provoke that.

MARY: You only provoke it by assuming any kind of equality. The moment you begin to assume equality is that moment that it's provoked—if you want to use that word.

GLORIA: That's why the man stopped Vivian. And called her what he did. Like, which was a cold bitch. But the thing is that it was because she was walking down the street as though she had a right to be there. And as though she, you know, she was walking into a store, she wasn't aware of anybody, she wasn't looking at anybody . . . we were just talking. But I've noticed more and more that whenever we're together there's less of an attempt to pick us up than an attempt to be violent, because it's happened a couple of times.

SEBERN: Then there's the story of a friend of mine who went into a coffee shop-bar setup with her child in Pennsylvania. And the proprietor of the place came over and said that "You'll have to get that out of here." And she thought he was speaking of the chicken leg which the little boy was eating, and she went to great lengths to assure him that she was going to buy some food for herself. And he said, "No, I don't mean that, I mean your child. He is too young to be up so late." It was nine o'clock.

She became incensed, enraged. He was not only telling her that—that she couldn't partake of the services everybody else had, but he was also putting it in the context of her being a bad mother. She'd no other way than, you know, giving him a very hard time, trying to rouse up the other customers who were bored with the whole scene, to get any kind of action going, and the feeling was overwhelming.

Her husband picked the child up and left because he didn't want a fight, which not only had undercut her argument, but really fulfilled a fear that, sure, that guy could and would beat somebody up over the issue of a child being up too late for his ethical standard.

And, as he pushed her out the door, he said, "You know, you're a woman, and I could really beat you up."

GLORIA: It's so depressing.

SEBERN: But the level at which we take that in. You know, it's not only the circumstances that come from outside. It's the level to which you accept that in day-to-day situations which doesn't allow you to have an instantaneous reaction, and know that you're taking somebody off guard and chopping them or kicking them, but tells you rather that you have to submit to constant punishment of this kind.

KATE: Has anybody here . . . has anybody here ever been . . . I meant my husband really beat me up once. I mean really just absolutely tore me apart.

The way this arose, really, had a great deal to do with my own inability to express anger at him. And what I would do instead was burst into tears. I mean, there's some kind of relationship between bursting into tears and being beaten up.

And whenever I would do that with him, he would say, "I can't deal with you when you're so upset. Come back and talk to me when you're in a rational frame of mind." I would've liked to do anything to him. I just don't know quite what. To me this was just the most totally frustrating thing that he ever said: "Go away while you're so upset and then come back."

Now of course he couldn't deal with anger at all—we kind of complemented each other on that. I cried and he withdrew. The thing is, though, that finally the dam just broke and he lost control of himself completely. This was a thing where I was—I was just hysterical and upset with him, and I just wouldn't go away and control myself. I just kept coming back at him and coming back at him and finally he had just had as much as he could take and, though he was a very, very controlled person and found my anger hard to deal with and found his own anger hard to deal with, right in front of our son, who was two at the time, and who came over to me after, when I was lying on the ground and really just—just—I mean for about ten minutes my husband just absolutely pummeled me like he was crazy.

But when I look back on that now, I think, you see, it was a time when I was asking him to move out and nothing was happening. The very next day he went out and got himself an apartment and moved out right like that. And so in a certain kind of way, it seemed to me at that time that at least Wayne finally *did* something. I mean, he saw only two alternatives: total withdrawal or the total opposite.

SEBERN: Because of the anger that has been repressed in us, the six of us in the room could eventually, you know, send this city like they had never seen King Kong.

GLORIA: But you see men allow themselves that option of becoming violent. Women don't. Not even with other women who they *can* beat up! Or even particularly maybe with their children. But that's the only visible way we allow ourselves an outlet: toward something totally powerless like a child or an animal.

SEBERN: Or yourself.

GLORIA: Or even yourself. But anything that has a modicum of consciousness, I mean, you just can't do it.

MARY: I was thinking just in relation to what you were saying, Kathy, about how we cry and they hit. Even when it doesn't come to that. Even when it's just a simple argument, there's always the potential for that kind of violence, even if you're in a situation where you're not getting hit or never have been.

Still, sometimes just the anger of my husband has made me realize, you know, why any anger is so intimidating, because ultimately for it to become physical is the only place it can go unless you begin to defuse that anger by doing something else or stopping the conversation or redirecting things, or becoming passive, or dropping the whole thing. It's always there with men.

KATE: I married my husband, who was 6'4", and I married him because he was tall and because I'm 5'8" and I somehow had a thing that finally I was accepting my role because he was big and strong.

And so, I mean I didn't *ask* to be beaten up, although in looking at it afterwards it seemed like a very masculine thing for him to do somehow since I had been nagging him because he never really asserted himself.

GLORIA: The thing that concerns me about the whole incident on Eighth Street tonight was the fact that if I had thought about it, and I guess I *did* think about it, in the split second of Vivian walking through the door and him standing there just totally smug, you know, smiling—I could have, you know, kicked him or hit him. I could have hit him back and I didn't. I could have taken him totally by surprise and really hurt him, and I didn't. I was within three inches of him and he was totally secure about the fact that no one was going to retaliate. And I didn't *do* anything.

And I can kind of back that up even further because when I was young I played with boys all the time. I was a tomboy. And we used to roughhouse and kid around and wrestle, and I was equally as strong as them. I never felt weaker than them because they were all about my age and I didn't really think in terms of strength . . . that these people were more powerful than me.

At ten I was having this puppy love kind of thing with this little boy on the block. And something I had done—I think I beat him in baseball or something like that—something ridiculous—and he turned around and he punched me in the arm. And my first reaction was to hit him back. And I had my hand up to hit him and I just stopped. There was no fear that he was going to beat me up, because we were equally strong at that point. I'm sure he's now stronger than me physically, but a boy of ten and girl of ten are about equally matched, since I was even bigger than him physically. He was a little boy, and I didn't hit back. And I think somehow that was a turning point for me.

MARY: The interesting thing to me is Gloria's being ten years old and an equal physical match and still not doing anything about it, which seems to me even more distressing.

I was thinking about my children who are very used to fighting with their father—roughhousing. My daughter is two years older than my son, so you'd think she'd be better at it, and she *was* up to a certain point. But now, at the age of eight, she's begun to play all sorts of so-called "feminine" games where instead of coming in punching, she runs around or pinches toes or does all kind of devious things that really are not part of the scene. Whereas my son, who's smaller than she is, you know, still fights very directly with his fists or butts with his head, but it's all very direct, head-on. She's already pulling away—not liking real physical contact— would rather play tricks or use an implement, something to get distance between her and her father. So it starts at a very early age where women begin to dislike or be conditioned to dislike any kind of real aggressive behavior.

VIVIAN: I don't travel the subway too much any more, but when

I did every day I encountered two or three incidents always with extremely well-dressed businessmen, and slapped them each time across the face. And it works. Because they were really horrified. And I think it tends to make them think twice about doing it again. I don't recommend it at twelve midnight when the train is empty and you're looking at a man who possibly might have a knife on him. But if it's a packed subway and the man looks like he can be intimidated, I would say slap him across the face. But I should add to that that in the subway, most of the people were outraged at my behavior.

SEBERN: Yeah. That's what happened to me.

VIVIAN: Very strange. But the men especially thought I was just really horrendous.

GLORIA: The men, of course, because they've probably done it to a hundred women. I mean, I don't think it takes anything perverted or abnormal about a man making advances towards a woman in the subway. It happens every day. I see it. You know, you can see the men just walking around, going from one woman to another. The big thing seems to be to impose yourself in front of a woman and to make her aware that you're there and you have the power to do something. More than even doing it. I mean I've had men just stand over me ominously, and you can always pick up those vibrations whether or not they're doing anything to you—you can just kind of look up and know that these men are just really gloating about the fact that you're uncomfortable and you're suddenly rearranging yourself and you're checking to see that nothing's showing and you're really upset and uncomfortable. And eventually maybe you'll even get up and move your seat. And I think that's an element too about it. That it's the feeling of power over you, aside from any cheap thrills they might get from rubbing up against you.

I remember a movie related to this. It was about a girl, a very normal young high school student. The girl was coming home from school. She got off the subway. She had this whole picture of romantic love, because she'd seen this couple that she knew on the train and they were holding hands and stuff and it was very obvious that she was this very romantic kind of schoolgirl. So she's walking home through the park in broad daylight, and she's pulled into the bushes and raped. And the whole rest of the story focused on the changes that this girl went through and her inability to accept the fact that violence had come into her life, and had shattered so many illusions at once. And the whole inability to—not only react to the violence while it was happening, but to accept the existence of it in her own head. She couldn't even accept the fact that it existed at all.

For many of us, during a great deal of our lives, we have been protected in one way or another by either our family or by a strong male—a man who was going to shield us in some sort of way from the existence of violence. It's that lack of ease in that situation. That lack of knowing what your chances are. What your chances for escape are, what your chances to hurt that person are, the way any good fighter could estimate. A woman, I don't think, has that ability, and can only say "Well, he's going to kill me if I even raise my hand." So you don't do anything. When, in fact, maybe it would be better to fight because maybe the element of surprise would allow you to get away. Maybe it wouldn't. But the thing is you have no real way of assessing it because you have no experience. I think that's a part of it.

KATE: It seems to me that the reason we have such difficulty responding adequately either to being attacked or being put down or being used in some way, being disregarded, whistled at or whatever, is that on the one hand there is objectively a great deal of real danger, and to a certain extent if we're sensible we're going to back away. I mean that's a sensible reaction to real danger. But on the other hand we have internalized our fear of invoking male anger, and that we carry around within us—this powerlessness. We've allowed it to shape us on the inside so that internally we're debilitated and there are also external conditions that are really threatening. The combination of the two really, I think, is too much.

Speaking Out on Prostitution

by Susan Brownmiller

Susan Brownmiller is a writer and critic and an active member of New York Radical Feminists. The following paper was presented at an all-day filibuster of a New York State Legislature hearing on "Prostitution as a Victimless Crime."

SUSAN BROWNMILLER: Gentlemen, you state that the purpose of your hearing today is to listen to testimony on the subject of prostitution, what you refer to as "a victimless crime." Prostitution is a crime, gentlemen, but it is not victimless. There is a victim, and that is the woman.

I understand in the last week you received some urgent phone calls from several women who consider themselves your peers— women from the New Democratic Coalition, a district leader or two —and they asked you to suspend the hearing. They told you that the women's liberation movement considers prostitution to be a women's issue, along with child care, along with equal pay for equal work, along with marriage, abortion, contraception, and rape. These women told you that they were planning a joint conference on prostitution with the Radical Feminists, and that this conference, to be held before the start of the legislative session, would evolve a new approach, a woman's approach, to the issue of prostitution. But you refused to cancel this hearing, giving ample evidence, I think, to the weight you give to the political power of women. And so, against our will, we are forced to use your hearing as our forum. We do this with regret, in heat and haste, without the proper thought, consideration, and democratic spirit of inquiry that our women's conference will have.

As with most other issues of women's liberation, the problem of prostitution is unbelievably complex, resting as it does on economics, psychology, sexuality, and the male power principle. There are some who'd say that the male power principle embodies the first three points I've mentioned: economics, psychology, and sexuality. To be perfectly honest, that's what I'd say. (*Applause*)

One fact about prostitution I'm sure has not escaped your notice: the buyers, the ones who hold the cash in their hand, the ones who create the market by their demand, they are all men, gentlemen, the same sex as yourselves.

In the 1940s, the Kinsey Report—which was probably the last really documented report on sexuality—the Kinsey Report stated that two-thirds of all American men have some experience with a prostitute. In 1964, R.E.L. Masters estimated that the figure was closer to 80 percent. Now, having counted the men in this room, I don't think we need to play a shell game to figure out which one of you might have a clean slate.

Now the stock your sex is buying with their dollar bills is human flesh, for the most part, but not always, the same sex as myself. And I say parenthetically "not always," because in this city at the present time, you can go any evening to the corner of 53rd Street and Third Avenue, and see men buying other men for sex. This is seldom talked about, but it is relevant. Again the buyers are always men.

Now the myth has it that the female prostitute is the seller of her own flesh, that she is a free participant in her act, that she has made a conscious choice to sell her body. That is a male myth, gentlemen, one that your sex has rather successfully popularized for your own self-interest. It has not only absolved you of your responsibility in this terrible crime of buying another human being's body, it has conveniently shifted your guilt onto our shoulders. The law in this city is applied to punish the woman and let the man go scot-free.

Now there is something else that the male sex has always tried to do to cover up its crime: it has tried to separate the woman engaged in prostitution from the rest of the women in the culture. It calls her "the other," it marks her the bad woman, it sends her to jail, and it tells the rest of us that we are very good and virtuous and we have nothing in common with her.

Well, gentlemen, I have good news for you. We have seen through *that* little myth: the feminist movement identifies itself with the female victim of the male-created institution known as prostitution. (*Applause*)

MAN: I take it you don't object to being interrupted.

BROWNMILLER: Now, I am white, and middle-class and ambitious, and I have no trouble identifying with either the call girl or the street hustler, and I can explain why in one sentence: I've been working to support myself in the city for fifteen years, and I've had more offers to sell my body for money than I have had to be an executive. According to John Kenneth Galbraith, in a recent issue of *The New York Times Magazine,* 96 percent of all jobs over $15,-000 in this country are held by white men. The remaining 4 percent are divided among blacks, browns, and women. Now when I see a young girl hustling on the street, I see a young girl like myself who has ambition. But she has no options. I mean, what else could she be? She could be a waitress, she could be a comptometer operator, she could be a welfare mother, she could be somebody's wife.

There was a time when I was an unemployed actress, and working to support myself as a waitress and a file clerk. The disparity between my reality situation and my ambition for a better life was so great that I gave serious consideration to the social pressure to do a little hustling. And that is something, gentlemen, I really don't think that you comprehend. I don't think that anyone has ever asked you to sell your body, or presumed that your body was for sale. I wonder if a cab driver has ever turned around to you and remarked, "I see you're a little short of change. Perhaps we could work together. I could steer some customers your way." I wonder if a man has ever walked up to you in a hotel lobby, and muttered, "What's your price? Ten? Twenty? I'll pay it. I'll pay it." That happened to me in the Hotel Astor. I wonder if you've ever applied for work in a bar-restaurant, and the owner, or perhaps he was only the manager, looked you up and down and said, "Are you sure you're over twenty-one? Why don't you come downstairs with me and prove it?"

Now these were all experiences that happened to me at a time of my life when perhaps I looked more vulnerable than I am today, and when I was certainly more desperate. And I want to say without theatricality that I was lucky. I had options that most other women don't have. I managed to use my ambition in a positive manner. I managed to become a writer, what Caroline Bird called "a loophole woman." There was, of course, one other option I could have exercised. I could've gotten married.

So now, perhaps you can understand why I identify with the prostitute, and why, when I see a front page headline in the *New York Times*, "Mayor Stepping Up Drive on Prostitutes and Smut," I know that in a very real sense it is me and my entire sex that the mayor and the *New York Times* are talking about. And when this mayor appoints a task force of six men and no women to study the problems of pimps, pornography, and prostitution, giving equal moral weight to each category, I know that his failure to appoint even one woman to this task force is not an oversight, it's just that the boys decided they've got to get together and do a little superficial something to preserve their fun.

Now I am worried that your purpose in holding this hearing today is to open the doors to the legalization of prostitution. Mr. Pete Hamill, for one, has waxed eloquent on the subject in *New York* magazine and in the *Village Voice*, extolling the virtues of a legal brothel he had visited in Curaçao, where he got a clean lay at a fair price with a medical guarantee of no venereal disease. A recent article in *Look* magazine reports on the first legal American brothel outside of Reno, Nevada. Perhaps you saw the story. In an interview with the pimp in charge, a white man described as sporting two diamond rings on his fingers, this pig said, "First of all, the customer doesn't have to worry about getting V.D. The girls are checked every week by a doctor, and once a month they get a blood test."

Gentlemen, if you intend to extend the definition of government-inspected meat to the sale of human flesh, you will do it over our dead bodies. The women's movement will not tolerate the legalization of sexual slavery in this state. Yes, there is a prostitution problem. It is expressed by Judge John A. Murtagh, who has written: "Most of the men who visit prostitutes would be considered normal." It is expressed by Judge Morris Schwalb, who began to hold prostitutes in his court without bail after he got some complaints from friends of his who were in town for a Bar Association hearing. They claimed that they were actually being harassed by women on the street. Well, if Judge Schwalb were to put on a skirt and walk down 42nd Street, or even Fifth Avenue, any afternoon, despite his hairy legs, I think he would begin to understand for the first time in his life what street harassment is all about. It is women who are being harassed on these streets in New York City, day and night, and they are being harassed by men and not the reverse. Yes, there is a prostitution problem, and it is expressed by Mr. Pete Hamill who daydreams about women in clean little stalls, medically approved and at a price a workingman can afford.

There is a serious problem in our society, when women with ambition must sell their bodies because there is no other way that they can earn fifteen thousand a year. There is a serious problem in our society when men think that access to the female body is, if not a divine right, at least a monetary right.

There has been but one in-depth study on the gratification men get from paying for sex, and that study was conducted in the 1920's. And perhaps that is the area in which you gentlemen could begin your research. Perhaps it is the only valid study a man could make in this day and age on the subject of prostitution. You might begin with Marshall Helfand, who, according to the *New York Times* of July 24th, was arrested and charged with promoting prostitution. Mr. Helfand is the owner of Tune Time Fashions at 520 Eighth Avenue, if you want to know how to reach him. Or perhaps you may want to fly in Mr. Weldon Case of Elyria, Ohio. Mr. Case was arrested along with Mr. Helfand and charged with patronizing a prostitute. He said in court that he was the president of the Midwest Intercontinental Telephone Company, which operates in twelve states. I think a garment center boss and a major corporation president might have some very interesting insights on their concept of manhood and their psychological need to pay a woman for the use of her body.

Prostitution will not end in this country until men see women as equals. And men will never see women as equals until there's an end to prostitution. So it seems that we will have to work for the full equality of women and the end of prostitution side by side. One cannot occur without the other. In the meantime, it seems to me, it's foolish to prosecute a woman for a crime in which she is the victim. But it is equally reprehensible to let a man go free for the criminal act of purchasing another's body.

Now that concludes the formal part of my testimony. I had a great deal of difficulty writing these words down because, as the poet Adrienne Rich once said in another context, "this is the oppressor's language." And it's very clear when you start to write about prostitution that you're using the oppressor's language, which is the male language. The institution is defined by the woman: prostitution; but it is the man who does the buying. There is no formal word to describe that man; we just have a couple of slang words like "john," "trick," that the prostitute uses. There is no formal word. Perhaps that's because it's all men, and men have never felt the need to use the specific word in the language that defines something that is their province. Anyway, I've had trouble, and because of that I feel that other women from the movement must speak now. . . .

Man-Hating

by Pamela Kearon

Pamela Kearon was a founding member of Redstockings. She is now active in The Feminists.

The question of man-hating among radical women seems like the most difficult one to get up a serious discussion on. And you really feel crummy dragging it all out again only to encounter the raised eyebrows, the surprised expressions, voices vibrating with moral indignation; or worse yet, some cute joke and a round of hearty chuckles—completely destroying your point. But hold on! Before you get indignant, before you make your little joke, allow me to try to convince you that man-hating is a valid and vital issue.

Hatred is certainly an observable human fact. And since women are human—not a link between man and the ape—not some innocuous, shadowy, fairy-tale version of the Man—since this is so, hatred, hostility and resentment probably exist somehow in us. And, further, since many of us have already come to the conclusions of feminism —that equal status and opportunity with the male is necessary to our full human existence—the realization of our past and continued subjugation has most likely aroused in us some sentiment resembling hatred. Now, each of us, in denying our hatred and explaining our astonishing magnanimity, relies upon some common argument. Among the most common:

Argumentum ad Sexus:

"Men and women are made for each other sexually. I am perfectly 'normal.' Therefore, I must certainly love men."

This article first appeared in *Notes From the Second Year*, and is reprinted here with the permission of the author.

Answer:

Many men engage in sexual intercourse, often extensively, even marry, while yet hating women. These men are called misogynists. Now, there is no shame in being a misogynist. It is a perfectly respectable attitude. Our whole society (including too many of the women in it) hates women. Perhaps we need a Latin or Greek derivative in place of "man-hating" to make the perfect symmetry of the two attitudes more obvious.[1]

Argumentum ad Superioritus:

"Hate man? No! Definitely not! We must understand them; they depend upon us to show them how to love."

Answer:

This argument is based upon the "Natural Superiority of Women."[2] We are congenitally incapable of hatred. It is our mysterious XX chromosomal structure. Failing to "understand" the man is a perversion of our second nature. Brushing aside forever the utterly unprovable fiction of our second nature, and speaking purely from personal experience, it would seem, on the whole, that people do not react to oppression with Love. I mean the poison seeps out somehow. Sometimes aggressively on those in an even meaner position; sometimes taking the form of an all-pervading and impotent resentment—a petty and spiteful attitude. When women take their hatred out on others, those others are likely to be other women, particularly their own daughters. In doing so they reconcile their own impulse for an object of hate with the demands of an authoritarian system which requires all hate and spite to be directed downward, while respect and "understanding" are reserved for higher-ups, thus keeping nearly everyone supplied with pre-ordained and relatively powerless victims.

Anyway, all arguments which tend to suppress the recognition of man-hating in our midst are reducible to this: *fear*. Man-hating is a subversive and therefore dangerous sentiment. Men, who control definition, have made of it a disgusting perversion. We have been unable to get out from under their definition. I've been at meetings where women actually left because they thought that "man-haters" were on the loose. One woman talked to me in awe and disgust about a woman who she felt had made an anti-male statement at a meeting. It has been the cause of a deep rift within Women's Liberation. It is a vital issue because it involves ultimately the way we feel about ourselves, and how far we are willing to go in our own behalf.

Hatred and Man-Hating

There is no dearth of hatred in the world, I agree. But the thing is, people keep on hating the wrong people. For instance, a lot of people apparently believe that we must fight to preserve our freedom against little Vietnam. Whites, just now stepping out of poverty themselves, arm against the "menace" of the Poor and the Blacks. Upper-middle-class radical snobs despise the class of Whites just beneath them. And men hate women. Our hatred is such a shoddy and confused emotion. We indulge in the most circuitous and illogical prejudices. We have never given the idea of hating someone who has actually done something hateful to us a chance. Oh, I know we ought to hate the sin and love the sinner. But too often we end up loving the sinner and hating his victim (as when one woman seeing another put down, or hearing about her unhappy affair, calls it masochism and that's the end of it).

If hatred exists (and we know it does), let it be of a robust variety. If it is a choice between woman-hating and man-hating, let it be the latter. Let us resolve to respond immediately and directly to injury instead of taking it all out on a more likely victim. It is a difficult stance because it requires a fidelity to what is real in us and neither innocuous nor attractive to oppressors, to that part of you which turned you on to feminism in the first place. That part which is really human and cannot submit.

Footnotes

[1] It is interesting that while the Greeks had a word for both man-hating and woman-hating, only the latter has been anglicized and incorporated into English—A likely word would be 'misandry.'

[2] From the book of that title by Ashley Montague.

Black Feminism

by Cellestine Ware

The following article is a revision of a chapter from Cellestine Ware's first book, Woman Power: Transitions in American Feminism *(Tower Publications, 1970). She was a founder of New York Radical Feminists, is active in the New York movement, and is currently at work on her second book.*

The rejection of black women by black men is a phenomenon best explained by the black man's hatred of blackness and by the need to dominate that underlies male-female relationships. As such, this rejection is an excellent study for feminists. The strength of the resistance to women's independence is shown by the strong epithets directed against black women. The black male's reaction is the forerunner of what all feminists will face as they grow in strength. As women begin to assume positions of equality with men, they will meet virulent abuse, much like that endured by black women now. They will also discover that men will reject them for more "feminine" women.

Black sociologist Calvin Hernton's *Sex and Racism in America* is filled with examples of the defamation and rejection, now subtle, now blatant, that are the lot of black women. For example:

> It is no mystery why white society is now tending to accept the black woman more readily than the black male. First of all, the Negro woman, like the white woman, does not represent to the white world as much of an aggressor against the present power structure as does the Negro man.

It wasn't true any time in the Sixties that black women were hired before black men. On the contrary, black women got little benefit from the drive to find black talent.

The rare black woman who had achieved a position of prominence was bitterly resented by black males. Black personnel men have been known to lose the resumés of promising black women. One such administrator at a famous radio and television station told a black woman applicant: "We already have enough sisters in the communications industry. It's time the brothers got ahead."

In the executive talent shortage of the 1960's, some organizations encouraged women in the patronizing way they had encouraged promotable Negroes when the Negro rights movement was popular; but the efforts to see that qualified women were promoted were much more half-hearted than those promoting Negroes. In 1967, for instance, 15 percent of a group of companies queried by the Bureau of National Affairs said they had undertaken aggressive recruiting of promotable Negroes in response to Title VII, but only one company reported an aggressive policy of recruiting women. In the business world sex is more of a barrier than race.

Yet history has made black women more independent than most American women. Unable to depend on the black man for the economic necessities or for protection, they did not acquire the habit of subordination to masculine authority. Because of this failure to develop subserviency to the male, black women are belittled by both middle- and lower-class black men. The middle-class black man, such as Mr. Hernton, sees the black woman as domineering and castrating. To wit:

> Repeatedly I have witnessed Negro women virtually dominating their white husbands. There may be fights, but she capitalizes on her Negroness and on her sex image by wielding a sort of *Amazon mastery* [my italics] over the white male. In all but a few black woman-white man relationships, it is the man who must do the adjusting—and what he must adjust to is nothing less than what is referred to as the Negro's mode of existence or the Negro's conceptualization of life in the United States.

Mr. Hernton is displaying common anxieties and fears in his emotionally charged statement about the "Amazon mastery" that he says black women develop over their white husbands. His translation of circumstantial necessity into a deliberate attempt at oppression ignores social realities: Discrimination and intolerance invariably force interracial couples to live in black communities, or at least in well-integrated ones.

The lower-class black male sees black women as bitches. The welfare check has made the poor black woman economically independent of the men who come and go in her life, and on whom she cannot rely. Poor black males complain of being told to "Get out! And don't bring your ass back here until you've got a job!" There is antagonism between black males and females, especially in the poorest segments of the community. The women are contemptuous of the men for not being able to find work and provide for their families, or for throwing their money away on gambling, other women, and drinking. The men curse the women for not being feminine and comforting.

The mistake that sociologists are making and that black men seem to be making is the assumption that these women have chosen to be heads of their families. They have become heads of households by default—as the only responsible adults in their families. It is interesting to note that the state menaces and subordinates these women in much the same way that the salary-earning male head of the house does his wife. Protection has its price.

It is the pressures of poverty and slum life that grind down the black family and destroy the role of the male as father-protector. It is these pressures, not black women, that make the confidence man the ghetto hero. In Harlem, in Watts, in Hough, the admired man beats the game: dresses sharp, has a string of girl friends, and doesn't have a steady job. He gets by doing a little of this and a little of that. For the poor black man, there is no ego aggrandizement in the traditional role of the head of the house. Economic and social racism force him to be inadequate in such a role. And so the black bitch was created to justify the confidence man.

According to Fletcher Knebel, Abbey Lincoln first verbalized the current black female unrest (it is as yet unorganized) in the face of this projection of the mythical black bitch. "We are the women," she declared, "whose nose is 'too big,' whose mouth is 'too big and loud,' whose behind is 'too big and broad,' whose feet are 'too big and flat,' whose face is 'too black and shiny,' who's just too damned much for everybody." She was referring to Sapphire, the Amazon of the black male imagination.

The distortions that underlie the transformation of the black mother into a witch-like figure with magical powers to destroy are obviously found in the educated as well as the ignorant. Recently a black educator said: "For the black man, the black woman is too much like his mother. He sees her as domineering, bossy, a woman who runs things. He wants a desirable, easy sex companion, and he finds her in the white woman." What will happen when this desirable white doll becomes real? Perhaps she will be rejected for an easygoing Oriental?

A black college student asserts: "We kind of *fear* [my italics] the middle-class black girl we meet around school. She's snobbish, uppity, and inclined to sneer at a black man unless he excels at something. White girls, for a lot of reasons, are easier, less Victorian, and let's face it, they have their own money."

It is the fear and anxiety of the black male that lead to the construction of the "evil" black female. By now, the superstructure of the "black bitch" bears as little relation to the real black woman as any myth to the reality. The preceding quotes suggest that the men speaking have no honest contact with women of either race. The magical approach of the male to the female is an ancient orientation toward women as the aliens of the human world.

The complaint that black women challenge black men is further proof of the threatening nature of female independence to most men. Philip Roth's indictment of the omnipotent Jewish mother with her all-devouring love has become a familiar theme of our literature just as Jews have been assimilated into the power centers of American life. Although the parallels in the black and Jewish traditions are slight, both cultures are now remarkable for the vehemence of the attacks on their women. I suggest that black literature will increasingly consist of virulent attacks on the evil black mother as black men move into positions of power.

Loving Another Woman

The following is from a taped interview with a woman who talked about her love relationship with another woman. Both of these women, who requested anonymity, had previously had only heterosexual relationships; both are feminists. The interview was conducted by Anne Koedt.

QUESTION: *You said you had been friends for a while before you realized you were attracted to each other. How did you become aware of it?*

ANSWER: I wasn't conscious of it until one evening when we were together and it all just sort of exploded. But, looking back, there are always signs, only one represses seeing them.

For example, I remember one evening—we are in the same feminist group together—and we were all talking very abstractly about love. All of a sudden, even though the group was carrying on the conversation in a theoretical way, we were having a personal conversation. We were starting to tell each other that we liked each other. Of course one of the things we discussed was: What is the thin line between friendship and love?

Or, there were times when we were very aware of having "accidentally" touched each other. And Jennie told me later that when we first met she remembered thinking, "abstractly" again, that if she were ever to get involved with a woman, she'd like to get involved with someone like me.

The mind-blowing thing is that you aren't at all conscious of what you are feeling; rather, you subconsciously, and systematically, refuse to deal with the implications of what's coming out. You just let it hang there because you're too scared to let it continue and see what it means.

Q: *What did you do when you became aware of your mutual attraction?*

A: We'd been seeing a lot of each other, and I was at her house for dinner. During the evening—we were having a nice time, but I remember also feeling uncomfortable—I became very aware of her as we were sitting together looking at something. There was an unusual kind of tension throughout the whole evening.

It was quite late by the time we broke up, so she asked me whether I wanted to stay over and sleep on her couch. And I remember really being very uptight—something I certainly wouldn't have felt in any other situation with a friend. Yet, even when I was uptight and felt that in some way by staying I would get myself into something, I wasn't quite sure what—something new and dangerous—I decided to stay anyway.

It wasn't really until I tried to fall asleep, and couldn't, that all of a sudden I became very, very aware. I was flooded with a tremendous attraction for her. And I wanted to tell her, I wanted to sleep with her, I wanted to let her know what I was feeling. At the same time I was totally bewildered, because here I was—not only did I want to tell her, but I was having a hard time just facing up to what was coming out in myself. My mind was working overtime trying to deal with this new thing.

She was awake too, and so we sat and talked. It took me about two hours to build up the courage to even bring up the subject. I think it is probably one of the most difficult things I ever had to do. To say—to in any way whatsoever open up the subject—to say anything was just so hard.

When I did bring it up in an oblique way and told her that I was attracted to her, she replied somewhat generally that she felt the same way. You see, she was as scared as I was, but I didn't know it. I thought she seemed very cool, so I wasn't even sure if she was interested. Although I think subconsciously I knew, because otherwise I wouldn't have asked her—I think I would have been too scared of rejection.

But when I finally did bring it up, and she said she felt the same way, well, at that point there was really no space left for anything in your mind. So we agreed to just drop it and let things happen as they would at a later time. My main, immediate worry was that maybe I had blown a good friendship which I really valued. Also, even if she did feel the same way, would we know what to do with it?

Q: *When you first realized that you were possibly getting involved with a woman, were you afraid or upset?*

A: No. The strange thing is that the next morning, after I left, I felt a fantastic high. I was bouncing down the street and the sun was shining and I felt tremendously good. My mind was on a super high.

When I got home I couldn't do any kind of work. My mind kept operating on this emergency speed, trying to deal with my new feelings for her. So I sat down and wrote a letter to myself. Just wrote it free association—didn't try to work it out in any kind of theory—and as I was writing I was learning from myself what I was feeling. Unexpectedly I wasn't feeling guilty or worried. I felt great.

Q: *When did you start sleeping with each other?*

A: The next time we were together. Again, we really wanted each other, but to finally make the move, the same move that with a man would have been automatic, was tremendously difficult... and exhilarating. Although we did sleep together, it wasn't sexual; just affectionate and very sensual. After that evening we started sleeping together sexually as well.

I guess it was also a surprise to find that you weren't struck down by God in a final shaft of lightning. That once you fight through that initial wall of undefined fears (built to protect those taboos), they wither rapidly, and leave you to operate freely in a new self-defined circle of what's natural. You have a new sense of boldness, of daring, about yourself.

Q: *Was it different from what you had thought a relationship with a woman would be like?*

A: Generally, no. Most of the things that I had thought intellectually in fact turned out to be true in my experience. One thing, however, was different. Like, I'd really felt that very possibly a relationship with a woman might not be terribly physical. That it would be for the most part warm and affectionate. I think I probably thought this because with men sex is so frequently confused with conquest. Men have applied a symbolic value to sex, where the penis equals dominance and the vagina equals submission. Since sensuality has no specific sex and is rather a general expression of mutual affection, its symbolic value, power-wise, is nil. So sex with a man is usually genitally oriented.

Perhaps I wasn't quite sure what would happen to sexuality once it was removed from its conventional context. But one of the things I discovered was that when you really like somebody, there's a perfectly natural connection between affection and love and sensuality and sexuality. That sexuality is a natural part of sensuality.

Q: *How is sex different with a woman?*

A: One of the really mind-blowing things about all this has been that it added a whole new dimension to my own sexuality. You can have good sex, technically, with a woman or a man. But at this point in time I think women have a much broader sense of sensuality. Since she and I both brought our experiences as women to sexuality, it was quite something.

Another aspect of sexuality is your feelings. Again, this is of course an area that has been delegated to women; we are supposed to provide the love and affection. It is one of our duties in a male-female relationship. Though it has been very oppressive in the context that we've been allowed it, the *ability* to show affection and love for someone else is, I think, a fine thing—which men should develop more in themselves, as a matter of fact. Love and affection are a necessary aspect of full sexuality. And one of the things I really enjoy with Jennie is this uninhibited ability to show our feelings.

Q: *Is the physical aspect of loving women really as satisfying as sex with a man?*

A: Yes.

Q: *You've been together a while now. What's your relationship like?*

A: Once we got over the initial week or so of just getting used to this entirely new thing, it very quickly became natural—natural is really the word I'd use for it. It was like adding another dimension to what we'd already been feeling for each other. It is quite a combination to fall in love with your friend.

We don't have any plans, any desire, to live together, although we do see a great deal of each other. We both like our own apartments, our own space.

I think one of the good things we did in the beginning was to say: Let's just see where it will go. We didn't say that we loved each other, just that we liked each other. We didn't immediately proclaim it a "relationship," as one is accustomed to do with a man —you know, making mental plans for the next ten years. So each new feeling was often surprising, and very intensely experienced.

Q: *What would you say is the difference between this relationship and those you have had with men?*

A: Well, one of the biggest differences is that for the first time I haven't felt those knots-in-the-stomach undercurrents of trying to figure out what's *really* happening under what you *think* is happening.

I think it all boils down to an absence of role-playing; I haven't felt with Jen that we've fallen into that. Both of us are equally strong persons. I mean, you can ask yourself the question, if there were going to be roles, who'd play what? Well, I certainly won't play "the female," and I won't play "the male," and it's just as absurd to imagine her in either one of them. So in fact what we have is much more like what one gets in a friendship, which is more equalized. It's a more above-board feeling.

I don't find the traditional contradictions. If I do something strong and self-assertive, she doesn't find that a conflict with her having a relationship with me. I don't get reminded that I might be making myself "less womanly." And along with that there's less *self*-censorship, too. There's a mutual, unqualified, support for daring to try new things that I have never quite known before.

As a result, my old sense of limits is changing. For example, for the first time in my life I'm beginning to feel that I don't have a weak body, that my body isn't some kind of passive baggage. The other day I gritted my teeth and slid down a fireman's pole at a park playground. It may sound ordinary, but it was something I had never dared before, and I felt a very private victory.

Q: *Given the social disapproval and legal restrictions against lesbianism, what are some of the external problems you have faced?*

A: One thing is that I hesitate to show my affection for her in public. If you're walking down the street and you want to put your arm around someone or give them a kiss—the kind of thing you do without thinking if it is a man—well, that's hardly considered romantic by most people if it's done with someone of your own sex. I know that if I were to express my feelings in public with Jennie, there would be a lot of social intrusion that I would have to deal with. Somehow, people would assume a license to intrude upon your privacy in public; their hostile comments, hostile attitudes, would ruin the whole experience. So you're sort of caught in a bind. But we have in fact begun to do it more and more, because it bothers me that I can't express my feeling as I see fit, without hostile interference.

Q: *What made you fall in love with a woman?*

A: Well, that's a hard question. I think maybe it's even a bit misleading the way you phrased it. Because I didn't fall in love with "a woman," I fell in love with Jen—which is not exactly the same thing. A better way to ask the question is: How were you able to *overcome* the fact that it was a woman? In other words, how was I able to overcome my heterosexual training and allow my feelings for her to come out?

Certainly in my case it would never have happened without the existence of the women's movement. My own awareness of "maleness" and "femaleness" had become acute, and I was really probing what it meant. You see, I think in a sense I never wanted to be either male *or* female. Even when I was quite little and in many ways seemed feminine and "passive"—deep down, I never felt at home with the kinds of things women were supposed to be. On the other hand, I didn't particularly want to be a man either, so I didn't develop a male identity. Before I even got involved with the women's movement, I was already wanting something new. But the movement brought it out into the open for me.

Another thing the movement helped me with was shedding the notion that, however independent my life was, I must have a man; that somehow, no matter what I did myself, there was something that needed that magical element of male approval. Without confronting this I could never have allowed myself to fall in love with Jennie. In a way, I am like an addict who has kicked the habit.

But most important of all, I like her. In fact I think she's the healthiest person I have ever been involved with. See, I think we were lucky, because it happened spontaneously and unexpectedly from both sides. We didn't do it because we felt compelled to put our ideological beliefs into reality.

Many feminists are now beginning to at least theoretically consider the fact that there's no reason why one shouldn't love a woman. But I think that a certain kind of experimentation going on now with lesbianism can be really bad. Because even if you do ideologically think that it is perfectly fine—well, that's a *political* position; but being able to love somebody is a very personal and private thing as well, and even if you remove political barriers, well, then you are left with finding an individual who particularly fits *you*.

So I guess I'm saying that I don't think women who are beginning to think about lesbianism should get involved with anyone until they are really attracted to somebody. And that includes refusing to be seduced by lesbians who play the male seduction game and tell you, "you don't love women," and "you are oppressing us" if you don't jump into bed with them. It's terrible to try to seduce someone on ideological grounds.

Q: *Do you now look at women in a more sexual way?*

A: You mean, do I now eye all women as potential bed partners? No. Nor did I ever see men that way. As a matter of fact, I've never found myself being attracted to a man just because, for example, he had a good physique. I had a sexual relationship with whatever boy friend I had, but I related to most other men pretty asexually. It's no different with women. My female friends—well, I still see them as friends, because that's what they are. I don't sit around and have secret fantasies of being in bed with them.

But there's a real question here: What is the source, the impetus, for one's sexuality? Is it affection and love, or is it essentially conquest in bed? If it's sex as conquest in bed, then the question you just asked is relevant, for adding the category of women to those you sleep with would mean that every woman—who's attractive enough to be a prize worth conquering, of course—could arouse your sexuality. But if the sexual source lies in affection and love, then the question becomes absurd. For one obviously does not immediately fall in love with every woman one meets simply because one is *able* to sleep with women.

Also, one thing that really turns me off about this whole business of viewing women as potential bedmates is the implied possessiveness of it. It has taken me this long just to figure out how men are treating women sexually; now when I see some lesbians doing precisely the same kinds of things, I'm supposed to have instant amnesia in the name of sisterhood. I have heard some lesbians say things like, "I see all men as my rivals," or have heard them proudly discuss how they intimidated a heterosexual couple publicly to "teach the woman a political lesson." This brings out in me the same kind of intense rage that I get when, for example, I hear white men discussing how black men are "taking their women" (or vice versa). Who the hell says we belong to anyone?

Q: *Do you think that you would have difficulty relating to a man again if this relationship broke up? That is, can you "go back" to men after having had a relationship with a woman?*

A: It's an interesting thing that when people ask that question, most often what they're really asking is, are you "lost" to the world of what's "natural"? Sometimes I find myself not wanting to answer the question at all just because they're starting out by assuming that something's wrong with having a relationship with a woman. That's usually what's meant by "go back to men"—like you've been off someplace wild and crazy and, most of all, unsafe, and can you find your way home to papa, or something. So first of all it wouldn't be "going back."

And since I didn't become involved with a woman in order to make a political statement, by the same token I wouldn't make the converse statement. So, sure I could have a relationship with a man if he were the right kind of person and if he had rejected playing "the man" with me—that leaves out a lot of men here, I must add. But if a man had the right combination of qualities, I see no reason why I shouldn't be able to love him as much as I now love her.

At a certain point, I think, you realize that the final qualification is not being male or female, but whether they've joined the middle. That is—whether they have started from the male or the female side—they've gone toward the center where they are working toward combining the healthy aspects of so-called male and female characteristics. That's where I want to go and that's what I'm beginning to realize I respond to in other people.

Q: *Now that you've gotten involved with a woman, what is your attitude toward gay and lesbian groups?*

A: I have really mixed feelings about them. To some extent, for example, there has been a healthy interplay between the gay movement and the feminist movement. Feminists have had a very good influence on the gay movement because women's liberation challenges the very nature of the sex role system, not just whether one may be allowed to make transfers within it. On the other hand, the gay movement has helped open up the question of women loving other women. Though some of this was beginning to happen by itself, lesbians made a point of pressing the issue and therefore speeded up the process.

But there is a problem to me with focusing on sexual choice, as the gay movement does. Sleeping with another woman is not *necessarily* a healthy thing by itself. It does not mean—or prove, for that matter—that you therefore love women. It doesn't mean that you have avoided bad "male" or "female" behavior. It doesn't guarantee you anything. If you think about it, it can be the same game with new partners: On the one hand, male roles are learned, not genetic; women can ape them too. On the other, the feminine role can be comfortably carried into lesbianism, except now instead of a woman being passive with a man, she's passive with another woman. Which is all very familiar and is all going nowhere.

The confusing of sexual *partners* with sexual *roles* has also led to a really bizarre situation where some lesbians insist that you aren't really a radical feminist if you are not in bed with a woman. Which is wrong politically and outrageous personally.

Q: *Did the fact that lesbians pushed the issue in the women's movement have a major effect upon your own decision to have a relationship with a woman?*

A: It's hard to know. I think that the lesbian movement has escalated the thinking in the women's movement, and to that extent it probably escalated mine.

But at the same time I know I was slowly getting there myself anyway. I'd been thinking about it for a long time. Because it is a natural question; if you want to remove sexual roles, and if you say that men and women are equal human beings, well, the next question is: Why should you only love men? I remember asking myself that question, and I remember it being discussed in many workshops I was in—what is it that make us assume that you can only receive and give love to a man?

A Feminist Look
at Children's Books

by the Feminists on Children's Media

Feminists on Children's Media is a collective formed in the summer of 1970 by women concerned about the stereotyped female image prevalent in children's literature. Their program of slides, tapes and readings on sexism in children's books has been shown to a variety of audiences, and their bibliography of non-sexist children's books, Little Miss Muffet Fights Back,* *has been widely distributed.*

Is the portrayal of females in children's books sexist? That is, are girls and women assigned only traditional female roles and personalities? And when the female foot fails to fit that often too-tight shoe, is the girl or woman then seen as an unfortunate, troubled human being?

These questions were the basis of a group effort to scrutinize some of the more highly praised children's books. In our view, a non-sexist portrayal would offer the girl reader a positive image of woman's physical, emotional, and intellectual potential; it would encourage her to reach her own full personhood, free of traditionally imposed limitations.

In selecting books to examine, we consulted a number of influential lists. These were the *Notable Books of 1969* (American Library Association), the Child Study Association's annual recommendations for that same year, and the Newbery Award winners.

Reprinted from School Library Journal, January, 1971, published by R. R. Bowker Company (A Xerox Company). Copyright © 1971, Xerox Corporation, and reprinted with the permission of the publisher. This article appeared in *Notes From the Third Year*.
* For a copy of this bibliography send 50 cents in coin plus a stamped (16 cents) self-addressed 4 x 9½ envelope to Feminists on Children's Media, P.O. Box 4315, Grand Central Station, New York, N.Y. 10017.

It was a shock to discover almost immediately that relatively few of the books on these lists even feature female characters, let alone what we would consider *positive* female characters. Of all forty-nine Newbery Award winners, books about boys outnumbered books about girls by about three to one. On that score, the years have brought little improvement. The ALA list for 1969 gave us a ratio of over two to one.

The Child Study Association list for the same year proved more difficult to analyze. It is very long, divided into innumerable categories, and many of the books can't yet be found in the libraries. However, we made a separate check of several categories. Under the heading of "Boys and Girls" we found a male to female ratio of two to one. Under "Growing Up" the ratio was over three to one. And "Sports," of course, like certain bars we could formerly name, was 100 percent male. The rest of the book list may not follow the pattern of this sampling, but suspicion runs high!

The thoughtful introduction to the Child Study Association list makes the following statement: The books a child reads "should not shield him from knowledge of destructive forces in the world, but rather help him to cope with them." We agree, for the most part. But why does the sentence read "shield *him*" and "help *him*"? Sexism is such a destructive force in the world that we feel the implicit sexism in this sentence should not be overlooked.

The introduction states also that a book's "possible emotional and intellectual impact on a young reader" must be considered. Right on! Not even a problem of gender there. The CSA continues: "... From its inception, it has been aware of the mental health aspects of reading and asks that books for children present basically honest concepts of life, positive ethical values, and honest interpersonal relationships." We ask no more than that. The CSA has clearly been struggling to encourage greater sensitivity to racism in books for children. If only their future book selections could be made with an equally growing sensitivity to the impact of sexism! Many of the present selections fail to realize the promise of their own introduction. The list is guilty of sexism—if only through indifference.

Of course, a greater sensitivity to sexism would greatly curtail the current lists of recommended children's books, at least for the next few years. Yet a scrupulous attitude on the part of prestigious organizations would surely serve powerfully in raising the general feminist consciousness of the children's book world, making forever obsolete Eve Merriam's recent and accurate comment that "sex prejudice is the only prejudice now considered socially acceptable." Habit dies hard.

We'd like to apologize for seeming to pick on CSA. It is just that such a praiseworthy introduction deserved attention in terms of its implications for the female image. Nor were we being picky in our examination of specific books: Checking the prevalence of so virulent a disease as sexism requires the isolation of even potential carriers.

What would we like to see in children's books? What were our criteria? We wanted to see girl readers encouraged to develop physical confidence and strength without the need to fear any corresponding loss of "femininity." We would have liked to see the elimination of all those tiresome references to "tomboys." Why can't a girl who prefers baseball to ballet simply be a girl who prefers baseball to ballet?

Many women have to—or simply prefer to—earn a living. Can't we encourage girls to find satisfaction and fulfillment in work, and lay aside forever the suspicion that for a woman, work outside the home is primarily proof of her inability to love a man, or to land a sufficiently lucrative one? Women do study seriously, work with enjoyment—or at least pride in their competence—get promoted, and (of course) fight sexism at work and in their families in order to progress. Let's show them as no less "feminine," despite the assertiveness and firm sense of self required in this untraditional role.

Margaret Mead has written that "man is unsexed by failure, woman by success." That is another brutal truth we would like to see changed. And while we're about it, let's not overlook the fact that boys, too, are denigrated and cramped by sexism. Our current rigid role definitions require that a boy be all that a girl should not be: unafraid, competent at "male" jobs, strong. A weeping boy is a "sissy." Words like "sissy"—and "hero," too—should be dissected and exposed for the inhuman demands they make on growing boys. Children's books could help.

We object to a woman's being defined by the man she marries, or the children she bears, or the father she once obeyed. Let's see women who are people in their own right—independent of such compensatory affiliations. And if a woman doesn't want children, or even a husband, must this be seen as peculiar? Why not encourage girls in a search for alternate life styles? Give a girl all the possible options for her future life choices that you give a boy, all his freedom to inquire and explore and achieve. Her options don't have to be slanted toward certain currently socially imposed preferences.

There are books on superwomen. Okay. Superwomen do exist. But many more books are needed on women who simply function very well and freely wherever they choose—or are forced—to apply their abilities.

We are bitterly tired of seeing depictions of the woman as castrator. Even a well-known writer, whose portrayal of girls we frequently admire, slipped badly in some recent picture books. In one of these, the mother reproves her son for spilling the mud he is playing with—even though the scene is outdoors! In another, little sister (and we know where she learned *her* lesson) reproves brother for accidentally spilling paint off his easel. Little girls are as capable of making a casual mess and as freely lost in creative play as little boys. A picture book that shows this beautifully is *Rain Rain Rivers* by Uri Shulevitz (Farrar, 1969) which we were delighted to find on both the ALA and CSA lists. (We were as pleased to find the two previously mentioned books ignored by both lists.)

And when, as must sometimes happen if books portray real life, there is an overcontrolling or too-bossy woman, she should not be made a fool or villain. A little understanding—of her problem, her frustration at not being allowed to play an equal role in her family or her world, and her consequent misuse of energy to project her ideas and ego through the lives of others—is long overdue.

How about books showing more divorced and single-parent families? And, for heaven's sake, every divorced or widowed mother does not solve her problems through remarriage—or even wish to do so. (Few do, you know!) Maybe she can start on the career she never had, and discover a new concept of herself. The difficulties and the loneliness are real, as are the child care problems. But let the woman find a new self-reliance in fighting her own battles, and joy in winning at least some of them.

There is also the question of language. No more automatic use of "he" to mean "child," or "mankind" to mean "humankind." If at first the alternatives seem forced, and they will, they won't sound that way for long.

Despite our criticism of socially assigned roles, we don't mean to diminish or ignore the mother or housewife. She is often a strong, wonderfully rich human being. Her role can be vital, and sometimes she finds satisfaction in it. But let's not insist on that as *her* role. Men can also cope skillfully with household tasks, and not necessarily look for a woman or daughter to take them off the hook.

Sexist Books

The books we read—most from the lists mentioned earlier—fell, or were pushed by our merciless analysis, into several categories. One, plain and simple, was the Sexist Book, in which girls and women are exclusively assigned traditional female roles, although the material may, unhappily, be fairly true to life.

We were forcibly struck by the purposeful sexist propaganda between the covers of some of the recommended children's books. Young women who have found it an uphill struggle to identify with the popular female image will recognize it as propaganda and not simply as a natural reflection of life. Unfortunately the girl reader is not yet so experienced. Books that outline a traditional background role for women, praising their domestic accomplishments, their timidity of soul, their gentle appearance and manners, and at the same time fail to portray initiative, enterprise, physical prowess, and genuine intellect, deliver a powerful message to children of both sexes. Such books are a social poison.

Take, for a horrible example, the attitude exemplified in the following line: "Accept the fact that this is a man's world and learn how to play the game gracefully." Those words fell from the lips of a *sympathetic* male character in Irene Hunt's 1967 Newbery winner *Up the Road Slowly* (Follett, 1966). Or take this juicy bit from the 1957 winner *Miracles on Maple Hill* by Virginia Sorenson (Harcourt, 1956):

> For the millionth time she was glad she wasn't a boy. It was all right for girls to be scared or silly or even ask dumb questions. Everybody just laughed and thought it was funny. But if anybody caught Joe asking a dumb question or even thought he was the littlest bit scared, he went red and purple and white. Daddy was even something like that, old as he was.

Does that passage describe real life? Indeed it does! But a good book for children should comment and leave the child feeling something is wrong here. This one does not. In fact, we voted it our supreme example of the most thoroughly relentless type of sexism found in children's literature. The girl, Marly, never overcomes her hero worship of brother Joe or her comparative inferiority. And it certainly would have been relevant to explore the toll that maintaining hero status takes on Joe's character.

Such perfect examples, of course, are not the rule. But there was a surplus of books whose thesis might seem less obvious, but whose refrain was predictably the same. A little girl in the 1955 Newbery winner *The Wheel on the School* (Harper, 1954) asks her boy playmate: "Can I go, too?" And the response is "No! Girls are no good at jumping. It's a boy's game." Meindert DeJong leaves it at that—and another eager little girl reader is squelched.

Those fictional girls who join the prestigious ranks of male adventurers often do so at the expense of other members of their sex. And small wonder, the tomboy-turned-token-female is simply the other side of the coin. The message is clear: If a girl wishes to join the boys in their pranks and hell-raising, or to use her imagination and personality in leading them, she renounces all claim to supposedly feminine characteristics—tears and fears and pink hair ribbons. The line between traditionally assigned sex roles is drawn sharp and clear. The girl who crosses that line is forced to desert her sex rather than allowed to act as a spokeswoman for a broader definition.

Take *Lulu's Back in Town* (Funk & Wagnall, 1968). The proof provided by author Laura Dean to show Lulu's final acceptance by the boys is the clubhouse sign: "FOR BOYS ONLY. No Girls Allowed. (Except Lulu.)" This is seen by the author, who unfortunately happens to be a woman, as a satisfactory ending. But our committee was not so pleased. (Except to find that neither ALA nor CSA had listed it.)

Cop-Outs

The Cop-Out Book is often the most insidious. At its worst, it promises much and delivers nothing. But the better ones are the most infuriating, for often they are only a step away from being the exact kind of literature we'd like to see for girls *and* boys *about* girls. The actual cop-out may be only a crucial line, a paragraph, the last chapter. But somewhere a sexist compromise is made, somewhere the book adjusts to the stereotyped role of woman, often for the sake of social pressure and conformity. The compromise brings with it a change, and this change is not only disturbing, but often distorts the logical development of the character herself. Suddenly her development is redirected, or, rather, stunted.

The many Cop-Out Books we found are probably a fair reflection of the social uncertainties and inner conflicts of writers, publishers, and reviewers in our sexist society.

Caddie Woodlawn by Carol R. Brink (Macmillan, 1935) is a Newbery winner. Not a recent one, but still extremely popular. Caddie is a young pioneer girl, allowed to run free with her brothers. She is happy and strong in her so-called tomboy role. Though her mother pressures her to become more of a "lady," the reader feels serenely certain that Caddie will remain her own person. Alas, as the book draws to a close, Caddie's father pleads: "It's a strange thing, but somehow we expect more of girls than of boys. It is the sisters and wives and mothers, you know, Caddie, who keep the world sweet and beautiful. . . ." Thus subdued, she joins the insipidly depicted girls at the weaving loom. True, the boys do ask her to teach them how to weave. Apparently they may choose to join women at their work, but no longer may Caddie choose to run free in the woods. And we are left feeling cheated. Why should it be the *right* choice for her obediently to join the "sweet and beautiful" women of the world on their pedestals? Why shouldn't she continue to struggle for a life in which she might fulfill some inner potential?

The linking of a girl's growing up to the abandoning of her "tomboy" ways is a depressingly frequent theme in these books. As a stage in growing up, tomboy behavior appears to be acceptable. But the girl must in the end conform to more socially approved behavior. In a widely used bibliography compiled by Clara Kirchner in 1966 entitled *Behavior Patterns in Children's Books,* there is an entire section called "From Tomboy to Young Woman." Here are two random descriptions:

A Girl Can Dream by Betty Cavanna (Westminster, 1948): Loretta Larkin, tops in athletic but poor in social graces and jealous of a classmate who shines socially, finds out that being "just a girl" can be fun.

Billie by Esphyr Slobodkina (Lothrop, 1959): Billie, who wore faded jeans and played boys' games because she didn't like being a girl, came to think differently after she took ballet lessons to limber up a sprained ankle.

These books fit into the following categories: Womanliness, Growing Up, and Popularity.

Young readers of such grievous cop-outs are forced to believe that the spunk, individuality, and physical capability so refreshingly portrayed in tomboy heroines must be surrendered when girls grow up, in order to fit the passive, supposedly more mature image of a young woman. But where is that earlier energy to be spent? Is depression in the adult woman perhaps linked to the painful suppression of so many sparks of life? In a way we could call the Cop-Out Book the "co-op" book, for it permits the tomboy reader to believe she can pass comfortably over into that other world at a safely future date. Real life is rarely like that.

A new book recommended on both the ALA and the CSA lists is Constance Green's *A Girl Called Al* (Viking, 1969). The main character comes across as a nonconformist who truly enjoys her individuality, and throughout most of the book she eschews traditional female worries—how she looks, hooking boy friends, etc. Wonderful. But the ending is a neat little all-American package. Al gets thin, gets pretty, and now she will be popular. All these sudden switches hit the reader in the last few pages. Her pigtails make room for a feminine hairdo. Her closest friend explains:

> Her mother took her to the place she gets her hair done and had the man wash and set Al's hair, and now she wears it long with a ribbon around it. It is very becoming, my mother says. She is right. But I miss Al's pigtails. I wanted her to wear it this way but now that she does I'm kind of sorry. She looks older and different, is all I know.

Again, we are led to believe that another character in our long line of individual heroines will conform to the role society has rigidly defined for her. We find it hard to buy the sudden change in Al. And we also miss the pigtails.

Sometimes it is the focus of a book that makes it a cop-out. When we read in 1959 Newbery winner, Elizabeth Speare's *The Witch of Blackbird Pond* (Houghton Mifflin, 1958), we praised Kit's independent spirit, her rejection of bigoted values, and her truly striking courage at a time when women were burned for witchcraft. From a feminist standpoint, the book is marred only by the plot's revolving around the standard question: "Whom shall Kit marry?" In too many books we find the male character worrying about *what* shall he be while the female character worries about *who* shall he be.

Only a few hairs are out of place in *Next Door to Xanadu* by Doris Orgel (Harper, 1969), also listed by ALA and CSA. The main character faces the too-often very real hatred of pre-teen boys toward girls. She meets it with strength, earning respect. The only boy-crazy girl in the book is deemphasized. But one scene allows our society's pervasive sexism to come shining through.

At a going-away party for one of the girls, a woman parades as a fortuneteller. "She took out a bowl, put it on the table, filled it with all sorts of strange little things. Then she said 'Who among you dares to delve into the secrets the future holds in store?' " Here were the fortunes of the girls: The girl who pulled out two safety pins would be "the mother of a fine pair of twins." Chalk meant another would be a teacher. The one who picked a little sack of soil would be "a farmer's wife." One pulled a penny: she would be very rich. One picked a little plastic boy doll and she would meet a "fine young man." "Great happiness" was in store for the one who got a bluebird's feather. When one of the girls pulled out a jack, the fortuneteller chanted: "Butcher, baker, candlestick-maker; tailor, sailor, teacher, preacher; doctor, lawyer, carpenter, smith—she would have kept it up, but Helen guessed it. Betsy would marry a jack-of-all-trades."

Not *be* a Jack-of-all-trades, but *marry* one. Not *be* a farmer, but be a farmer's wife. The only vocation predicted was that of teacher. Unfortunately, fortunetellers will be like that, until we have feminist fortunetellers. That would certainly bring brighter futures.

At the risk of carping, we felt that such a fine book as *A Wrinkle in Time* by Madeline L'Engle (Farrar, 1962), the 1963 Newbery winner, had a hint of acceptance of woman's second-class status. This is almost the only science fiction book in which a girl is the main character. We even find a mother who is a scientist, perhaps one of the only scientist moms in juvenile fiction. But why did father have to be a super scientist, topping mom by a degree or two?

Positive Images

Happily, if not of course, there are some books for children which show female characters in flexible, diverse roles. They allow for character development beyond the stereotype, and do not disappoint us in the end. At first we tried calling these "Non-Sexist." But we found many books were not precisely either Sexist or Cop-Out, though somehow they did not quite fit our exacting feminist standards, usually because they did not deal with the questions they posed in a sufficiently clear, real, and affirmative way. The rare book that did succeed, even in this, is our Positive-Image Book.

Certainly, these categories overlap a bit. *A Wrinkle in Time* really belongs among the Positive-Image Books. We just couldn't resist putting down papa's degrees. Unfair, we admit, because of the especially fine, honest relationship between Calvin (the boy who is a friend, as opposed to Boy Friend) and the girl protagonist. They respect each other's heads, and his ego does not stand in the way of her saving the day with an act of courage that rescues her little brother from it. We also applauded the image of the mother as a brilliant scientist who instills pride in her children.

Another Newbery we salute is the 1961 winner, *Island of the Blue Dolphins* by Scott O'Dell (Houghton Mifflin, 1960), one of the rare books showing a girl with strong physical skills. She kills wild dogs, constructs weapons, kills a giant tentacled sea fish, and hauls a six-man canoe by herself. The Indian girl protagonist, Karana, spends eighteen years alone on a bleak and lonely island. And there we are indeed tempted to ask why such a marvelous heroine can only be encountered alone on an island—and never in the midst of society?

While on the subject of positive images, there is a new book we hope will appear on the 1970 recommended lists. *Rufus Gideon Grant* by Leigh Dean (Scribners, 1970) is about a boy, but we were taken by the following reference to a woman: "There inside this magazine was this lady, climbing giant trees and playing with wild chimpanzees. . . ." And Rufus asks: "Can a boy be a zoologist?"

If we had time we would also like to discuss such essentially positive-image books as *Strawberry Girl* by Lois Lenski (Lippincott, 1945), *From the Mixed-Up Files of Mrs. Basil E. Frankweiler* by E. L. Konigsburg (Atheneum, 1967), Vera and Bill Cleaver's *Where the Lilies Bloom* (Lippincott, 1969), and *Pippi Longstocking* by Astrid Lindgren (reissued in paper by Viking, 1969). Padding our Positive-Image list a bit we might add commendable classics like Lewis Carroll's *Alice in Wonderland* (first published in 1865), *Anne of Green Gables* by Lucy M. Montgomery (Grosset & Dunlap, 1908), and *Rebecca of Sunnybrook Farm* by Kate Douglas Wiggin (Macmillan, 1903). Of course there are some positive books that escaped our notice, just as some of the negative ones may have slipped by, but we wanted to cover a fourth and extra category that seems to overlap all the others.

Especially for Girls

This category appears on a number of publishers' lists and on lists of recommended books. It is called "especially for girls." The reason advanced by librarians and publishers for having such a category at all is that while girls are perfectly happy to read "boys' " books, no self-respecting boy will read books about girls. In our male-dominated society, unfortunately, this is probably true. But listing a separate group of books for girls provides boys with a list of books *not* to read, further polarizing the sexes.

There seems only one possible justification for a separate category of books for girls: to spot and recommend those books which, according to our highest, most stringent feminist standards are not sexist. Pursuing this logic, when children's literature no longer supports sexism, there will no longer be any reason to list books "especially for girls."

The current lists of girls' books promoted by publishers show a preponderance of stories about love, dating, and romance. And there are the companion books about young girls with problems like shyness, overweight, glasses, acne, and so on, that are supposed to interfere with romance. Certainly, problems facing young girls should be dealt with in the books they read, but we resent the implication forced on young girls that romance is the only fulfilling future for them. Boys, too, are involved in romance, but their books are about other things.

The lists for girls also include career books about nurses, secretaries, ballet dancers, stewardesses. Why not more female doctors?

Bosses? Pilots? Aquanauts? Present books simply reinforce the sex roles imposed by society, and even then virtually all the careers end in a cop-out. When the girl marries she gives up the career. But *must* marriage and career be mutually exclusive? For their publishers, these books are justified by the market—they are meant to sell rather than edify. We happen to believe that career books that edify will also sell, and far more lastingly, as women gain in the struggle for their freedom.

But what about those lists of currently recommended books that *are* intended to edify? In 1969, for example, the Child Study Association listed eight books "Especially for Girls." Of these, we were disheartened to find that only one was free—or almost free—of sexism. Two more were Cop-Out Books. The rest were middling to very bad.

Let's start with the best. *The Motoring Millers* by Alberta Wilson Constant (Crowell, 1969) not only shows delightful girls and women behaving responsibly and delightfully and doing many things that men do, but the question of sex roles is specifically aired. In the story, the winner of an auto race turns out to be a young girl. When the wife of a college president says to her, "I want you to know that I am highly in favor of your driving in this race. Women should advance their cause in every field," the winner replies, "I didn't think about that. I just love to drive. Taught myself on our one-cylinder Trumbull when I was ten." We welcome both reactions.

Two more books on this list, *A Girl Called Al* and *Next Door to Xanadu,* have already been described above as Cop-Outs, though we did consider them both *almost* commendable. To those three acceptable books, we would also add *Julie's Decision* by Rose A. Levant (Washburn, 1969) except that we were disturbed by what seemed a paternalistic white attitude especially inappropriate in a book about a black girl.

But, after these titles, the CSA girls' list deteriorates into sexism. It is shocking to find "recommended for girls" a book like *The Two Sisters* by Honor Arundel (Meredith, 1969), which not only reinforces the stereotype of girls as romantic, clothes-crazy, and spendthrift, but whose moral says that, when all is said and done, love is a woman's proper vocation and her future ought to be subordinated to her husband's. The young heroine in *The Two Sisters* has just told her father that she may abandon her university scholarship to follow her husband who has gone off to find a better job in another city. Her father says gently: "Geoff's quite right to be ambitious and you're right not to stand in his way. A man who doesn't get a chance to fulfill his ambition makes a terrible husband." It doesn't occur to either that a woman who sacrifices her potential can also end up making a terrible wife.

John Rowe Townsend's *Hell's Edge* (Lothrop, 1969) is just as bad. The motherless teenage heroine cooks all the meals and does the housework for her teacher-father, whose domestic ineptitude is paraded as one of his endearing qualities. A pair of sisters in the book are set up with mutually exclusive stereotyped female traits— and then shot down for them. One is described as a "half-wit" for being concerned with looks and clothes; the other sister, a book-worm, is denigrated for not caring about her looks or clothes. Damned if you do and damned if you don't.

In another CSA recommendation, the boys in the family are considered more important than the girls, even though the book is supposedly for girls. (Well, it happens in real life too!) The name of that prize is *One to Grow On* by Jean Little (Little, Brown, 1969).

In *A Crown for a Queen* by Ursula Moray Williams (Meredith, 1969), the plot revolves around—get ready—a *beauty* contest with the boys as judges! The most memorable (and most offensive) line occurs when the heroine, Jenny, finally gets the beauty crown. As we might predict, she "never felt happier in her life." This is scarcely the positive female image we'd been looking for, even if we could all be beauty queens.

As our consciousness of "woman's place" changes, our recommendations of books for girls must change. As must books themselves. Eventually, we will have no more need for any list recommended "Especially for Girls."

Independence from the Sexual Revolution

by Dana Densmore

Dana Densmore has been active in the women's movement in Boston since June, 1968. She helped start A Journal of Female Liberation (No More Fun and Games, The Female State), *and her main energies have been devoted to it, as she believes that the dissemination of ideas and analysis is the most critical need in making the feminist revolution. Her second priority is self-defense. She has studied Tae Kwon Do for two and a half years, the last six months with Jayne West's Feminist Tae Kwon Do School. She is a member of Cell 16, which puts out the* Journal, *and is in a feminist study group.*

We human beings are not creatures who spring from the earth, our integrity round and tight, our will free and objective. We are not only influenced by what goes on around us, we are conditioned and created by it.

Desires and even needs can be created. We are all familiar with the ingenious techniques of Madison Avenue to generate insecurity in order to offer their product or service as a means of assuaging the insecurity. The most effective techniques zero in on our fears of not being socially acceptable, not being loved, not being sexually attractive.

The seeds of this insecurity exist already in a society whose ideology of individualism isolates people and throws the blame for all maladjustment and failure onto the individual. We constantly hear the variations on this theme. It is used to avoid admitting that anything could be wrong with the way our society is set up. "If you can't make a satisfactory adjustment to life, it's your own problem: perhaps some professional help is in order." "Don't try to change the world—you'd better free your mind instead."

And we hear it thrown at us in response to the threat of female liberation. "You should *be* intimidated by being put down by men." "*Leave* your family if it's so oppressive." "If you don't like the way your lover treats you, you can get out of bed." "It's your own fault if you don't get good jobs—you *let* yourself be discouraged, you *took* the unchallenging, 'feminine' courses of study in school."

The assumption implicit in all these things is the individualist ideology that if you are unable to do something which is theoretically possible (or which is thought to be theoretically possible) it is because of a personal hang-up and consequently you have no legitimate gripe. This isolates people and tends to make them insecure and unself-confident. They often can be brought to despise themselves because they see in themselves so many supposed weaknesses and psychological problems that prevent them from being happy, well-adjusted, and effective. This is a characteristic of our society and isolates all of us, not just the women. (However, women, being the most oppressed, are forced to blame themselves the most for their impotence and thus despise themselves the most and are most isolated and afraid and anxious that no one will love them.)

The very isolation the individualist ideology imposes makes us desire even more to be loved and accepted, and fear even more being unlovable. But we cannot escape our fears of being unlovable. "Who would want me?" we ask; "I have all these hang-ups." The solution offered to all this is often to open yourself up until you can merge selflessly with another person. In many cases it is explicitly sex. But the solutions all point to sex one way or another. Sex becomes magic, assumes a life of its own, making anything interesting, everything worthwhile. It's for this that we spend those hours trying on micro-dresses, loading up with jingle-jangle chains, smoothing on lacy white stockings and Instant Glow Face Gleamer.

It is this that many girls who would be most free to fight in the female liberation struggle are squandering valuable energy pursuing as an indispensable part of their lives. They lavish and dissipate their valuable time and talents and emotional strength on attempts to be attractive to men and to work things out with lovers so that "love" might be less degrading. And too often all they reap is demoralization, damaged egos, emotional exhaustion.

Under the banner of "not denying our sexuality" and pointing to repression in the past when women were denied the right to any pleasure in their bodies at all, many of us now embrace sexuality and its expression completely uncritically. As if present excess could make up for past deprivation. As if even total sexual fulfillment would change anything. Except . . . is this true?—except private dead-of-the-night fears that maybe we really are the sexually frustrated, neurotic freaks our detractors accuse us of being. Are we chasing sexual fulfillment so earnestly because we have to prove that our politics are not just a result of our needing a good fuck?

Then there is the issue of orgasms. Among those who were never well-adjusted and womanly enough to psych themselves into an orgasm while being vaginally stimulated by a man, there are some who, when they discover that their shame and misery were not only not unique but in fact extremely common and due to very straightforward anatomical causes, react to this discovery by feeling that they must make it up by demanding all the physical fulfillment they had been providing the men all along and missing themselves.

What we lost wasn't just X many instances of physical pleasure. The suffering that countless women have endured because they were told that if they didn't have vaginal orgasms they were frigid—that they were neurotic and selfish and unwomanly and sexually maladjusted and unable to let go and give and secretly resented the power of their husbands and envied them—this suffering is staggering and heartbreaking.

The liberation of sexual equality and the right to sexual pleasure is the solution for the future. But is there any solution for the past? Is it a solution to go out and collect orgasms in order to make up for all those frustrated, self-loathing years? I say you can never make up for all that suffering, and certainly not through a mere physical sensation. And as for the psychological rewards of getting my due at last, I can feel no triumph in that, especially when I'm still fighting the old habits and old guilts that remain long after the intellect and the will have plunged on.

The worst part about it is that even with perfect sexual fulfillment, mutual guilt-free pleasure, we are still oppressed. After all, some women managed to have vaginal orgasms all along, and they were still oppressed; in fact, that was how you were supposed to *achieve* orgasm—by surrendering completely to the man's will, by loving being a woman and everything that that implied. Sexual relations in the world today (and perhaps in all past ages) are oppressive. The fact that your lover gives you an orgasm changes only one small part of that oppression (namely the part that dictated that you had to see yourself as a creature who was allowed only the muted, sensuous, semi-masochistic pleasure of getting fucked and never the direct active transcendent pleasure of orgasm).

If that were the only injustice, or even the major injustice, done us, we would be very well off indeed. In fact, we would probably be able to bear it without concern, certainly without misery and self-loathing. It's the general oppression and degradation we suffer in the world that causes us to be humiliated in the sex act, as Simone de Beauvoir points out. If it weren't for the sense of inadequacy and impotency we learn from all other aspects of our lives, we *would* kick our lover out of bed if he was arrogant, inconsiderate, or ungentle.

Some men do the dinner dishes every night. That doesn't make their wives free. On the contrary, it's just one more thing she has to feel grateful to him for. He, in the power and glory of his maleness, condescended to do something for her. It will never mean more than that until the basic power relations are changed. As long as men are the superior caste and hold the political power in the class relationship between men and women, it *will* be a favor your lover is doing you, however imperiously you demand it. And beyond that one thing, nothing else need have changed.

But the issue isn't just orgasm. We weren't even allowed to engage in sexual intercourse without giving up social dignity and the respect of men. We weren't allowed to love, to make love, to enjoy making love, even with our *husbands*. Husbands were commanded to love their wives, wives to obey their husbands. It was cruel and insufferably hypocritical.

But whatever we were denied in the past, it cannot be argued that access to sexual pleasure is denied to us now. Our "right" to enjoy our own bodies has not only been bestowed upon us: it is almost a duty. In fact, things have been turned around to the point where the "fact" (actually a smear device) that we do *not* engage in sex is whispered about and used by men to discourage "their" women from having anything to do with us. This is one development that makes me laugh out loud whenever I think about it. What would "Ask Beth" think about that! How can men pull this off with a straight face? They must be terrified indeed at the thought of losing their power to define what is proper for proper women. (For that power is exactly what we are challenging.)

The right that is a duty. Sexual freedom that includes no freedom to decline sex, to decline to be defined at every turn by sex. Sex becomes a religion, existing independently of the individuals who share its particular physical consummation. The media totally bombard us with it. Sex is everywhere. It's forced down our throats. It's the great sop that keeps us in our place. The big lift that makes our dreary worlds interesting. Everywhere we are sexual objects, and our own enjoyment just enhances our attractiveness. We are wanton. We wear miniskirts and see-through tops. We're sexy. We're free. We run around and hop into bed whenever we please. This is the self-image we have built up in us by advertising and the media. It's self-fulfilling. And very profitable. It keeps us in our place and feeling lucky about it (the freedom to consume, consume, consume, until we swallow the world). It makes us look as if we're free and active (actively, freely, we solicit sex from men).

And people seem to *believe* that sexual freedom (even when it is only the freedom to actively offer oneself as a willing object) is freedom. When men say to us, "But aren't you already liberated?" what they mean is, "We *said* it was okay for you to let us fuck you, that guilt was neurotic, that chaste makes waste; you're already practically giving it away on the street, what more do you want or could you stomach?" The unarticulated assumption behind this misunderstanding is that women are purely sexual beings, bodies and sensuality, fucking machines. Therefore freedom for women could only mean sexual freedom.

Spiritual freedom, intellectual freedom, freedom from invasions of privacy and the insults of degrading stereotypes—these are appropriate only to men, who care about such things and can appreciate them. Woman, remember, is a sexual being, soft, emotional, expressive, giving, close to the earth, physical, imprisoned by the frightening, disgusting, delicious, all too perishable flesh. For such a creature to presume upon the territory of transcendence is horrifying, unthinkable, polluting the high, pure realms of the will and spirit, where we rise *above* the flesh.

Unfortunately, the oppressed often adopt the psychoses of the ruling class, transformed, sometimes, until they seem no longer vicious and intellectually dishonest projections but a reasonable acceptance of reality (and for the oppressed, reality *is* in a sense what the ruling class believes). So we recognize that we have something of an intellect, and perhaps even use it openly with tolerant or sophisticated men. But we still recognize that insofar as we are also *women,* we are soft, emotional, expressive, giving, close to the earth, ruled at times by our sensuality, our profound, undeniable sexuality.

There are rewards for us in this. In losing ourselves in sexual surrender we bring that masterful, rational, hard, unemotional analytical man to abject, total, frenzied *need* of the flesh he likes to fancy himself above. And there is no question that for a woman sexual love contains as a strong component the desire to become powerful by merging with the powerful. She sees herself as impotent and ineffectual, him as masterful and competent. She longs for that sense of competence and the confidence that comes to him from knowing it's "his world." In the intimacy and ecstasy of sex she seeks to lose herself, become one with him.

Children who are told over and over that they are liars or thieves become liars or thieves. People who are told over and over that they are crazy become crazy. If you are told over and over that you are a being who has profound sexual needs the odds are very good that you will discover that you do. Particularly when other outlets are forbidden or discouraged. Particularly when it is emphasized that those who do *not* feel these needs are frigid, neurotic, sexually maladjusted (which for a woman means *essentially* maladjusted), dried up, barren, to be pitied.

This stereotype too is self-fulfilling. A woman who cannot enjoy sex, for whatever reason (her husband, it may be, is repulsive to her either because of his style as a lover or because of the contempt with which he treats her out of bed), may become bitter believing she is missing her womanly fulfillment, the great soul-shaking pleasure that would make the rest of the misery of being a woman worthwhile. It's useless to claim that we aren't programmed to desire sex, to reach for it, to need it. Even when we know something is false our conditioning drives us to continue to act it out. In this case it is very difficult even to sort out what is true and what is false.

A woman in her forties wrote to me as follows: "Now I realize all that about its being an instinct, but I think there's something more to the story. When I reflect on my own past experience, I can rarely find a time when I was driven to it from inside need. I'm not saying if I didn't have it for a long period (which hasn't ever happened to me), I might not feel the instinct, but I'm saying we need some evidence or just how much because I suspect that even the minimum is far, far less than is believed. . . . I know I talked myself into most sex probably looking for the 'earth-moving orgasm' which maybe was a hoax anyway. What if no one had given me those words with which I talked myself into it? I begin to distrust it all. Reminds me of that line from *Notes From the First Year:* sometimes you'd rather play ping pong."

No doubt there are some innate needs, or at least propensities. But a propensity can be culturally built into an obsession or culturally killed off, sometimes simply by never reinforcing it. I personally suspect that some form of sex urge may turn out to be innate. Human beings reproduced before they had an elaborate social organization institutionalizing sexual intercourse and before full-page color ads in magazines urged women to "Be Some Body."

And if it turns out that this urge is not that strong, it might still be worth keeping (i.e., reinforcing) if it affords people physical pleasure or pleasures of intimacy. But it should be taken for granted that it must be pleasurable to *both parties,* always: which means it must never be institutionalized by law or culture. And if it *is* a basic "drive" felt by both men and women, there is no need to institutionalize it to ensure its survival.

What we "see" when we look inside may correspond very poorly with reality. We're saturated with a particular story about what's inside. Moreover, we've been saturated with this all our lives, and it has conditioned us and made us what we are. We *feel* that we need sex, but the issue is very confused. What is it we really need? Is it orgasms? Intercourse? Intimacy with another human being? Stroking? Companionship? Human kindness? And do we "need" it physically or psychologically?

Intercourse, in the sense of the physical act which is the ultimate aim of so much anxiety, plotting, and consuming, is not necessarily the thing we are really longing for, any more than, in the more obvious cases, it is the consumer products advertising builds up neurotic longing for. Physically, there is a certain objective tension and release, at least for a man, when excitation proceeds to orgasm. With a woman even this physical issue is much less clear: most women don't have orgasms at all, and very few always have them. I think we might all agree that *that* isn't why we go to bed with a man. In any case an orgasm for a woman isn't a release in the same sense that it is for a man, since we are capable of an indefinite number, remaining aroused the whole time, limited only by exhaustion. The release we feel, therefore, is psychological. A psychological tension to get this man, to possess him in a certain intimate sense, is released when we "get him" through *his* orgasm. We then enjoy the pleasure of closeness because *he* is more open to us (provided he *is* open, and doesn't just turn over and go to sleep, or jump up to attend to something else on his mind, his attention easily distracted now).

Without denying that sex can be pleasurable, I suggest that the real thing we seek is closeness, merging, perhaps a kind of oblivion of self that dissolves the terrible isolation of individualism. The pleasure argument doesn't impress me very much. A lot of things are pleasurable without our getting the idea that we can't live without them, even in a revolutionary context. I can think of certain foods, certain music, certain drugs, whose physical pleasurableness compares favorably even to good sex.

Moreover, destruction of the sense of isolation through communication, community, human kindness, and common cause are all available from other women as you work together in the struggle against oppression. With other women you are more than friends, you are sisters. It would be a mistake to brush off too quickly the spiritual strength to be gained from sisterhood or to overestimate the solace in the arms of a man, just because that is, traditionally, women's only resort.

What I want to suggest is not that sex is by its *nature* evil and destructive, but that it is not an absolute physical need: the assumption that it *is* an absolute physical need is evil, and the patterns of behavior that grow out of that assumption are destructive. Most of us recognize that sexual relationships often turn out to be evil and destructive in a society where dehumanization, exploitation, and oppression of women is so deeply embedded into the culture. What we seek is the exception, the rare case where we have, or think for a little while that we might have, the right guy and the right circumstances.

But even in love we are limited when we believe that we must screw to express love. We are programmed to think that not only is sex the only way to demonstrate or prove our love, it is the only (or best) way to *express* it. And in this dangerous and alienating society we are always very anxious to demonstrate, to prove, and to express our love, and to have the affections of our lover demonstrated, proved, and expressed to us. For men this is doubly compelling because sex for a man is the only or best way to prove or express his virility, both by the demonstration of sexual potency and by the imposing of his will on her.

To the extent that this is true, then, we are conditioned to that one mode of expression and turn to it uncritically. But we need to develop new nonsexual ways of relating to people, to men as well as women. The obsession with genital sexuality, and screwing in particular, cheats us out of a world of rich possibilities. We think that love is sex love, genital sex love. Therefore we can't love women or men we aren't sexually involved with or interested in. Affection too is identified with genital sex and except for children, pets, and a few close relatives, all physical affection must be limited to our assigned male sex partner. Even communication, human contact and understanding, is assumed to be available only in the intimacy of genital sexual contact.

All desire for love, companionship, physical affection, communication, and human kindness therefore translate to us into a desire for sex. This is pathetically narrow, impossibly limiting. Especially since it can be asked with some justice whether it is very common to obtain this communication, this human kindness, this companionship and affection we seek. It's what we want, all right, but we must ask of it, as we ask of the patent medicine which promises just what we want: does it really do that? And if not, perhaps it is, in practice, a fraud.

In fact, as women have frequently observed, sex can be a fast way to ruin a good relationship. Either because the man just can't treat her as an equal when he's so personally involved, or because he doesn't know how to treat a woman equally in a sexual relationship, or because he was secretly or subconsciously after the conquest all along.

Another problem is that men have a different view of love and sex than women and for the most part women do not know this. They assume they are making equal and similar investments. Studies have been made of what men and women think love is, what love means to them. Affection and companionship are first on the women's lists, with security and other elements following, and sex turns up as number 8. Men reverse this with sex first. Companionship and affection are *secondary* goals for men. This orientation of men, coupled with the set of cultural attitudes (and fears) men have toward women, make the sexual love relationship a poor place for a woman to seek communication and human understanding.

However, as long as we are able to make clear demands of a relationship, to insist that the man fulfill certain requirements or we shall do without him, thank you, then we can keep our heads above water. These requirements might be: (1) He is sexually interested in me, not just interested in sex with me the one who is closest at hand. (2) He is not indifferent to me aside from the sex; he has tender feelings, loyalty, perhaps even love for me. (3) He respects me as a person, is willing to discuss things with me, does not browbeat me, lecture me, or disparage my opinion or projects.

It is when we are not free, or do not feel free, to make such a set of minimum demands on a relationship that the serious trouble arises. And we are not free when we are in the grip of the false conditioning that decrees that we need sex. We are not free if we believe the culture's ominous warnings that we will become "horny" (what a callous, offensive word) and frustrated and neurotic and finally shrivel up into prunes and have to abandon hope of being good, creative, effective people. We are not free if we believe that we, like the lower animals, are driven by something which is not only instinctual but mindlessly, hopelessly, ineluctable. If we believe all that, then, due to the rarity of good, healthy, constructive relationships between men and women in the world today, we will be forced to accept, even seek out, evil and destructive relationships where we are used, and accept that humiliation in return for the privilege of "using him."

If it were true that we needed sex from men, it would be a great misfortune, one that might almost doom our fight. (Meanwhile, the belief that it is true can serve the same function.) Fortunately, it is not true. When we seek sex it is by conscious, intelligent choice. We wish to experience through intimacy human kindness, communication, back-to-the-womb merging and oblivion, childlike openness. We do it because we think it's the right thing to do. We may be mistaken. We may only think it's the right thing because we think that we will turn into neurotic bitches if we don't. But we *don't* do it because we are sexual beings who cannot "deny our sexuality." According to this argument, to have sexual feelings, or an energy that could be rapidly converted into sexual energy, and yet to choose not to engage in sexual intercourse but rather to expend that energy on something else which seems, at the moment, of higher priority, is to "deny" our sexuality.

This is what men have done to us all along. (They do not apply this same logic to themselves.) Because they only relate to us sexually they conclude that we are just sexual beings. If we then function on any other level, something is seriously out of joint since in effect we are "denying" that we are primarily sexual beings. But in fact, it is only if we are *merely* sexual beings, *exclusively* sexual beings, that choosing to put our energy elsewhere indicates any kind of denial. (The great scientist or artist or writer who puts all his energy in his work is not *denying* anything—that would be to insult him; he simply feels that the day is only so long and for this particular time his work is the most important thing to him.)

Personally, I recognize that I have sexual feelings. Their exact nature and origin is open to debate, but I have no doubt that there is an objective, physical reality involved at least to some extent. However, I and I alone will decide what importance these feelings have in my life as a human being. We are not living in an ideal society, and "post-revolutionary" characters or life styles might well hinder revolution or make it impossible. The fact that in a good society women might want to produce children, at least until the perfection of the artificial womb, is no reason for me to take myself out of the struggle by having children now under these conditions. Similarly, the belief that sex would have a place in a good society does not necessarily mean that we must engage in it now. That decision must be based on the objective conditions of the present.

Let me say something about the objective conditions of the present. We are crippled people living in an evil and destructive world. We have a great deal to do beyond the mere business of living. There is much work that needs to be done, and not, by any means, just the work of liberating people and making a revolution. There is the work of rebuilding ourselves, learning to know ourselves and our potentials, learning to respect ourselves, learning to respect and work with other women. We must overcome all the self-destructive patterns we have been taught in a lifetime of being female.

This work of reclaiming ourselves and making a revolution in women's minds in order to free all of us is the most important work. If a particular sexual relationship or encounter is convenient, appropriate, and pleasurable, if it is not demeaning or possessive or draining in any way, you might decide to choose to invest some of your precious self in it.

But remember how precious your time and your energy and your ego is, and respect yourself enough to insist that the rewards be equal to the investment.

Feminist Graffiti

by Ellen Levine

Ellen Levine is co-author of Rebirth of Feminism, *a photographer, and an editor of* Notes From the Third Year. *She is presently at work on a book,* All She Needs, *from which the following excerpts are taken.*

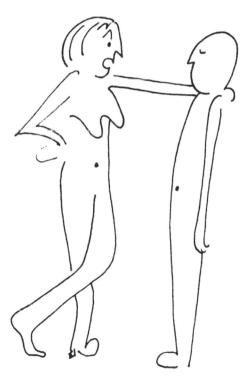

I SOMETIMES WONDER
IF YOU'RE THE RIGHT ONE
FOR ME TO BE SUBMISSIVE TO

Copyright © 1972 by Ellen Levine.

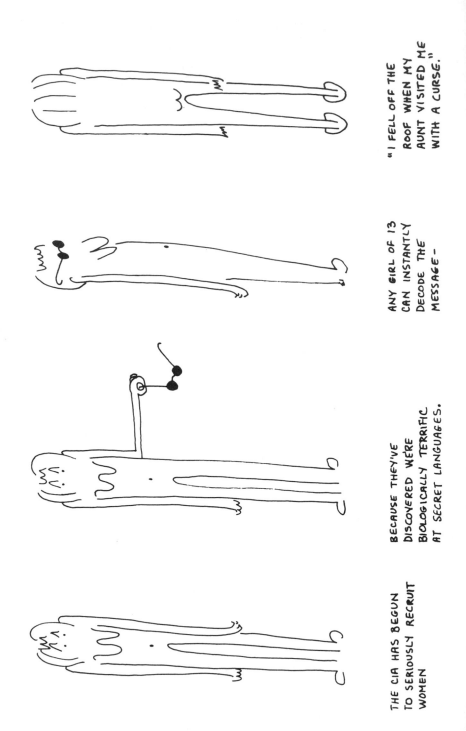

THE CIA HAS BEGUN
TO SERIOUSLY RECRUIT
WOMEN

BECAUSE THEY'VE
DISCOVERED WE'RE
BIOLOGICALLY TERRIFIC
AT SECRET LANGUAGES.

ANY GIRL OF 13
CAN INSTANTLY
DECODE THE
MESSAGE —

"I FELL OFF THE
ROOF WHEN MY
AUNT VISITED ME
WITH A CURSE."

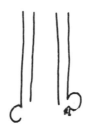

I WISH MEN NEVER
MADE PASSES AT GIRLS
WHO WEAR GLASSES

IF ALL WOMEN SECRETLY
WANT TO BE RAPED,

YOU'RE NOT A REAL WOMAN
IF YOU DON'T WANT TO BE
RAPED.

BUT SINCE
YOU ALWAYS GET
WHAT YOU REALLY WANT,

IF I HAVEN'T
BEEN RAPED,

MAYBE I SECRETLY
DON'T WANT TO BE
A WOMAN.

I'VE GOT TO FIND A SHRINK
TO HELP ME GET RAPED.

I'M WORKING HARD
AT THINKING LIKE
A MAN

Theory
and
Analysis

The Building of the Gilded Cage

by Jo Freeman

Jo Freeman is a graduate student in political science who, with any luck, will be the University of Chicago's first (unofficial) Ph.D. in women's studies. She has written extensively on women and women's liberation in feminist journals, and publications such as Nation, Trans-Action, *and the* Valparaiso Law Review. *Currently she is compiling an anthology of feminist writings to serve as an introductory textbook for courses on women.*

Hidden somewhere in the byways of social science is an occasionally discussed, seldom studied, frequently employed and rarely questioned field generally referred to as social control. We have so thoroughly absorbed our national ideology about living in a "free society" that whatever else we may question, as radicals or academics, we are reluctant to admit that all societies, ours included, do an awful lot of controlling of *everyone's* lives. We are even more reluctant to face the often subtle ways that our own attitude and our own lives are being controlled by that same society.

This is why it has been so difficult for materially well-off, educated whites—women as well as men—to accept the idea that women are oppressed. "Women can have a career (or do something else) if they really want to" is the oft-heard refrain. "Women are where they are because they like it" is another. There are many more. "Women are their own worst enemies." "Women prefer to be wives and mothers rather than compete in the hard, aggressive male world." "Women enjoy being feminine. They like to be treated like ladies." These are just variations on the same "freedom of choice" argument which maintains that women are free (don't forget, we are living in a *free* society) to do what they want and never question why they think they want what they say they want.

But what people think they want is precisely what society must control if it is to maintain the *status quo*. As the Bems put it, "We overlook the fact that the society that has spent twenty years carefully marking the woman's ballot for her has nothing to lose in that twenty-first year by pretending to let her cast it for the alternative of her choice. Society has controlled not her alternatives but her motivation to choose any but one of those alternatives."[1]

There are many mechanisms of social control and some are more subtle than others. The socialization process, the climate of opinion in which people live, the group ideology (political or religious), the kind of social structures available, the legal system, and the police are just some of the means society has at its disposal to channel people into the roles it finds necessary for its maintenance. They are all worthy of study, but here we are going to look only at two of them—one overt and one covert—to see what they can tell us about women.

The easiest place to start when trying to determine the position of any group of people is with the legal system. This may strike us as a little strange since our national ideology also says that "all men are equal under the law" until we remember that the ideology is absolutely correct in its restriction of this promise to "men." Now there are three groups who have never been accorded the status and the rights of manhood—blacks, children (minors) and women. Children at least are considered to be in their inferior, dependent status only temporarily because some of them (white males) eventually graduate to become men. Blacks (the 47% who are male) have "been denied their manhood" since they were kidnapped from Africa and are currently demanding it back. But women (51% of the population, black and white)—how can a woman have manhood?

This paradox illustrates the problem very well: because there is a longstanding legal tradition, reaching back to early Roman law, which says that women are perpetual children and the only adults are men. This tradition, known as the "Perpetual Tutelage of Women"[2] has had its ups and downs, been more or less enforced, but the definition of women as minors who never grow up, who therefore must always be under the guidance of a male (father, brother, husband or son), has been carried down in modified form to the present day and vestiges of it can still be seen in our legal system.

Even Roman law was an improvement over Greek society. In that cradle of democracy only men could be citizens in the polis. In fact most women were slaves, and most slaves were women.[3] In ancient Rome both the status of women and slaves improved slightly as they were incorporated into the family under the rule of *patria potestas* or Power of the Father. This term designated not so much a familial relationship as a property relationship. All land was owned by families, not individuals, and was under the control of the oldest male. Women and slaves could not assume proprietorship and in fact frequently were considered to be forms of property. The woman in particular had to turn any income she might receive over to the head of the household and had no rights to her own children, to divorce, or to any life outside the family. The relationship of woman to man was designated by the concept of *manus* (hand) under which the woman stood. Women had no rights under law—not even legal recognition. In any civil or criminal case she had to be represented by the *pater* who accepted legal judgment on himself and in turn judged her according to his whims. Unlike slaves, women could not be *emancipated* (removed from under the hand). She could only go from under one hand to another. This was the nature of the marital relationship. (From which comes our modern practice of asking a woman's father for her *hand* in marriage.) At marriage a woman was "born again" into the household of the bridegroom's family and became the "daughter of her husband."[4]

Although later practice of Roman Law was much less severe than the ancient rules, some of the most stringent aspects were incorporated into Canon Law and from there passed to the English Common Law. Interpretation and spread of Roman Law varied throughout Europe, but it was through the English Common Law that it was brought to this country and made part of our own legal tradition.

Even here history played tricks on women. Throughout the sixteenth and seventeenth centuries, tremendous liberalizations were taking place in the Common Law attitude toward women. This was particularly true in the American colonies where rapidly accelerating commercial expansion often made it profitable to ignore the old social rules. In particular, the development of property other than land facilitated this process as women had always been held to have some right in *movable* property while only male heirs could inherit the family lands.[5]

But when Blackstone wrote his soon-to-be-famous *Commentaries on the Laws of England,* he chose to ignore these new trends in favor of codifying the old Common Law rules. Published in 1765, his work was used in Britain as a textbook. But in the Colonies and new Republic it became a legal Bible. Concise and readable, it was frequently the only book to be found in law libraries in the United States up until the middle of the nineteenth century, and incipient lawyers rarely delved past its pages when seeking the roots of legal tradition.[6] Thus when Edward Mansfield wrote the first major analysis of *The Legal Rights, Liabilities and Duties of Women* in 1845, he still found it necessary to pay homage to the Blackstone doctrine that "the husband and wife are as one and that one is the husband." As he saw it three years before the Seneca Falls Convention would write the *Woman's Declaration of Independence* "it appears that the husband's control over the person of his wife is so complete that he may claim her society altogether; that he may reclaim her if she goes away or is detained by others; that he may maintain suits for injuries to her person; that she cannot sue alone; and that she cannot execute a deed or valid conveyance without the concurrence of her husband. In most respects she loses the power of personal independence, and altogether that of separate action in legal matters."[7] The husband also had almost total control over all the wife's real and personal property or income.

Legal traditions die hard even when they are mythical ones. So the bulk of the activities of feminists in the nineteenth century were spent chipping away at the legal nonexistence that Blackstone had defined for married women. Despite the passage of Married Women's Property Acts and much other legislative relief during the nineteenth century, the core idea of the Common Law that husbands and wives have reciprocal—not equal—rights and duties remains. The husband must support the wife and children, and she in return must render services to the husband. Thus the woman is legally required to do the domestic chores, to provide marital companionship and sexual consortium. Her first obligation is to him. If he moves out of town, she cannot get unemployment compensation if she quits her job to follow him, but he can divorce her on grounds of desertion if she doesn't. Likewise, unless there has been a legal separation, she cannot deny him access to their house even if she has good reason to believe that his entry on a particular occasion would result in physical abuse to her and her children. He must maintain her, but the amount of support beyond subsistence is at his discretion. She has no claim for direct compensation for any of the services rendered.[8]

Crozier commented on this distribution of obligations: "... Clearly, that economic relationship between A and B whereby A has an original ownership of B's labor, with the consequent necessity of providing B's maintenance, is the economic relationship between an owner and his property rather than that between two free persons. It was the economic relationship between a person and his domesticated animal. In the English Common Law the wife was, in economic relationship to the husband, his property. The financial plan of marriage law was founded upon the economic relationship of owner and property."[9]

This basic relationship still remains in force today. The "domesticated animal" has acquired a longer leash, but the legal chains have yet to be broken. Common Law practices, assumptions, and attitudes still dominate the law. The property, real and personal, brought by the woman to the marriage now remains her separate estate, but such is not always the case for property acquired during the marriage.

There are two types of property systems in the United States—common law and community. In the nine community property states (Arizona, California, Hawaii, Idaho, Louisiana, Nevada, New Mexico, Texas and Washington), all property or income acquired by either husband or wife is community property and is equally divided upon divorce. However "the general rule is that the husband is the head of the 'community' and the duty is his to manage the property for the benefit of his wife and family. Usually, as long as the husband is capable of managing the community, the wife has no power of control over it and acting alone, cannot contract debts chargeable against it."[10] Included in the property is the income of a working wife which, under the law, is managed by the husband with the wife having no legal right to a say in how it shall be spent.

In common law states each spouse has a right to manage his own income and property. However, unlike community property states, this principle does not recognize the contribution made by a wife who works only in the home. Although the wife generally contributes domestic labor to the maintenance of the home far in excess of that of her husband, she has no right to an allowance, wages or an income of any sort. Nor can she claim joint ownership upon divorce.[11]

Marriage incurs a few other disabilities as well. A married woman cannot contract on the same basis as her husband or a single woman in most states. In only five states does she have the same right to her own domicile. In many states a married woman can now live separately from her husband but his domicile is still her address for purposes of taxation, voting, jury service, etc.[12]

Along with the domicile regulations, those concerning names are most symbolic of the theory of the husband's and wife's legal unity. Legally, every married woman's surname is that of her husband and no court will uphold her right to go by a different name. Pragmatically, she can use another name only so long as her husband does not object. If he were legally to change his name, hers would automatically change too, though such would not necessarily be the case for the children. "In a very real sense, the loss of a woman's surname represents the destruction of an important part of her personality and its submersion in that of her husband."[13]

When we move out of the common law and into the statutory law we find an area in which, until recently, the dual legal status of women has increased in the last seventy years. This assault was particularly intense around the turn of the century, but has solidified considerably since then. Some of the earliest sex discriminatory legislation was against prostitutes; but this didn't so much prohibit the practice of their profession as regulate their hours and place of work. The big crackdown against prostitutes didn't come until World War I when there was fear that the soldiers would contract venereal disease.[14]

There was also a rise in the abortion laws. Originally abortion was illegal only when performed without the husband's consent and the only crime was a "wrong to the husband in depriving him of children."[15] Prior to passage of the nineteenth century laws which made it a criminal offense it was largely regarded as a Church offense punishable by religious penalties.[16]

The most frequent new laws were sex specific labor legislation. Under common law and in the early years of this country there was very little restrictive legislation on the employment of women. It was not needed. Custom and prejudice alone sufficed to keep the occupations in which women might be gainfully employed limited to domestic servant, factory worker, governess, and prostitute. As women acquired education and professional skills in the wake of the Industrial Revolution, they increasingly sought employment in fields which put them in competition with men. In some instances men gave way totally and the field became dominated by women, losing prestige, opportunities for advancement, and pay in the process. The occupation of secretary is the most notable. In most cases men fought back and were quick to make use of economic, ideological, and legal weapons to reduce or eliminate their competition. "They excluded women from trade unions, made contracts with employers to prevent their hiring women, passed laws restricting the employment of married women, caricatured working women, and carried on ceaseless propaganda to return women to the home or keep them there."[17]

The restrictive labor laws were the main weapon. Among the earliest were those prohibiting women from practicing certain professions, such as law and medicine. But most were directed toward regulating work conditions in factories. Initially such laws were aimed at protecting both men and women workers from the sweatshop conditions that prevailed during the nineteenth century. The extent to which women, and children, were protected more than men varied from state to state, but in 1905 the heated struggle to get the state to assume responsibility for the welfare of workers received a major setback. The Supreme Court invalidated a New York law that no male or female worker could be required or permitted to work in bakeries more than sixty hours a week and in so doing made all such protective laws unconstitutional.[18]

Three years later the court upheld an almost identical Oregon statute that applied to females only, on the grounds that their physical inferiority and their function as "mothers to the race" justified special class legislation.[19] With this decision as a precedent, the drive for protective legislation became distorted into a push for laws that applied to women only. It made some strange allies, who had totally opposing reasons for supporting such laws. On the one hand social reformers and many feminists were in favor of them on the principle that half a loaf was better than none and the hope that at some time in the future the laws would apply to men as well.[20] Many male union leaders were also in favor of them, but not because they would protect women. As President Strasser of the International Cigarmakers Union expressed it, "We cannot drive the females out of the trade but we can restrict this daily quota of labor through factory laws."[21]

Strasser soon proved to be right, as the primary use of "protective" laws has been to protect the jobs of men by denying overtime pay, promotions, and employment opportunities to women. The Supreme Court has long since rejected its ruling that prevented protective legislation from applying to men, yet there has been no move by male workers to have the laws extended to them. Most of the real benefits made available by such laws have been obtained through federal law or collective bargaining, while the state restrictive laws have been quoted by unions and employers alike to keep women in an inferior competitive position. The dislike of these laws felt by the women they affect can be seen in the numerous cases challenging their legitimacy that have been filed since Title VII of the Civil Rights Act was passed (prohibiting sex discrimination in employment).

These laws do more than restrict the hours which women may work. An examination of the state labor laws reveals a complex, confusing, inconsistent chaos. As of 1970, before the courts began voiding many sex specific labor laws on the grounds they were in conflict with Title VII, thirteen states had minimum wage laws which applied only to women and minors, and two which applied only to women. Adult women were prohibited from working in specified occupations or under certain working conditions considered hazardous in twenty-six states; in ten of these women could not work in bars.[22]

Laws restricting the number of hours a woman may work—generally to eight per day and forty-eight per week—were found in forty-one states and the District of Columbia. Twenty states prohibited night work and limitations were made in twelve on the amount of weight that could be lifted by a woman. These maximums ranged from fifteen to thirty-five pounds (the weight of a small child).[23]

The "weight and hours" laws have proved to be the most onerous and are the ones usually challenged in the courts. In *Mengelkoch et al. v. the Industrial Welfare Commission of California and North American Aviation, Inc.*, the defending corporation has admitted that the women were denied overtime and promotions to positions requiring overtime, justifying their actions by the California maximum hours law. In *Koig v. Southern Bell Telephone and Telegraph Co.*, the plaintiffs are protesting that their current job is exempt from the Louisiana maximum hours law but that the higher paying job to which they were denied promotion is not. One major case which challenged the Georgia weight lifting law is *Weeks v. Southern Bell Telephone and Telegraph*. It received a favorable ruling from the Fifth Circuit Court but the plaintiff has yet to be given the promotion for which she sued.

But perhaps most illustrative of all is an Indiana case,[24] in which the company tried to establish maximum weight lifting restrictions even though its plant and the plaintiffs were located in a state which did not have such laws. By company policy, women were restricted to jobs whose highest pay rate was identical with the lowest pay rate for men. Many of the women, including the defendants, were laid off while men with less seniority were kept on, on the grounds that the women could not lift over thirty-five pounds. This policy resulted in such anomalies as women having to lift seventeen and a half tons of products a day in separate ten-pound loads while the male supervisors sat at the head of the assembly line handling the controls and lifting one forty-pound box of caps each hour. "In a number of other instances, women were doing hard manual labor until the operations were automated; then they were relieved of their duties, and men were employed to perform the easier and more pleasant jobs."[25] In its defense, the company claimed it reached this policy in accordance with the union's wishes, but the Seventh Circuit Court unanimously ruled against it anyway. This is only one of many instances in which corporations and unions have taken advantage of "protective" legislation to protect themselves from giving women equal job opportunities and equal pay.

With the passage of Title VII, the restrictive labor legislation is slowly being dissolved by the courts. But these laws are just vestiges of what has been an entirely separate legal system applicable particularly to women. At their base lies the fact that the position of women under the Constitution is not the same as that of men. The Supreme Court has ruled several times that the Fourteenth Amendment prohibits any arbitrary class legislation, except that based on sex. The last case was decided in 1961, but the most important was in 1874. In *Minor v. Happerset* (88 U.S. 21 Wall, 162 1873), the court first defined the concept of "second-class citizenship" by saying that some citizens could be denied rights which others had. The "equal protection" clause of the Fourteenth Amendment did not give women equal rights with men.

Other groups in society have also had special bodies of law created for them as a means of social control. Thus an examination of the statutes can clearly delineate those groups which society feels it necessary to control.

The statutes do not necessarily indicate *all* of the groups which a particular society excludes from full participation, but they do show those which it most adamantly excludes. In virtually every society that has existed, the caste cleavages, as distinct from the class lines, have been imbedded in the law. Differentiating between class and caste is often difficult as the two differ in degree that only at the extremes is seen as a difference in kind. It is made more difficult by our refusal to acknowledge that castes exist in our society. Here too we have allowed our thinking to be subverted by our national ideology. Our belief in the potentiality, if not the current existence, of high social mobility determined only by the individual's talents, leads us to believe that mobility is hampered by one's socio-economic origins but not that it is made impossible if one comes from the wrong caste. Only recently have we reluctantly begun to face the reality of the "color line" as a caste boundary. Our consciousness of the caste nature of the other boundaries, particularly that of sex, is not yet this high.

The law not only shows the caste boundaries, it also gives a fairly good history of the changes in boundaries. If the rigidity of caste lines fades into more permeable class lines, the legislation usually changes with it. The Middle Ages saw separate application of the law to the separate estates. In the early years of this country certain rights were reserved to those possessing a minimum amount of property. Today, nobility of birth or amount of income may affect the treatment one receives from the courts, but it is not expressed in the law itself. For the past 150 years, the major caste divisions have been along the lines of age, sex, and ethnic origin; these have been the categories for which special legislation has existed.

The law further indicates when restricted castes are seen to be most threatening and the ways in which they are felt to be threatening. If members of a group will restrict their own activities, or these activities are inconsequential, law is unnecessary. No law need be made to keep people out of places they never considered going. It is when certain prerogatives are threatened by an outgroup that it must be made illegal to violate them. Thus Jim Crow laws were not necessary during slavery and restrictive labor legislation was not extensively sought for until women entered the job market in rapidly accelerating numbers at the end of the nineteenth century.

Frequently, members of the lower castes are lumped together and the same body of special law applied to all. Most of the labor legislation discussed earlier applies to "women and minors." The state of New York once worded its franchise law to include everyone but "women, minors, convicts and idiots." When a legal status had to be found for Negro slaves in the seventeenth century, the "nearest and most natural analogy was the status of women."[26] But the clearest analogy of all was stated by the Southern slave-owning class when trying to defend the system prior to the Civil War. One of the most widely read rationalizations was that of George Fitzhugh, who wrote in his 1854 *Sociology for the South* that "The kind of slavery is adapted to the men enslaved. Wives and apprentices are slaves, not in theory only, but often in fact. Children are slaves to their parents, guardians and teachers. Imprisoned culprits are slaves. Lunatics and idiots are slaves also."[27]

The progress of "out castes," particularly those of the wrong race and sex, also have been parallel. The language of the Nineteenth Amendment was borrowed directly from that of the Fifteenth. The "sex" provision of Title VII (only the second piece of corrective legislation pertaining to women that has been passed)[28] was stuck into the Civil Rights Act of 1964 as a joke by octogenarian representative Howard W. Smith of Virginia.[29]

Many of the same people were involved in both movements as well. Sojourner Truth and Frederick Douglass were staunch feminists. Douglass urged the first Convention at Seneca Falls in 1848 to demand the franchise when many of the women were reluctant to do so. Similarly, the early feminists were ardent abolitionists. The consciousness of two of the most active is dated from the World Anti-Slavery Convention in London in 1840 when Lucretia Mott and Elizabeth Cady Stanton were compelled to sit in the galleries rather than participate in the convention.[30] Many of today's new feminists also come out of an active background in the civil rights and other social movements.[31] Almost without exception, when one of the lower castes in our society begins to revolt, the others quickly perceive the similarities to their own condition and start the battle on their own grounds.

Thus it is not surprising that these groups quickly find that they have more in common than a similar legal situation. All of them, when comparing themselves to the culture of the middle-aged white male,[32] find that they are distinctly in the minority position. This minority position involves a good deal more than laws and a good deal more than economic and social discrimination. Discrimination *per se* is only one aspect of oppression and not always the most significant one. There are many other social and psychological aspects. Likewise, being subject to separate laws and having poorer access to the socio-economic system are only some of the characteristics of being in a minority group. This point has been well explored by Hacker, who has shown the similarities in the caste-like status of women and blacks.[33]

The Negro analogy has been challenged many times on the grounds that women do not suffer from the same overt segregation as blacks. This point is well noted. But it is important to realize that blatant discrimination is just one mechanism of social control. There are many more subtle ones employed long before such coercion becomes necessary. It is only when these other methods fail to keep a minority group in its place that harsher means must be found. Given that a particular society needs the subservience of several different groups of people, it will use its techniques to a different degree with each of them depending on what is available and what they are most susceptible to. It is a measure of the blacks' resistance to the definition which white society has tried to impose on them that such violent extremes have had to be used to keep the caste lines intact.

Women, however, have not needed such stringent social chains.

Their bodies can be left free because their minds are chained long before they become functioning adults. Most women have so thoroughly internalized the social definitions which tell them that their only significant role is to serve men as wives and raise the next generation of men and their servants that no laws are necessary to enforce this.

The result is that women, even more than other minority groups, have their identities derived first as members of a group and only second, if at all, as unique persons. "Consider the following—When a boy is born, it is difficult to predict what he will be doing twenty-five years later. We cannot say whether he will be an artist or a doctor or a college professor because he will be permitted to develop and fulfill his own identity. But if the newborn child is a girl, we can predict with almost complete certainty how she will be spending her time twenty-five years later. Her individuality does not have to be considered; it is irrelevant."[34]

Yet until very recently, most women have refused to recognize their own oppression. They have openly accepted the social definition of who and what they are. They have refused to be conscious of the fact that they are seen and treated, before anything else, as women. Many still do. This very refusal is significant because no group is so oppressed as one which will not recognize its own oppression. Women's denial that they must deal with their oppression is a reflection of just how far they still have to go.

There are many reasons why covert mechanisms of social control have been so much more successful with women than with most other minority groups. More than most they have been denied any history. Their tradition of subjection is long and even this history is purged from the books so that women cannot compare the similarities of their current condition with that of the past. In a not-so-subtle way both men and women are told that only men make history and women are not important enough to study.

Further, the agents of social control are much nearer to hand than those of any other group. No other minority lives in the same household with its master, separated totally from its peers and urged to compete with them for the privilege of serving the majority group. No other minority so thoroughly accepts the standards of the dominant group as its own and interprets any deviance from those values as a sign of degeneracy. No other minority so readily argues for the maintenance of its own position as one that is merely "different" without questioning whether one must be the "same" to be equal.

Women reach this condition, this acceptance of their secondary role as right and just, through the most insidious mechanism of social control yet devised—the socialization process. That is the mechanism that we want to analyze now.

To understand how most women are socialized we must first understand how they see themselves and are seen by others. Several studies have been done on this. Quoting one of them, McClelland stated that "the female image is characterized as small, weak, soft and light. In the United States it is also dull, peaceful, relaxed, cold, rounded, passive and slow."[35] A more thorough study which asked men and women to choose out of a long list of adjectives those which most clearly applied to themselves showed that women strongly felt themselves to be such things as uncertain, anxious, nervous, hasty, careless, fearful, dull, childish, helpless, sorry, timid, clumsy, stupid, silly, and domestic. On a more positive side women felt they were: understanding, tender, sympathetic, pure, generous, affectionate, loving, moral, kind, grateful and patient.[36]

This is not a very favorable self-image but it does correspond fairly well with the social myths about what women are like. The image has some nice qualities, but they are not the ones normally required for that kind of achievement to which society gives its highest social rewards. Now one can justifiably question both the idea of achievement and the qualities necessary for it, but this is not the place to do so. Rather, because the current standards are the ones which women have been told they do not meet, the purpose here will be to look at the socialization process as a mechanism to keep them from doing so. We will also need to analyze some of the social expectations about women and about what they define as a successful *woman* (not a successful person) because they are inextricably bound up with the socialization process. All people are socialized to meet the social expectations held for them and it is only when this process fails to do so (as is currently happening on several fronts) that it is at all questioned.

First, let us further examine the effects on women of minority group status. Here, another interesting parallel emerges, but it is one fraught with more heresy than any previously observed. When we look at the *results* of female socialization we find a strong similarity between what our society labels, even extols, as the typical "feminine" character structure and that of oppressed peoples in this country and elsewhere.

In his classic study *The Nature of Prejudice* Allport devotes a chapter to "Traits Due to Victimization." Included are such personality characteristics as sensitivity, submission, fantasies of power, desire for protection, indirectness, ingratiation, petty revenge and sabotage, sympathy, extremes of both self and group hatred and self and group glorification, display of flashy status symbols, compassion for the underprivileged, identification with the dominant group's norms, and passivity.[37] Allport was primarily concerned with Jews and Negroes but compare his characterization with the very thorough review of the literature on sex differences among young children made by Terman and Tyler. For girls, they listed such traits as: sensitivity, conformity to social pressures, response to environment, ease of social control, ingratiation, sympathy, low levels of aspiration, compassion for the underprivileged, and anxiety. They found that girls, compared to boys, were more nervous, unstable, neurotic, socially dependent, submissive, had less self-confidence, lower opinions of themselves and of girls in general, and were more timid, emotional, ministrative, fearful, and passive.[38] These are also the kinds of traits found in the Indians when under British rule,[39] in the Algerians under the French,[40] and elsewhere.

Two of the most essential aspects of this "minority group character structure" are the extent to which one's perceptions are distorted and one's group is denigrated. These two things in and of themselves are very effective means of social control. If one can be led to believe in one's own inferiority then one is much less likely to resist the status that goes with the inferiority.

When we look at women's opinions of women we find the notion that they are inferior very prevalent. Young girls get off to a very good start. They begin speaking, reading, and counting sooner. They articulate more clearly and put words into sentences earlier. They have fewer reading and stuttering problems. Girls are even better in math in the early school years. They also make a lot better grades than boys do until late high school. But when they are asked to compare their achievements with those of boys, they rate boys higher in virtually every respect. Despite factual evidence to the contrary, girls' opinion of girls grows progressively worse with age while their opinion of boys and boys' abilities grows better. Boys, likewise, have an increasingly better opinion of themselves and worse opinion of girls as they grow older.[41]

These distortions become so gross that, according to Goldberg, by the time girls reach college they have become prejudiced against women. Goldberg gave college girls sets of booklets containing six identical professional articles in traditional male, female and neutral fields. The articles were identical, but the names of the authors were not. For example, an article in one set would bear the name "John T. McKay" and in another set the same article would be authored by "Joan T. McKay." Questions at the end of each article asked the students to rate the articles on value, persuasiveness, and profundity and the authors for writing style and competence. The male authors fared better in every field, even in such "feminine" areas as art history and dietetics. Goldberg concluded that "Women are prejudiced against female professionals and, regardless of the actual accomplishments of these professionals, will firmly refuse to recognize them as the equals of their male colleagues."[42]

But these unconscious assumptions about women can be very subtle and cannot help but to support the myth that women do not produce high-quality professional work. If the Goldberg findings hold in other situations, and the likelihood is great that they do, it explains why women's work must be of a much higher quality than that of men to be acknowledged as merely equal. People in our society simply refuse to believe that a woman can cross the caste lines and be competent in a "man's world."

However, most women rarely get to the point of writing professional articles or doing other things which put them in competition with men. They seem to lack what psychologists call the "achievement motive."[43] When we look at the little research that has been done we can see why this is the case. Horner's recent study of undergraduates at the University of Michigan showed that 65% of the women but only 10% of the men associated academic success with having negative consequences. Further research showed that these college women had what Horner termed a "motive to avoid success" because they perceived it as leading to social rejection and role conflict with their concept of "femininity."[44] Lipinski has also shown that women students associate success in the usual sense as something which is achieved by men, but not by women.[45] Pierce suggested that girls did in fact have achievement motivation but that they had different criteria for achievement than did boys. He went on to show that high achievement motivation in high school women correlates much more strongly with early marriage than it does with success in school.[46]

Some immediate precedents for the idea that women should not achieve too much academically can be seen in high school, for it is here that the performance of girls begins to drop drastically. It is also at this time that peer group pressures on sex role behavior increase and conceptions of what is "properly feminine" or "masculine" become more narrow.[47] One need only recall Asch's experiments to see how peer group pressures, coupled with our rigid ideas about "femininity" and "masculinity," could lead to the results found by Horner, Lipinski, and Pierce. Asch found that some 33% of his subjects would go contrary to the evidence of their own senses about something as tangible as the comparative length of two lines when their judgments were at variance with those made by the other group members.[48] All but a handful of the other 67% experienced tremendous trauma in trying to stick to their correct perceptions.

These experiments are suggestive of how powerful a group can be in imposing its own definition of a situation and suppressing the resistance of individual deviants. When we move to something as intangible as sex role behavior and to social sanctions far greater than simply the displeasure of a group of unknown experimental stooges, we can get an idea of how stifling social expectations can be. It is not surprising, in light of our cultural norm that a girl should not appear too smart or surpass boys in anything, that those pressures to conform, so prevalent in adolescence, prompt girls to believe that the development of their minds will have only negative results.

But this process begins long before puberty. It begins with the kind of toys young children are given to play with, with the roles they see their parents in, with the stories in their early reading books, and the kind of ambitions they express or actions they engage in that receive rewards from their parents and other adults. Some of the early differentiation along these lines is obvious to us from looking at young children and reminiscing about our own lives. But some of it is not so obvious, even when we engage in it ourselves. It consists of little actions which parents and teachers do every day that are not even noticed but can profoundly affect the style and quality of a child's developing mind.

Adequate research has not yet been done which irrefutably links up child-rearing practices with the eventual adult mind, but there is evidence to support some hypotheses. Let us take a look at one area where strong sex differences show up relatively early: mathematical reasoning ability. No one has been able to define exactly what this ability is, but it has been linked up with number ability and special perception or the ability to visualize objects out of their context. As on other tests, girls score higher on number ability until late high school, but such is not the case with analytic and special perception tests. These tests indicate that boys perceive more analytically while girls are more contextual—although the ability to "break set" or be "field independent" also does not seem to appear until after the fourth or fifth year.[49]

According to Maccoby, this contextual mode of perception common to women is a distinct disadvantage for scientific production. "Girls on the average develop a somewhat different way of handling incoming information—their thinking is less analytic, more global, and more perseverative—and this kind of thinking may serve very well for many kinds of functioning but it is not the kind of thinking most conducive to high-level intellectual productivity, especially in science."[50]

Several social psychologists have postulated that the key developmental characteristic of analytic thinking is what is called early "independence and mastery training," or "whether and how soon a child is encouraged to assume initiative, to take responsibility for himself, and to solve problems by himself, rather than rely on others for the direction of his activities."[51] In other words, analytically inclined children are those who have not been subject to what Bronfenbrenner calls "over-socialization,"[52] and there is a good deal of indirect evidence that such is the case. Levy has observed that "overprotected" boys tend to develop intellectually like girls.[53] Bing found that those girls who were good at special tasks were those whose mothers left them alone to solve the problems by themselves while the mothers of verbally inclined daughters insisted on helping them.[54] Witkin similarly found that mothers of analytic children had encouraged their initiative while mothers of non-analytic children had encouraged dependence and discouraged self-assertion.[55] One writer commented on these studies that "this is to be expected, for the independent child is less likely to accept superficial appearances of objects without exploring them for himself, while the dependent child will be afraid to reach out on his own and will accept appearances without question. In other words, the independent child is likely to be more *active*, not only psychologically but physically, and the physically active child will naturally have more kinesthetic experience with spatial relationships in his environment."[56]

When we turn to specific child-rearing practices we find that the pattern repeats itself according to the sex of the child. Although comparative studies of parental treatment of boys and girls are not extensive, those that have been made indicate that the traditional practices applied to girls are very different from those applied to boys. Girls receive more affection, more protectiveness, more control, and more restrictions. Boys are subjected to more achievement demands and higher expectations.[57] In short, while girls are not always encouraged to be dependent *per se,* they are usually not encouraged to be *independent* and physically active. "Such findings indicate that the differential treatment of the two sexes reflects in part a difference in goals. With sons, socialization seems to focus primarily on directing and constraining the boys' impact on the environment. With daughters, the aim is rather to protect the girl from the impact of environment. The boy is being prepared to mold his world, the girl to be molded by it."[58]

This relationship holds true cross-culturally even more than it does in our own society. In studying child socialization in 110 nonliterate cultures, Barry, Bacon, and Child found that "pressure toward nurturance, obedience, and responsibility is most often stronger for girls, whereas pressure toward achievement and self-reliance is most often stronger for boys."[59] They also found that strong differences in socialization practices were consistent with highly differentiated adult sex roles.

These cross-cultural studies show that dependency training for women is widespread and has results beyond simply curtailing analytic ability. In all these cultures women were in a relatively inferior status position compared to males. In fact, there was a correlation with the degree of rigidity of sex-role socialization, and the subservience of women to men.

In our society also, analytic abilities are not the only ones valued.

Being person-oriented and contextual in perception are very valuable attributes for many fields where, nevertheless, very few women are found. Such characteristics are valuable in the arts and the social sciences where women are found more than in the natural sciences—yet even here their achievement is not deemed equivalent to that of men. One explanation of this, of course, is the repressive effect of role conflict and peer group pressures discussed earlier. But when one looks further it appears that there is an earlier cause here as well.

As several studies have shown, the very same early independence and mastery training which has such a beneficial effect on analytic thinking also determines the extent of one's achievement orientation[60]—that drive which pushes one to excel beyond the need of survival. And it is precisely this kind of training that women fail to receive. They are encouraged to be dependent and passive—to be "feminine." In that process the shape of their mind is altered and their ambitions are dulled or channeled into the only socially rewarded achievement for a woman—marriage.

Now we have come almost full circle and can begin to see the vicious nature of the trap in which our society places women. When we become conscious of the many subtle mechanisms of social control—peer group pressures, cultural norms, parental training, teachers, role expectations, and negative self concept—it is not hard to see why girls who are better at most everything in childhood do not excel at much of anything as adults.

Only one link remains and that requires taking a brief look at those few women who do manage to slip through a chance loophole. Maccoby provided the best commentary on this when she noted that the girl who does not succumb to overprotection and develop the appropriate personality and behavior for her sex has a major price to pay: the anxiety that comes from crossing the caste lines. Maccoby feels that "it is this anxiety which helps to account for the lack of productivity among those women who do make intellectual careers—because [anxiety] is especially damaging to creative thinking." The combination of all these factors tells "something of a horror story. It would appear that even when a woman is suitably endowed intellectually and develops the right temperament and habits of thought to make use of her endowment, she must be fleet of foot indeed to scale the hurdles society has erected for her and to remain a whole and happy person while continuing to follow her intellectual bent."[61]

The plot behind this horror story should by now be clearly evident. There is more to oppression than discrimination and more to the condition of women than whether or not they want to be free of the home. All societies have many ways to keep people in their places, and we have only discussed a few of the ones used to keep women in theirs. Women have been striving to break free of these bonds for many hundreds of years and once again are gathering their strength for another try. It will take more than a few changes in the legal system to significantly change the condition of women, although those changes will be reflective of more profound changes taking place in society. Unlike blacks, the women's liberation movement does not have the thicket of Jim Crow laws to cut through. This is a mixed blessing. On the one hand, the women's liberation movement lacks the simple handholds of oppression which the early civil rights movement had; but at the same time it does not have to waste time wading through legal segregation before realizing that the real nature of oppression lies much deeper. It is the more basic means of social control that will have to be attacked as women and men look into their lives and dissect the many factors that made them what they are. The dam of social control now has many cracks in it. It has held women back for years, but it is about to break under the strain.

Footnotes

[1] Sandra and Daryl Bem, "We're All Non-Conscious Sexists," *Psychology Today*, Nov. 1970, p. 26.

[2] Sir Henry Sumner Maine, *Ancient Law* (London: John Murray, 1905), p. 135.

[3] Alvin W. Gouldner, *Enter Plato* (New York, London: Basic Books), 1965, p. 10.

[4] Numa Denis Fustel de Coulanges, *The Ancient City* (Garden City, N.Y.: Doubleday & Co., 1959), pp. 126–128.

[5] Richard B. Morris, *Studies in the History of American Law* (Philadelphia: Mitchell & Co., 1959), pp. 126–8.

[6] Mary Beard, *Woman as a Force in History* (New York: Macmillan, 1946), pp. 108–109.

[7] Edward Mansfield, *The Legal Rights, Liabilities and Duties of Women* (Salem, Mass.: Jewett & Co., 1945), p. 273.

[8] Sophonisba Breckinridge, *The Family and the State* (Chicago: University of Chicago Press, 1934), pp. 109–110.

[9] Blanche Crozier, "Marital Support," 15 *Boston University Law Review* 28 (1935).

[10] Philip Francis, *The Legal Status of Women* (New York: Oceana Publications, 1963), p. 23.

[11] Citizens Advisory Council on the Status of Women, *Report of the Task Force on Family Law and Policy*, 1968, p. 2.

[12] *Ibid.*, p. 39.

[13] Leo Kanowitz, *Women and the Law: The Unfinished Revolution* (Albuquerque: University of New Mexico Press, 1969), p. 41.

[14] George Gould and Ray F. Dickenson, The American Social Hygiene Association, *Digest of State and Federal Laws Dealing with Prostitution and Other Sex Offenses*, 1942.

[15] Bernard M. Dickens, *Abortion and the Law* (Bristol: MacGibbon & Kee, Ltd., 1966), p. 15.

[16] Alan F. Guttmacher, "Abortion—Yesterday, Today and Tomorrow," *The Case for Legalized Abortion Now*, Guttmacher, ed. (Berkeley: Diablo Press, 1967), p. 4.

[17] Helen Mayer Hacker, "Women as a Minority Group," *Social Forces*, Vol. 31, Oct. 1951, p. 67.

[18] *Lockner v. New York*, 198 U.S. 45 (1905).

[19] *Muller v. Oregon*, 208 U.S. 412 (1908).

[20] British feminists always opposed such laws for their country on the grounds that any sex specific laws were fraught with more evil than good.

[21] Alice Henry, *The Trade Union Woman* (New York: Appleton & Co., 1915), p. 24.

[22] U.S. Department of Labor, *Summary of State Labor Laws for Women*, Feb. 1967, passim.

[23] *Ibid.*

[24] *Sellers, Moore and Case v. Colgate Palmolive Co. and the International Chemical Workers Union, Local No. 15*, 272 Supp. 332; Minn. L. Rev. 52: 1091.

[25] *Brief for the Plaintiffs/Appellants in the Seventh Circuit Court of Appeals*, No. 16, 632, p. 5.

[26] Gunnar Myrdal, *An America Dilemma* (New York: Harper, 1944), p. 1073.

[27] George Fitzhugh, *Sociology for the South* (Richmond, Va.: A. Morris, 1854), p. 86.

[28] The first was the Equal Pay Act of 1963 which took 94 years to get through Congress.

[29] Caroline Bird, *Born Female: The High Cost of Keeping Women Down* (New York: David McKay Co., 1968), Chapter I.

[30] Eleanor Flexner, *Century of Struggle* (New York, Atheneum, 1959), p. 71. They were joined by one white and one black man, William Lloyd Garrison and John Cronan.

[31] Jo Freeman, "The New Feminists," *The Nation*, Feb. 24, 1969, p. 242.

[32] Myrdal, p. 1073.

[33] Hacker, pp. 10–19.

[34] Bem and Bem, p. 7.

[35] David McClelland, "Wanted: A New Self-Image for Women," *The Woman in America*, ed. by Robert J. Lifton (Boston: Beacon Press, 1965), p. 173.

[36] Edward M. Bennett and Larry R. Cohen, "Men and Women: Personality Patterns and Contrasts," *Genetic Psychology Monographs*, Vol. 59, 1959, pp. 101–155.

[37] Gordon W. Allport, *The Nature of Prejudice* (Reading, Mass.: Addison-Wesley Co., 1954), pp. 142–161.

[38] Lewis M. Terman and Leona E. Tyler, "Psychological Sex Differences," *Manual of Child Psychology*, ed. by Leonard Carmichael (New York: Wiley & Sons, 1954), pp. 1080–1100.

[39] Lewis Fisher, *Gandhi* (New York: New American Library, 1954).

[40] Franz Fanon, *The Wretched of the Earth* (New York: Grove Press, 1963).

[41] S. Smith, "Age and Sex Differences in Children's Opinion Concerning Sex Differences," *Journal of Genetic Psychology*, Vol. 54, 1939, pp. 17–25.

[42] Philip Goldberg, "Are Women Prejudiced Against Women?," *Transaction*, April, 1969.

[43] McClelland, passim.

[44] Matina S. Horner, "Woman's Will to Fail," *Psychology Today*, Vol. 3, No. 6, Nov. 1969, p. 36. See also: S. Horner, *Sex Differences in Achievement Motivation and Performance in Competitive and Non-Competitive Situations*, unpublished doctoral dissertation, University of Michigan, 1968.

[45] Beatrice Lipinski, *Sex-Role Conflict and Achievement Motivation in College Women*, unpublished doctoral dissertation, University of Cincinnati, 1965.

[46] James V. Pierce, "Sex Differences in Achievement Motivation of Able High School Students," Co-operative Research Project No. 1097, University of Chicago, Dec. 1961.

[47] Lionel J. Neiman, "The Influence of Peer Groups Upon Attitudes Toward the Feminine Role," *Social Problems*, Vol. 2, 1954, p. 104–111.

[48] S. E. Asch, "Studies of Independence and Conformity: A Minority of One Against a Unanimous Majority," *Psychological Monographs*, Vol. 70, 1956, No. 9.

[49] Eleanor E. Maccoby, "Sex Differences in Intellectual Functioning," *The Development of Sex Differences*, ed. by E. Maccoby (Calif.: Stanford University Press, 1966), p. 26ff. The three most common tests are the Rod and Frame test, which requires the adjustment of a rod to a vertical position regardless of the tilt of a frame around it; the Embedded Figures Test, which determines the ability to perceive a figure embedded in a more complex field; and an analytic test in which one groups a set of objects according to a common element.

[50] Eleanor E. Maccoby, "Woman's Intellect," *The Potential of Women*, ed. by Farber and Wilson (New York: McGraw-Hill, 1963), p. 30.

[51] Maccoby, *ibid.*, p. 31. See also: Julia A. Sherman, "Problems of Sex Differences in Space Perception and Aspects of Intellectual Functioning," *Psychological Review*, Vol. 74, No. 4, July, 1967, pp. 290–299; and Philip E. Vernon, "Ability Factors and Environmental Influences," *American Psychologist*, Vol. 20, No. 9, Sept. 1965, pp. 723–733.

[52] Urie Bronfenbrenner, "Some Familiar Antecedents of Responsibility and Leadership in Adolescents," *Leadership and Interpersonal Behavior,* ed. by Luigi Petrullo and Bernard M. Bass (New York: Holt, Rinehart, and Winston, 1961), p. 260.

[53] D. M. Levy, *Maternal Overprotection* (New York: Columbia University Press, 1943).

[54] Maccoby, "Woman's Intellect," p. 31.

[55] H. A. Witkin, R. B. Dyk, H. E. Patterson, D. R. Goodenough, and S. A. Karp, *Psychological Differentiation* (New York: Wiley, 1962).

[56] James Clapp, "Sex Differences in Mathematical Reasoning Ability," unpublished paper, 1968.

[57] R. R. Sears, E. Maccoby, and H. Levin, *Patterns of Child Rearing* (Evanston, Ill.: Row and Peterson, 1957).

[58] Bronfenbrenner, p. 260.

[59] Herbert Barry, M. K. Bacon, and Irving L. Child, "A Cross-Cultural Survey of Some Sex Differences in Socialization," *The Journal of Abnormal and Social Psychology,* Vol. 55, Nov. 1957, p. 328.

[60] Marian R. Winterbottom, "The Relation of Need for Achievement to Learning Experiences in Independence and Mastery," *Basic Studies in Social Psychology,* ed. by Harold Proshansky and Bernard Seidenberg (New York: Holt, Rinehart and Winston, 1965), pp. 294–307.

[61] Maccoby, "Woman's Intellect," p. 37.

Abortion Law Repeal (sort of): a Warning to Women

by Lucinda Cisler

Lucinda Cisler has worked full-time in the feminist movement since early 1968 when she was part of New York Radical Women. As an architect and city planner, she concerns herself with the place of women in the design fields; she is also the author of the several on-going editions of Women: a Bibliography. However, she has devoted most of her day-to-day efforts for feminism to working for repeal of all abortion and contraception laws especially through writing and direct political activity. She is involved with New' Yorkers for Abortion Law Repeal, NOW, Zero Population Growth, and the newspaper, Majority Report. In 1955 she received the Betty Crocker Homemaker of Tomorrow Award for her California High School. Her home is not neat.

One of the few things everyone in the women's movement seems to agree on is that we have to get rid of the abortion laws and make sure that any woman who wants an abortion can get one. We all recognize how basic this demand is; it sounds like a pretty clear and simple demand, too—hard to achieve, of course, but obviously a fundamental right just like any other method of birth control.

But just because it *sounds* so simple and so obvious and is such a great point of unity, a lot of us haven't really looked below the surface of the abortion fight and seen how complicated it may be to get what we want. The most important thing feminists have done and have to keep doing is to insist that the basic reason for repealing the laws and making abortions available is JUSTICE: women's right to abortion.

Everyone recognizes the cruder forms of opposition to abortion traditionally used by the forces of sexism and religious reaction. But a feminist philosophy must be able to deal with *all* the stumbling blocks that keep us from reaching our goal, and must develop a consciousness about the far more subtle dangers we face from many who honestly believe they are our friends.

In our disgust with the extreme oppression women experience under the present abortion laws, many of us are understandably tempted to accept insulting token changes that we would angrily shout down if they were offered to us in any other field of the struggle for women's liberation. We've waited so long for anything to happen that when we see our demands having any effect at all we're sorely tempted to convince ourselves that everything that sounds good in the short run will turn out to be good for women in the long run. And a lot of us are so fed up with "the system" that we don't even bother to find out what it's doing so we can fight it and demand what *we* want. This is the measure of our present oppression; a chain of aluminum *does* feel lighter around our necks than one made of iron, but it's still a chain, and our task is still to burst entirely free.

The abortion issue is one of the very few issues vital to the women's movement that well-meaning people outside the movement were dealing with on an organized basis even before the new feminism began to explode a couple of years ago. Whatever we may like to think, there *is* quite definitely an abortion movement that is distinct from the feminist movement, and the good intentions of most of the people in it can turn out to be either a tremendous source of support for our goals or the most tragic barrier to our ever achieving them. The choice is up to us: we must subject every proposal for change and every tactic to the clearest feminist scrutiny, demand only what is good for *all* women, and not let some of us be bought off at the expense of the rest.

Until just a couple of years ago the abortion movement was a tiny handful of good people who were still having to concentrate just on getting the taboo lifted from public discussions of the topic. They dared not even think about any proposals for legal change *beyond* "reform" (in which abortion is grudgingly parceled out by hospital committee fiat to the few women who can "prove" they've been raped, or who are crazy, or are in danger of bearing a defective baby). They spent a lot of time debating with priests about When Life Begins, and Which Abortions Are Justified. They were mostly doctors, lawyers, social workers, clergymen, professors, writers, and a few were just plain women usually not particularly feminist.

Part of the reason the reform movement was very small was that it appealed mostly to altruism and very little to people's self-interest: the circumstances covered by "reform" *are* tragic but they affect very few women's lives, whereas repeal is compelling because most women know the fear of unwanted pregnancy and in fact get abortions for that reason.

Some people were involved with "reform"—and are in the abortion movement today—for very good reasons: they are concerned with important issues like the public health problem presented by illegal abortions, the doctor's right to provide patients with good medical care, the suffering of unwanted children and unhappy families, and the burgeoning of our population at a rate too high for *any* economic system to handle.

But all these good reasons to be concerned with abortion are, in the final analysis, based on simple expediency. Such reasons are peripheral to the central rationale for making abortion available: justice for women. And unless a well-thought-out feminism underlies the dedication of these people, they will accept all kinds of token gains from legislators and judges and the medical establishment in the name of "getting something done NOW"—never mind what that is, or how much it cuts the chances for real changes later by lulling the public into a false sense of accomplishment.

These people do deserve a lot of credit for their lonely and dogged insistence on raising the issue when everybody else wanted to pretend it didn't exist. But because they invested so much energy earlier in working for "reform" (and got it in several states), they have an important stake in believing that their approach is the "realistic" one—that one must accept the small, so-called "steps in the right direction" that can be wrested from reluctant politicians, that it isn't quite dignified to demonstrate or shout about what you want, that raising the women's rights issue will "alienate" politicians, and so on.

Others, however (especially in centers of stylish liberalism like New York City), are interested in abortion because they are essentially political fashion-mongers: Some of them aspire to public office and some just like to play around the pool. For them, it's "groovy" to be for something racy like abortion. You can make a name for yourself faster in a small movement, such as this one still is, than in something huge like the peace movement, and it's sexier than supporting the grape strikers in their struggle.

Unfortunately, the "good people" share with these pseudo-militants an overawed attitude toward politicians, doctors, lawyers, and traditional "experts" of all kinds; they tend to view the women's movement as rather eccentric troops they can call upon to help them with colorful things like unavoidable demonstrations, rather than as the grassroots force whose feminist philosophy should be leading *them* in the right direction. Even those who have begun to say that the woman's right to abortion *is* the central issue show a good deal of half-concealed condescension toward the very movement that has brought this issue to the fore and inspired the fantastic change in public opinion witnessed in the last year or so.

Because of course, it *is* the women's movement whose demand for *repeal*—rather than "reform"—of the abortion laws has spurred the general acceleration in the abortion movement and its influence. Unfortunately, and ironically, the very rapidity of the change for which we are responsible is threatening to bring us to the point where we are offered something so close to what we want that our demands for true radical change may never be achieved.

Most of us recognize that "reforms" of the old rape-incest-fetal deformity variety are not in women's interest and in fact, in their very specificity, are almost more of an insult to our dignity as active, self-determining humans than are the old laws that simply forbid us to have abortions unless we are about to die. But the *new* reform legislation now being proposed all over the country is not in our interest either: it looks pretty good, and the improvements it seems to promise (at least for middle-class women) are almost irresistible to those who haven't informed themselves about the complexities of the abortion situation or developed a feminist critique of abortion that goes beyond "it's our right." And the courts are now handing down decisions that look good at a glance but that contain the same restrictions as the legislation.

All of the restrictions are of the kind that would be extremely difficult to get judges and legislators to throw out later (unlike the obvious grotesqueries in the old "reform" laws, which are already being challenged successfully in some courts and legislatures). A lot of people are being seriously misled because the legislation and the court decisions that incorporate these insidious limitations are being called abortion law "repeal" by the media. It's true that the media are not particularly interested in accuracy when they report news of interest to women, but the chief reason for this dangerous misuse of language is that media people are getting their information from the established abortion movement, which wants very badly to think that these laws and decisions *are* somehow repeal. (It seems pretty clear that when you repeal an abortion law you just get rid of it; you do not put things back into the statutes or make special rules that apply to abortion but not to other medical procedures.)

The following are the four major restrictions that have been cropping up lately in "repeal" bills, and some highly condensed reasons why feminists (and indeed anyone) must oppose them. No one can say for sure whether sexist ill-will, political horsetrading, or simple ignorance played the largest part in the lawmakers' decisions to include them, but all of them codify outmoded notions about medical technology, religion, or women's "role":

1. Abortions may only be performed in licensed hospitals. Abortion is almost always a simple procedure that can be carried out in a clinic or a doctor's office. Most women do need a place to lie down and rest for a while after a D&C or even a vacuum aspiration abortion, but they hardly need to occupy scarce hospital beds and go through all the hospital rigmarole that ties up the woman's money and the time of overworked staff people.

Hospital boards are extremely conservative and have always wanted to minimize the number of abortions performed within their walls: the "abortion committees" we now have were not invented by lawmakers but by hospital administrators. New laws that insure a hospital monopoly will hardly change this attitude. (The same committees regulate which women will be able to get the sterilizations they seek—even though voluntary sterilization is perfectly legal in all but one or two states.) The hospitals and accreditation agencies set up their own controls on who will get medical care, and doctors who want to retain their attending status are quite careful not to do "too many" abortions or sterilizations.

Hawaii's new law has this kind of restriction, and hospitals there are already busy setting up a new catechism of "guidelines," none of which insures that women will get more abortions and all of which insure that they will have to ask a lot of strangers for "permission" before they are allowed to spend the considerable amount of money hospitalizations inevitably cost. The legislation proposed in several other states contains the same provisions that essentially shift the locus of control over women's decisions from the state to the hospital bureaucracies and their quasi-legal "regulations."

2. *Abortions may only be performed by licensed physicians.* This restriction sounds almost reasonable to most women who have always been fairly healthy and fairly prosperous, who are caught up in the medical mystique so many doctors have cultivated, and who accept the myth that abortion is incredibly risky and thus should cost a lot. But it is one of the most insidious restrictions of all, and is most oppressive to poor women.

Most doctors are not at all interested in performing abortions: even the ones who don't think it's dirty and who favor increasing the availability of abortion generally consider it a pretty boring procedure that they don't especially want to do. One reason they do find it tedious is that it is basically quite a simple operation, especially when the new vacuum aspiration technique is used, rather than the old dilation and curettage. The physicians who would like to see paramedical specialists trained to perform abortions with the aspirator (or who would like to perfect other promising new methods, such as hormone injections) would be completely thwarted by this restriction in their desire to provide efficient, inexpensive care on a mass basis. The general crisis in the medical delivery system in fact demands that paramedical people be trained to do a great many things that physicians do now.

If physicians themselves were to try to perform all the abortions that are needed, they would be swamped with requests and would have to charge a great deal for their specialized training. Childbirth is statistically eight or ten times more dangerous than abortion, and yet nurses are now being trained as midwives in many medical centers. Why can't they and other medical personnel also be specially trained to use the aspirator so that five or six of them can perform clinic abortions under the general supervision of one physician? Only if paramedicals are allowed to do abortions can we expect to have truly inexpensive (and eventually free) abortions available to all women.

In the fall of 1969 a Washington, D.C. court threw out the District's limitations on a doctor's right to perform abortions—but upheld the conviction of a doctor's paramedical aide who said she had wanted to help poor women. Anyone who knows what the present situation in D.C. is will know that abortion is *not* readily available when its performance is limited to doctors only. The public hospital where poor women go had to be forced by court order to provide this service; private hospitals that serve middle-class women still operate restrictively and charge a lot, a few doctors willing to brave the stigma of being "abortionists" are performing abortions in their offices for $300 or so. Although they work long hours, they are inundated with patients (one has a backlog of five weeks). Another is so swamped, partly because he continues to muddle through with D&C, that he does not even take the time to give the women an anesthetic (although they are assured before they arrive that they will get one).

Several attempts have been made to get D.C. doctors to devote a few volunteer hours each week to a free clinic for the poor; doctors have refused, expressing either indifference or fear of professional censure.

Some women insist that because *they* would prefer to go to a doctor, *all* women must be compelled by law to go to one. It is each woman's right to choose to spend $300 for an abortion from a doctor, but she is obviously oppressing other women when she insists that all must do as she does. An abortion performed by a paramedical person with special training in a given modern procedure could easily, in fact, be safer than a D&C performed by a physician who hasn't done many abortions before.

In any case, it is only when doctors have the right to train the people they need to help them meet the demand, and women have the right to get medical care at a price they can afford, that butchers and quacks will be put out of business. Existing medical practice codes provide for the punishment of quacks, but as long as poor women cannot find good abortions at a price they can pay, so long will butchers elude the law and women continue to die from their ministrations.

Looking not so far into the future, this restriction would also deny women themselves the right to use self-abortifacients when they are developed—and who is to say they will not be developed soon? The laws regulating contraception that still exist in thirty-one states were made before contraceptive foam was invented, at a time when all effective female contraception involved a visit to the doctor. That visit was frozen into a legal requirement in some states, and we still have the sad and ludicrous example of Massachusetts, where non-prescriptive foam cannot legally be bought without a prescription.

The "doctors only" clause is a favorite in legislation that masquerades as repeal. New York, Hawaii, Maryland, Alaska and Washington State are among the important states where this restriction was (rather quietly) included.

3. *Abortions may not be performed beyond a certain time in pregnancy, unless the woman's life is at stake.* Significantly enough, the magic time limit varies from bill to bill, from court decision to court decision, but this kind of restriction essentially says two things to women: (a) at a certain stage, your body suddenly belongs to the state and it can force you to have a child, whatever your own reasons for wanting an abortion late in pregnancy; (b) because late abortion entails more risk to you than early abortion, the state must "protect" you even if your considered decision is that you want to run that risk and your doctor is willing to help you. This restriction insults women in the same way the present "preservation-of-life" laws do: it assumes that we must be in a state of tutelage and cannot assume responsibility for our own acts. Even many women's liberation writers are guilty of repeating the paternalistic explanation given to excuse the original passage of U.S. laws against abortion: in the nineteenth century abortion was more dangerous than childbirth, and women had to be protected against it. Was it somehow less dangerous in the eighteenth century? Were other kinds of surgery safe then? And, most important, weren't women wanting and getting abortions, even though they knew how much they were risking? "Protection" has often turned out to be but another means of control over the protected; labor law offers many examples. When childbirth becomes as safe as it should be, perhaps it will be safer than abortion: will we put back our abortion laws, to "protect women"?

And basically, of course, no one can ever know exactly when *any* stage of pregnancy is reached until birth itself. Conception can take place at any time within about three days of intercourse, so that any legal time limit reckoned from "conception" is, meaningless because it cannot be determined precisely. All the talk about "quickening," "viability," and so on, is based on old religious myths (if the woman believes in them, of course, she won't look for an abortion) or tied to ever-shifting technology (who knows how soon a three-day-old fertilized egg may be considered "viable" because heroic mechanical devices allow it to survive and grow outside the woman's uterus?). To listen to judges and legislators play with the ghostly arithmetic of months and weeks is to hear the music by which angels used to dance on the head of a pin.

There are many reasons why a woman might seek a late abortion, and she should be able to find one legally if she wants it. She may suddenly discover that she had German measles in early pregnancy and that her fetus is deformed; she may have had a sudden mental breakdown; or some calamity may have changed the circumstances of her life: whatever her reasons, *she belongs to herself and not to the state.*

This limitation speaks to the hang-ups many people have, and it would be almost impossible to erase from a law once it were enacted—despite its possible constitutional vulnerability on the grounds of vagueness. It is incorporated in New York State's amended abortion law, among many others, and in a Federal court decision in Wisconsin that has been gravely misrepresented as judicial "repeal." The Washington, D.C. decision discussed the "issue," and concluded that Congress should probably enact new laws for different stages of pregnancy. This is not repeal, it is a last-ditch attempt at retaining a little of the state ownership of pregnant women provided for under the worst laws we have now.

4. Abortions may only be performed when the married woman's husband or the young single woman's parents give their consent. The feminist objection to vesting a veto power in anyone other than the pregnant woman is too obvious to need any elaboration. It is utterly fantastic, then, to hear that some women's liberation groups in Washington State have actually been *supporting* an abortion bill with a consent provision. Although such a debasing restriction is written into law in most of the states that have "reform," some legal writers consider it of such little consequence that they fail to mention it in otherwise accurate summaries of U.S. abortion laws.

The women's collective now putting out *Rat* in New York recently printed a very good map of the U.S., showing in ironic symbols the various restrictions on abortion in each state. For their source these radical women had used a legal checklist that did not include a mention of husband's consent—so their map didn't show this sexist restriction existing anywhere.

This may be the easiest of these restrictions to challenge constitutionally, but why should we have to? Instead we could prevent its enactment and fight to eradicate the hospital regulations that frequently impose it even where the law does not.

All women are oppressed by the present abortion laws, by old-style "reforms," and by seductive new fake-repeal bills and court decisions. But the possibility of fake repeal—if it becomes reality—is the most dangerous: it will divide women from each other. It can buy off most middle-class women and make them believe things have really changed, while it leaves poor women to suffer and keeps us all saddled with abortion laws for many more years to come. There are many nice people who would like to see abortion made more or less legal, but their reasons are fuzzy and their tactics acquiescent. Because no one else except the women's movement is going to cry out against these restrictions, it is up to feminists to make the strongest and most precise demands upon the lawmakers —who ostensibly exist to serve *us*. We will not accept insults and call them "steps in the right direction."

Only if we know what we *don't* want, and why, and say so over and over again, will we be able to recognize and reject all the clever plastic imitations of our goal.

April, 1970

Postscript

Despite dogged efforts to disprove the predictions in this article, they have come true with a vengeance. At this writing the New York legislature is again playing not only with "the ghostly arithmetic of months and weeks" but also with attempts to return to the old abortion law where a woman can get help only if her life is in danger.

Their efforts ignored even by the "feminist" media, small numbers of feminists along with others who agree with us on these issues have continued to slave away at abortion law repeal in New York and other states. In fact, it was only through a 1971 and 1972 campaign to go *forward* to repeal of abortion and contraception laws that the New York status quo has so far been preserved against *backward* moves—and survived to face the current attack.

Most middle-class women have indeed been bought off by New York's law: even when they live in other states they can go to New York for their own abortions and go home, less impelled to work for repeal; they can afford $150 for an abortion, never realizing that this price is still 3 times what it could be if doctors were allowed to have trained assistants working with them; they come in early for their own abortions, hardly knowing about other women who are "too far along" in pregnancy to get legal help, and must have a baby or resort to the same old illegal-abortion game (they are only 1 in 50, and don't matter, it seems). Both the media and the establishment groups who have ego stakes or economic stakes in "preserving" laws like New York's don't tell them that the admissions rate for women with botched *illegal* abortions has dropped only about 50% in New York City hospitals, and that some of these women still die.

Courts seem to be declaring various state laws invalid, but a close reading of what they actually say still reveals a half-hearted approach and much weaseling about the "stages of pregnancy." The U.S. Supreme Court is expected to rule soon on Texas' old law and on parts of Georgia's old-style "reform" law. But legislatures have already shown they still have the upper hand: after Florida's law was overturned, its legislature immediately enacted a new restrictive law; and in Vermont, where the courts had acted favorably, the legislature barely adjourned just before passing a law that would have been worse than the old one in several respects—especially in a new criminalization of the woman herself. Litigation is fine, but courts are basically passive: they must wait for actions to be brought before them, while legislatures can initiate their own actions at any time.

Recent research in the history of abortion laws shows that English and American women were legally freer in 1799 than any of us is today: until special statutes were enacted in the early 19th century—to "protect" women from making dangerous choices— abortion *at any stage of pregnancy* was not a crime under common law. Common law is not codified in writing, and abortion law repeal would return us to the common-law state of legal silence. Even the Catholic bishops of Texas, foreseeing that some legal changes will be taking place regardless of their own desires, have expressed a willingness to settle for the legal neutrality of repeal *in preference to* positive statements of government approval of abortion. Is it really so wild, then, to say "let's bring the Anglo-American world into the 18th century"?

Since April 1970, the Catholic and other anti-feminist opposition has waked up and created powerful, tightly-knit organizations all over the country, aided by reactionary political groups, richly funded, and cheered on by the President of the United States. Poor pro-abortion groups still struggle uphill for repeal, not only against this fearsome opposition but also against the stunning apathy of most of the people who say they favor the "right to abortion" but find the topic—and any effort to achieve that right—tedious and unfashionable. Millions of dollars are being made on abortion in New York, for instance, but political action for repeal is still carried on by the pennies and sacrifices of individual citizens.

In the area of language, the old confusion between "reform" and "repeal" still poses great problems. But in New York "repeal" has suddenly become a veritable nightmare: late in 1970 anti-abortion forces began deliberately to use this word to mean its very opposite —to describe their attempts to bring back the old law. They no longer need to call their activities "repeal," and their own literature usually avoids the word: their Orwellian usage has now taken firm root in the daily media, among politicians of all stripes, and in "liberal" circles where the status quo is very profitable and feminist efforts to move on to real repeal are a terrifying threat.

Since communication among human beings is difficult at best, and language is still our best bridge between minds, it seems worthwhile to keep words sorted out somewhat, so that, for instance, "up" doesn't mean "down," "freedom" doesn't mean "slavery," and "repeal abortion laws" doesn't mean "add still more abortion laws." But beneath the sick equation of the third pair of opposites lies a profound contempt for women and for feminist efforts on the abortion front. This instant capitulation to anti-feminist Newspeak, even by many who call themselves feminists, shows that the *idea* of repeal is now so dead that its very *name* is an empty husk, up for grabs. The enemy is winning by infiltrating our own thoughts and language, and each isolated show of resistance is considered fruitless and even quaint, by the same individuals who froth at the mouth when they are called "girl" or "Mrs."

. . .

No women's group, even the stodgiest, ever considered accepting compromise on the Equal Rights Amendment; we demanded what we wanted, in unison, and we got it—seeing clearly that compromises once enacted are almost impossible to budge. Why then have we behaved so differently when it comes to so basic and personal a right as the legal capacity to decide what is to happen inside our very bodies? Why do we refuse to see that "justifiable" abortion granted to some is *not* a right but a most tenuous privilege, and that as long as *any* woman belongs to the state every women is a chattel?

Can it be that we really like being property after all?

Author's note/May 7, 1972

. . .

Abortion Information

A. How to find an abortion: Contact

1. **Women's Health and Abortion Project,** 212-691-3396 or 2063 (c/o Women's Liberation Center, 243 W. 20th St., New York City, N.Y. 10010). The Project works closely with doctors to bring prices down; it's still about $100 for a first-trimester outpatient abortion. The Project asks those who can pay to give a $10 donation to help them carry on their work.

2. **Family Planning Information Service,** 212-677-3040 (c/o Planned Parenthood of New York City, 300 Park Avenue South, New York City, N.Y. 10010). As of mid-1972, the prices of abortions through PP were still relatively high, but they do have suggestions for sources outside New York State, if you live far away.

(Lists of clinics and doctors are quickly outdated, but the reliable referral sources like those listed above have the most current information. Post-16-week abortions and free or low-cost abortions are harder to arrange, but each of these services does try, so ask them if they can help. Post-16-week abortions cost more: $250 and up; after 24 weeks, abortion is illegal in New York unless your life is in danger.)

B. **How to find out more by reading:** Send a stamped envelope to the Society for Humane Abortion, P.O. Box 1862, San Francisco, Calif. 94101, and ask for the SHA literature list.

C. **How to start solving the problem by getting rid of the laws in your state:** *Every state* has laws against abortion; about 30 states still have laws restricting contraception. If you want to work to erase them, **New Yorkers for Abortion Law Repeal** has material that can probably help you; NYALR is still working on both kinds of repeal in New York and has literature useful to people in every state (50¢ for a sample packet). NYALR will help you draw up actual repeal bills to have your legislature introduce, and has made up a chart (50¢) showing all state and federal restrictions on both contraception and abortion. $5 puts you on the mailing list for a year. NYALR, P.O. Box 240, Planetarium Station, New York, N.Y. 10024.

Jane Crow
and the Law:
Sex Discrimination
and Title VII
by Pauli Murray and Mary Eastwood

Mary Eastwood is a founder and one of the directors of Human Rights For Women. Pauli Murray is a Professor of American Studies at Brandeis University and teaches a course in women's studies. Both were founding members of NOW; both recently wrote articles for the Valparaiso University Law Review, Symposium on Women and the Law (Spring, 1971), and both have been active in the women's movement since it began. This article is an abridgment of a 1965 article by Pauli Murray and Mary Eastwood published in 34 Geo. Wash. L. Rev. 232, with 1971 notes by the authors.

1971 NOTE: This was the first article dealing with Title VII of the Civil Rights Act of 1964 written by feminist lawyers. In 1965, most lawyers and government officials charged with enforcing the equal employment opportunity provisions of Title VII regarded the sex discrimination prohibition as unimportant and openly asserted that this aspect of the law need not be enforced with the same seriousness as discrimination by reason of race. This attitude directly contributed to the rise of the new feminist movement. Today, much of the legal theory on Title VII, and some of the constitutional theory, presented in "Jane Crow and the Law" has become a part of the law of the land.

Antifeminism and Racism

Discriminatory attitudes toward women are strikingly parallel to those regarding Negroes. Women have experienced both subtle and explicit forms of discrimination comparable to the inequalities imposed upon minorities. Contemporary scholars have been impressed by the interrelation of these two problems in the United States, whether their point of departure has been a study of women or of racial theories. In *The Second Sex*, Simone de Beauvoir makes frequent reference to the position of American Negroes. In *An American Dilemma*, Gunnar Myrdal noted that the similarity of the two problems was not accidental, but originated in the paternalistic order of society. "From the very beginning," Dr. Myrdal observed, "the fight in America for the liberation of the Negro slaves was closely coordinated with the fight for women's emancipation. . . . The women's movement got much of its public support by reason of its affiliation with the Abolitionist movement."

The United Nations Charter and the Universal Declaration of Human Rights both stress respect for human rights and fundamental freedoms for all persons without distinction as to race, sex, language, or religion. Until the enactment of the Civil Rights Act of 1964, "sex" generally had not been included with "race, color, religion and national origin" in federal laws and regulations designed to eliminate discrimination. As a practical matter, "civil rights" had become equated with Negro rights, which created bitter opposition and divisions. The most serious discrimination against both women and Negroes today is in the field of employment. The addition of "sex" to Title VII of the Civil Rights Act, making it possible for a second large group of the population to invoke its protection against discrimination in employment, represents an important step toward implementation of our commitment to human rights.

Equality of Rights Under the Constitution

In three nineteenth century cases, the Supreme Court held that the privileges and immunities clause of the fourteenth amendment did not confer upon women the right to vote or the right to practice law within a state. Between 1908 and 1937, the Supreme Court upheld various state labor laws applicable to women but not men, on the ground that sex furnishes a reasonable basis for legislative classification. The Court upheld in 1948 a state law forbidding the licensing of females (with certain exceptions) as bartenders and in 1961 a state law providing that no female may be taken for jury service unless she registers with the clerk of court her desire to serve.

The courts generally have over-simplified the question of reasonableness of classification by sex by applying the principle that "sex is a valid basis for classification." The blanket application of such a doctrine totally defeats the meaning of equal protection of the law for women.

Ironically, the 1908 case, *Muller v. Oregon,* cited as leading precedent for this doctrine, upheld an Oregon maximum hour law for women in certain industries, partly "to secure a real equality of right" for women in the unequal struggle for subsistence. The thrust of the decision was to equalize the bargaining position of women in industry. The other ground for sustaining the legislation was the relation of woman's health needs to her maternal functions and the public interest in preserving "the well-being of the race." The decision was rendered against a background of the common law position of women before they had gained political equality and on the basis of medical knowledge available more than fifty years ago.

Later decisions, disregarding the rationale of *Muller,* seized upon the Court's language and extended the doctrine of sex as a basis for legislative classification to remote or unrelated subjects. *Muller* has been cited in support of jury exclusion, differential treatment in licensing occupations, and the exclusion of women from a state supported college.

Although the Supreme Court has in no case found a law distinguishing on the basis of sex to be a violation of the fourteenth amendment, the amendment may nevertheless be applicable to sex discrimination. The genius of the American Constitution is its capacity, through judicial interpretation, for growth and adaptation to changing conditions and human values. Recent Supreme Court decisions in cases involving school desegregation, reapportionment, the right to counsel, and the extension of the concept of state action illustrate the modern trend toward insuring equality of status and recognizing individual rights. Courts have not yet fully realized that women's rights are part of human rights; but the climate appears favorable to renewed judicial attacks on sex discrimination.

1971 NOTE: The Supreme Court has not yet ruled that a law discriminating on the basis of sex is unconstitutional. However, a law giving preference to male relatives in the administration of decedents' estates, held by the Idaho Supreme Court to be constitutional, will be heard by the high court next term. Lower courts have found the following violative of the fifth or fourteenth amendments' due process or equal protection guarantees: the exclusion of women from juries; exclusion of women from a state university; heavier criminal penalties for women than for men convicted of the same crimes; and a prohibition against women working as bartenders. A U.S. Court of Appeals recently ruled that the issue of whether California's special restrictions on working hours of women, having the effect of preserving the better jobs for men, raised a substantial constitutional question. This case, Mengelkoch v. Industrial Welfare Commission, *is currently pending in the U.S. District Court in Los Angeles. But other federal courts have found that sex distinctions in computing social security benefits and the exclusion of women from the draft do not violate the Constitution. The position of women under the Constitution is still unclear.*

Before attempting to formulate any principle of equal protection of the laws, certain assumptions that have confused the issue must be reexamined. The first is the assumption that equal rights for women is tantamount to seeking identical treatment with men. This is an oversimplification. As individuals, women seek equality of opportunity for education, employment, cultural enrichment, and civic participation without barriers built upon the myth of the stereotyped "woman." As women, they seek freedom of choice: to develop their maternal and familial functions primarily, or to develop different capacities at different stages of life, or to pursue some combination of these choices.

The second assumption confusing the "woman problem" is that, because of inherent differences between the sexes, differential treatment does not imply inequality or inferiority. The inherent differences between the sexes, according to this view, make necessary the application of different principles to women than to minority groups.

To the degree women perform the function of motherhood, they differ from other special groups. But maternity legislation is not sex legislation; its benefits are geared to the performance of a special service much like veterans' legislation. When the law distinguishes between the "two great classes of men and women," gives men a preferred position by accepted social standards, and regulates the conduct of women in a restrictive manner having no bearing on the maternal function, it disregards individuality and relegates an entire class to inferior status.

The doctrine of "classification by sex" extracted from *Muller* is too sweeping. Courts have sanctioned inequalities as "protection" and "privilege"; suggestions of "chivalry" and concern for the "ladies" conceal continued paternalism. Deriving their respectability from a principle of equality, these applications remain anachronisms in the law.

It may not be too far-fetched to suggest that this doctrine as presently applied has implications comparable to those of the now discredited doctrine of "separate but equal." It makes the legal position of women not only ambiguous but untenable. Through unwarranted extension, it has penalized all women for the biological function of motherhood far in excess of precautions justified by the findings of advanced medical science. Through semantic manipulation, it permits a policy originally directed toward the protection of a segment of a woman's life to dominate and inhibit her development as an individual. It reinforces an inferior status by lending governmental prestige to sex distinctions that are carried over into those private discriminations currently beyond the reach of the law.

Although the "classification by sex" doctrine was useful in sustaining the validity of progressive labor legislation in the past, perhaps it should now be shelved alongside the "separate but equal" doctrine. It could be argued that, just as separate schools for Negro and white children by their very nature cannot be "equal," classification on the basis of sex is today inherently unreasonable and discriminatory.

There are a few laws that refer to women or men or males or females, but that in reality do not classify by sex and accordingly would not be constitutionally objectionable if classification by sex were prohibited. For example, a law that prohibits rape can apply only to men; a law that provides for maternity benefits can apply only to women. If these laws were phrased in terms of "persons" rather than "men" or "women," the meaning or effect could be no different. Thus, the legislature by its choice of terminology has not made any sex classification.

A second category of law or official practice that would not become invalid if the "classification by sex" doctrine were discarded are those that do not treat men and women differently, but only separately: for example, separate dormitory facilities for men and women in a state university or separate toilet facilities in public buildings. Unlike separation of the races, in our culture separation of the sexes in these situations carries no implication of inferiority for either sex.

If this reappraisal of sex discrimination under the fifth and fourteenth amendments were accepted by the courts, one might speculate as to the effect on various other laws. Alimony based on sex would not be permitted, but alimony not based on sex but provided for the non-paid homemaker could be proper, as would be alimony that takes into account the relative income of the two parties. Any equitable division of property between spouses not based on sex would be permitted. Also permissible, because not based on classification by sex, would be equitable arrangements upon dissolution of a marriage that require one parent to furnish all or a major portion of the financial support and the other parent to bear all or a major portion of responsibility for the care, custody, and education of the children. Laws that provide benefits for wives or widows where the same benefits were not provided for husbands or widowers would be inconsistent, unless based on the non-sex factor of dependency.

To be consistent with the principle of equality of rights, different minimum ages for marriage for boys and girls (if different, lower for girls than for boys) and different ages in state child labor laws (if different, higher for girls than for boys) should be equalized. State labor standards legislation would have to apply equally to men and women. Both sexes would be subject to compulsory military service and jury service, but exemptions could be made for activities, such as care of dependent children or other family members, if based on performance of the function rather than sex.

If laws classifying persons by sex were prohibited by the Constitution, and if it were made clear that laws recognizing functions, *if performed*, are not based on sex per se, much of the confusion as to the legal status of women would be eliminated. Moreover, this may be the only way to give adequate recognition to women who are mothers and homemakers and who do not work outside the home—it recognizes the intrinsic value of child care and homemaking. The assumption that financial support of a family by the husband-father is a gift from the male sex to the female sex and, in return, the male is entitled to preference in the outside world is all too common. Underlying this assumption is the unwillingness to acknowledge any value for child care and homemaking because they have not been ascribed a dollar value.

The Bona Fide Occupational Qualification Exception

The most important issue in administering the sex discrimination provisions of Title VII is the interpretation of the bona fide occupational qualification exception. Section 703(a) of the Civil Rights Act provides:

> It shall be an unlawful employment practice for an employer—
> (1) to fail or refuse to hire or to discharge any individual, or otherwise to discriminate against any individual with respect to his compensation, terms, conditions, or privileges of employment, because of such individual's race, color, religion, sex, or national origin; or (2) to limit, segregate, or classify his employees in any way which would deprive or tend to deprive any individual of employment opportunities or otherwise adversely affect his status as an employee, because of such individual's race, color, religion, sex, or national origin.

Sections 703(b) and (c) contain comparable provisions defining unlawful employment practices of employment agencies and labor organizations. Section 703(e) provides that it is not an unlawful employment practice for an employer to hire an individual "on the basis of his religion, sex, or national origin in those certain instances where religion, sex, or national origin is a bona fide occupational qualification reasonably necessary to the normal operation of that particular business or enterprise. ..." Section 704(b) provides that it is an unlawful employment practice for an employer, labor organization, or employment agency to print or publish a notice or advertisement relating to employment, specifying sex, except when sex is a bona fide occupational qualification for employment.

A loose definition of bona fide occupational qualification as to sex could subvert the purpose of Title VII, which is to provide equal employment opportunity. The language of this exception in section 703(e), providing that it shall apply "in those certain instances" where it is reasonably necessary "to the normal operation of that particular business or enterprise," does not permit exclusion of women (or men) in any broad or general category of jobs.

The Federal Employment Experience. Section 701(b) of the act defines the term "employer" to exclude the United States, but provides "that it shall be the policy of the United States to insure equal employment opportunities for Federal employees without discrimination because of race, color, religion, sex, or national origin and the President shall utilize his existing authority to effectuate this policy." The federal policy of non-discrimination as to sex has been defined by the Civil Service Commission at the direction of the President. Two categories of position are excepted: (1) law enforcement positions requiring the bearing of firearms, and (2) institutional or custodial positions where the duties may be properly performed only by a person of the same sex as the individuals under care or for whom services are rendered. Other exceptions are permissible "in certain unusual circumstances when it can be clearly and logically concluded from the facts at hand that a *particular individual* under consideration cannot reasonably be expected to perform effectively the duties of the position."

Under the federal policy, employment conditions generally are not considered a proper basis for limiting hiring opportunities to males or to females as the case may be. Examples of conditions that may not be used as bases for sex discrimination are listed in the Federal Personnel Manual:

—Travel, including extensive travel, travel in remote areas, or travel with a person or persons of the opposite sex.
—Rotating assignments or other shift work.
—Geographical location, neighborhood environment, or outdoor work.
—Contact with public or a particular group or groups.

—Exposure to weather.

—Living or working facilities, except where the sharing of common living quarters with members of the opposite sex would be required.

—Working with teams or units of opposite sex.

—Monotonous, detailed, or repetitious duties.

—Limited advancement opportunities.

Excuses For Sex Discrimination. The federal guidelines might be viewed as negatively defining "bona fide occupational qualification," by setting forth factors that may *not* be used to justify exclusion of one sex or the other. There would seem to be little reason for a federal policy under Title VII that differs greatly from that demonstrated to be workable by the federal government.

Several types of excuses are likely to be claimed as bona fide occupational qualifications that have no relationship to ability to perform a job. One might be based on assumptions of the life patterns of women in general: for example, the assumption that women are only temporary workers because they leave to marry and raise children, or the assumption that turnover among women is high because they must leave the job if the family moves. Such assumptions are often mythical. However, even if it could be proved that women are likely to leave the job earlier, this should not justify pre-judging a particular individual.

A second excuse an employer might use for refusing to hire a woman is sex prejudice on the part of the public, customers, other employees, or some other group. Similarly, this assumption may be false; even if the assumption could be proved true, the prejudice may not affect the particular woman's performance of the job; she may even be able to overcome the prejudice and perhaps change the discriminatory attitudes. Sex prejudice is one of the negative factors listed in the Federal Personnel Manual that fails to justify discrimination in hiring.

A third excuse employers might offer as a bona fide occupational qualification is based on the assumption that certain attributes are peculiar to one sex. For example, women express emotions differently than men; men may be considered less capable of operating intricate equipment; men are stronger than women; women have more endurance than men, and so forth. Individual variations are, of course, more significant than any generality as to characteristics, even if the generality can be shown to be valid and the characteristic be relevant to performance of the job.

1971 NOTE: The Equal Employment Opportunity Commission guidelines on discrimination because of sex include the above three types of discrimination as not justifying exclusion of persons of one sex under the bona fide occupational qualification provision. The EEOC added a fourth situation—that of providing "separate facilities" for the opposite sex, as not a "b.f.o.q." "unless the expense would be clearly unreasonable." The EEOC guidelines further would permit sex discrimination for jobs such as actor or actress.

Employment Advertisements

Under section 704(b) of the Civil Rights Act, employment advertisements may not indicate a preference, limitation, specification, or discrimination based on sex except where sex is a bona fide occupational qualification for employment.

The continued use of sex-segregated newspaper advertisements indicates that compliance with section (704(b) of the Civil Rights Act is very slow. Newspapers could assist employers and employment agencies in complying with this provision and comparable state provisions by discontinuing separate help-wanted columns for men and women. A few newspapers—for example *The Blade* (Toledo, Ohio), *Toledo Times, The Phoenix Gazette*, the *Honolulu Star Bulletin*—have done this.

1971 NOTE: Although the EEOC initially announced that job advertisements under sex-segregated want ad headings would not be considered violative of Title VII, it subsequently reversed its position, and the present guidelines state that such sex labeled job advertisements are violative of Title VII. However, the job ad provision of Title VII remains largely unenforced. In a suit to try to directly subject newspapers themselves to the prohibition against identifying job ads by the desired sex of applicant, a Federal court in California ruled that newspapers are not "employment agencies" within the meaning of Title VII. The case has been appealed to the U.S. Court of Appeals in San Francisco.

Some newspapers have discontinued separate male and female

columns because they were required to by state or local fair employ-
ment laws (e.g. New York, Washington, D.C., Pittsburgh).

Effect of Title VII on State Laws
Regulating the Employment of Women

The major types of state laws regulating the employment of
women are: laws prohibiting the employment of women in certain
occupations, such as employment in bars and mines; maximum
hour laws for women; minimum wage laws for women; laws prohibiting the employment of women during certain hours of the
night in certain industries; weight lifting limitations for women;
and laws requiring special facilities for women employees, such as
seats and restrooms.

The debate in the House of Representatives when "sex" was
added to Title VII of the civil rights bill indicates that both proponents and opponents of the amendment thought it might remove
the "restriction" or "protection," depending on the point of view,
of these state labor laws. Speaking in favor of the sex amendment,
Representative Griffiths stated, "[I]f labor is seeking to maintain
the old distinction, they will do far better to support this amendment and ask for a savings clause in this law. ...." A "savings
clause" for state protective laws for women was not added to Title
VII. Section 708 of the act provides:

> Nothing in this title shall be deemed to exempt or relieve any per-
> son from any liability, duty, penalty, or punishment provided by
> any present or future law of any State or political subdivision of
> a State, other than any such law which purports to require or per-
> mit the doing of any act which would be an unlawful employment
> practice under this title.

There was no discussion of the effect of this provision on state laws
regulating the employment of women. It seems clear, however, that
an employer would have to continue to comply with a state labor
law regulating the employment of women unless the law "purports
to require or permit" him to refuse to hire an individual because of
sex or to discriminate with respect to compensation, terms, conditions, or privileges of employment or to do any other act unlawful
under section 703. A law prohibiting the employment of women in
certain occupations might require an employer to do an act that

would be an unlawful employment practice under the Civil Rights Act; such a state law would require an employer to refuse to hire a woman because of her sex even though she were otherwise qualified.

On the other hand, a minimum wage law for women does not require an employer to discriminate in payment of compensation. Such a law merely prescribes a standard for women; the lack of a legal standard for men does not affirmatively permit discrimination against men. Under this reasoning, the employer would not be relieved from complying with state minimum wage laws for women. To comply with Title VII, however, he would have to pay male employees the same wage he pays female employees doing the same work. As a practical matter, there are relatively few cases where men are paid less than women at the minimum wage level.

Similarly, state laws requiring rest periods and special facilities, such as seats, dressing rooms, or restrooms, for women would not necessarily permit discrimination in the conditions of employment merely because the requirements are imposed only for women employees. Nor do they affirmatively permit an employer to refuse to hire a woman. To comply with Title VII, the employer could provide for male employees what the state law requires him to provide for female employees.

More difficult problems are presented by state laws prohibiting the employment of women in excess of a specified maximum hours per day or week, laws prohibiting the employment of women between certain hours at night, and laws imposing weight lifting limitations. These laws would be consistent with Title VII only if the employer could readjust the manner of operating his business so that the treatment of all his employees, male or female, met the standards prescribed for females under state law. This would mean, however, that an employer might have to discontinue overtime employment entirely, close his business during certain hours of the night, or reduce the weight of his equipment or product. This result, of course, would be unrealistic and far removed from the purpose of the Civil Rights Act to prohibit class discrimination.

It could be argued that, since compliance with these state laws would impose unreasonable requirements on employers, compliance may be tantamount to requiring employers to refuse to hire women at all for certain jobs; such a requirement would be unlawful under Title VII except in cases where being a male is a bona fide occupational qualification.

1971 NOTE: Federal courts in several Title VII cases have held that special weight lifting and hours restrictions on women employees deny women equal employment opportunities in violation of the federal statute. Some of these cases are still pending. A number of states have repealed their hours restrictions on women only. And in some, the restrictive laws are not enforceable because of Attorney Generals' opinions ruling them inconsistent with the non-discrimination requirements of the federal law, which, of course, supersedes conflicting state law under Article VI of the Constitution.

The First Title VII case to be heard by the Supreme Court involved the question of whether an employer could refuse to hire women with pre-school age children while hiring men with such children (Phillips v. Martin-Marietta). *The Court held that employers subject to Title VII could not have one hiring policy for women and another for men.*

Conclusion

According women equality of rights under the Constitution and equal employment opportunity, through positive implementation of Title VII of the Civil Rights Act of 1964, would not likely result in any immediate, drastic change in the pattern of women's employment. But great scientific and social changes have already taken place, such as longer life span, smaller families, and lower infant death rate, with the result that motherhood consumes smaller proportions of women's lives. Thus, the effects of sex discrimination are felt by more women today.

The recent increase in activity concerning the status of women indicates that we are gradually coming to recognize that the proper role of the law is not to protect women by restrictions and confinement, but to protect both sexes from discrimination.

Psychology Constructs the Female

or
The Fantasy Life
of the Male Psychologist
(with some attention
to the fantasies
of his friends,
the male biologist
and the male anthropologist)

by Naomi Weisstein

Naomi Weisstein holds a Ph.D in psychology from Harvard University and has completed her NSF postdoctoral fellowship in mathematical biology at the University of Chicago. She is now teaching psychology at Loyola University in Chicago, is a member of a women's liberation rock band, and has been a long time activist in the feminist movement.

It is an implicit assumption that the area of psychology which concerns itself with personality has the onerous but necessary task of describing the limits of human possibility. Thus when we are about to consider the liberation of women, we naturally look to psychology to tell us what 'true' liberation would mean: what would give women the freedom to fulfill their own intrinsic natures.

Psychologists have set about describing the true natures of women with a certainty and a sense of their own infallibility rarely found in the secular world. Bruno Bettelheim, of the University of Chicago, tells us (1965) that

> We must start with the realization that, as much as women want to be good scientists or engineers, they want first and foremost to be womanly companions of men and to be mothers.

Erik Erikson of Harvard University (1965), upon noting that young women often ask whether they can 'have an identity before they know whom they will marry, and for whom they will make a home', explains somewhat elegiacally that

> Much of a young woman's identity is already defined in her kind of attractiveness and in the selectivity of her search for the man (or men) by whom she wishes to be sought...

Mature womanly fulfillment, for Erikson, rests on the fact that a woman's

> ... somatic design harbors an 'inner space' destined to bear the offspring of chosen men, and with it, a biological, psychological, and ethical commitment to take care of human infancy.

Some psychiatrists even see the acceptance of woman's role by women as a solution to societal problems. 'Woman is nurturance ...,' writes Joseph Rheingold (1964), a psychiatrist at Harvard Medical School, '... anatomy decrees the life of a woman... When women grow up without dread of their biological functions and without subversion by feminist doctrine, and therefore enter upon motherhood with a sense of fulfillment and altruistic sentiment, we shall attain the goal of a good life and a secure world in which to live it.' (p. 714)

These views from men who are assumed to be experts reflect, in a surprisingly transparent way, the cultural consensus. They not only assert that a woman is defined by her ability to attract men, they see no alternative definitions. They think that the definition of a woman in terms of a man is the way it should be; and they back it up with psychosexual incantation and biological ritual curses. A woman has an identity if she is attractive enough to obtain a man, and thus, a home; for this will allow her to set about her life's task of 'joyful altruism and nurturance'.

Business certainly does not disagree. If views such as Bettelheim's and Erikson's do indeed have something to do with real liberation for women, then seldom in human history has so much money and effort been spent on helping a group of people realize their true potential. Clothing, cosmetics, home furnishings, are multi-million dollar businesses: if you don't like investing in firms that make weaponry and flaming gasoline, then there's a lot of cash in 'inner space'. Sheet and pillowcase manufacturers are concerned to fill this inner space:

> Mother, for a while this morning, I thought I wasn't cut out for married life. Hank was late for work and forgot his apricot juice and walked out without kissing me, and when I was all alone I started crying. But then the postman came with the sheets and towels you sent, that look like big bandana handkerchiefs, and you know what I thought? That those big red and blue handkerchiefs are for girls like me to dry their tears on so they can get busy and do what a housewife has to do. Throw open the windows and start getting the house ready, and the dinner, maybe clean the silver and put new geraniums in the box. *Everything to be ready for him when he walks through that door.* (Fieldcrest 1966; emphasis added.)

Of course, it is not only the sheet and pillowcase manufacturers, the cosmetics industry, the home furnishings salesmen who profit from and make use of the cultural definitions of man and woman. The example above is blatantly and overtly pitched to a particular kind of sexist stereotype: the child nymph. But almost all aspects of the media are normative, that is, they have to do with the ways in which beautiful people, or just folks, or ordinary Americans, or extraordinary Americans, should live their lives. They define the possible; and the possibilities are usually in terms of what is male and what is female. Men and women alike are waiting for Hank, the Silva Thins man, to walk back through that door.

It is an interesting but limited exercise to show that psychologists and psychiatrists embrace these sexist norms of our culture, that they do not see beyond the most superficial and stultifying media conceptions of female nature, and that their ideas of female nature serve industry and commerce so well. Just because it's good for business doesn't mean it's wrong. What I will show is that it *is wrong;* that there isn't the tiniest shred of evidence that these fantasies of servitude and childish dependence have anything to do with women's true potential; that the idea of the nature of human possibility which rests on the accidents of individual development of genitalia, on what is possible today because of what happened yesterday, on the fundamentalist myth of sex organ causality, has strangled and deflected psychology so that it is relatively useless in describing, explaining or predicting humans and their behavior. It then goes without saying that present psychology is less than worthless in contributing to a vision which could truly liberate—men as well as women.

The central argument of my paper, then, is this. Psychology has nothing to say about what women are really like, what they need and what they want, essentially because psychology does not know. I want to stress that this failure is not limited to women; rather, the kind of psychology which has addressed itself to how people act and who they are has failed to understand, in the first place, why people act the way they do, and certainly failed to understand what might make them act differently.

The kind of psychology which has addressed itself to these questions divides into two professional areas: academic personality research, and clinical psychology and psychiatry. The basic reason for failure is the same in both these areas: the central assumption for most psychologists of human personality has been that human behavior rests on an individual and inner dynamic, perhaps fixed in infancy, perhaps fixed by genitalia, perhaps simply arranged in a rather immovable cognitive network. But this assumption is rapidly losing ground as personality psychologists fail again and again to get consistency in the assumed personalities of their subjects (Block, 1968). Meanwhile, the evidence is collecting that what a person does and who she believes herself to be, will in general be a function of what people around her expect her to be, and what the overall situation in which she is acting implies that she is. Compared to the influence of the social context within which a person lives, his or her history and 'traits', as well as biological make-up, may simply be random variations, 'noise' superimposed on the true signal which can predict behavior.

Some academic personality psychologists are at least looking at the counter evidence and questioning their theories; no such corrective is occurring in clinical psychology and psychiatry: Freudians and neo-Freudians, Nudic-marathonists and Touchy-feelies, classicists and swingers, clinicians and psychiatrists, simply refuse to look at the evidence against their theory and practice. And they supply their theory and practice with stuff so transparently biased as to have absolutely no standing as empirical evidence.

To summarize: the first reason for psychology's failure to understand what people are and how they act is that psychology has looked for inner traits when it should have been looking for social context; the second reason for psychology's failure is that the theoreticians of personality have generally been clinicians and psychiatrists, and they have never considered it necessary to have evidence in support of their theories.

Theory without Evidence

Let us turn to this latter cause of failure first: the acceptance by psychiatrists and clinical psychologists of theory without evidence. If we inspect the literature of personality, it is immediately obvious that the bulk of it is written by clinicians and psychiatrists, and that the major support for their theories is 'years of intensive clinical experience'. This is a tradition started by Freud. His 'insights' occurred during the course of his work with his patients. Now there is nothing wrong with such an approach to theory formulation; a person is free to make up theories with any inspiration that works: divine revelation, intensive clinical practice, a random numbers table. But he/she is not free to claim any validity for his/her theory until it has been tested and confirmed. But theories are treated in no such tentative way in ordinary clinical practice. Consider Freud. What he thought constituted evidence violated the most minimal conditions of scientific rigor. In *The Sexual Enlightenment of Children* (1963), the classic document which is supposed to demonstrate empirically the existence of a castration complex and its connection to a phobia, Freud based his analysis on the reports of the father of the little boy, himself in therapy, and a devotee of Freudian theory. I really don't have to comment further on the contamination in this kind of evidence. It is remarkable that only recently has Freud's classic theory on the sexuality of women—the notion of the double orgasm—been actually tested physiologically and found just plain wrong. Now those who claim that fifty years of psychoanalytic experience constitute evidence enough of the essential truths of Freud's theory should ponder the robust health of the double orgasm. Did women, until Masters and Johnson (1966), believe they were having two different kinds of orgasm? Did their psychiatrists badger them into reporting something that was not true? If so, were there other things they reported that were also not true? Did psychiatrists ever learn anything different than their theories had led them to believe? If clinical experience means anything at all, surely we should have been done with the double orgasm myth long before the Masters and Johnson studies.

But certainly, you may object, 'years of intensive clinical experience' is the only reliable measure in a discipline which rests for its findings on insight, sensitivity, and intuition. The problem with insight, sensitivity, and intuition, is that they can confirm for all time the biases that one started out with. People used to be absolutely convinced of their ability to tell which of their number were engaging in witchcraft. All it required was some sensitivity to the workings of the devil.

Years of intensive clinical experience is not the same thing as empirical evidence. The first thing an experimenter learns in any kind of experiment which involves humans is the concept of the 'double blind'. The term is taken from medical experiments, where one group is given a drug which is presumably supposed to change behavior in a certain way, and a control group is given a placebo. If the observers or the subjects know which group took which drug, the result invariably comes out on the positive side for the new drug. Only when it is not known which subject took which pill is validity remotely approximated. In addition, with judgments of human behavior, it is so difficult to precisely tie down just what behavior is going on, let alone what behavior should be expected, that one must test again and again the reliability of judgments. How many judges, blind, will agree in their observations? Can they replicate their own judgments at some later time? When, in actual practice, these judgment criteria are tested for clinical judgments, then we find that the judges cannot judge reliably, nor can they judge consistently: they do no better than chance in identifying which of a certain set of stories were written by men and which by women; which of a whole battery of clinical test results are the products of homosexuals and which are the products of heterosexuals (Hooker, 1957), and which, of a battery of clinical test results *and* interviews (where questions are asked such as 'Do you have delusions?', Little & Schneidman, 1959) are products of psychotics, neurotics, psychosomatics, or normals. Lest this summary escape your notice, let me stress the implications of these findings. The ability of judges, chosen for their clinical expertise, to distinguish male heterosexuals from male homosexuals on the basis of three widely used clinical projective tests—the Rorschach, the TAT, and the MAP—was *no better than chance*. The reason this is such devastating news, of course, is that sexuality is supposed to be of fundamental importance in the deep dynamic of personality; if what is considered gross sexual deviance cannot be caught, then what are psychologists talking about when they, for example, claim that at the basis of paranoid psychosis is 'latent homosexual panic'? They can't even identify what homosexual anything is, let alone 'latent homosexual panic'.* More frightening, expert clinicians cannot be consistent on what diagnostic category to assign to a person, again on the basis of both tests and interviews; a number of normals in the Little & Schneidman study were described as psychotic, in such categories as 'schizophrenic with homosexual tendencies' or 'schizoid character with depressive trends'. But most disheartening, when the judges were asked to rejudge the test protocols some weeks later, their diagnoses of the same subjects on the basis of the same protocol differed markedly from their initial judgments. It is obvious that even simple descriptive conventions in clinical psychology cannot be consistently applied; if clinicians were as faulty in recognizing food from non-food, they'd poison themselves and starve to death. That their descriptive conventions have any explanatory significance is therefore, of course, out of the question.

As a graduate student at Harvard some years ago, I was a member of a seminar which was asked to identify which of two piles of clinical test, the TAT, had been written by males and which by females. Only four students out of twenty identified the piles correctly, and this was after one and a half months of intensively study-

---

* It should be noted that psychologists have been as quick to assert absolute truths about the nature of homosexuality as they have about the nature of women. The arguments presented in this paper apply equally to the nature of homosexuality; psychologists know nothing about it; there is no more evidence for the 'naturalness' of heterosexuality than for the 'naturalness' of homosexuality. Psychology has functioned as a pseudo-scientific buttress for patriarchal ideology and patriarchal social organization: women's liberation and gay liberation fight against a common victimization.

ing the differences between men and women. Since this result is below chance—that is, this result would occur by chance about four out of a thousand times—we may conclude that there *is* finally a consistency here; students are judging knowledgeably within the context of psychological teaching about the differences between men and women; the teachings themselves are simply erroneous.

You may argue that the theory may be scientifically 'unsound' but at least it cures people. There is no evidence that it does. In 1952, Eysenck reported the results of what is called an 'outcome of therapy' study of neurotics which showed that, of the patients who received psychoanalysis the improvement rate was 44%; of the patients who received psychotherapy the improvement rate was 64%; and of the patients who received no treatment at all the improvement rate was 72%. These findings have never been refuted; subsequently, later studies have confirmed the negative results of the Eysenck study. (Barron & Leary, 1955; Bergin, 1963; Cartwright and Vogel, 1960; Truax, 1963; Powers and Witmer, 1951) How can clinicians and psychiatrists, then, in all good conscience, continue to practice? Largely by ignoring these results and being careful not to do outcome-of-therapy studies. The attitude is nicely summarized by Rotter (1960) (quoted in Astin, 1961): 'Research studies in psychotherapy tend to be concerned more with psychotherapeutic procedure and less with outcome.... To some extent, it reflects an interest in the psychotherapy situation as a kind of personality laboratory.' Some laboratory.

The Social Context

Thus, since we can conclude that since clinical experience and tools can be shown to be worse than useless when tested for consistency, efficacy, agreement, and reliability, we can safely conclude that theories of a clinical nature advanced about women are also worse than useless. I want to turn now to the second major point in my paper, which is that, even when psychological theory is constructed so that it may be tested, and rigorous standards of evidence are used, it has become increasingly clear that in order to understand why people do what they do, and certainly in order to change what people do, psychologists must turn away from the theory of the causal nature of the inner dynamic and look to the social context within which individuals live.

Before examining the relevance of this approach for the question of women, let me first sketch the groundwork for this assertion.

In the first place, it is clear (Block, 1968) that personality tests never yield consistent predictions; a rigid authoritarian on one measure will be an unauthoritarian on the next. But the reason for this inconsistency is only now becoming clear, and it seems overwhelmingly to have much more to do with the social situation in which the subject finds himself than with the subject himself.

In a series of brilliant experiments, Rosenthal and his co-workers (Rosenthal and Jacobson, 1968; Rosenthal, 1966) have shown that if one group of experimenters has one hypothesis about what they expect to find, and another group of experimenters has the opposite hypothesis, both groups will obtain results in accord with their hypotheses. The results obtained are not due to mishandling of data by biased experimenters; rather, somehow, the bias of the experimenter creates a changed environment in which subjects actually act differently. For instance, in one experiment, subjects were to assign numbers to pictures of men's faces, with high numbers representing the subject's judgment that the man in the picture was a successful person, and low numbers representing the subject's judgment that the man in the picture was an unsuccessful person. Prior to running the subjects, one group of experimenters was told that the subjects tended to rate the faces high; another group of experimenters was told that the subjects tended to rate the faces low. Each group of experimenters was instructed to follow precisely the same procedure: they were required to read to subjects a set of instructions, and to *say nothing else*. For the 375 subjects run, the results showed clearly that those subjects who performed the task with experimenters who expected high ratings gave high ratings, and those subjects who performed the task with experimenters who expected low ratings gave low ratings. How did this happen? The experimenters all used the same words; it was something in their conduct which made one group of subjects do one thing, and another group of subjects do another thing.†

The concreteness of the changed conditions produced by expectation is a fact, a reality: even with animal subjects, in two separate studies (Rosenthal & Fode, 1960; Rosenthal & Lawson, 1961), those

---

† I am indebted to Jesse Lemisch for his valuable suggestions in the interpretations of these studies.

experimenters who were told that rats learning mazes had been especially bred for brightness obtained better learning from their rats than did experimenters believing their rats to have been bred for dullness. In a very recent study, Rosenthal & Jacobson (1968) extended their analysis to the natural classroom situation. Here, they tested a group of students and reported to the teachers that some among the students tested 'showed great promise'. Actually, the students so named had been selected on a random basis. Some time later, the experimenters retested the group of students: those students whose teachers had been told that they were 'promising' showed real and dramatic increments in their IQs as compared to the rest of the students. Something in the conduct of the teachers towards those who the teachers believed to be the 'bright' students, made those students brighter.

Thus, even in carefully controlled experiments, and with no outward or conscious difference in behavior, the hypotheses we start with will influence enormously the behavior of another organism. These studies are extremely important when assessing the validity of psychological studies of women. Since it is beyond doubt that most of us start with notions as to the nature of men and women, the validity of a number of observations of sex differences is questionable, even when these observations have been made under carefully controlled conditions. Second, and more important, the Rosenthal experiments point quite clearly to the influence of social expectation. In some extremely important ways, people are what you expect them to be, or at least they behave as you expect them to behave. Thus, if women, according to Bettelheim, want first and foremost to be good wives and mothers, it is extremely likely that this is what Bruno Bettelheim, and the rest of society, want them to be.

There is another series of brilliant social psychological experiments which point to the overwhelming effect of social context. These are the obedience experiments of Stanley Milgram (1965) in which subjects are asked to obey the orders of unknown experimenters, orders which carry with them the distinct possibility that the subject is killing somebody.

In Milgram's experiments, a subject is told that he is administering a learning experiment, and that he is to deal out shocks each time the other 'subject' (in reality, a confederate of the experimenter) answers incorrectly. The equipment appears to provide graduated shocks ranging upwards from 15 volts through 450 volts; for each of four consecutive voltages there are verbal descriptions such as 'mild shock', 'danger, severe shock', and, finally, for the 435 and 450 volt switches, a red XXX marked over the switches. Each time the stooge answers incorrectly, the subject is supposed to increase the voltage. As the voltage increases, the stooge begins to cry in pain; he demands that the experiment stop; finally, he refuses to answer at all. When he stops responding, the experimenter instructs the subject to continue increasing the voltage; for each shock administered the stooge shrieks in agony. Under these conditions, about 62½% of the subjects administered shock that they believed to be possibly lethal.

No tested individual differences between subjects predicted how many would continue to obey, and which would break off the experiment. When forty psychiatrists predicted how many of a group of 100 subjects would go on to give the lethal shock, their predictions were orders of magnitude below the actual percentages; most expected only one-tenth of one per cent of the subjects to obey to the end.

But even though *psychiatrists* have no idea how people will behave in this situation, and even though individual differences do not predict which subjects will obey and which will not, it is easy to predict when subjects will be obedient and when they will be defiant. All the experimenter has to do is change the social situation. In a variant of Milgram's experiment, two stooges were present in addition to the 'victim'; these worked along with the subject in administering electric shocks. When these two stooges refused to go on with the experiment, only ten per cent of the subjects continued to the maximum voltage. This is critical for personality theory. It says that behavior is predicted from the social situation, not from the individual history.

Finally, an ingenious experiment by Schachter and Singer (1962) showed that subjects injected with adrenalin, which produces a state of physiological arousal in all but minor respects identical to that which occurs when subjects are extremely afraid, became euphoric when they were in a room with a stooge who was acting euphoric, and became extremely angry when they were placed in a room with a stooge who was acting extremely angry.

To summarize: If subjects under quite innocuous and non-coercive social conditions can be made to kill other subjects and under other types of social conditions will positively refuse to do so; if subjects can react to a state of physiological fear by becoming euphoric because there is somebody else around who is euphoric or angry because there is somebody else around who is angry; if students become intelligent because teachers expect them to be intelligent, and rats run mazes better because experimenters are told the rats are bright, then it is obvious that a study of human behavior requires, first and foremost, a study of the social contexts within which people move, the expectations as to how they will behave, and the authority which tells them who they are and what they are supposed to do.

Biologically Based Theories

Biologists also have at times assumed they could describe the limits of human potential from their observations not of human, but of animal behavior. Here, as in psychology, there has been no end of theorizing about sexes, again with a sense of absolute certainty surprising in 'science.' These theories fall into two major categories.

One category of theory argues that since females and males differ in their sex hormones, and sex hormones enter the brain (Hamburg & Lunde in Maccoby, 1966), there must be innate behavioral differences. But the only thing this argument tells us is that there are differences in physiological state. The problem is whether these differences are at all relevant to behavior.

Consider, for example, differences in levels of the sex hormone testosterone. A man who calls himself Tiger* has recently argued (1970) that the greater quantities of testosterone found in human males as compared with human females (of a certain age group) determines innate differences in aggressiveness, competitiveness, dominance, ability to hunt, ability to hold public office, and so forth. But Tiger demonstrates in this argument the same manly and courageous refusal to be intimidated by evidence which we have already seen in our consideration of the clinical and psychiatric tradition. The evidence does not support his argument, and in most cases, directly contradicts it. Testosterone level does not seem to be

---

* Schwarz-Belkin (1914) claims that the name was originally Mouse, but this may be a reference to an earlier L. Tiger (putative).

related to hunting ability, or dominance, or aggression, or competitiveness. As Storch has pointed out (1970), all normal *male mammals* in the reproductive age group produce much greater quantities of testosterone than females; yet many of these males are neither hunters nor are they aggressive (e.g., rabbits). And among some hunting mammals, such as the larger cats, it turns out that more hunting is done by the female than the male. And there exist primate species where the female is clearly more aggressive, competitive, and dominant than the male (Mitchell, 1969; and see below). Thus, for some species, being female and therefore having less testosterone than the male of that species means hunting more, or being more aggressive, or being more dominant. Nor does having *more* testosterone preclude behavior commonly thought of as "female": there exist primate species where females do not touch infants except to feed them; the males care for the infants at all times (Mitchell, 1969; see fuller discussion below). So it is not clear what testosterone or any other sex-hormonal difference means for differences in nature, or sex-role behavior.

In other words, one can observe identical types of behavior which have been associated with sex (e.g., "mothering") in males and females, despite known differences in physiological state, i.e., sex hormones, genitalia, etc. What about the converse to this? That is, can one obtain differences in behavior given a single physiological state? The answer is overwhelmingly yes, not only as regards non-sex-specific hormones (as in the Schachter and Singer 1962 experiment cited above), but also as regards gender itself. Studies of hermaphrodites with the same diagnosis (the genetic, gonadal, hormonal sex, the internal reproductive organs, and the ambiguous appearances of the external genitalia were identical) have shown that one will consider oneself male or female depending simply on whether one was defined and raised as male or female (Money, 1970; Hampton & Hampton, 1961):

"There is no more convincing evidence of the power of social interaction on gender-identity differentiation than in the case of congenital hermaphrodites who are of the same diagnosis and similar degree of hermaphroditism but are differently assigned and with a different postnatal medical and life history." (Money, 1970, p. 432).

Thus, for example, if out of two individuals diagnosed as having the adrenogenital syndrome of female hermaphroditism, one is raised as a girl and one as a boy, each will act and identify her/himself accordingly. The one raised as a girl will consider herself a girl; the one raised as a boy will consider himself a boy; and each will conduct her/himself successfully in accord with that self-definition.

So, identical behavior occurs given different physiological states; and different behavior occurs given an identical physiological starting point. So it is not clear that differences in sex hormones are at all relevant to behavior.

The other category of theory based on biology, a reductionist theory, goes like this. Sex-role behavior in some primate species is described, and it is concluded that this is the 'natural' behavior for humans. Putting aside the not insignificant problem of observer bias (for instance, Harlow, 1962, of the University of Wisconsin, after observing differences between male and female rhesus monkeys, quotes Lawrence Sterne to the effect that women are silly and trivial, and concludes that 'men and women have differed in the past and they will differ in the future'), there are a number of problems with this approach.

The most general and serious problem is that there are no grounds to assume that anything primates do is necessary, natural or desirable in humans, for the simple reason that humans are not nonhumans. For instance, it is found that male chimpanzees placed alone with infants will not 'mother' them. Jumping from hard data to ideological speculation, researchers conclude from this information that *human* females are necessary for the safe growth of human infants. It would be as reasonable to conclude, following this logic, that it is quite useless to teach human infants to speak, since it has been tried with chimpanzees and it does not work.

One strategy that has been used is to extrapolate from primate behavior to 'innate' human preference by noticing certain trends in primate behavior as one moves phylogenetically closer to humans. But there are great difficulties with this approach. When behaviors from lower primates are directly opposite to those of higher primates, or to those one expects of humans, they can be dismissed on evolutionary grounds—higher primates and/or humans grew out of that kid stuff. On the other hand, if the behavior of higher primates is counter to the behavior considered natural for humans, while the behavior of some lower primate is considered the natural one for humans, the higher primate behavior can be dismissed also, on the grounds that it has diverged from an older, prototypical pattern. So either way, one can select those behaviors one wants to prove as innate for humans. In addition, one does not know whether the sex-role behavior exhibited is dependent on the phylogenetic rank, or on the environmental conditions (both physical and social) under which different species live.

Is there then any value at all in primate observations as they relate to human females and males? There is a value but it is limited: its function can be no more than to show some extant examples of diverse sex-role behavior. It must be stressed, however, that this is an extremely limited function. The extant behavior does not begin to suggest all the possibilities, either for non-human primates or for humans. Bearing these caveats in mind, it is nonetheless interesting that if one inspects the limited set of observations of existing non-human primate sex-role behaviors, one finds, in fact, a much larger range of sex-role behavior than is commonly believed to exist. 'Biology' appears to limit very little; the fact that a female gives birth does not mean, even in non-humans, that she necessarily cares for the infant (in marmosets, for instance, the male carries the infant at all times except when the infant is feeding [Mitchell, 1969]); 'natural' female and male behavior varies all the way from females who are much more aggressive and competitive than males (e.g., Tamarins, see Mitchell, 1969) and male 'mothers' (e.g., Titi monkeys, night monkeys, and marmosets; see Mitchell, 1969) to submissive and passive females and male antagonists (e.g., rhesus monkeys).

But even for the limited function that primate arguments serve, the evidence has been misused. Invariably, only those primates have been cited which exhibit exactly the kind of behavior that the proponents of the biological fixedness of human female behavior wish were true for humans. Thus, baboons and rhesus monkeys are generally cited: males in these groups exhibit some of the most irritable and aggressive behavior found in primates, and if one wishes to argue that females are naturally passive and submissive, these groups provide vivid examples. There are abundant counter examples, such as those mentioned above (Mitchell, 1969); in fact, in general, a counter example can be found for every sex-role behavior cited, including, as mentioned in the case of marmosets, male 'mothers'.

But the presence of counter examples has not stopped florid and overarching theories of the natural or biological basis of male privilege from proliferating. For instance, there have been a number of theories dealing with the innate incapacity in human males for monogamy. Here, as in most of this type of theorizing, baboons are a favorite example, probably because of their fantasy value: the family unit of the hamadryas baboon, for instance, consists of a highly constant pattern of one male and a number of females and their young. And again, the counter examples, such as the invariably monogamous gibbon, are ignored.

An extreme example of this maiming and selective truncation of the evidence in the service of a plea for the maintenance of male privilege is a recent book, *Men in Groups* (1969) by Tiger. (See above, especially footnote.) The central claim of this book is that females are incapable of 'bonding' as in 'male bonding'. What is 'male bonding'? Its surface definition is simple: '. . . a particular relationship between two or more males such that they react differently to members of their bonding units as compared to individuals outside of it' (pp. 19–20). If one deletes the word male, the definition, on its face, would seem to include all organisms that have any kind of social organization. But this is not what Tiger means. For instance, Tiger asserts that females are incapable of bonding; and this alleged incapacity indicates to Tiger that females should be restricted from public life. Why is bonding an exclusively male behavior? Because, says Tiger, it is seen in male primates. All male primates? No, very few male primates. Tiger cites two examples where male bonding is seen: rhesus monkeys and baboons. Surprise, surprise. But not even all baboons: as mentioned above, the hamadryas social organization consists of one-male units; so does that of the Gelada baboon (Mitchell, 1969). And the great apes do not go in for male bonding much either. The 'male bond' is hardly a serious contribution to scholarship; one reviewer for *Science* has observed that the book '. . . shows basically more resemblance to a partisan political tract than to a work of objective social science', with male bonding being '. . . some kind of behavioral phlogiston' (Fried, 1969, p. 884).

In short, primate arguments have generally misused the evidence; primate studies themselves have, in any case, only the very limited function of describing some possible sex-role behavior; and at present, primate observations have been sufficiently limited so that even the range of possible sex-role behavior for non-human primates is not known. This range is not known since there is only minimal observation of what happens to behavior if the physical or social environment is changed. In one study (Itani, 1963), different troops of Japanese macaques were observed. Here, there appeared to be cultural differences: males in 3 out of the 18 troops observed differed in their amount of aggressiveness and infant-caring behavior. There could be no possibility of differential evolution here; the differences seemed largely transmitted by infant socialization. Thus, the very limited evidence points to some plasticity in the sex-role behavior of non-human primates; if we can figure out experiments which massively change the social organization of primate groups, it is possible that we might observe great changes in behavior. At present, however, we must conclude that, given a constant physical environment, non-human primates do not change their social conditions by themselves very much, and thus the 'innateness' and fixedness of their behavior is simply not known. Thus, even if there were some way, which there isn't, to settle on the behavior of a particular primate species as being the 'natural' way for humans, we would not know whether or not this were simply some function of the present social organization of that species. And finally, once again it must be stressed that even if non-human primate behavior turned out to be relatively fixed, this would say little about our behavior. More immediate and relevant evidence, i.e., the evidence from social psychology, points to the enormous plasticity in human behavior, not only from one culture to the next, but from one experimental group to the next. One of the most salient features of human social organization is its variety; there are a number of cultures where there is at least a rough equality between men and women (Mead, 1949). In summary, primate arguments can tell us very little about our 'innate' sex-role behavior; if they tell us anything at all, they tell us that there is no one biologically 'natural' female or male behavior, and that sex-role behavior in non-human primates is much more varied than has previously been thought.

Conclusion

In brief, the uselessness of present psychology (and biology) with regard to women is simply a special case of the general conclusion: one must understand the social conditions under which humans live if one is going to attempt to explain their behavior. And, to understand the social conditions under which women live, one must understand the social expectations about women.

How are women characterized in our culture, and in psychology? They are inconsistent, emotionally unstable, lacking in a strong conscience or superego, weaker, 'nurturant' rather than productive, 'intuitive' rather than intelligent, and, if they are at all 'normal', suited to the home and the family. In short, the list adds up to a typical minority group stereotype of inferiority (Hacker, 1951): if they know their place, which is in the home, they are really quite lovable, happy, childlike, loving creatures. In a review of the intellectual differences between little boys and little girls, Eleanor Maccoby (1966) has shown that there are no intellectual differences until about high school, or, if there are, girls are slightly ahead of boys. At high school, girls begin to do worse on a few intellectual tasks, such as arithmetic reasoning, and beyond high school, the achievement of women now measured in terms of productivity and accomplishment drops off even more rapidly. There are a number of other, non-intellectual tests which show sex differences; I choose the intellectual differences since it is seen clearly that women start becoming inferior. It is no use to talk about women being different but equal; all of the tests I can think of have a 'good' outcome and a 'bad' outcome. Women usually end up at the 'bad' outcome. In light of social expectations about women, what is surprising is not that women end up where society expects they will; what is surprising is that little girls don't get the message that they are supposed to be stupid until high school; and what is even more remarkable is that some women resist this message even after high school, college, and graduate school.

My paper began with remarks on the task of the discovery of the limits of human potential. Psychologists must realize that it is they who are limiting discovery of human potential. They refuse to accept evidence, if they are clinical psychologists, or, if they are rigorous, they assume that people move in a context-free ether, with only their innate dispositions and their individual traits determining what they will do. Until psychologists begin to respect evidence, and until they begin looking at the social context within which people move, psychology will have nothing of substance to offer in this task of discovery. I don't know what immutable differences exist between men and women apart from differences in their genitals; perhaps there are some other unchangeable differences; probably there are a number of irrelevant differences. But it is clear that until social expectations for men and women are equal, until we provide equal respect for both men and women, our answers to this question will simply reflect our prejudices.

References

Astin, A. W., "The functional autonomy of psychotherapy." *American Psychologist*, 1961, *16*, 75–78.

Barron, F. & Leary, T., "Changes in psychoneurotic patients with and without psychotherapy." *J. Consulting Psychology*, 1955, *19*, 239–245.

Bregin, A. E., "The effects of psychotherapy: negative results revisisted." *Journal of Consulting Psychology*, 1963, *10*, 244–250.

Bettelheim, B., "The Commitment required of a woman entering a scientific profession in present day American society." *Woman and the Scientific Professions*, The MIT symposium on American Women in Science and Engineering, 1965.

Bleck, J., "Some reasons for the apparent inconsistency of personality." *Psychological Bulletin*, 1968, *70*, 210–212.

Cartwright, R. D. & Vogel, J. L., "A comparison of changes in psychoneurotic patients during matched periods of therapy and no-therapy." *Journal of Consulting Psychology*, 1960, *24*, 121–127.

Erikson, E., "Inner and outer space: reflections on womanhood." *Daedalus*, 1964, *93*, 582–606.

Eysenck, H. J., "The effects of psychotherapy: an evaluation." *Journal of Consulting Psychology*, 1952, *16*, 319–324.

Fieldcrest—Advertisement in the *New Yorker*, 1965.

Fried, M. H., "Mankind excluding woman," review of Tiger's *Men in Groups*. *Science*, 1969, *165*, 883–884.

Freud, S., *The Sexual Enlightenment of Children*, Collier Books Edition, 1963.

Goldstein, A. P. & Dean, S. J., *The Investigation of Psychotherapy: Commentaries and Readings*. John Wiley & Sons, New York: 1966.

Hacker, H. M., "Women as a minority group." *Social Forces*, 1951, *30*, 60–69.

Hamburg, D. A. & Lunde, D. T., "Sex hormones in the development of sex differences in human behavior." In Maccoby, ed., *The Development of Sex Differences*, pp. 1–24, Stanford University Press, 1966.

Hampton, J. L. & Hampton, J. C., "The Ontogenesis of Sexual Behavior in Man." In *Sex and Internal Secretions*, Ed. W. C. Young, 1966, 1401–1432.

Harlow, H. F., "The heterosexual affectional system in monkeys." *The American Psychologist*, 1962, *17*, 1–9.

Hooker, E., "Male homosexuality in the Rorschach." *Journal of Projective Techniques*, 1957, *21*, 18–31.

Itani, J., "Paternal care in the wild Japanese monkeys, *Macaca fuscata*." In C. H. Southwick (ed.), *Primate Social Behavior*, Princeton: Van Nostrand, 1963.

Little, K. B. & Schneidman, E. S., "Congruences among interpretations of psychological and anamestic data. *Psychological Monographs*, 1959, *73*, 1–42.

Maccoby, Eleanor E., "Sex differences in intellectual functioning." In Maccoby, ed., *The development of sex differences*, 25–55. Stanford U Press: 1966.

Masters, W. H. & Johnson, V. E., *Human Sexual Response*, Little Brown: Boston, 1966.

Mead, M., *Male and Female: A Study of the Sexes in a Changing World*, William Morrow: New York, 1949.

Milgram, S., "Some conditions of obedience and disobedience to authority." *Human Relations*, 1965a, *18*, 57–76.

Milgram, S., "Liberating effects of group pressures." *Journal of Personality and Social Psychology*, 1965b, *1*, 127–134.

Mitchell, G. D., "Paternalistic behavior in primates." *Psychological Bulletin*, 1969, *71*, 399–417.

Money, J. "Sexual dimorphism and homosexual gender identity," *Psychological Bulletin*, 1970, *6*, 425–440.

Powers, E. & Witmer, H., *An Experiment in the Prevention of Delinquency*, New York: Columbia University Press, 1951.

Rheingold, J., *The Fear of Being a Woman*, Grune & Stratton: New York, 1964.

Rosenthal, R., "On the social psychology of the psychological experiment: the experimenter's hypothesis as unintended determinant of experimental results." *American Scientist*, 1963, *51*, 268–283.

Rosenthal, R., *Experimenter Effects in Behavioral Research*, New York: Appleton-Century Crofts, 1966.

Rosenthal, R. & Jacobson, L., *Pygmalion in the Classroom: Teacher Expectation and Pupil's Intellectual Development*, New York: Holt Rinehart & Winston, 1968.

Rosenthal, R. & Lawson, R., "A longitudinal study of the effects of experimenter bias on the operant learning of laboratory rats." Unpublished manuscript, Harvard University, 1961.

Rosenthal, R. & Pode, K. L., "The effect of experimenter bias on the performance of the albino rat." Unpublished manuscript, Harvard U., 1960.

Rotter, J. B., "Psychotherapy." *Annual Review of Psychology*, 1960, *11*, 381–414.

Schachter, S. & Singer, J. E., "Cognitive, social and physiological determinants of emotional state." *Psychological Review*, 1962, *63*, 379–399.

Schwarz-Belkin, M., "Les Fleurs de Mal." In *Festschrift for Gordon Piltdown*, Ponzi Press, New York, 1914.

Storch, M. "Reply to Tiger," 1970. Unpublished Manuscript.

Tiger, L. "Male dominance? Yes. A Sexist Plot? No." *New York Times Magazine*, October 25, 1970.

Tiger, L., *Men in Groups*, New York: Random House, 1969.

Truax, C. B., "Effective ingredients in psychotherapy: an approach to unraveling the patient-therapist interaction." *Journal of Counseling Psychology*, 1963, *10*, 256–263.

The Myth of the Vaginal Orgasm

by Anne Koedt

Anne Koedt was a founder of the radical feminist movement in New York (New York Radical Women, The Feminists, and New York Radical Feminists). She has worked with Notes from its beginnings as a mimeographed journal (Notes From the First Year), and was an editor of Notes From the Second and Third Years. She is at work on a book about feminism and sexuality, to be published by Random House.

Whenever female orgasm and frigidity are discussed, a false distinction is made between the vaginal and the clitoral orgasm. Frigidity has generally been defined by men as the failure of women to have vaginal orgasms. Actually the vagina is not a highly sensitive area and is not constructed to achieve orgasm. It is the clitoris which is the center of sexual sensitivity and which is the female equivalent of the penis.

I think this explains a great many things: First of all, the fact that the so-called frigidity rate among women is phenomenally high. Rather than tracing female frigidity to the false assumptions about female anatomy, our "experts" have declared frigidity a psychological problem of women. Those women who complained about it were recommended psychiatrists, so that they might discover their "problem"—diagnosed generally as a failure to adjust to their role as women.

The facts of female anatomy and sexual response tell a different story. Although there are many areas for sexual arousal, there is only one area for sexual climax; that area is the clitoris. All orgasms are extensions of sensation from this area. Since the clitoris is not necessarily stimulated sufficiently in the conventional sexual positions, we are left "frigid."

Aside from physical stimulation, which is the common cause of orgasm for most people, there is also stimulation through primarily mental processes. Some women, for example, may achieve orgasm through sexual fantasies, or through fetishes. However, while the stimulation may be psychological, the orgasm manifests itself physically. Thus, while the cause is psychological, the *effect* is still physical, and the orgasm necessarily takes place in the sexual organ equipped for sexual climax—the clitoris. The orgasm experience may also differ in degree of intensity—some more localized, and some more diffuse and sensitive. But they are all clitoral orgasms.

All this leads to some interesting questions about conventional sex and our role in it. Men have orgasms essentially by friction with the vagina, not the clitoral area, which is external and not able to cause friction the way penetration does. Women have thus been defined sexually in terms of what pleases men; our own biology has not been properly analyzed. Instead, we are fed the myth of the liberated woman and her vaginal orgasm—an orgasm which in fact does not exist.

What we must do is redefine our sexuality. We must discard the "normal" concepts of sex and create new guidelines which take into account mutual sexual enjoyment. While the idea of mutual enjoyment is liberally applauded in marriage manuals, it is not followed to its logical conclusion. We must begin to demand that if certain sexual positions now defined as "standard" are not mutually conducive to orgasm, they no longer be defined as standard. New techniques must be used or devised which transform this particular aspect of our current sexual exploitation.

Freud—A Father of the Vaginal Orgasm

Freud contended that the clitoral orgasm was adolescent, and that upon puberty, when women began having intercourse with men, women should transfer the center of orgasm to the vagina. The vagina, it was assumed, was able to produce a parallel, but more mature, orgasm than the clitoris. Much work was done to elaborate on this theory, but little was done to challenge the basic assumptions.

To fully appreciate this incredible invention, perhaps Freud's general attitude about women should first be recalled. Mary Ellman, in *Thinking About Women*, summed it up this way:

> Everything in Freud's patronizing and fearful attitude toward women follows from their lack of a penis, but it is only in his essay *The Psychology of Women* that Freud makes explicit ... the deprecations of women which are implicit in his work. He then prescribes for them the abandonment of the life of the mind, which will interfere with their sexual function. When the psychoanalyzed patient is male, the analyst sets himself the task of developing the man's capacities; but with women patients, the job is to resign them to the limits of their sexuality. As Mr. Rieff puts it: For Freud, "Analysis cannot encourage in women new energies for success and achievement, but only teach them the lesson of rational resignation."

It was Freud's feelings about women's secondary and inferior relationship to men that formed the basis for his theories on female sexuality.

Once having laid down the law about the nature of our sexuality, Freud not so strangely discovered a tremendous problem of frigidity in women. His recommended cure for a woman who was frigid was psychiatric care. She was suffering from failure to mentally adjust to her "natural" role as a woman. Frank S. Caprio, a contemporary follower of these ideas, states:

> ... whenever a woman is incapable of achieving an orgasm via coitus, provided the husband is an adequate partner, and prefers clitoral stimulation to any other form of sexual activity, she can be regarded as suffering from frigidity and requires psychiatric assistance. (*The Sexually Adequate Female*, p. 64.)

The explanation given was that women were envious of men— "renunciation of womanhood." Thus it was diagnosed as an anti-male phenomenon.

It is important to emphasize that Freud did not base his theory upon a study of woman's anatomy, but rather upon his assumptions of woman as an inferior appendage to man, and her consequent social and psychological role. In their attempts to deal with the ensuing problem of mass frigidity, Freudians embarked on elaborate mental gymnastics. Marie Bonaparte, in *Female Sexuality*, goes so far as to suggest surgery to help women back on their rightful path. Having discovered a strange connection between the non-frigid woman and the location of the clitoris near the vagina,

> it then occurred to me that where, in certain women, this gap was excessive, and clitoridal fixation obdurate, a clitoridal-vaginal reconciliation might be effected by surgical means, which would then benefit the normal erotic function. Professor Halban, of Vienna, as much a biologist as surgeon, became interested in the problem and worked out a simple operative technique. In this, the suspensory ligament of the clitoris was severed and the clitoris secured to the underlying structures, thus fixing it in a lower position, with eventual reduction of the labia minora. (p. 148.)

But the severest damage was not in the area of surgery, where Freudians ran around absurdly trying to change female anatomy to fit their basic assumptions. The worst damage was done to the mental health of women, who either suffered silently with self-blame, or flocked to psychiatrists looking desperately for the hidden and terrible repression that had kept from them their vaginal destiny.

Lack of Evidence

One may perhaps at first claim that these are unknown and unexplored areas, but upon closer examination this is certainly not true today, nor was it true even in the past. For example, men have known that women suffered from frigidity often during intercourse. So the problem was there. Also, there is much specific evidence. Men knew that the clitoris was and is the essential organ for masturbation, whether in children or adult women. So obviously women made it clear where *they* thought their sexuality was located. Men also seem suspiciously aware of the clitoral powers during "foreplay," when they want to arouse women and produce the necessary lubrication for penetration. Foreplay is a concept created for male purposes, but works to the disadvantage of many women, since as soon as the woman is aroused the man changes to vaginal stimulation, leaving her both aroused and unsatisfied.

It has also been known that women need no anesthesia inside the vagina during surgery, thus pointing to the fact that the vagina is in fact not a highly sensitive area.

Today, with extensive knowledge of anatomy, with Kelly, Kinsey, and Masters and Johnson, to mention just a few sources, there is no ignorance on the subject. There are, however, social reasons why this knowledge has not been popularized. We are living in a male society which has not sought change in women's role.

Anatomical Evidence

Rather than starting with what women *ought* to feel, it would seem logical to start out with the anatomical facts regarding the clitoris and vagina.

The Clitoris is a small equivalent of the penis, except for the fact that the urethra does not go through it as in the man's penis. Its erection is similar to the male erection, and the head of the clitoris has the same type of structure and function as the head of the penis. G. Lombard Kelly, in *Sexual Feeling in Married Men and Women,* says:

> The head of the clitoris is also composed of erectile tissue, and it possesses a very sensitive epithelium or surface covering, supplied with special nerve endings called genital corpuscles, which are peculiarly adapted for sensory stimulation that under proper mental conditions terminates in the sexual orgasm. No other part of the female generative tract has such corpuscles. (Pocketbooks; p. 35.)

The clitoris has no other function than that of sexual pleasure.

The Vagina—Its functions are related to the reproductive function. Principally, 1) menstruation, 2) receive penis, 3) hold semen, and 4) birth passage. The interior of the vagina, which according to the defenders of the vaginally caused orgasm is the center and producer of the orgasm, is:

> like nearly all other internal body structures, poorly supplied with end organs of touch. The internal entodermal origin of the lining of the vagina makes it similar in this respect to the rectum and other parts of the digestive tract. (Kinsey, *Sexual Behavior in the Human Female,* p. 580.)

The degree of insensitivity inside the vagina is so high that "Among the women who were tested in our gynecologic sample, less than 14% were at all conscious that they had been touched." (Kinsey, p. 580.)

Even the importance of the vagina as an *erotic* center (as opposed to an orgasmic center) has been found to be minor.

Other Areas—Labia minora and the vestibule of the vagina. These two sensitive areas may trigger off a clitoral orgasm. Because they can be effectively stimulated during "normal" coitus, though infrequently, this kind of stimulation is incorrectly thought to be vaginal orgasm. However, it is important to distinguish between areas which can stimulate the clitoris, incapable of producing the orgasm themselves, and the clitoris:

> Regardless of what means of excitation is used to bring the individual to the state of sexual climax, the sensation is perceived by the genital corpuscles and is localized where they are situated: in the head of the clitoris or penis. (Kelly, p. 49.)

Psychologically Stimulated Orgasm—Aside from the above mentioned direct and indirect stimulations of the clitoris, there is a third way an orgasm may be triggered. This is through mental (cortical) stimulation, where the imagination stimulates the brain, which in turn stimulates the genital corpuscles of the glans to set off an orgasm.

Women Who Say They Have Vaginal Orgasms

Confusion—Because of the lack of knowledge of their own anatomy, some women accept the idea that an orgasm felt during "normal" intercourse was vaginally caused. This confusion is caused by a combination of two factors. One, failing to locate the center of the orgasm, and two, by a desire to fit her experience to the male-defined idea of sexual normalcy. Considering that women know little about their anatomy, it is easy to be confused.

Deception—The vast majority of women who pretend vaginal orgasm to their men are faking it to "get the job." In a new best-selling Danish book, *I Accuse*, Mette Ejlersen specifically deals with this common problem, which she calls the "sex comedy." This comedy has many causes. First of all, the man brings a great deal of pressure to bear on the woman, because he considers his ability as a lover at stake. So as not to offend his ego, the woman will comply with the prescribed role and go through simulated ecstasy. In some of the other Danish women mentioned, women who were left frigid were turned off to sex, and pretended vaginal orgasm to hurry up the sex act. Others admitted that they had faked vaginal orgasm to catch a man. In one case, the woman pretended vaginal orgasm to get him to leave his first wife, who admitted being vaginally frigid.

Later she was forced to continue the deception, since obviously she couldn't tell him to stimulate her clitorally.

Many more women were simply afraid to establish their right to equal enjoyment, seeing the sexual act as being primarily for the man's benefit, and any pleasure that the woman got as an added extra.

Other women, with just enough ego to reject the man's idea that they needed psychiatric care, refused to admit their frigidity. They wouldn't accept self-blame, but they didn't know how to solve the problem, not knowing the physiological facts about themselves. So they were left in a peculiar limbo.

Again, perhaps one of the most infuriating and damaging results of this whole charade has been that women who were perfectly healthy sexually were taught that they were not. So in addition to being sexually deprived, these women were told to blame themselves when they deserved no blame. Looking for a cure to a problem that has none can lead a woman on an endless path of self-hatred and insecurity. For she is told by her analyst that not even in her one role allowed in a male society—the role of a woman—is she successful. She is put on the defensive, with phony data as evidence that she'd better try to be even more feminine, think more feminine, and reject her envy of men. That is, shuffle even harder, baby.

Why Men Maintain the Myth

1. *Sexual Penetration Is Preferred*—The best physical stimulant for the penis is the woman's vagina. It supplies the necessary friction and lubrication. From a strictly technical point of view this position offers the best physical conditions, even though the man may try other positions for variation.

2. *The Invisible Woman*—One of the elements of male chauvinism is the refusal or inability to see women as total, separate human beings. Rather, men have chosen to define women only in terms of how they benefited men's lives. Sexually, a woman was not seen as an individual wanting to share equally in the sexual act, any more than she was seen as a person with independent desires when she did anything else in society. Thus, it was easy to make up what was convenient about women; for on top of that, society has been a function of male interests, and women were not organized to form even a vocal opposition to the male experts.

3. *The Penis as Epitome of Masculinity*—Men define their lives primarily in terms of masculinity. It is a universal form of ego-boosting. That is, in every society, however homogeneous (i.e., with the absence of racial, ethnic, or major economic differences) there is always a group, women, to oppress.

The essence of male chauvinism is in the psychological superiority men exercise over women. This kind of superior-inferior definition of self, rather than positive definition based upon one's own achievements and development, has of course chained victim and oppressor both. But by far the most brutalized of the two is the victim.

An analogy is racism, where the white racist compensates for his feelings of unworthiness by creating an image of the black man (it is primarily a male struggle) as biologically inferior to him. Because of his position in a white male power structure, the white man can socially enforce this mythical division.

To the extent that men try to rationalize and justify male superiority through physical differentiation, masculinity may be symbolized by being the *most* muscular, the most hairy; having the deepest voice, and the biggest penis. Women, on the other hand, are approved of (i.e., called feminine) if they are weak, petite; shave their legs; have high soft voices.

Since the clitoris is almost identical to the penis, one finds a great deal of evidence of men in various societies trying to either ignore the clitoris and emphasize the vagina (as did Freud), or, as in some places in the Mideast, actually performing clitoridectomy. Freud saw this ancient and still practiced custom as a way of further "feminizing" the female by removing this cardinal vestige of her masculinity. It should be noted also that a big clitoris is considered ugly and masculine. Some cultures engage in the practice of pouring a chemical on the clitoris to make it shrivel up into "proper" size.

It seems clear to me that men in fact fear the clitoris as a threat to masculinity.

4. *Sexually Expendable Male*—Men fear that they will become sexually expendable if the clitoris is substituted for the vagina as the center of pleasure for women. Actually this has a great deal of validity if one considers *only* the anatomy. The position of the penis inside the vagina, while perfect for reproduction, does not necessarily stimulate an orgasm in women because the clitoris is located

externally and higher up. Women must rely upon indirect stimulation in the "normal" position.

Lesbian sexuality could make an excellent case, based upon anatomical data, for the irrelevancy of the male organ. Albert Ellis says something to the effect that a man without a penis can make a woman an excellent lover.

Considering that the vagina is very desirable from a man's point of view, purely on physical grounds, one begins to see the dilemma for men. And it forces us as well to discard many "physical" arguments explaining why women go to bed with men. What is left, it seems to me, are primarily psychological reasons why women select men at the exclusion of women as sexual partners.

5. *Control of Women*—One reason given to explain the Mideastern practice of clitoridectomy is that it will keep the women from straying. By removing the sexual organ capable of orgasm, it must be assumed that her sexual drive will diminish. Considering how men look upon their women as property, particularly in very backward nations, we should begin to consider a great deal more why it is not in men's interest to have women totally free sexually. The double standard, as practiced for example in Latin America, is set up to keep the woman as total property of the husband, while he is free to have affairs as he wishes.

6. *Lesbianism and Bisexuality*—Aside from the strictly anatomical reasons why women might equally seek other women as lovers, there is a fear on men's part that women will seek the company of other women on a full, human basis. The recognition of clitoral orgasm as fact would threaten the heterosexual *institution*. For it would indicate that sexual pleasure was obtainable from either men *or* women, thus making heterosexuality not an absolute, but an option. It would thus open up the whole question of *human* sexual relationships beyond the confines of the present male-female role system.

Books Mentioned in This Essay

Sexual Behavior in the Human Female, Alfred C. Kinsey, Pocketbooks, 1953.
Female Sexuality, Marie Bonaparte, Grove Press, 1953.
Sex Without Guilt, Albert Ellis, Grove Press, 1958 and 1965.
Sexual Feelings in Married Men and Women, G. Lombard Kelly, Pocketbooks, 1951 and 1965.

I Accuse (Jeg Anklager), Mette Ejlersen, Chr. Erichsens Forlag (Danish), 1968.

The Sexually Adequate Female, Frank S. Caprio, Fawcett Gold Medal Books, 1953 and 1966.

Thinking About Women, Mary Ellman, Harcourt, Brace & World, 1968.

Human Sexual Response, Masters and Johnson, Little, Brown, 1966.

Housework: Slavery or Labor of Love

by Betsy Warrior

This is part of a longer article published in A Journal of Female Liberation—The First Revolution *by Cell 16, 2 Brewer St., Cambridge, Massachusetts. Betsy Warrior is a feminist and an anarchist.*

In every period of labor reform, the lot of the houseworker has lain outside the sphere of interest of reformers and radicals alike, and has remained untouched by any improvements accruing to those workers whose jobs are outside the home. This continues to be the case today. Energy is being directed at improving the conditions of migrant workers, minority groups in the labor force, and even women if they happen to be in the "outside" labor force, i.e., in work situations analogous to male workers. No such energy is being directed at the situation of the household worker. The oppression of females who work outside the home is more easily recognizable because general standards that are accepted for male workers can theoretically be applied to females also. Thus their inequality in relation to male workers can be exposed. There are no such standards for houseworkers nor has the labor they perform ever been recognized as such.

The most obvious reason that no attention has been given to the situation of the houseworker is simply the fact that men aren't engaged in this work. As this position is unique to women, men don't see any direct benefit for themselves in the improvement of it; therefore, it remains unchanged. In this respect, as in many others, men constitute an upper caste who have a monopoly on economic and political power and will use it only when it is directly in their interest. Females, on the other hand, although they would benefit from improvements in this area, are relatively powerless and so unable to implement the necessary changes. The failure of men to use their power to improve the situation of the houseworker is also due to the fact that they rightly feel that any major changes in this area would undermine male supremacy. Men now have their domestic work done for them free. If a change occurred in this area it might mean that men would have to share this now low-prestige work and/or pay to have someone else do it.

It has been suggested that women will gain equality only when they are all employed in the "public" labor force and that this step will by some magic free them from the status of unpaid domestic slavery. The solution to this dilemma can't lie in the hope that all women will leave the home and join the outside paid labor force. First of all, women working outside the home receive the lowest wages and fill the lowest positions in the paid labor force. Secondly, even in time of economic expansion when new jobs are created, there aren't enough jobs to go around.

Besides these two factors that deprive women of incentive to join the "outside" labor force, there are other deterrents. One of the main deterrents is the fact that there are no facilities set up by society for child care or home maintenance in the event that a woman decides to work outside the home. The few existing facilities can't even be considered by the majority of women because of their prohibitive cost and their inability to accommodate more than a tiny percentage of those who might have use for them. Someone has to perform the vast amount of labor entailed in raising children and maintaining living quarters. This labor continues to devolve on women even when they have jobs outside the home. Doubly burdened, women are unable to devote their full attention to either job and are effectively kept at the lowest levels of the paid labor force. On top of that they have been used as scapegoats for every ill of society because they are unable to give their full attention to the roles of mother, wife, and housekeeper.

There are other equally discouraging deterrents of a psychological nature such as the belief that it is the duty of a woman to be solely a wife and mother and that she can't overstep these limits except at the risk of losing her "true" identity. Also a woman's education isn't geared to facilitate a successful or fulfilling career outside the home. Indoctrination and tracking take care of this. If in spite of this, a woman decides to work outside the home, it can be taken for granted that some of the psychological deterrents have been at least partially overcome. But having decided to work outside the home, she comes up against other obstacles that are impossible to remove by a mere change of thinking.

This brings us back to the problem of child care and housework. In other countries attempts have been made to improve the status of women and release them from their unpaid drudgery by drawing them into the paid labor force. These attempts failed and were doomed to failure from the outset because no adequate provisions were made for housework or the care of children. Because of the reformist nature of the changes in the role of women in these societies, the very basis of woman's oppression remained untouched. Females didn't actively share in the decision-making of these revolutions and in fact weren't equally represented in any important areas of these revolutions.

I don't think the feebleness of these reformist attempts is wholly attributable to innocent error or a faulty analysis on the part of male socialist planners but more likely to the unwillingness of males to share the responsibility for home maintenance and child care and an indifference on their part to something they think need not concern them. To equalize the status of the female would have entailed such major and drastic reorganization of society that, judging by the results of the revolutions, it was something the "revolutionary" leaders were unwilling or afraid to undertake. This attitude led them to attack only a symptom of the problem (i.e., the inequality of women in the paid labor force) rather than its root, woman's primary oppression as unpaid domestic—the underlying reason for this inequality. The revolutionary goal of complete emancipation for the female half of the human race has in all revolutions been a goal of low priority which has later been neglected and finally betrayed. But this is an old story to the woman's movement.

> The reorganization of ordinary home maintenance service is long overdue. Household workers have, historically, been low paid, without standards of hours and working conditions, without collective bargaining, without most of the protections accorded by legislation and accepted as normal by other workers, and without

means and opportunity adequately to maintain their homes. (From *American Women (1963–1968)* : *Report on the Status of Women —Interdepartmental Committee*)

This quote from *The Report on the Status of Women* gives an understated and inaccurate account of the situation of houseworkers: In fact it is meant only to apply to the tiny minority of houseworkers who actually do get paid! To say that a segment of the labor force is low-paid is quite different from stating that roughly half of the labor force is un-paid—the half that produces and maintains all labor power. Also the quote doesn't recognize that this situation will exist by necessity under the present economy and a real change can be effected only along with a complete change in the sex role system. The situation of the paid houseworker is indelibly tainted by the economic status of the majority of unpaid houseworkers. How much remuneration is society willing to give for a service that is usually provided free?

In another pamphlet put out by the Woman's Bureau of the US Department of Labor, this question is posed, "What is Equal Pay?" It goes on to explain that "Equal pay means payment of 'rate for the job' without regard to sex—in the factory, in the office, in the school, in the store—and in all other places where men and women perform work of a *comparable* character."

In other pamphlets put out by the Department of Labor, it is cited that women on an average work anywhere between 36 and 99.6 hours a week in the home. This a job at which *all* women are employed at one time or another in their lives, if not all their lives. But there is no mention of "rate for the job" for this work, and this oversight holds true for socialist publications as well. The socialist analyses, including those by women, state that woman's oppression arises at the point of production. What production? They mean, of course, the production that men are engaged in—the production of the "public" sector of the economy! The maddening persistence of this oversight lies in the male orientation of all this literature which does not recognize labor except "where men and women perform work of a comparable character."

The phrase "comparable character" betrays the pseudo-equality offered by these analyses. The main function of woman, which she is confined to because of sex and which distinguishes her from the male, is just what is responsible for her inferior status in the outside labor force and everywhere. This function is in no way comparable to anything done by males. To offer the illusion that women will be equal by receiving equal pay for work that is also done by males, is a conscious effort to keep women's slavery intact. Women are not just laborers in the male-defined sense of the word. Women are the source of all labor in that they are the producers of all laborers. This is the basic means of production (reproduction) in any society. It creates the first commodity, female and male laborers, who in turn create all other commodities and products. Men as the ruling class profit from this commodity through its labor. These profits come in two sizes: king-size and super. The individual man who is king of his castle (the patrilineal family) has his labor power produced, prepared, and maintained for him free. When he sells his labor power on the market he is selling a commodity he owns but did not produce, thereby profiting from the slave labor that went into the making of this product. The *male* capitalist class makes a super-profit when it buys this labor power and then receives the surplus value of its "outside" economy production.

It is clear to me that women will not be freed from their sexual status (slavery) by being given equal opportunity in the "outside" labor force; it has been tried already and has failed. Rather they will be given the basis for equal opportunity by being freed of their function as domestic slaves and its form, the patrilineal family. If we attempt to improve the situation of the houseworker without attacking the economy and sex role attitudes which make this situation possible, then, in effect, we will be trying to make the slavery of women more palatable.

As it is not possible to make any improvements in the institution of slavery, and this is the only accurate counterpart we can find for housework, we must take housework out of the realm of slavery and thereby change its very nature and social meaning. This means, in effect, the abolition of "housework" and "domestic" service in the sense that it is now known. Once this work has to be paid for, it will be incorporated into the "public" economy. This means that the work that was formerly done in separate, duplicated, single units will be collectivized and industrialized on a large basis with a more efficient use of both time and labor and without the waste, alienation, and duplication now involved in child care and home maintenance. Only when this is accomplished will women be able to fight for their equality on a more nearly equal footing with men.

WHY IS this REDHEAD STRIKING?

Lane   *August 26 March,*
New York, 1970.

David Robison   Ladies' Home Journal *sit-in,*
New York, 1970.

...el Hardy   *Abortion March, New York, 1970.*

ABOLISH Abortion LAWS

STOP BUTCHER ABORTIONS

Michael Hardy   Abortion March, New York

David Robison   International Women's Day, New York,

August 26 March down Fifth Avenue, New York, 1970.

Bettye Lane

Older Women's Liberation Conference (OWL), New York,

Small group rap session.

Bettye Lane　　　　　*Playboy Club Picket,*
　　　　　　　　　　　New York, 1970.

Bettye Lane　　　　　*August 26 M*
　　　　　　　　　　　New York,

Joreen

Abortion Demonstration, Chicago,

Shumsky

Ellen Levine

Levine

THE LONG Island Press DISCRIMINATES!

Paper Routes For Girls Too

Girls La

Bettye Lane

Long Island Press *picket, New York, 1*

Levine

Amy Stromsten

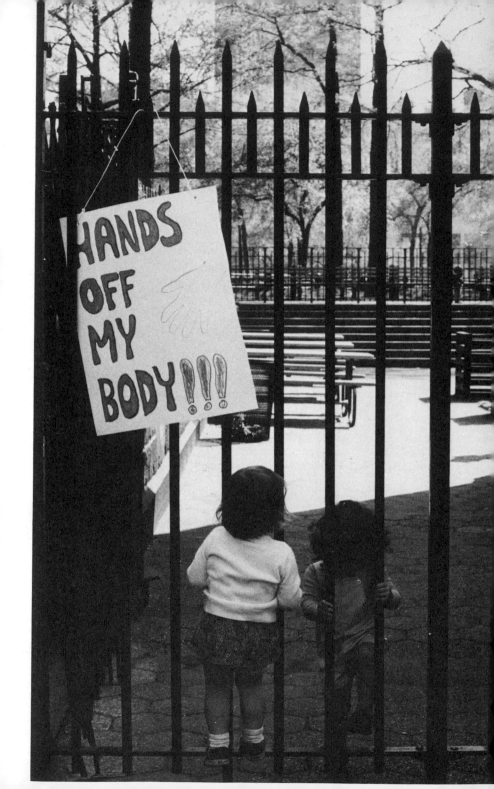

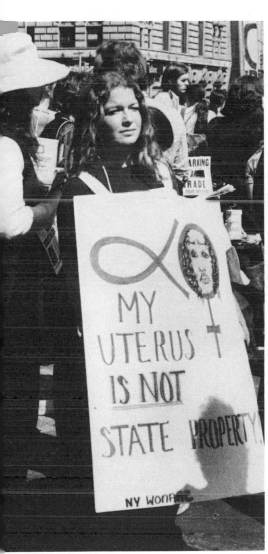

os: Robert Hirschfield

...rtion Demonstration in New York, 1972.

Michael Hardy

Marriage

by Sheila Cronan

Sheila Cronan was a founding member of Redstockings and was active in THE FEMINISTS for more than two years. At present she is attending law school at the University of California, Berkeley.

Marriage has been a subject which has generated considerable controversy in the Women's Movement. So far as I know, no group other than The Feminists has publicly taken a stand against marriage, although I'm sure it has been a topic of discussion in most.

One widely held view in the Movement is represented in the following statement:

> We women can use marriage as the "dictatorship of the proletariat" in the family revolution. When male supremacy is completely eliminated, marriage, like the state, will wither away.[1]

The basic assumption behind this concept, and one that I myself shared at one time, is that marriage benefits women. This idea is very much part of the male culture and is always being reinforced by men's complaints about marriage and by the notion that women are the ones who want to get married. We've all heard plenty of jokes about how women "snare" husbands, and popular songs with lines like "the boy chases the girl until she catches him." Mothers give their daughters advice on how to get their boy friends to marry them, etc. The propaganda tells us that marriage laws are operating in the interest of women and in fact exist to provide protection for the woman. From this assumption it is logical to conclude that we must retain the institution of marriage until such time as discrimination against women no longer exists and consequently "protection" is no longer necessary.

The Feminists decided to examine the institution of marriage as it is set up by law in order to find out whether or not it did operate in women's favor. It became increasingly clear to us that the institution of marriage "protects" women in the same way that the institution of slavery was said to "protect" blacks—that is, that the word "protection" in this case is simply a euphemism for oppression.

We discovered that women are not aware of what marriage is really about. We are given the impression that love is the purpose of marriage—after all, in the ceremony, the wife promises to "love, honor, and cherish" her husband and the husband promises to "love, honor, and protect" his wife. This promise, which women believe to be central to the marriage contract, is viewed as irrelevant by the courts. For example, in a well-known case here in New York State, a woman attempted to obtain an annulment on the grounds that her husband had told her that he loved her prior to the marriage and then afterward admitted that he did not and never would. This was held *not* to give grounds for annulment,[2] despite the fact that the man committed fraud, which is normally grounds for nullifying any contract.

There is nothing in most marriage ceremonies specifically referring to sex, yet the courts have held that "the fact that a party agrees to and does enter into the marriage implies a promise to consummate the marriage by cohabitation, so that failure to do so gives grounds for annulment on the basis of fraud in the inducement."[3] An annulment was granted a New York man on the grounds that his wife was unable to have sex with him due to an incurable nervous condition.[4]

But then, one might ask, how is this particularly oppressive to women? After all, men also enter into marriage with the understanding that love is central. Many of us, in examining our personal histories, however, have suspected that "love" has a different meaning for men than it does for women. This has been substantiated by a study done by a man, Clifford R. Adams of Penn State University, who spent thirty years studying 4000 couples, researching the subconscious factors involved in mate selection. His conclusion was:

> When a man and a woman gaze into each other's eyes with what they think are love and devotion, they are not seeing the same thing. . . . For the woman, the first things she seeks are love, affection, sentiment. She has to feel loved and wanted. The second is security, then companionship, home and family, community ac-

ceptance, and sixth, sex. But for the man sex is at the top of the list, not at the bottom. It's second only to companionship. The single category of love-affection-sentiment is *below* sex.[5]

Sex is compulsory in marriage. A husband can legally force his wife to have sexual relations with him against her will, an act which if committed against any other woman would constitute the crime of rape. Under law, "a husband cannot be guilty of raping his own wife by forcing her to have sexual intercourse with him. By definition, the crime [of rape] is ordinarily that of forcing intercourse on someone other than the wife of the person accused."[6] Thus the threat of force is always present even if it is not necessary for the man to exert it—after all, most women are aware of the " 'right' of the husband to insist on and the 'duty' of the wife to 'submit' "[7] to sexual intercourse.

It is clear that the compulsory nature of sex in marriage operates to the advantage of the male. The husband theoretically has the duty to have intercourse with his wife also, but this normally cannot occur against his will. Furthermore, as far as the enjoyment of the sex act is concerned, figures show that men (with the exception of impotent men who generally cannot have sex at all) nearly always experience orgasm when they have sex. Women, however, are not so fortunate. Surveys have shown that:

> fifteen to twenty percent of all [American] married women have never had an orgasm. About fifty percent reach orgasm on a "now and then" basis, meaning that they experience full culmination about one sex act out of three. Thirty to thirty-five percent of American wives say that they "usually" reach orgasm, meaning that they get there two out of three times or thereabouts. Only a very few women can claim that they have an orgasm every time they take part in sexual activities.[8]

Thus sex as practiced in American marriages clearly benefits the male far more than the female. Despite the emphasis that has recently been put on the husband's duty to give pleasure to his wife, this is not happening most of the time, and we all know that intercourse without orgasm is at best a waste of time. From the above figures we see that 70 percent of American wives have this boring and often painful experience over two-thirds of the time.

> In Alabama's legal code of 1852 two clauses, standing in significant juxtaposition, recognized the dual character of the slave.
> The first clause confirmed his status as property—the right of

the owner to his "time, labor and services" and to his obedient compliance with all lawful commands. . . .

The second clause acknowledged the slave's status as a person. The law required that masters be humane to their slaves, furnish them adequate food and clothing, and provide care for them during sickness and in old age. In short, the state endowed masters with obligations as well as rights and assumed some responsibility for the welfare of the bondsmen.[9]

The following is a description of marital responsibilities:

The legal responsibilities of a wife are to live in the home established by her husband; to perform the domestic chores (cleaning, cooking, washing, etc.) necessary to help maintain that home; to care for her husband and children.

The legal responsibilities of a husband are to provide a home for his wife and children; to support, protect and maintain his wife and children.[10]

The word "slave" is usually defined as a person owned by another and forced to work without pay for, and obey, the owner. Although wives are not bought and sold openly, I intend to show that marriage is a form of slavery. We are told that marriage is an equitable arrangement entered into freely by both husband and wife. We have seen above that this is not true with regard to the sexual aspect of marriage—that in this respect marriage is clearly set up to benefit the male. It also is not true with regard to the rest of the marital responsibilities.

Women believe that they are voluntarily giving their household services, whereas the courts hold that the husband is legally entitled to his wife's domestic services and, further, that she *cannot be paid* for her work.

As part of the rights of consortium, the husband is entitled to the services of his wife. If the wife works outside the home for strangers she is usually entitled to her own earnings. But domestic services or assistances which she gives the husband are generally considered part of her wifely duties. The wife's services and society are so essential a part of what the law considers the husband is entitled to as part of the marriage that it will not recognize any agreement between the spouses which provides that the husband is to pay for such services or society. In a Texas case David promised his wife, Fannie, that he would give her $5000 if she would stay with him while he lived and continue taking care of his house and farm accounts, selling his butter and doing all the other tasks which she had done since their marriage. After David's death, Fannie sued his estate for the money which had been promised her. The court held that the contract was unenforceable since Fannie had agreed to do nothing which she was not already legally and morally bound to do as David's wife.[11]

Whereas the legal responsibilities of the wife include providing all necessary domestic services—that is, maintaining the home (cleaning, cooking, washing, purchasing food and other necessities, etc.), providing for her husband's personal needs and taking care of the children—the husband in return is obligated only to provide her with basic maintenance—that is, bed and board. Were he to employ a live-in servant in place of a wife, he would have to pay the servant a salary, provide her with her own room (as opposed to "bed"), food, and the necessary equipment for doing her job. She would get at least one day a week off and probably would be required to do considerably less work than a wife and would normally not be required to provide sexual services.

Thus, being a wife is a full-time job for which one is not entitled to receive pay. Does this not constitute slavery? Furthermore, slavery implies a lack of freedom of movement, a condition which also exists in marriage. The husband has the right to decide where the couple will live. If he decides to move, his wife is obligated to go with him. If she refuses, he can charge her with desertion. This has been held up by the courts even in certain cases where the wife would be required to change her citizenship.[12] In states where desertion is grounds for divorce (forty-seven states plus the District of Columbia), the wife would be the "guilty party" and would therefore be entitled to no monetary settlement.

The enslavement of women in marriage is all the more cruel and inhumane by virtue of the fact that it appears to exist with the consent of the enslaved group. Part of the explanation for this phenomenon lies in the fact that marriage has existed for so many thousands of years—the female role has been internalized in so many successive generations. If people are forced into line long enough, they will begin to believe in their own inferiority and to accept as natural the role created for them by their oppressor. Furthermore, the society has been so structured that there is no real alternative to marriage for women. Employment discrimination, social stigma, fear of attack, sexual exploitation are only a few of the factors that make it nearly impossible for women to live as single people. Furthermore, women are deceived as to what the nature of marriage really is. We have already seen how we are made to believe that it is in our interest. Also, marriage is so effectively disguised in glowing, romantic terms that young girls rush into it excitedly, only to discover too late what the real terms of the marriage contract are.

The marriage contract is the only important legal contract in which the terms are not listed. It is in fact a farce created to give women the illusion that they are consenting to a mutually beneficial relationship when in fact they are signing themselves into slavery.

The fact that women sign themselves into slavery instead of being purchased has significance from another point of view. A purchased slave is valuable property who would not be merely cast aside if the master no longer liked him, but would be sold to someone else who would be obligated to care for him. Furthermore, the necessity for purchasing slaves ensured that only people with money could be slave masters, whereas almost any man can have a wife.

Given the existence of marriage and the fact that women work for no pay but with the expectation of security—that is, that their husbands will continue to "support" them—divorce is against the interests of women. Many of us have suspected this for some time because of the eagerness with which men have taken up the cause of divorce reform (i.e., making it easier to get one). When a man "takes a wife" he is obtaining her unpaid labor in return for providing her with basic maintenance. After twenty years of marriage in which she has provided him with domestic and sexual services, given birth to and raised his children, and perhaps even put him through medical school and helped him build a thriving practice, he is free to cast her aside in order to replace her with someone more exciting. If there are minor children involved, he will probably be required to provide child support—which is only fair since they are his children. If he is well off financially and the judge is sympathetic to the woman, he may be required to pay alimony; if this occurs you can be sure that he will complain bitterly and claim that it constitutes oppression for him. But what is alimony after all? Isn't it ridiculous to require an employer to give his employee severance pay when he in fact owes him twenty years' back wages?

Very few women get alimony anyway. Often child support payments are camouflaged as alimony because it is beneficial to the man tax-wise to do so.[13]

It is hardly necessary to go into the situation a woman finds herself in after the divorce, particularly if the marriage has lasted any length of time. Her productive years have been devoted to her husband's interests rather than her own and she is consequently in no position to fend for herself in this society. She is not trained for any job besides that of domestic servant. Her only hope is to find another husband, and if she is past a certain age this may be very difficult. In other forms of slavery this tragic situation would not occur as the monetary value of the slave would ensure his security.

While wives are "owned" by their husbands in the same sense that slaves are owned by their masters—that is, that the master is entitled to free use of the slave's labor, to deny the slave his human right to freedom of movement and control over his own body— the scarcity of slaves resulted in their monetary value. Any man can take a wife and although he is legally required to support her, there is very little anyone can do if he is unable to fulfill this responsibility. Thus many women are forced to work outside the home because their husbands are unemployed or are not making enough money to support the family. This in no way absolves us from our domestic and child care duties, however.[14]

Since marriage constitutes slavery for women, it is clear that the Women's Movement must concentrate on attacking this institution. Freedom for women cannot be won without the abolition of marriage. Attack on such issues as employment discrimination is superfluous; as long as women are working for nothing in the home we cannot expect our demands for equal pay outside the home to be taken seriously.

Furthermore, marriage is the model for all other forms of discrimination against women. The relationships between men and women outside of marriage follow this basic pattern. Although the law does not officially sanction the right of a man to force his sweetheart to have sex with him, she would find it very difficult to prove rape in the courts, especially if they have had a regular sexual relationship. Also, it is not unusual for a man to expect his girl friend to type his term papers, iron his shirts, cook dinner for him, and even clean his apartment. This oppressive relationship carries over into employment and is especially evident in the role of the secretary, also known as the "office wife."

One of the arguments in the Movement against our attacking marriage has been that most women are married. This has always seemed strange to me as it is like saying we should not come out against oppression since all women are oppressed. Clearly, of all the oppressive institutions, marriage is the one that affects the most women. It is logical, then, that if we are interested in building a mass movement of women, this is where we should begin.

Another argument against attacking marriage has been that it is dying out anyway. The evidence cited for this is usually the growing rate of divorce. But the high rate of remarriage among divorced persons shows that divorce is not evidence for the decline of marriage. We have seen that divorce is in fact a further abuse so far as women's interests are concerned. And the fact is that marriage rates have been on the increase. From 1900 to 1940 approximately one half of all American women over twenty years of age were married at any given time. After 1940 the figure began to rise noticeably: by 1960 it had reached the rate of two-thirds of all women over twenty.[15]

The Women's Movement must address itself to the marriage issue from still another point of view. The marriage relationship is so physically and emotionally draining for women that we must extricate ourselves if for no other reason than to have the time and energy to devote ourselves to building a feminist revolution.

The Feminists have begun to work on the issue of marriage. It is only a beginning, however; all women must join us in this fight.

Footnotes

[1] Kathie Sarachild, "Hot and Cold Flashes," in *The Newsletter*, Vol. I, No. 3, May 1, 1969.

[2] *Schaeffer v. Schaeffer*, 160 AppDiv 48, 144 NYS 774.

[3] Eugene R. Canudo, *Law of Marriage, Divorce and Adoption* (Gould Publications, 1966), p. 20.

[4] *Hiebink v Hiebink*, 56 NYS(2) 394, aff'd 269 AppDiv 786, 56 NYS(2) 397.

[5] Reported in *Glamour Magazine*, November, 1969, p. 214.

[6] Harriet F. Pilpel and Theodora Zavin, *Your Marriage and the Law* (New York: Collier Books, 1964), p. 215.

[7] *Ibid.*, p. 64.

[8] L. T. Woodward, M.D., *Sophisticated Sex Techniques in Marriage* (New York: Lancer Books, 1967), p. 18.

[9] Kenneth M. Stampp, *The Peculiar Institution* (New York: Vintage Books, 1956), p. 192.

[10] Richard T. Gallen, *Wives' Legal Rights* (New York: Dell Publishing Co., 1967), pp. 4–5.

[11] Pilpel and Zavin, *op. cit.*, p. 65. For a New York case similar to the Texas one cited, see *Garlock v Garlock*, 279 NY 337.

[12] Gallen, *op. cit.*, p. 6.

[13] *Report of the Task Force on Family Law and Policy to the Citizen's Advisory Council on the Status of Women*, April, 1968, p. 7.

[11] Gallen, *op. cit.*, p. 7.

[15] *American Women: Report of the President's Commission on the Status of Women*, 1963, p. 6.

ADC:
Marriage to the State

by André Leo

Most women on welfare are on ADC (Aid to Dependent Children) because they have children and they left the man they were living with or he left them. Maybe their husband died, or they were never living with a man but got pregnant and had a child. The majority of people on welfare live under ADC and the majority of women receiving ADC are white (contrary to myth); the average length of time on ADC is approximately two to three years. Almost all ADC clients are women, and the only parent in the home; they are referred to as "ADC mothers" in this article.

The average ADC mother has three children and applied for assistance when she and her husband separated because she had no income and needed financial help. I have never had an ADC case where the woman received alimony. According to a lawyer I know, the vast majority of divorces do not involve alimony, but often do involve child support payments. However, when the courts track down a father to pay for his children (which isn't too often) he will have to pay only about $10–15 a week per child. None of the ADC mothers I serviced ever got more than $15 a week, if they got that. Child support payments ordered by the courts are well under subsistence level and so ADC is available and pays the woman very little more.

In Michigan the budgets are set up to include $44 per month per person in the family. A *maximum* budget for a four-person family (one parent and three children) looks like this:

$176 food, clothing, incidentals
100 maximum for rent or home purchase
 29 utilities (heat, electricity, and water)
Total $305 monthly allotment

(If the woman gets support payments from the man they are *subtracted* from this total and she gets the remainder—she's not ahead.)

That's hardly enough to live on, and there's nothing for an emergency. On top of that, the ADC is "given" out by the Department of Social Services as if the mother is begging for it, and the state is doing her a "favor" by doling out money to "help" her family.

A social worker next to me at work said, "These women have no pride. Why don't they go out and work instead of getting handouts from ADC?" That same social worker's mother never "worked." But she is proud of her mother and would be thoroughly insulted if you said to her, "Why didn't your mother have enough pride to go out and work instead of taking handouts from her husband?"

The fact is that ADC is just a subsitute MAN and I will refer to ADC as "The Man" from now on as it makes the whole issue a lot more clear. Let me explain.

"Woman's Work"

The principal economic fact about this society is the division of labor between male and female with "man's labor" being paid for and "woman's work" not. Woman's work is defined as child bearing, child raising, and housework. That's what every little girl is told she will do when she "grows up." She is taught to think of "women's work" as her *main* goal in life, and to be proud of thinking this way—since everything in the culture engraves this image upon her mind. Probably her mother was a housewife and she will be one too. Such is the rigidity of the sexual caste system.

In the conventional image the girl will become a housewife and child raiser only if she lands a man in marriage. The man has to bring in the bread for her to play house. So the essential thing to being a housewife and child raiser is having a man to dole out the money for food, clothes, and rent from *his* check which *he* gets from "working."

Work has been defined by male-dominated culture to mean work which you get paid for. Housework has been excluded from this definition of work because male-controlled society has made sure that women do not get paid for their labor as housekeepers and child raisers. All things in this materialistic society are given a monetary value, but household work and child raising have no monetary value if done by a wife and mother for a man. The only time women get paid for housework is when they go to another woman's house and do "her" work for her, either because she's working outside her home (and she certainly can't get a house-husband to do this work for her), or because her husband is wealthy enough to give her money to get out of the low-status house-wifely chores. Rich or poor, the woman still has the responsibility to do the housework or to get someone else to do it for her.

The fact that housework is low-status work is important. House-work when done by a "domestic worker"—i.e., paid for—is one of the lowest paid jobs in this society. But really, what is the difference between the actual work done by a housewife and the work done by a maid or domestic worker? It's clear that almost all women are domestic workers, whether paid or unpaid. Women in male-domi-nated society are primarily a servant caste. With the passing of the days of cheap and plentiful servants, one vast class of servants still remains with us: women. Women are servants in their roles as wives, housekeepers, child raisers, etc. Women's real and ancient servant status and function in male society remains basically un-changed in spite of industrialism and modern technology.

The male-dominated Left also defines work as what you get paid for. When talking about the "working class," they include those domestic laborers who work for other women for pay. But they conveniently exclude all women who work as housewives full- or part-time for men, because they don't get wages—only room and board and handouts now and then from their man (employer). The male supremacism of the Left has time and again interfered with the development of a clear perception of how women are econom-ically in bondage to men of all classes and races.

The Working "Unemployed"

What if a housewife and mother, working without pay, is sud-denly without that man who got paid for *his* work? Does it enter this woman's mind to now demand pay for the work she is doing? No. She has been too well conditioned to think that her work is "special women's work," "you can't put a price on motherhood," and "it's not a job—it's unselfish devotion."

But where would she go, who would pay her for her work, if she did demand pay? No one. They'd even laugh her out of the unemployment security commission offices if she applied for unemployment compensation. Besides, she's still doing "her work" and not getting paid for it. It's the only layoff where the employee has to keep right on working.

So she goes to the only place that is available, to the S.S. (Social Services, that is) to get "welfare." She is made to feel that she is being "given" something for nothing. Meanwhile she's still doing that housework and child raising she was supposed to devote her life to. But now she's bad, lazy, and a leech for doing all that hard work.

The ADC mother learns that there are two kinds of housewives, the "good" ones and the "bad" ones. The "good" ones do the same work as she does but they are still living with a man who "provides" them with their needs from *his* pay from *his* work. The "bad" ones are those who are not living with or being paid for by *a man* and so the state replaces him in the form of an ADC check ("The Man").

"They Should All Go To Work"

What about the argument that ADC mothers could find jobs to support their families if they had enough pride to get off welfare? The stigma of ADC is so great that many ADC mothers believe this themselves. But the argument is shallow and does not hold up for the majority of ADC mothers. If a woman has a large family (two or more children), she will most likely not be able to support her family on a woman's wage rate. If you don't believe this, here are figures on women's wages (they are for 1966 but the situation has gotten worse for female labor since then): In 1966 the median income for a white man was $7,164; for a nonwhite man, $4,528; a white woman, $4,152; a nonwhite woman, $2,949 (full-time year-round work only).

Things are getting worse, and the gap between men's and women's

income has been widening. More than two thirds of all women working full-time, year-round jobs had incomes under $5,000, while
fewer than one fourth of all men were in this bracket. Men often
make more money than women in the same job. Women sales
workers earn 60 percent less than male sales workers. Women man-
agers, officials, and proprietors earn 45 percent less than men in
those same jobs. Women clerks earn 44 percent less than male
clerks. Besides, women are systematically kept out of the labor market and discriminated against more strongly than any other group,
their unemployment rates are highest.

Even if a woman does get a job, she's likely to get more money
on ADC than from work outside her home. She will also have problems finding and paying for baby-sitters or day care. This has been
a very effective way, so far, for this male-controlled economy to
keep mothers with pre-school children out of the labor market. When
she has finally got her job, she will realize why so many ADC
mothers stay home. Now she has two full-time jobs, and only one
for pay! Her life will be a continual round of back-breaking labor
with hardly any time for leisure or the enjoyment of her children.
And all that for poverty-level wages.

The Man and Patriarchal Society

When you put all these facts together some curious patterns begin
to emerge. "The Man" (ADC) has been set up to preserve the family system in which men get paid and the women are unpaid and
kept in a colonized position economically and psychologically. This
is done by refusing to pay women for honest work done in the home,
but rather treating them as "welfare recipients"; by making ADC
checks so low that women have to live with a man to be adequately
"provided" for; by not providing child care centers, and, in fact,
making it difficult to set them up; by perpetuating sex discrimination in the Work Incentive Program and throughout the agency;
etc. ADC makes a concerted effort to strengthen the patriarchal family system and works to prevent the development of other forms of
social structure for child raising and work division. The agency
literature is full of patriarchal male-supremacist dribble all sugar-
coated in terms of "helping" these women who are ADC mothers.

There is no just solution to the situation of women under welfare within the present male-dominated family system. The only way out is for women to get together themselves and to create new structures which do not treat women as a caste labor group or oppress children. Structures where women and men share all tasks and decisions of the society for equal rewards and treatment. The women's liberation movement has already begun to bring women together to try to work out alternatives to the present family system; women on welfare are also beginning to organize themselves to confront the welfare system. The two groups need to work more closely with each other as they are confronting many of the same issues—and the same white male-controlled system.

The saddest thing about "The Man" is that "he" turns woman against woman. Some women say with pride, "Well *I* got along without ADC [The Man], why can't they?" But chances are, those same women couldn't have made it without *some* man to pay for them. For remember, sister, if you have a child or the potential to bear a child—in other words, if you're a woman—you are a potential recipient of "The Man."

Rape:
An Act of Terror

by Barbara Mehrhof and Pamela Kearon

Pamela Kearon and Barbara Mehrhof were founding members of Red-stockings and are now active in The Feminists.

To see rape within the system of female oppression is to understand its non-accidental and non-arbitrary nature and to gain insight into its special purpose for the class of men. There is no group other than slaves that has been singled out for such systematic and total exploitation and suppression as the class of women. The condition of woman exceeds the bounds of the definition of oppression and in the modern Western world her situation is unique.

We are given to understand that in Western society the rule of law operates in contradistinction to the rule of men. This implies that society is built upon *principles* derived from Nature or God which are generally assented to by the governed. By its nature law deals in generalities; the governed are viewed as equal and indistinguishable. Women and slaves, however, have traditionally existed outside this rule of law, since law is the means by which the *public* affairs of freemen are stabilized. The public realm is where male interest groups vie with each other to create history and the world of things. Its essence is visibility and therefore it constitutes accepted Reality. Women and slaves are relegated to the private sphere which is the vague, hidden, unseen world of superior/inferior relationships. The definitive activity of the private sphere is labor—that is, the maintenance of biological life for oneself and others. This is the function of women and slaves.

The imposition of the duty to labor exemplified in marriage cancels out whatever "paper rights" (i.e., legal or public) women might possess because it maintains her private status—servant to the male. It is in this that women are distinguished as a group and subjected to a rule of governance by which they are treated differently from other citizens. This rule of governance is the direct rule by men. This fact, that woman qua woman exists outside the protection of the law, is crucial in understanding rape and how it can be used by men as a terror tactic.

The justification of this rule of women by men is the *Ideology of Sexism*, which from a single assumption seeks to explain the meaning of human life. It posits the human male as the highest expression of Nature, his destiny as Nature's development. Thus, anything which interferes with this destiny, or his needs or desires, must be controlled or suppressed—all of the natural world, including the human female. Male dominance over the female is therefore a *natural* condition. If man is the highest expression of Nature, it follows that man is the Good. Woman, having a will and her own self-interest, is a potential obstruction to male destiny and is therefore a priori Bad, Evil, the Criminal—and consequently the justifiable Victim.

The Ideology of Sexism is totally inured to experience or history. Its basis is not male achievement but rather maleness itself. So the ideology is not subject to criticism or adjustment despite the obvious existence of droves of grotesque or pathetic male individuals. Like Nazism and racism which also posit superiority a priori, sexism is grounded in a physical manifestation of the assumed superiority. For Nazism it is blond hair and blue eyes, for racism skin color, for sexism the penis. But skin, eye and hair color are physical traits which are simply exist. They cannot engage in activity. There is, then, no unique *act* which affirms the polarity Aryan/Semite or white/black. Sexual intercourse, however, since it involves the genitals (that particular difference between the sexes selected by the Ideology of Sexism to define superiority/inferiority), provides sexism with an inimitable act which perfectly expresses the polarity male/female. The Reality created by the Ideology makes the sexual act a renewal of the feeling of power and prestige for the male, of impotence and submission for the female. Rape adds the quality of terror.

Terror is an integral part of the oppression of women. Its purpose is to ensure, as a final measure, the acceptance by women of the inevitability of male domination. The content of terror includes the threat of death, destitution and/or inhuman isolation for the female. The most important aspect of terrorism is its indiscriminateness with respect to members of the terrorized class. There are no actions or forms of behavior sufficient to avoid its danger. There is no sign that designates a rapist since each male is potentially one.[1] While simple fear is utilitarian, providing the impetus to act for one's safety, the effect of terror is to make all action impossible.

The earlier and more thoroughly the woman is terrorized, the more completely she is incapable of acting against the existing Reality modeled on the Sexist Ideology and brought into being by the power of the male class. As long as one is free to act one can invalidate and transform reality. When free action is eliminated one can only incorporate reality as created by others, or go mad or die. The woman assaulted by a rapist is not merely hampered by real or imagined lack of kinetic energy relative to the attacker; she is also restricted by her fragile sense of her own reality and worth. Rape is a punishment without crime or guilt—at least not subjective guilt. It is punishment rather for the *objective* crime of femaleness. That is why it is indiscriminate. It is primarily a lesson for the whole class of women—a strange lesson, in that it does not teach a form of behavior which will save women from it. *Rape teaches instead the objective, innate and unchanging subordination of women relative to men.*[2]

Rape is justified by the Ideology of Sexism. Its most explicit justification is the least publicly expressed. But all rationales exhibit the same tendency to favor the male over the female:

1. In the first instance (going from most extreme to most liberal), rape is seen as arising directly from the overwhelming male sex urge and/or need for violence. But since man is good, to tamper with those powerful forces which are part of his nature is harmful and detrimental. Men must be conditioned in order not to rape. To rape is the highest expression of male freedom, therefore *rape is good.* Though an extreme position among males, or, more specifically, one that is not often openly articulated except by certain

---

[1] Psychologists, for example, have revealed that there are no significant emotional differences between rapists and other men.

[2] This refers as well to other terror tactics aimed at women—including sex murders and gender-determined assaults and murders.

male "revolutionaries," this basic attitude reinforces and gives validity to all other rationales for rape.

2. Rape arises from the provocation of the female—in the very existence of her body or in conscious or unconscious signals indicating she would like to be "taken." This view has more popular currency, but instead of locating the source in the male, it is found in the female. Here rape is bad—but the fault and the shame belong to the woman.

3. Rape is the result of *frustration* to the male sex urge or need for violence. The fault here is with civilization or society, which has limited legitimate male outlets. Deprived of a universal sex orgy or the legendary promiscuity of yore when no girl ever said "no," and denied the supposed exhilaration of the much-glorified hunt, men are forced to act in a way which even they do not approve of. However, the socializing tendency is designated as female, so that woman is still the source of the act—though this time indirectly.

4. A male has been hurt. He is a member of an oppressed class or has been defeated by early psychological experiences. Rape is an understandable expression of hostility toward "society," which has cheated him of his ambition and fulfillment in the world. That the woman is his victim is unfortunate. But he has looked around and seen women who are more forceful than himself or more educated and knowledgeable. This is the greatest sacrilege recognized by Sexist Ideology. It is only to be expected that he would strike out against women in general to regain his manhood. Depending on the politics of the particular rape apologist, it is argued that we must all work for a socialist revolution or to restore the father to his rightful place in the family. But this is the most sentimental and insidious explanation of rape because it ensnares countless women into jeopardizing their own safety and freedom by leading them to pity the male and his "lost manhood."

5. The rapist is crazy. This is an apolitical explanation of rape which, if it appears in its pure form (and it usually doesn't), excuses the male without condemning the female. It says that rape is something void of self-purpose—like lightning, like thunder, like erupting volcanos. It ignores the difference in class between the male rapist and the female victim. His choice of victim and the form his hostility takes are dictated by his rights and her function in the male world. In the conduct of the Boston Strangler case, for

example, the police constantly sought the reasons for the death of his thirteen victims either in the women's own conscious behavior or in some unconscious signals they may have been emitting. Yet they sought to explain the actions of Albert deSalvo, the confessed killer, by his past sufferings. The search was clearly for *the criminal in the victim, the victim in the criminal.*

Rape supports the male class by projecting its power and aggressiveness on the world. For the individual male, the possibility of rape remains a prerogative of his in-group; its perpetration rekindles his faith in maleness and his own personal worth.

Rape is only a slightly forbidden fruit. It is assumed to be condemned by law in our society, yet an examination of law reveals that it's forbidden quality is more of a delectable fantasy than reality. In New York State, for instance, the law stipulates that the woman must prove she was raped by force, that "penetration" occured, *and* that someone witnessed the rapist in the area of the attack. Although the past rape convictions of the defendant are not admissible evidence in a rape trial, the "reputation" of the rape victim is. The police will refuse to accept charges in many cases, especially if the victim is alone when she comes in to file them. In New York City only certain hospitals will accept rape cases and they are not bound to release their findings to the courts. Finally, the courts consistently refuse to indict men for rape. Rape is never defined in marriage in the U.S.A. This simply means that a husband always has the right to take his wife by force regardless of her inclinations. It is next to impossible to press rape charges against a boy friend, male acquaintance, or male with whom one has had a single date. In North Carolina, only a virgin can claim to have been the victim of rape.

It is clear that women do not come under the law on anything like an equal footing with men—or rather, that women as women do not enjoy the protection of law at all. Women as victims of rape, unlike the general victim of assault, are not assumed to be independent, indistinguishable and equal citizens. They are viewed by the law as subordinate, dependent and an always potential hindrance to male action and male prerogative. Rape laws are designed to protect males against the charge of rape. The word of a peer has a special force; the word of a dependent is always suspicious, presumed to be motivated by envy, revenge, or rebellion.

Rape, then, is an effective political device. It is not an arbitrary act of violence by one individual on another; it is a political act of *oppression* (never rebellion) exercised by members of a powerful class on members of the powerless class. Rape is supported by a consensus in the male class. It is preached by male-controlled and all-pervasive media with only a minimum of disguise and restraint. It is communicated to the male population as an act of freedom and strength and a male right never to be denied.

Women, through terror unable to act, do not test the Reality dictated by Sexist Ideology. When an individual woman manages to see that rape is an act which oppresses and degrades her and limits her freedom, when she sees it as political and useful to all males, she cannot count upon support from other women. Many women believe that rape is an act of sick men or is provoked by the female. Thus women as a class do not yet have a consensus. We have no media providing instant and constant communication; we are physically, economically and socially isolated by the institution of marriage which requires lonely labor in service to the male and primary loyalty to him.

The first step toward breaking the debilitating hold on us of the Sexist Ideology is the creation of a counter-reality, a mutually guaranteed support of female experience undistorted by male interpretation. We must build a consensus among us. Power for a group is consensus and organization. Terror depends upon the scattered, confused character of the terrorized class. We *must* understand rape as essentially an act of terror against women—whether committed by white men or minority group males. This is the only means of freeing our imagination so that we can act together—or alone if it comes to it—against this most perfect of political crimes.

October, 1971.

Radical Feminism 1

by Bonnie Kreps

Bonnie Kreps is a founder of the radical feminist movement in Canada. This article is based on a brief presented to the Royal Commission on the Status of Women in Canada in June, 1968. It was the basis for a speech used widely during the formation of the Toronto New Feminists, Canada's first radical feminist group. Bonnie Kreps is a feminist film maker whose films include "After the Vote: A Report From Down Under" and "Portrait of My Mother."

Put very bluntly, the traditional view of woman can be summed up in the words of Aristotle:

> The female is a female by virtue of a certain *lack* of qualities; we should regard the female nature as afflicted with a natural defectiveness.

This may be a rather crass over-statement of the male chauvinist attitude, but the philosophical assumption exhibited here lies at the crux of the problem at hand: that is, man has consistently defined woman not in terms of herself but in relation to him. She is not regarded as an autonomous being; rather, he is the Subject, he is Absolute—she is the Other. Simone de Beauvoir has argued convincingly that, throughout history, one group has never set itself up as the One without at once setting up in opposition the Other, which then tends to become an object. Otherness, she argues, is a fundamental category of human thought. Thus, good-evil, right-wrong, nationalism, racism, anti-Semitism, and male chauvinism.

In accepting the traditional view of herself as secondary and inferior, woman has provided justification for the charge of inferiority. We are all familiar with the contention that women are different *in their nature* from men. Biological differences which no one can deny are used with great enthusiasm by those who wish to justify the status quo *vis-à-vis* women, by those to whom freedom for women seems a profound threat to something deep in themselves.

Whatever biology may determine for us all—and the question is debatable—I think it is an obvious truth that one is not born, but rather becomes, a woman or a man. One is born a female or male child with certain given characteristics and certain potentials which are hereditarily and environmentally determined and must, therefore, be viewed developmentally. To understand woman's so-called "nature," we must, therefore, examine her situation: her history, the myths about her, her social environment, her education, and so forth. A look at history and mythology, for instance, will show that women have been written out of history and represented from a male point of view in mythology. The great figures of history and mythology are always male; as de Beauvoir says:

> Representation of the world, like the world itself, is the work of men; they describe it from their own point of view, which they confuse with absolute truth.

Woman's immediate social environment puts enormous pressure on her to submit to male dominance. She is exhorted to play out the role of Cinderella, expecting fortune and happiness from some Prince Charming rather than to venture out by herself. Be pretty, be pleasant, use mouthwash and deodorant, never have an intellectual thought, and Prince Charming will sweep you off to his castle, where you will live happily ever after. Such is the carrot, and behind it is the stick: "Men don't make passes at girls who wear glasses," "wall flower," "spinster," "old maid," "loose woman," . . . the list goes on, and its message is: to have caught a man is proof of a woman's desirability as a human being; to be without a man is a social and moral disgrace.

The economic discrimination against the working woman is highly conducive to her seeing marriage as a liberation from ill-paid drudgery. She usually faces the prospect of being an underpaid worker in society's lowest echelons. She faces a discrimination based on sex which racial groups no longer tolerate. So it is little wonder that her desire to find a husband is reinforced.

Society's most potent tool for making female human beings into dependent adults is a socialization process. We have a society which is based on arbitrary and strictly enforced sex roles. We may see a loosening of this condition with the next generation, but it is still unhappily true that a certain role is now ascribed purely on the basis of sex. And what does this mean for the female sex? It means that the essential characteristic of the so-called "feminine" character is passivity. Through her upbringing and education, from girlhood up, a girl's sense of self is progressively crushed. Whereas boys get experimental, control-oriented toys, girls get role-playing toys. Boys get tractors, rockets, microscopes, etc.; girls get dolls and vacuum cleaners. Whereas boys are dressed practically and are expected to get dirty, little girls are all too often dressed to be "ladylike"—in other words, they are dressed to be pretty objects, like dolls. Whereas boys are encouraged to be rough, tough and aggressive, girls are trained to become timid and docile (put euphemistically: good listeners, feminine, real helpmates, etc.) Whereas boys prepare themselves to become creators of their own future, girls are trained to relate through others and taught that to please they must *try* to please and therefore renounce their autonomy.

To please is to abdicate. That is the lesson the young girl learns. It is the lesson which finds its apotheosis in a recent best-seller by the American movie star, Arlene Dahl—its commercial success is redoubtable, its title totally indicative of its message: *Always Ask a Man.*

As long as marriage and motherhood are conceived of as a woman's entire destiny and the fulfillment of her "nature," her lot will involve the acceptance of a situation imposed from the outside rather than a free choice according to her individuality. As long as woman accepts this situation, she will endanger her individuality and possibility for growth as a human being. She will, in short, be abdicating the potential of her nature by giving in to the demands of her situation.

We all know about the alcohol and pill consumption of women, the large influx of female psychiatric patients with unspecified ailments, and the myriad symptoms which suggest that something is troubling a great many women. When we add to that the enormous success of feminist books like *The Second Sex* and *The Feminine Mystique,* and the rising waves of new feminists in Europe and America, I think it becomes apparent to all but the most pig-headed that the picture of the happy housewife, the fulfilled woman who has bought all the garbage of the Feminine Mystique, that this picture is a gross distortion. The true picture spells out in large letters: FRUSTRATION.

For those many women who have acknowledged their sense of emptiness, their frustration, there has often followed a feeling of guilt. They feel that there must be something peculiarly wrong with them and that they should be able somehow to cope with their frustration. (Note here the rising success of the tension-reducing pill named COPE.) We are still the beneficiaries of Freud's claim that neurosis is a sign of sickness.

There has emerged recently, however, a new school of psychology with a new definition of sickness and health. Called, loosely, "The Third Force," it contrasts sharply with Freud and the behaviorists. Some of its major tenets are these: Each of us has an essential core, a potential and personality, which tends strongly to persist. One might liken it to the body's drive for health. If this psychological drive for health is frustrated or stunted, sickness results. No psychological health is possible unless this essential core of the person is fundamentally accepted, loved, and respected by others and by himself. And, they add, "adjustment is, very definitely, *not* necessarily synonymous with psychological health."

On this basis, it would seem that woman's present situation is not consonant with her optimal growth; further, that the frustrations engendered by attempting to force these disparities into consonance —these frustrations are a sign, not of mental sickness, but of mental health.

The most reasonable conclusion reached from the above arguments is therefore, I would think, that the traditional view of women and its attendant Feminine Mystique are a fraud. While they are to men's advantage in many (though ultimately not all) respects, they mean loss of growth, of full-humanness, to the woman who submits to their edicts. Such a woman will risk a loss of identity, she will risk becoming a thing.

Modern woman is in the grip of a vicious circle and in urgent need of liberation. The more she resigns herself to the demands of her situation, the more she will stunt her human growth, and the more she will thus be unable to escape from her situation. The ultimate success of the slave system was, after all, that it ultimately convinced the slaves themselves that they were fit for nothing else but being slaves and that being a slave wasn't all that bad. We women can learn a lot from the emergence of black people who are fighting for black dignity. The question for women is, what are the mechanics of our particular kind of oppression and how do we best fight it?

First of all, we must recognize that the liberation of women must be collective, it must be aimed at freedom for all women. Our goal must be that any and all women who want to escape from the sex role foisted upon them will have the freedom to do so. Therefore, no "token integration," no relieving of symptoms without getting at the causes. Secondly, we must get full economic rights for women, because only economic liberty can guarantee women that their theoretic civil liberties will provide them with liberty in practice. We must do away with the woman-as-economic-parasite notion. Thirdly, women must be freed from their present partial or complete slavery to the species. They must have the right to decide over their own bodies. Fourthly, and most generally, girls and women must be encouraged to seek self-fulfillment as human beings rather than merely as females.

The statement that girls should seek fulfilment as human beings rather than as females has enormous implications. It is the starting point for the very large philosophical and political area known as radical feminism.

To explain somewhat further: The Women's Liberation Movement is a generic term covering a large spectrum of positions. Broadly speaking, the movement can be divided into three areas: (1) The largely economically oriented (usually Marxist) segment which sees liberation for women as part of a socialist revolution; (2) liberal groups like the National Organization for Women. This segment is analogous to the NAACP in the black struggle; it is working for some kind of integration of women into the main fabric of society; and (3) radical feminism, which chooses to concentrate exclusively on the oppression of women *as women* (and not as workers, students, etc.). This segment therefore concentrates its analysis on institutions like love, marriage, sex, masculinity and femininity. It would be opposed specifically and centrally to sexism, rather than capitalism (thus differing from the

Marxists), and would not be particularly concerned with "equal rights," "equal pay for equal work" and other major concerns of the NOW segment.

The point I would like to make is that all three broad segments have their own validity, all three are important. One belongs in one segment rather than another because of personal affinity with the aims being striven for. Personally, I find radical feminism most congenial, because it seems to me to get at the fundamentals of the sexual oppression which is so prevalent in today's society. Most of the really important books which recently have come out on the subject are written by radical feminists. Kate Millett's *Sexual Politics*, for example, and the very important *Notes From the Second Year* and *Notes From the Third Year*.

In short, radical feminism is concerned with the analysis of the oppression of women *as women*. Its basic aim could fairly be stated as "There shall be no characteristics, behaviour, or roles ascribed to any human being on the basis of sex." In other words, we must fight the myth of the so-called "female" character (men should fight the myth of the "male"); we must fight the corrupt notion we now call "love," which is based on control of another rather than on love for the growth of another; we must fight the institutionalization of the oppression of women—especially the institution of marriage.

Radical feminism is called "radical" because it is struggling to bring about really fundamental changes in our society. We, in this segment of the movement, do not believe that the oppression of women will be ended by giving them a bigger piece of the pie, as Betty Friedan would have it. We believe that the pie itself is rotten. We do not believe that women should be integrated into the male world so that they can be "just as good as men." We believe that the male world as it now exists is based on the corrupt notion of "maleness vs. femaleness," that the oppression of women is based on this very notion and its attendant institutions. "Separate but equal" will get us nowhere; we must eradicate the sexual division on which our society is based. Only then do men and women have a hope of living together as human beings.

The Woman Identified Woman

by Radicalesbians

Our awareness is due to all women who have struggled and learned in consciousness raising groups, but particularly to gay women whose path has delineated and focused the women's movement on the nature and underlying causes of our oppression.

What is a lesbian? A lesbian is the rage of all women condensed to the point of explosion. She is the woman who, often beginning at an extremely early age, acts in accordance with her inner compulsion to be a more complete and freer human being than her society—perhaps then, but certainly later—cares to allow her. These needs and actions, over a period of years, bring her into painful conflict with people, situations, the accepted ways of thinking, feeling and behaving, until she is in a state of continual war with everything around her, and usually with her self. She may not be fully conscious of the political implications of what for her began as personal necessity, but on some level she has not been able to accept the limitations and oppression laid on her by the most basic role of her society—the female role. The turmoil she experiences tends to induce guilt proportional to the degree to which she feels she is not meeting social expectations, and/or eventually drives her to question and analyze what the rest of her society more or less accepts. She is forced to evolve her own life pattern, often living much of her life alone, learning usually much earlier than her "straight" (heterosexual) sisters about the essential aloneness of life (which the myth of marriage obscures) and about the reality of illusions. To the extent that she cannot expel the heavy socialization that goes with being female, she can never truly find peace with herself. For she is caught somewhere between accepting society's view of her—in which case she cannot accept herself—and coming to understand what this sexist society has done to her and why it is functional and necessary for it to do so. Those of us who work that through find ourselves on the other side of a tortuous journey through a night that may have been decades long. The perspective gained from that journey, the liberation of self, the inner peace, the real love of self and of all women, is something to be shared with all women—because we are all women.

It should first be understood that lesbianism, like male homosexuality, is a category of behavior possible only in a sexist society characterized by rigid sex roles and dominated by male supremacy. Those sex roles dehumanize women by defining us as a supportive/serving caste *in relation to* the master caste of men, and emotionally cripple men by demanding that they be alienated from their own bodies and emotions in order to perform their economic/political/military functions effectively. Homosexuality is a by-product of a particular way of setting up roles (or approved patterns of behavior) on the basis of sex; as such it is an inauthentic (not consonant with "reality") category. In a society in which men do not oppress women, and sexual expression is allowed to follow feelings, the categories of homosexuality and heterosexuality would disappear.

But lesbianism is also different from male homosexuality, and serves a different function in the society. "Dyke" is a different kind of put-down from "faggot," although both imply you are not playing your socially assigned sex role . . . are not therefore a "real woman" or a "real man." The grudging admiration felt for the tomboy, and the queasiness felt around a sissy boy point to the same thing: the contempt in which women or those who play a female role—are held. And the investment in keeping women in that contemptuous role is very great. Lesbian is the word, the label, the condition that holds women in line. When a woman hears this word tossed her way, she knows she is stepping out of line. She knows that she has crossed the terrible boundary of her sex role. She recoils, she protests, she reshapes her actions to gain approval. Lesbian is a label invented by the Man to throw at any woman who dares to be his equal, who dares to challenge his prerogatives (including that of all women as part of the exchange medium among men), who dares to assert the primacy of her own needs. To have the label applied to people active in women's liberation is just the most recent instance of a long history; older women will recall that not so long ago, any woman who was successful, independent, not orienting her whole life about a man, would hear this word. For in this sexist society, for a woman to be independent means she *can't be* a woman—she must be a dyke. That in itself should tell us where women are at. It says as clearly as can be said: women and person are contradictory terms. For a lesbian is not considered a "real woman." And yet, in popular thinking, there is really only one essential difference between a lesbian and other women: that of sexual orientation—which is to say, when you strip off all the packaging, you must finally realize that the essence of being a "woman" is to get fucked by men.

"Lesbian" is one of the sexual categories by which men have divided up humanity. While all women are dehumanized as sex objects, as the objects of men they are given certain compensations: identification with his power, his ego, his status, his protection (from other males), feeling like a "real woman," finding social acceptance by adhering to her role, etc. Should a woman confront herself by confronting another woman, there are fewer rationalizations, fewer buffers by which to avoid the stark horror of her dehumanized condition. Herein we find the overriding fear of many women toward being used as a sexual object by a woman, which not only will bring her no male-connected compensations, but also will reveal the void which is woman's real situation. This dehumanization is expressed when a straight woman learns that a sister is a lesbian; she begins to relate to her lesbian sister as her potential sex object, laying a surrogate male role on the lesbian. This reveals her heterosexual conditioning to make herself into an object when sex is potentially involved in a relationship, and it denies the lesbian her full humanity. For women, especially those in the movement, to perceive their lesbian sisters through this male grid of role definitions is to accept this male cultural conditioning and to oppress their sisters much as they themselves have been oppressed by men. Are we going to continue the male classification system of defining all females in sexual relation to some other category of people? Affixing the label lesbian not only to a woman who aspires to be a person, but also to any situation of real love, real solidarity, real primacy among women, is a primary form of divisiveness among women: it is the condition which keeps women within the confines of the feminine role, and it is the debunking/scare term that keeps women from forming any primary attachments, groups, or associations among ourselves.

Women in the movement have in most cases gone to great lengths to avoid discussion and confrontation with the issue of lesbianism. It puts people up-tight. They are hostile, evasive, or try to incorporate it into some "broader issue." They would rather not talk about it. If they have to, they try to dismiss it as a "lavender herring." But it is no side issue. It is absolutely essential to the success and fulfillment of the women's liberation movement that this issue be dealt with. As long as the label "dyke" can be used to frighten a woman into a less militant stand, keep her separate from her sisters, keep her from giving primacy to anything other than men and family—then to that extent she is controlled by the male culture. Until women see in each other the possibility of a primal commitment which includes sexual love, they will be denying themselves the love and value they readily accord to men, thus affirming their second-class status. As long as male acceptability is primary— both to individual women and to the movement as a whole—the term lesbian will be used effectively against women. Insofar as women want only more privileges within the system, they do not want to antagonize male power. They instead seek acceptability for women's liberation, and the most crucial aspect of the acceptability is to deny lesbianism—i.e., to deny any fundamental challenge to the basis of the female. It should also be said that some younger, more radical women have honestly begun to discuss lesbianism, but so far it has been primarily as a sexual "alternative" to men. This, however, is still giving primacy to men, both because the idea of relating more completely to women occurs as a negative reaction to men, and because the lesbian relationship is being characterized simply by sex, which is divisive and sexist. On one level, which is both personal and political, women may withdraw emotional and sexual energies from men, and work out various alternatives for those energies in their own lives. On a different political/psychological level, it must be understood that what is crucial is that women begin disengaging from male-defined response patterns. In the privacy of our own psyches, we must cut those cords to the core. For irrespective of where our love and sexual energies flow, if we are male-identified in our heads, we cannot realize our autonomy as human beings.

But why is it that women have related to and through men? By virtue of having been brought up in a male society, we have internalized the male culture's definition of ourselves. That definition consigns us to sexual and family functions, and excludes us from defining and shaping the terms of our lives. In exchange for our psychic servicing and for performing society's non-profitmaking functions, the man confers on us just one thing: the slave status which makes us legitimate in the eyes of the society in which we live. This is called "femininity" or "being a real woman" in our cultural lingo. We are authentic, legitimate, real to the extent that we are the property of some man whose name we bear. To be a woman who belongs to no man is to be invisible, pathetic, inauthentic, unreal. He confirms his image of us—of what we have to be in order to be acceptable by him—but not our real selves; he confirms our womanhood—as he defines it, in relation to him—but cannot confirm our personhood, our own selves as absolutes. As long as we are dependent on the male culture for this definition, for this approval, we cannot be free.

The consequence of internalizing this role is an enormous reservoir of self-hate. This is not to say the self-hate is recognized or accepted as such; indeed most women would deny it. It may be experienced as discomfort with her role, as feeling empty, as numbness, as restlessness, as a paralyzing anxiety at the center. Alternatively, it may be expressed in shrill defensiveness of the glory and destiny of her role. But it does exist, often beneath the edge of her consciousness, poisoning her existence, keeping her alienated from herself, her own needs, and rendering her a stranger to other women. They try to escape by identifying with the oppressor, living through him, gaining status and identity from his ego, his power, his accomplishments. And by not identifying with other "empty vessels" like themselves. Women resist relating on all levels to other women who will reflect their own oppression, their own secondary status, their own self-hate. For to confront another woman is finally to confront one's self—the self we have gone to such lengths to avoid. And in that mirror we know we cannot really respect and love that which we have been made to be.

As the source of self-hate and the lack of real self are rooted in our male-given identity, we must create a new sense of self. As long as we cling to the idea of "being a woman," we will sense some conflict with that incipient self, that sense of I, that sense of a whole person. It is very difficult to realize and accept that being "feminine" and being a whole person are irreconcilable. Only women can give to each other a new sense of self. That identity we have to develop with reference to ourselves, and not in relation to men. This consciousness is the revolutionary force from which all else will follow, for ours is an organic revolution. For this we must be available and supportive to one another, give our commitment and our love, give the emotional support necessary to sustain this movement. Our energies must flow toward our sisters, not backward toward our oppressors. As long as woman's liberation tries to free women without facing the basic heterosexual structure that binds us in one-to-one relationship with our oppressors, tremendous energies will continue to flow into trying to straighten up each particular relationship with a man, into finding how to get better sex, how to turn his head around—into trying to make the "new man" out of him, in the delusion that this will allow us to be the "new woman." This obviously splits our energies and commitments, leaving us unable to be committed to the construction of the new patterns which will liberate us.

It is the primacy of women relating to women, of women creating a new consciousness of and with each other, which is at the heart of women's liberation, and the basis for the cultural revolution. Together we must find, reinforce, and validate our authentic selves. As we do this, we confirm in each other that struggling, incipient sense of pride and strength, the divisive barriers begin to melt, we feel this growing solidarity with our sisters. We see ourselves as prime, find our centers inside of ourselves. We find receding the sense of alienation, of being cut off, of being behind a locked window, of being unable to get out what we know is inside. We feel a real-ness, feel at last we are coinciding with ourselves. With that real self, with that consciousness, we begin a revolution to end the imposition of all coercive identifications, and to achieve maximum autonomy in human expression.

Lesbianism and Feminism
by Anne Koedt

Female homosexuality is becoming an increasingly important problem. It is believed by some that women are becoming rapidly defeminized as a result of their overt desire for emancipation, and that this "psychic masculinization" of modern women contributes to frigidity.... Some sexologists fear that this defeminization trend may seriously affect the sexual happiness of modern women. They claim it will more than likely influence the susceptibility of many to a homosexual way of thinking and living.

—Frank S. Caprio, M.D.,
Variations in Sexual Behavior

Feminism is the theory; lesbianism is the practice.

—Attributed to Ti-Grace Atkinson

When Gertrude Stein entertained friends, she conversed only with the men and left Alice Toklas the duty of talking with the ladies.

—Simone de Beauvoir, *The Second Sex*

Only women can give each other a new sense of self.... We must be available and supportive to one another, [and] give our commitment and our love....

—Radicalesbians, "Woman Identified Woman"

I like her breasts and don't understand her legs.

—Jill Johnston

Lesbian Baiting

Feminists have been called "lesbian" long before they may have, in fact, considered its application in their personal lives; it has been an insult directed at them with escalated regularity ever since they began working politically for women's liberation. Their reaction to lesbian baiting has been mixed. On the one hand it was clear that feminism was threatening to men, and that men were retaliating with whatever verbal weapons were at hand. But the threat of being called lesbian touched real fears; to the extent that a woman was involved with a man, she feared being considered Unfeminine and Unwomanly, and thus being rejected. There was also the larger threat: the fear of male rejection in general. Since it is through husbands that women gain economic and social security, through male employers that they earn a living, and in general through male power that they survive, to incur the wrath of men is no small matter. Women knew this long before they put it in feminist terms. Thus it is not just vanity and personal idiosyncrasy for women to wish to remain in the good graces of men. It is a practical reflection of reality.

For feminists the main educational value of lesbian baiting has been its exposure of the very clear connection in men's minds between being "unfeminine" and being independent. Being called unfeminine is a comparatively gentle threat informing you that you are beginning to waver, whereas being called a lesbian is the danger signal—the final warning that you are about to leave the Territory of Womanhood altogether.

Acts of feminine trangression may take different forms. A woman may appear too self-reliant and assertive; she may work politically for women's rights; she may be too smart for her colleagues; or she may have important close friends who are women. Often women have been called "lesbian" by complete strangers simply because they were sitting in a cafe obviously engrossed in their own conversation and not interested in the men around them. (Curiously enough it is precisely on the most seemingly "feminine" women that men will frequent this kind of abuse, since the purpose is more to scare the women back into "place" than to pinpoint any actual lesbianism.)

The consideration of lesbianism as a personal option grew out of very different reasons. For many feminists there had always been a logical, theoretical connection between the elimination of sex roles and the possibility of loving other women. With some this became a reality when they met a woman they were attracted to. For others, lesbianism has meant a freedom from male relationships in general, a release from the task of looking for that elusive "special" man who wasn't a male chauvinist. Other feminists saw a love relationship with a woman as a positive thing because they felt other women would not encourage the passivity and submissiveness that they had previously found themselves falling into with men. Most important of all, perhaps, women found that there were other women to love in their own right as persons.

Definitions

With the increased interaction between the gay and women's liberation movements, a heightened consciousness about lesbianism has evolved among feminists—and along with it a corresponding disagreement and confusion as to what exactly it means to be a lesbian. It is clear that more is being implied than the straight dictionary definition of women sleeping with members of their own sex. Some women define it as meaning having sex *exclusively* with women, a more rigid definition than the one commonly used. Other gay women see lesbianism as much more than a defining term for the sex of your bed partner; to them it is a "total life commitment to a life with women" and "an entire system of world view and life living."[1] Indeed, some gay women seek to equate their lesbianism with vanguard radical feminism since, as some of them say, "we rejected men and sex roles long before there even *was* a women's liberation movement." For the purposes of this discussion the meaning of the word lesbianism is restricted to its simplest definition of "women having sexual relations with women," so that the various "life style" arguments which are sometimes added to the basic definition can be looked at separately.

I think that the first thing to do is to define radical feminism: To me it means the advocacy of the total elimination of sex roles. A radical feminist, then, is one who believes in this and works politically toward that end.* Basic to the position of radical feminism is the concept that biology is not destiny, and that male and female roles are learned—indeed that they are male political constructs that serve to ensure power and superior status for men. Thus the bio-

---

* She does not by this definition live a life untouched by sex roles; there are no "liberated" women in that sense.

logical male is the oppressor not by virtue of his male biology, but by virtue of his *rationalizing* his *supremacy* on the basis of that biological difference. The argument that "man is the enemy" is then true only insofar as the man adopts the male supremacy role.

What then is the relationship between lesbianism and radical feminism? Taking even the most minimal definitions of lesbianism and feminism, you can find one major point of agreement: biology does not determine sex roles. Thus, since roles are learned there is nothing inherently "masculine" or "feminine" in behavior.

Beyond these basic assumptions, however, there are important differences. Radical feminism naturally incorporates the notion of lesbianism† but with strict reservations. Mainly I think that many radical feminists have resented the whole baggage of assumed implications that some gay women have tagged onto lesbianism. It has been presented too often as a package deal where if you accepted the idea of lesbianism, you would necessarily also have to accept a whole gay position which frequently runs contrary to radical feminism.

The following are some of the points of disagreement:

Homosexuality as "Sick" or "Healthy"

The agreement that there is nothing innately sick about persons having sex with someone of their own sex does not mean that therefore all gay behavior is healthy in feminist terms. A lesbian acting like a man or a gay man acting like a woman is not necessarily sicker than heterosexuals acting out the same roles; but it is not healthy. *All role playing is sick*, be it "simulated" or "authentic" according to society's terms.

The fact that there has occurred a role transfer, and that now it is being acted out by the "wrong" sex, does not change the nature of *what* is being acted out. A male homosexual who dresses up with make-up, makes catty remarks about other women, worries excessively about boy friend approval, and in general displays the insecurity and helplessness that have been the symptoms of women's oppression, is as far away from being the full person he could be as

† Reform feminism which envisions *only* an "equal partnership with men" clearly has in mind improved male-female relationships, not new possibilities for loving and relating sexually to women as well.

the woman acting out that same role. The point is that they are, in a sense, both in drag.

On the other hand, two lesbians who have chosen not to fall into imitative roles, but are instead exploring the positive aspects of both "masculine" and "feminine" behavior beyond roles—forming something new and equal in the process—would in my opinion probably be healthy.

Gay as Radical Feminist Vanguard

One position advanced by some lesbians is the idea that lesbians are the vanguard of the women's movement because 1) they broke with sex roles before there even was a feminist movement, and 2) they have no need for men at all. (Somehow they are the revolution.) The following is one example of this position:

> Feel the real glow that comes from "our" sisterhood. We can teach you something about being gentle and kind for we never felt competitive. Remember WE long before YOU have known discontent with male society and WE long before YOU knew and appreciated the full potential of everything female. . . . It is WE who say welcome to you, long blind and oppressed sisters, we have been fighting against male supremacy for a long time, join US! We are not intimidated by relational differences, for we have never felt mortgaged by society.[2]

Several points seem to be ignored with this kind of argument. For one, there is a confusion of a personal with a political solution. Sex roles and male supremacy will not go away simply by women becoming lesbians. It will take a great deal of sophisticated political muscle and collective energy for women to eliminate sexism. So at best a lesbian relationship can give a woman more happiness and freedom in her private life (assuming both women are not playing roles). But a radical feminist is not just one who tries to live the good non-sexist life at home; she is one who is working politically in society to destroy the institutions of sexism.

Another assumption implicit in the argument of "lesbian-as-the-vanguard-feminist" is that having balked at one aspect of sexism—namely, exclusive heterosexuality—they are therefore radical feminists. *Any* woman who defies her role—be it refusing to be a mother, wanting to be a biochemist, or simply refusing to cater to a man's ego—is defying the sex role system. It is an act of rebellion.

In the case of lesbianism, the act of rebellion often has earned the woman severe social ostracism. However, it becomes radical only if it is then placed in the context of wanting to destroy the system as a whole, that is, destroying the sex role system as opposed to just rejecting men. Indeed, there can be reformism within lesbianism too; when a lesbian says "I have nothing against men; I just don't want to be involved with them," she is really describing an accommodation within the sexist system even though she has performed the rebellious act of violating that system by being a lesbian. It is also in this context that a statement like "feminism is the theory; lesbianism is the practice" is erroneous. For not only is the sex of a woman's lover insufficient information to infer radical feminism, but there is also the false implication that to have no men in your personal life means you are therefore living the life of fighting for radical feminist change.

The notion that lesbians have no need for men at all also needs clarification. First of all, since we are all women living in a male society, we do in fact depend regularly upon men for many crucial things, even if we do not choose to have men in our personal relationships. It is for this reason that one woman alone will not be fully liberated until all women are liberated. However, taking the statement to mean having no need for men in *personal relationships* (which can be an important achievement for women, since one should obviously want the person, not the man), one must still ask the question: has the male role been discarded? Thus again the crucial point is not the sex of your bed partner but the sex role of your bed partner.

Gay Movement as a Civil Rights Movement

The organized gay movement seeks to protect the freedom of any homosexual, no matter what her or his individual style of homosexuality may be. This means protection of the transvestite, the queen, the "butch" lesbian, the couple that wants a marriage license, or the homosexual who may prefer no particular role. They are all united on one thing: the right to have sex with someone of one's own sex (i.e., "freedom of sexual preference").

As is clear from the wide range of homosexual behavior, not all modes necessarily reflect a dislike for sex roles *per se*. Nor was the choice necessarily made deliberately. The boy who grew up trained as a girl, or the girl who was somehow socialized more toward the male role, did not in their childhood choose to reverse sex roles. Each was saddled with a role (as were we all) and had to make the best of it in a society that scorned such an occurrence. Merle Miller in an article in the *New York Times* (January 17, 1971), where he "came out" as a homosexual, said: "Gay is good, Gay is proud. Well, yes, I suppose. If I had been given a choice (but who is?), I would prefer to be straight." His point was not that gay is sick but rather that he did not choose his gayness. And, furthermore, had he been trained heterosexually, society would have been a great deal easier on him. Which is a very understandable sentiment given the cruelty and discrimination that is practiced against homosexuals. In such cases the bravery and rebelliousness is to be found rather in the ability to act out homosexuality in spite of social abuse.

In uniting to change oppressive laws, electing officials who will work toward these ends, and changing social attitudes which are discriminatory against homosexuals, the gay movement is addressing itself to its civil rights. It is my feeling that the gay liberation issue is in fact a civil rights issue (as opposed to a radical issue) because it is united around the secondary issue of "freedom of sexual preference." Whereas in fact the real root of anti-homosexuality is sexism. That is, the *radical* gay person would have to be a feminist. This tracing of the roots of gay oppression to sexism is also expressed in Radicalesbian's "Woman Identified Woman":

> It should first be understood that lesbianism, like male homosexuality, is a category of behavior possible only in a sexist society characterized by rigid sex roles and dominated by male supremacy.... In a society in which men do not oppress women, and sexual expression is allowed to follow feelings, the categories of homosexuality and heterosexuality would disappear.

Bisexuality

One position taken by some lesbians is that bisexuality is a cop-out. This is usually argued in terms like "until all heterosexuals go gay, we are going to remain homosexual," or "lesbianism is more than having sex with women; it is a whole life style and commitment to women. Bisexuality is a sign of not being able to leave men and be free. We are *women-* (not men-) identified women."

The first position mentioned is an apparently tactical argument (though it has also been used by some, I think, to dismiss the discussion of bisexuality altogether by safely pushing it off into the Millennium), and makes the case for politically identifying yourself with the most discriminated against elements—even though you might really believe in bisexuality.*

Taking that argument at face value (and I don't completely), I think it is a dangerous thing to advocate politically. For by, in effect, promoting exclusive homosexuality, they lend political support to the notion that it *does* matter what the sex of your partner may be. While I recognize the absolute necessity for the gay movement to concentrate on the freedom of people to sleep with members of their own sex (since it is here that discrimination exists), it must at the same time always be referred back to its larger, radical perspective: that it is oppressive for that very question even to be asked. As a matter of fact, if "freedom of sexual preference" is the demand, the solution obviously must be a bisexuality where the question becomes irrelevant.

I think in fact that the reason why bisexuality has been considered such an unpopular word by most gays is not to be found primarily in the arguments just discussed, but rather in gay adherence to a kind of fierce homosexual counter-definition which has developed. That is, a counter identity—a "life style" and "world view"—has been created around the fact of their homosexuality. This identity is so strong sometimes that to even advocate or predict bisexuality is considered "genocide." The following is an example: In a response to a statement by Dotson Rader that "as bisexuality is increasingly accepted as the norm, the position of the homosexual *qua* homosexual will fade," one gay response was that "The homosexual, like the Jew, is offered the choice between integration or the gas chamber."[3]

It is not with the actual gay counterculture that I want to quarrel; I think it is a very understandable reaction to an intolerable exclusion of homosexuals from society. To be denied the ordinary benefits and interaction of other people, to be stripped of your identity by a society that recognizes you as valid only if your role and your biology are "properly" matched—to be thus denied must of course

* See for example *A Gay Manifesto* by Carl Wittman (Gay Flames Pamphlet No. 9).

result in a new resolution of identity. Since gays have been rejected on the basis of their homosexuality, it is not surprising that homosexuality has become the core of the new identity.

The disagreement with feminism comes rather in an attempt to make a revolutionary political position out of this adjustment. The often heard complaint from feminists that "we are being defined once again by whom we sleep with" is correct, I think. The lesson to be learned from a feminist analysis of sex roles is that there is no behavior implied from our biology beyond, as Wilma Scott Heide has noted, the role of sperm donor and wet nurse.[4] A woman has historically been defined, on the basis of biology, as incomplete without a man. Feminists have rejected this notion, and must equally reject any new definition which offers a woman her identity by virtue of the fact that she may love or sleep with other women.

It is for this reason, also, that I disagree with the Radicalesbian concept of the "woman-identified-woman." For we ought not to be "identified" on the basis of whom we have relationships with. And there is a confusion in such a term; it seems to mix up the biological woman with the political woman. I think the often used feminist definition of "woman-identified" as meaning having identified with the female *role* in society is more useful; it refers to a specific political phenomenon of internalization. So far as finding a term which describes women's solidarity or sisterhood on the basis of our common oppression, the term is feminism. Beyond that, what is left is the biological female—an autonomous being who gains her identity by virtue of her own achievements and characteristics, not by virtue of whom she has a love relationship with.

Once we begin to discuss persons as *persons* (a word which doesn't ask the sex of an individual), even the word "bisexuality" may eventually be dropped, since implicit in its use is still an eagerness to inform you that it is *both* sexes. Perhaps we will finally return to a simpler word like "sexuality," where the relevant information is simply "sex among persons."

If you don't sleep with women . . .

If you are a feminist who is not sleeping with a woman you may risk hearing any of the following accusations: "You're oppressing me if you don't sleep with women"; "You're not a radical feminist if you don't sleep with women"; or "You don't love women if you don't sleep with them." I have even seen a woman's argument about an entirely different aspect of feminism be dismissed by some lesbians because she was not having sexual relations with women. Leaving aside for a minute the motives for making such accusations, there is an outrageous thing going on here strictly in terms of pressuring women about their personal lives.

This perversion of "the personal is the political" argument, it must be noted, was not invented by those gay women who may be using it now; the women's movement has had sporadic waves of personal attacks on women—always in the guise of radicalism (and usually by a very small minority of women). I have seen women being told they could not be trusted as feminists because they wore miniskirts, because they were married (in one group quotas were set lest the group's quality be lowered by "unliberated women"), or because they wanted to have children. This rejection of women who are not living the "liberated life" has predictably now come to include rejection on the basis of the "unliberated" sex life.

The original genius of the phrase "the personal is political" was that it opened up the area of women's private lives to political analysis. Before that, the isolation of women from each other had been accomplished by labeling a woman's experience "personal." Women had thus been kept from seeing their common condition as women and their common oppression by men.

However, opening up women's experience to political analysis has also resulted in a misuse of the phrase. While it is true that there are political implications in everything a woman *qua* woman experiences, it is not therefore true that a woman's life is the political property of the women's movement. And it seems to me to show a disrespect for another woman to presume that it is any group's (or individual's) prerogative to pass revolutionary judgment on the progress of her life.

There is a further point: Even the most radical feminist is not the liberated woman. We are all crawling out of femininity into a new sense of personhood. Only a woman herself may decide what her next step is going to be. I do not think women have a political obligation to the movement to change; they should do so only if they see it in their own self-interest. If the women's movement believes that feminism *is* in women's self-interest, then the task at hand is to make it understood through shared insights, analysis, and experience. That is, feminism is an offering, not a directive, and one therefore enters a woman's private life at her invitation only. Thus a statement like "you don't love women if you don't sleep with them" must above all be dismissed on the grounds that it is confusing the right to discuss feminism with the right to, uninvited, discuss a woman's private life and make political judgments about it.

However, taking the issue presented in the above accusation (outside of its guilt-provoking personal context*), there are several points to consider. One element of truth is that some women are unable to relate sexually to other women because of a strong self-hatred for themselves as women (and therefore all women). But there may also be many other reasons. A woman may not be interested in sleeping with anyone—a freedom women are granted even less often than the right to sleep with other women. She may not have met a woman she's attracted to. Or she may be involved with a man whom she likes as a person, without this necessarily being a rejection of women. It should also be noted that the women who suffer from strong self-hatred may not necessarily find it impossible to relate sexually to women. They may instead find that taking the male part in a lesbian relationship will symbolically remove them from their feminine role. Such a woman then may become one who "balls" women so as not to be one.

All in all, as has been noted earlier, there is no magic that makes lesbianism proof positive of any high feminist motives. Rather, what the woman brings to her relationship as far as relinquishing sex roles will, I think, determine her ultimate attitude about really loving other women.

Conclusion

Homosexuality, with its obvious scorn for the "rules" of biology, challenges a cornerstone of sexist ideology and consequently makes most men nervous. There is at this time less fear of female homosexuality than of male homosexuality, possibly because men still feel secure that isolated lesbian examples will not tempt most women away from their prescribed feminine roles, and perhaps also because

* Regarding motives: provoking guilt is a tactic not so much for informing as it is for controlling others.

lesbianism is frequently seen by men as something erotic (it seems, alas, we can still remain sex objects in men's eyes even when making love to each other).

With male homosexuality, however, men (and thus male society) are more personally threatened. The precise irony of male supremacy is that it is a system rationalized on the basis of biology but actualized through socialization. Deviants who inadvertently were socialized differently, or who chose differently, are thus a threat to the *premise* that biology is destiny. Thus, to have another man break rank is to threaten all men's group-supremacy status. Also, for a man to leave the "superior" group is to go down—that is, become "inferior" or "feminine." Frequently male homosexuals may touch on the unspoken fears in many men that they are not powerful and "manly" enough to fulfill their supremacy destiny, and the gay male thus becomes the symbol of total male "failure." Still other men display a robust camaraderie (à la Mailer) where "buggering" a fellow male obviously means that one would have to play woman, and good fellowship wouldn't allow another man such degradation.

To understand men's fear of homosexuality, then, is above all to understand men's fear of losing their place of power in society with women. And to hold that power, men must preserve both the "absoluteness" of their ideology and the group unity of their members.

It must be kept in mind that while homosexuality does contain an implicit threat to sexist ideology, it is, at best, only a small part of the whole fight to bring down the sex role system. (Indeed, if the gay movement were to be seen as only the demand for the right of making role transfers within society, for example, it would work against feminism by supporting a reformed version of the sex role system.)

Thus it is only in the most radical interpretation that lesbianism becomes an organic part of the larger feminist fight. In this context it joins the multitude of other rebellions women have been making against their prescribed role—be it in work, in law, or in personal relationships. As with all such rebellions, they are only personal accommodations to living in a sexist society unless they are understood politically and fought for collectively. The larger political truth is still that we are women living in a male society where men have the power and we don't; that our "female role" is a creation that is nothing more than a male political expediency for maintaining that power; and that until the women's movement alters these ancient political facts we cannot speak of being free collectively or individually.

Footnotes

[1] Anon., *Vortex*, Lawrence, Kansas.

[2] T. B., letter, *Everywoman*, March 26, 1971.

[3] Letter to the Editor, *Evergreen*, May, 1971.

[4] Judith Hole and Ellen Levine, *Rebirth of Feminism* (Chicago: Quadrangle, 1971), p. 76.

The Spiritual Dimension of Women's Liberation

by Mary Daly

Mary Daly belongs to NOW and is active in the task force on women and organized religion. She is also active in women's liberation at Boston College, where she teaches, and is one of the organizers of the Catholic Women's Caucus. She holds several degrees in theology and philosophy and is the author of The Church and the Second Sex *(Harper & Row, 1968) which explores sexism in the history of the church.*

Women who are committed to achieving liberation and equality often turn away from organized religion, seeing it either as irrelevant or as a stubborn and powerful enemy, placing obstacles to all they seek to attain. Having been turned off by institutional religion they choose to leave it behind and forget it, except when it really shows muscle—as in the struggle over abortion laws. Some, on the other hand, have opted to continue their relationship with church or synagogue in the hope of changing sexist beliefs, laws, and customs in these institutions. The second choice is based upon a conviction that there are important values transmitted through these institutions that make it worth the pain and effort of staying in and fighting the system.

These are personal choices and no one can set down hard-and-fast rules for everyone to follow. However, it is important that women be aware of the issue of religion. First of all, it is necessary to understand institutional religion's role in the oppression of women, which it continues to exercise in this culture whether they personally relate to it or not. Second, women should be sensitive to the fact that the movement itself is a deeply spiritual event which has the potential to awaken a new and post-patriarchal spiritual consciousness.

Institutionalized Christianity and the Oppression of Women

The Judaic-Christian tradition has been patriarchal down through the millennia, although sometimes this has been modified or disguised.[1] The Bible reflected the oppressed condition of women in ancient times. In the Decalogue of the Old Testament a man's wife is listed among his possessions, along with his ox and his ass. The biblical story of Eve's birth, which has been called the hoax of the ages, fixed woman's place in the universe. The story of the Fall of Adam and Eve perpetuated the myth of feminine evil, giving a powerful image of woman as temptress—a dominant theme in Western culture for thousands of years. In the New Testament, the Apostle Paul put women in their place: veiled, silent, and subordinate. In the early centuries of Christianity the Fathers of the Church classified women as fickle, shallow, garrulous, weak, and unstable. In the Middle Ages, Thomas Aquinas decreed that they are misbegotten males, and theologians dutifully taught this for centuries.

In the modern period Popes and theologians greeted the first wave of feminism with the double-talk of the feminine mystique: Women should be equal but subordinate. On childbirth, Pope Pius XII pontificated: "She loves it [the child] the more, the more pain it has cost her." Today, some liberal Catholic and Protestant theologians admit that sexism exists in the churches but show little inclination to do anything about it. All of this, of course, is in blatant contradiction to Christian teaching about the worth and dignity of every human person.

Although there have been outstanding "exceptional women" in every period of Christian history, their existence has had almost no effect upon the official ideology and policies of the churches. This fact can be understood when it is realized that the Judaic-Christian tradition has functioned to legitimate male-dominated society. The image of God as exclusively a father and not a mother, for example, was spawned by the human imagination under the conditions of patriarchal society and sustained as plausible by patriarchy. Then, in turn, the image has served to perpetuate this kind of society by making its mechanisms for the oppression of women appear right and fitting. If God in "his" heaven is a father ruling "his" people, then it is in the "nature" of things and according to divine plan and the order of the universe that society be male-dominated. Within this context a mystification of roles takes place: the husband dominating his wife can feel that he represents God himself. A theologian such as Karl Barth could feel justified in writing that woman is "ontologically" subordinate to man.

It might seem that intelligent people do not really think of God as an old man with a beard, but it is quite possible for the mind to function on two different and even contradictory levels at the same time. For example, many speak of God as spirit and at the same time, on the imaginative level, envisage "him" as male. The widespread concept of the Supreme Being has been a not very subtle mask of the divine father figure, and it is not too surprising that it has been used to justify oppression, especially that of women, which is said to be "God's plan."

> **In the third chapter of Genesis:**
> **". . . And thy desire shall be to thy husband**
> **and he shall rule over thee . . . ."**

Doctrines about Jesus also have often reflected a kind of phallic obsession. Some theologians have argued that since Jesus was male and called only males to become apostles, women should not be ordained. The doctrine of a unique "incarnation" in Jesus reinforced the fixed idea of patriarchal religion that God is male and male is God. So also did the image of the Virgin kneeling in adoration before her own Son. The mechanism that can be seen in all of this is the familiar vicious circle in which the patterns of a particular kind of society are projected into the realm of religious beliefs and these in turn justify society as it is. The belief system becomes hardened and functions to resist social change, which would rob it of its plausibility. (In a matriarchal or a diarchal society, what credibility would the image of a divine patriarch have?)

Patriarchal religion tends to be authoritarian. Given the fact that the vicious circle is not foolproof, there is always the possibility that beliefs may lose their credibility. For this reason they are often buttressed by notions of "faith" that leave no room for dissent. For example, the believer is often commanded to assent blindly to doctrines handed down by authority (all male). The inculcation of anxieties and guilt feelings over "heresy" and "losing the faith" has been a powerful method used by institutional religion to immunize itself from criticism. Women especially have been victimized by this.

Traditional Christian ethics also have been to a great extent the product and support of sexist bias. Much of the theory of Christian virtue appears to be the product of reactions on the part of men—probably guilt reactions—to the behavioral excesses of the stereotypic male. There has been theoretical emphasis upon charity, meekness, obedience, humility, self-abnegation, sacrifice, service. Part of the problem with this moral ideology is that it became generally accepted not by men but by women, who have hardly been helped by an ethic which reinforced their abject situation.

This emphasis upon the passive virtues, of course, has not challenged exploitativeness, but supported it. Part of the whole syndrome has been the reduction of hope to passive expectation of a reward from the divine Father for following the rules. Love or charity has been interpreted to mean that people should turn the other cheek to their oppressors. Within the perspective of such a privatized morality, "sin" often becomes an offense against those in power, or against "God"—the two being more or less equated. The structures of oppression are not seen as sinful.

It is consistent with all of this that the traditional Christian moral consciousness has been fixated on the problems of reproductive activity to a degree totally disproportionate to its feeble concern for existing human life. The deformity of perspective was summed up several years ago in Archbishop Robers's remark that "if contraceptives had been dropped over Japan instead of bombs which merely killed, maimed, and shriveled up thousands alive, there would have been a squeal of outraged protest from the Vatican to the remotest Mass center in Asia." Pertinent also is Simone de Beauvoir's remark that the church has reserved its uncompromising humanitarianism for man in the fetal condition.

> "... But I suffer not a woman to teach, nor to usurp authority over the man but to be in silence; for Adam was first formed, then Eve; and Adam was not deceived, but the woman being deceived, was in the transgression."
>
> (Timothy 1,2:12-14)

Although both of these remarks are directed at the Catholic Church, the same attitudes are widespread in Protestantism. Many theologians today do, of course, acknowledge that this passive and privatized morality has failed to cope with structures of oppression. However, few seriously face the possibility that the roots of this distortion are deeply buried in the fundamental and all-pervasive sexual alienation which the women's movement is seeking to overcome.

The Spiritual Potential of the Movement

As the women's revolution begins to have an effect upon the fabric of society, beginning to transform it from patriarchy into something that never existed before—into a diarchal situation that is radically new—it will, I think, become the greatest single challenge to Christianity to rid itself of its oppressive tendencies or go out of business. Beliefs and values that have held sway for thousands of years will be questioned as never before. The movement, if it is true to its most authentic and prophetic dimensions, is possibly also the greatest single hope for the survival and development of authentic spiritual consciousness over against the manipulative and exploitative power of technocracy.

The caricature of a human being which is presented by the masculine stereotype depends for its existence upon the acceptance by women of the role assigned to them—the eternal feminine. By becoming whole persons women can generate a counterforce to the polarization of human beings into these stereotypes, forcing men to reexamine their own self-definition. This movement toward the becoming of whole human beings, to the degree that it succeeds, will transform the values and symbols of our society, including religious symbols.

The women's liberation movement is a spiritual movement because it aims at humanization of women and therefore of the species. At its core it is spiritual in the deepest sense of the word, because it means the self-actualization of creative human potential in the struggle against oppression. Since the projections of patriarchal religion serve to block the dynamics of creativity, self-actualization, and authentic community by enforcing reduction of people to stereotyped roles, the challenge to patriarchy which is now in its initial stages is a sign of hope for the emergence of more genuine religious consciousness. The becoming of women may be not only the doorway to deliverance from the omnipotent Father in all of his disguises, but, to many, also a doorway *to* something, namely, to a more authentic search for transcendence, that is, for God.

Women's liberation is an event that can challenge authoritarian, exclusivist, and non-existential ideas of faith and revelation. Since women have been extra-environmentals, that is, since we have not been part of the authority structure which uses "faith" and "revelation" to reinforce the mechanisms of alienation, our emergence can unmask the idolatry often hidden behind these ideas.

> **". . . The head of every man is Christ; and the head of every woman is man . . . ."**
> **Saint Paul (Corinthians, 1,11:3)**

There could result from this becoming of women a remythologizing of Western religion. If the need for parental symbols for God persists, something like the Father-Mother God of Mary Baker Eddy will be more acceptable to the new woman and the new man than the Father God of the past. A symbolization for incarnation of the divine presence in human beings may continue to be needed in the future, but it is highly unlikely that women or men will find plausible that symbolism which is epitomized in the Christ-Mary image. Perhaps this will be replaced by a bisexual imagery which is non-hierarchical.

The becoming of women can bring about a transvaluation of values. Faith can come to be understood in a non-authoritarian and universalist sense. Hope, rather than being restricted to expectation of rewards for conformity, can come to be experienced and understood as creative, political, and revolutionary. Love will mean uniting to overcome oppression. It will be understood that the most loving thing one can do for the oppressor is to fight the oppressive situation that destroys both the oppressor and the oppressed. Suffering, which has been so highly esteemed in Christianity, will be seen as acceptable not when abjectly and submissively endured, but when experienced in the struggle for liberation.

> "And if they will learn anything, let them ask their husbands at home; for it is a shame for women to speak in church."
> **(Corinthians 1,14:35)**

The ethic emerging in the struggle has as its main theme not prudence but existential courage. This is the courage to risk economic and social security for the sake of liberation. It means not only risking the loss of jobs, friends, and social approval, but also facing the nameless anxieties encountered in new and uncharted territory. There is the anxiety of meaninglessness that can be overwhelming at times when the old simple meanings, role definitions, and life expectations have been rooted out and rejected openly, and a woman emerges into a world without models. There is also the anxiety of guilt over refusing to do what society demands, an anxiety which can still hold a woman in its grip long after the guilt has been recognized as false. To affirm oneself and one's sisters in the face of all this requires courage.

> "Likewise, ye wives, be in subjection to your own husbands . . . ."
> **Saint Peter (Peter 1,3:1)**

Such courage expresses itself in sisterhood, which is not at all merely the female counterpart of brotherhood. Sisterhood is a revolutionary fact. It is the bonding of those who have never bonded before, for the purpose of overcoming sexism and its effects, both internal and external. It is the coming together of those who are oppressed by sexual definition. The Christian churches have been fond of preaching the "brotherhood of man," which included women incidentally, as baggage. However, the concept has never been realized because brotherhood in patriarchy, despite frequent attempts to universalize the term, is exclusive and divisive. "Brother" means us versus them. It begins by excluding women as "the other" and continues its divisiveness from there, cutting off "the other" by familial, tribal, racial, national, economic, and ideological categories.

Women are learning to be aware that brotherhood, even when it attempts to be universal, means a male universalism. The churches, the peace movement, the New Left, for the most part fail to notice the need for change in the situation of the more than 50 percent female membership of the groups to which they would extend their brotherhood.

The "sisterhoods" of patriarchal society have really been mini-brotherhoods, following male models and serving male purposes. The religious sisterhoods within the Catholic Church, for example, have been male-dominated according to Canon Law. These communities, though they have offered an alternative to marriage and attracted some gifted women, have used the word "sister" in an elitist and divisive sense and have supported the ideology of sexism.

The sisterhood of women's liberation involves a strategic polarization which is different from all of this. It implies polarization for the sake of women's internal wholeness or oneness, because as in the case of all oppressed groups, women suffer from a duality of consciousness. We have internalized the image that the oppressor has of us and are therefore divided against ourselves and against each other by self-hatred. We can only overcome this by bonding with each other. Sisterhood implies polarization also for the sake of political oneness, to achieve liberation. However, its essential dynamic is directed to overcoming the stereotypes that reduce people to the role of "the other." That is, it points toward a unity deeper than most theologians are capable of envisaging, despite the great amount of ink that has been spilled on the subject of "the bonds of charity."

Sisterhood is an event that is new under the sun. It is healing, revolutionary, and revelatory—which is what Christian brotherhood was claimed to be but failed to be. It is at war with the idols of patriarchal religion, but it is in harmony with what is authentic in the ideals of the religious traditions. In this sense, the movement in its deepest dimension is itself both anti-church and church. It has the potential to release the authentic values that have been distorted and suppressed by the sexism of synagogue and church.

Footnote

[1] A documented historical study and criticism of this can be found in my book, *The Church and the Second Sex* (New York: Harper and Row, 1968).

Building
A Movement

Free Space

by Pamela Allen

Introduction

I joined my group, Sudsofloppen, at its second meeting in September, 1968. I was new to San Francisco, having moved from New York City where I had been active in women's liberation. I brought to the group a political commitment to building a mass women's movement. The group experience has helped me to synthesize and deepen my emotional and intellectual understanding of the predicament of females in this society and of the concerns with which we must deal in building a women's movement.

We have defined our group as a place in which to think: to think about our lives, our society, and our potential for being creative individuals and for building a women's movement. We call this Free Space. We have had successes and failures in utilizing this space. Usually our problems stem from our failure to be completely honest with ourselves and each other—failing to question and disagree with another's ideas and perspectives and to say what we think is an alternative. Our failure to be truthful has always had a negative effect on the functioning of our group. Thus individual integrity—intellectual and emotional honesty—is our goal. It has been a difficult struggle.

Precisely because the group does become so meaningful to our lives as we start to separate ourselves from dependence on male values and institutions, it is a temptation to transfer our identities onto the group, to let our thinking be determined by group consensus rather than doing it ourselves. Although we are not sure that full autonomy is a possible goal, we believe that our hope lies in developing as individuals who understand themselves, their own needs, the workings of our society, and the needs of others. Thus we try to resist the temptation to submerge our individuality in the group and struggle instead to make contact with our own feelings and thoughts. Freedom is frightening and difficult to use. We are always struggling to take advantage of the Free Space we have created for ourselves.

We have developed four group processes to help us in our endeavor to become autonomous in thought and behavior. We call these processes "opening up," "sharing," "analyzing," and "abstracting." They are our way of keeping in touch with our emotions, giving one another information about experiences we have had, trying to understand the meaning of those events, and finally fitting that understanding into an overview of our potential as human beings and the reality of our society—i.e., developing an ideology.

The group processes are described below. It should be understood that they are not totally separate processes; rather there is a great deal of overlap. But the emphasis in opening up is on our feelings; in sharing, on our experiences; in analyzing, on our thinking; and in abstracting, on our evolving theory.

I have chosen to write about one structure that has developed in the women's movement, the small group, because I think the small group is especially suited to freeing women to affirm their own view of reality and to think independently of male-supremacist values. It is a space where women can come to understand not only the ways this society works to keep women oppressed but ways to overcome that oppression psychologically and socially. It is Free Space.

The group processes described in this paper were discussed and identified by Sudsofloppen after we had been meeting for over a year. This was one of the first times that we turned our growing ability to analyze onto ourselves and our own activity. The experience of working out these concepts collectively was very exciting for us all. For some, the processes may seem a little arbitrary and too structured, but we are a group which believes that there is always a structure, that the issue is to consciously choose one that will encourage our growth rather than just hope that it will happen. We think this way because our early activity was consciously unstructured—we thought—and we found that letting things just happen meant that the strongest personalities controlled the meetings and that it was very easy to avoid areas of discussion that were difficult.

The group processes as described here are impersonal and they ensure that those of us who find it hard to open up about our feelings will be challenged to do so. The same is true for women who fear analysis and would rather remain only on the subjective level. The total process is not easy but we feel that *each* process is necessary to understanding the human experience. We believe that theory and analysis which are not rooted in concrete experience (practice) are useless, but we also maintain that for the concrete, everyday experiences to be understood, they must be subjected to the processes of analysis and abstraction.

Opening Up

This is a very individual need: the need for a woman to open up and talk about her feelings about herself and her life. In the beginning of a group experience opening up is a reaching out to find human contact with other women. Later it becomes a way to communicate to others about one's subjective feelings about the group, about the women's movement, about one's life.

Our society alienates us from our feelings. However, this is less true for women than for men. It is imperative for our understanding of ourselves and for our mental health that we maintain and deepen our contact with our feelings. Our first concern must not be with whether these feelings are good or bad, but what they are. Feelings are a reality. To deny their existence does not get rid of them. Rather it is through admitting them that one can begin to deal with her feelings.

Opening up is an essential but difficult process for a group. In its early stages a group usually fosters a feeling of intimacy and trust which frees women to discuss their fears and problems. This is because most women have been isolated and alone and the group experience is the first time they have found others who like themselves are frustrated with their lot as women in this society. Every woman who has tried to articulate her loss of a sense of identity to her husband knows the despair of not being understood. Any woman who has tried to explain her driving need to have a life of her own and sees her words falling on the uncomprehending ears of family and friends knows the horror of being alone, being seen by others as some kind of freak. Any woman who has admitted that she is unhappy and depressed but can't explain why knows the pain of not being taken seriously. Isolated, always getting negative responses to her attempts to communicate her feelings about her condition, the woman finds it easy to begin to question herself, to see her problems as personal ones.

The group offers women a place where the response will be positive. "Yes, we know." "Yes, we understand." It is not so much the words that are said in response that are important as the fact that someone listens and does not ridicule; someone listens and acknowledges the validity of another's view of her life. It is the beginning of sisterhood, the feeling of unity with others, of no longer being alone.

The early group experience of closeness—the honeymoon period as some call it—fosters opening up about one's feelings toward oneself and one's life. But as the group begins to function on a long-term basis and the members participate in activities in a women's movement, it becomes harder to be honest about one's feelings for sometimes they are negative and may involve another woman. Yet such disclosures are necessary if trust and sisterhood are to become long-term realities. Neither a group nor a movement can function if there is latent distrust and hostility or overt backbiting going on. In addition an individual cannot be free to trust in herself and in others if she is suppressing feelings and allowing them to cloud her thinking and activity.

Opening up is a personal need to admit to and express one's emotions—her joys as well as her sorrows. In addition it is a group need in that no group can continue to function over a long period of time which does not deal with the feelings of its members. Unless women are given a *non-judgmental* space in which to express themselves, we will never have the strength or the perception to deal with the ambivalences which are a part of us all. It is essential that the group guarantee confidentiality, that we know that our feelings will not be revealed elsewhere or used against us. This is a group commitment without which there can be no trust.

Sharing

The opening up process is centered on the individual's expressive needs, and carried to an extreme it can become self-indulgence.

However, there is another experience that can take place in the group which is similar to the first yet different, for the emphasis is on teaching one another through sharing experiences. Not only do we respond with recognition to someone's account, but we add from our own histories as well, building a collage of similar experiences from all women present. The intention here is to arrive at an understanding of the social conditions of women by pooling descriptions of the forms oppression has taken in each individual's life. Revealing these particulars may be very painful, but the reason for dredging up these problems is not only the therapeutic value of opening up hidden areas. Through the common discussion comes the understanding that many of the situations described are not personal at all, and are not based on individual inadequacies, but rather have a root in the social order. What we have found is that painful "personal" problems may be common to many of the women present. Thus attention can turn to finding the real causes of these problems rather than merely emphasizing one's own inadequacies.

Almost any topic can be used for the sharing process. All that is necessary is that women have experience in that area. Some of the topics we have used for discussion have been communal living, job experiences, experiences in the civil rights movement, SDS, and the peace movement, relationships with men focusing on examples of male chauvinism, relationships with women with emphasis on our adolescent experiences and how these affect our present feelings toward women, and our self-images—how we perceive ourselves and how we think others perceive us. Agreeing on a topic and preparing for the discussion for a week or so seem to ensure the most productive sharing discussion.

The sharing occasions have shown us that the solutions to our problems will be found in joining with other women, because the basis of many of our problems is our status as women. It was not only sharing the stories of our childhood, school, marriage, and job experiences that led us to this realization. It was as much the positive feelings, the warmth and comradeship of the small group which reinforced the conviction that it is with other women both now and in the future that solutions will be found. The old stereotypes that women can't work together and don't like one another are shown in practice to be false.

After sharing, we *know* that women suffer at the hands of a male-supremacist society and that this male supremacy intrudes into every sphere of our existence, controlling the ways in which we are allowed to make our living and the ways in which we find fulfillment in personal relationships. We know that our most secret, our most private problems are grounded in the way women are treated, in the way women are allowed to live. Isolation turns frustration into self-doubt, but joining together gives women perspective that can lead to action. Through sharing they can see that they have been lied to, and begin to look critically at a society which so narrowly defines the roles they may play. But before they can take their destinies into their own hands, they must understand the objective condition of women and the many forms that oppression takes in the lives of women.

Analyzing

A third stage now takes place in the group: the experience of analyzing the reasons for and the causes of the oppression of women. This analysis rises out of the questions which are posed by the basic raw data of the opening up and sharing periods. It is a new way of looking at women's condition: the development of concepts which attempt to define not only the why's and how's of our oppression but ways of fighting that oppression. Because the analysis takes place *after* the sharing of individual examples of oppression, it is based on a female understanding of the reality of women's condition.

This period is important because it is the beginning of going beyond our personal experiences. Having gained a perspective on our lives through the sharing process, we now begin to look at woman's predicament with some objectivity. This new approach is difficult for many of us, for as women we exist predominantly in the realm of subjectivity; we perform functions but seldom get on top of a situation to understand how something works and why. Analyzing is a new and difficult procedure to learn.

In analyzing the role the group has played in our lives, for example, we have come to understand the ways in which women are kept from feeling they are worthwhile. We have discussed the need to have a social identity and the ways women are prevented from acquiring one. Women's roles as wife and mother have been analyzed. We have come to see that women are relegated to a private sphere, dependent both psychologically and financially on their husbands. The group is a first step in transcending the isolation. Here, sometimes for the first time in her life, a woman is allowed an identity independent of a man's. She is allowed to function intellectually as a thinker rather than as a sex object, servant, wife, or mother. In short, the group establishes the social worth of the women present, a necessity if women are to take themselves seriously.

We have had to face realistically the inability of many of us to think conceptually. This inability comes from being encouraged to stay in the private sphere and to relate to people on personal levels even when working. We are training ourselves to get out from under our subjective responses and to look at our reality in new ways. Although this is not easy for us, we see the absolute necessity of analysis, for our oppression takes both obvious and subtle forms which vary with our class and educational status. The complexity of women's situations necessitates our bringing information outside our individual experiences to bear on our analysis of women's oppression. This is the period when questions can be asked about how the entire society functions. This is the period when books and other documentation become crucial.

It is our contention, however, that this period of analysis belongs *after* the opening up and sharing experiences, for concepts we find must answer the questions which come from our problems as women. It is not in our interest to fit experiences into preconceived theory, especially one devised by men. This is not only because we must suspect all male thinking as being male-supremacist, but because we must teach ourselves to think independently. Our thinking must grow out of our questions if it is to be internalized and if we are to have the tools to look objectively at new experience and analyze it correctly. Thus a period of analysis will come after each new experience and will add new thinking to an ever growing ideology.

Abstracting

A synthesis of the analyses is necessary before decisions can be made as to priorities in problems and approach. For this to happen a certain distance must exist between us and our concerns. When we remove ourselves from immediate necessity, we are able to take the concepts and analysis we have developed and discuss abstract theory. We are able to look at the totality of the nature of our condition, utilizing the concepts we have formulated from discussions of the many forms our oppression takes. Further we begin to build (and to some extent, experience) a vision of our human potential. This does not mean we become more like men. Rather we come to understand what we could be if freed of social oppression. We see this abstracting experience as the purest form of Free Space.

We are only beginning to experience this Free Space, abstracting, now that we have had a year of opening up, sharing, and analyzing behind us. We are beginning to see how different institutions fulfill or prevent the fulfillment of human needs, how they work together and how they must be changed. We are beginning to gain an overview of what type of women's movement will be necessary to change the institutions that oppress women.

Specifically we have begun to have a clear understanding of what role the small group can and cannot play in this social revolution. It is clear to us that the small group is neither an action-oriented political group in and of itself nor is it an alternative family unit. Rather, this is where ideology can develop. And out of this emerging ideology will come a program grounded in a solid understanding of women's condition that will have its roots, but not its totality, in our own experience. Intellectually this is the most exciting stage. It is a joy to learn to think, to begin to comprehend what is happening to us. Ideas are experiences in themselves, freeing, joyous experiences which give us the framework for formulating our actions.

It is important to stress that opening up, sharing, analyzing, and abstracting are not limited to certain periods of time. One never completes any of the processes. Opening up is not limited to the past and one does not graduate through the various processes until one is abstracting to the exclusion of all else. Analyzing and abstracting are only valid processes if they continue to be rooted in the present feelings and experiences of participants. The order may be fixed but the processes themselves are ongoing.

The total group process is not therapy because we try to find the social causes for our experiences and the possible programs for changing these. But the therapeutic experience of momentarily relieving the individual of all responsibility for her situation does occur and is necessary if women are to be free to act. This takes place in both the opening up and sharing phases of the group activity and gives us the courage to look objectively at our predicament, accepting what are realistically our responsibilities to change and understanding what must be confronted societally.

Consciousness Raising

This introduction can serve as a working sheet for a beginning consciousness raising group.

The typical consciousness-raising group is composed of six to twelve women who meet on an average of once a week. Groups larger than ten or twelve are less conducive to lengthy personal discussion and analysis. The consciousness-raising process is one in which personal experiences, when shared, are recognized as a result not of an individual's idiosyncratic history and behavior, but of the system of sex-role stereotyping. That is, they are political, not personal, questions.

Generally consciousness-raising groups spend from three to six months talking about personal experiences and then analyzing those experiences in feminist terms. Thereafter they often begin working on specific projects including such activities as reading, analyzing and writing literature; abortion law repeal projects; setting up child care centers; organizing speak-outs (rape, motherhood, abortion, etc.); challenging sex discrimination in employment, education, etc.

The following is a list of topic areas generally discussed. Although listed by week, they are not in any particular order, nor is it necessary to rigidly adhere to a one-week/one-topic schedule. The questions are examples of the kinds of areas that can be explored.

Week 1 GENERAL: What are some of the things that got you interested in the women's movement?

Week 2 FAMILY: Discuss your parents and their relationship to you as a girl (daughter). Were you treated differently from brothers or friends who were boys?

Week 3 FAMILY: Discuss your relationships with women in your family.

Week 4 CHILDHOOD AND ADOLESCENCE: Problems of growing up as a girl. Did you have heroines or heros? Who were they? What were your favorite games? How did you feel about your body changing at puberty?

Week 5 MEN: Discuss your relationships with men—friends, lovers, bosses—as they evolved. Are there any recurring patterns?

Week 6 MARITAL STATUS: How do (or did) you feel about being single? Married? Divorced? What have been the pressures—family, social—on you?

Week 7 MOTHERHOOD: Did you consider having children a matter of choice? Discuss the social and personal pressures you may have felt to become a mother. What have been your experiences and thoughts regarding such issues as child care, contraception and abortion?

Week 8 SEX: Have you ever felt that men have pressured you into having sexual relationships? Have you ever lied about orgasm?

Week 9 SEX: Sex objects—When do you feel like one? Do you want to be beautiful? Do you ever feel invisible?

Week 10 WOMEN: Discuss your relationships with other women. For example, have you ever felt competitive with other women for men? Have you ever felt attracted to another woman?

Week 11 BEHAVIOR: What is a "nice girl"? Discuss the times you have been called selfish. Have you ever felt that you were expected to smile even when you didn't feel like it?

Week 12 AGE: How do you feel about getting old? Your mother getting old? What aspects of aging do you look forward to? Fear? Do you think it is a different problem for men and women?

Week 13 AMBITIONS: What would you most like to do in life? How does being a woman affect that?

Week 14 MOVEMENT ACTIVITY: What are some of the things you would like to see the women's movement accomplish?

Consciousness Raising: A Dead End?

by Carol Williams Payne

Carol Payne is a relative newcomer to the women's movement. She has been a member of an unaffiliated consciousness-raising group in New York for a year and a half.

For almost a year and a half I have been a member of a group of women which has met regularly on Thursday evenings. Some of us are married, some single, some divorced, some with children, some without, some established in professions, some trying to decide what kind of work to do. Our ages range from mid-20's to mid-30's. Membership in the group has shifted; some people have moved away; others became frustrated with the direction the group was taking or felt that they didn't want to contribute.

The group was formed when two women began talking to each other about starting a group to talk about starting a group to talk about problems women have in working and wondering whether their self-doubts and lack of self-confidence were related to their being women. They found enough friends and friends of friends interested in the same problems to start a group. There were seven of us to begin with; then two more joined. The number has remained between six and nine.

We have talked about many problems which concern us—work, competitiveness with other women, jealousy, relationships with men, our childhood, our parents. We have tried to understand how we have been shaped by society's expectations of us, how we share problems and fears and how we can help each other.

Sometimes we used the approved consciousness-raising technique of choosing a subject and having everyone speak about it. More often, whoever wanted to speak about something initiated the discussion. Doing this created problems because the people who were the most vocal or the most competitive tended to dominate meetings and we spent many evenings struggling with destructive tendencies and personality conflicts.

Periodically, we asked ourselves, "What is the purpose of this group? What are we trying to accomplish? What direction should we be going in?"

We argued about this. A women's group shouldn't be group therapy, we decided. But there were elements of group therapy in what we were trying to do, to help each other deal with personal problems. We finally realized that we could not handle confrontation and hostility in the manner of group therapy because we did not have a trained leader who could remain objective and call a halt if someone was being hurt. We decided that we should be supportive and avoid confrontation.

We never resolved the question of what a women's liberation group was supposed to do. There was always a conflict between those who favored the personal, psychological approach and those who felt that a women's group should be building a bridge between the personal insight gained by being in a small group and political action with a larger body of women.

We would discuss one person's problem in balancing work and family responsibilities, another's in handling the aftermath of a divorce, another's with her husband who felt threatened by her belonging to a women's liberation group, but we never tried to relate these problems to the structural problems of women in society nor did we think about how they could be dealt with beyond the personal level of these particular women in their particular situations.

Some women in our group were engaged in political action or work which involved them with other women and they looked upon the group as a haven from the hassles they were going through elsewhere. All of us were busy and could not spare much more than one evening a week. And it was easier to continue the way we had started than to find some meaningful action that we could all agree we wanted to do.

I kept asking myself, "What is the point of just continuing to talk about ourselves? Why bother? Where is it leading?" Some evenings we didn't get down to serious discussion until 10:30 or

11:00 when everyone was ready to go home. Some meetings degenerated to the level of comparing bra sizes and talking about what vitamins we bought at the health food store. At these meetings we were all unconsciously expressing our frustration with our purposelessness.

I continued to come for several months after I had realized that things would probably not change and that the majority of the members were not as frustrated as I was with what the group was doing. Because I had become attached to the group and didn't want to leave, I kept hoping that we would come to a resolution.

I left because the group did not change and I needed to relate to the women's movement in a different way. I felt that nothing could be accomplished by becoming more and more intimate with a small group of women and that if women's groups are not political then they are nothing more than amateur group therapy or social clubs.

The consciousness-raising group was one of the great successes of the beginning of the women's liberation movement. It was a great way to reach large numbers of women and to provide a setting in which women could develop self-confidence and a realization of what they shared. The groups met a need and they proliferated.

But now, my staying in a small group which just talks and which does not relate to the rest of the movement is stagnation. It is pointless to develop the self-confidence to challenge assumptions about women's roles and an understanding of the way society channels women without then collectively doing something about these problems. There must be a way to retain the intimacy and sense of belonging that comes from being part of a small group and link it to a sense of purpose and relationship with other groups.

I am not sure where to go from here. I feel isolated because I was not connected with any women's organization except the small group. Beyond the group I am related to nothing but the barrage of distorted images of women's liberation projected by the mass media.

Where should I fit in among the ideological schisms which are dividing the movement? What organizations are still in existence? At this point, is developing a theoretical base and a strategy for action more important than specific actions? And if action, what action?

I don't think my time in the group was wasted but now I need to work with women in a different way on specific projects with tangible results. The question is what? and how? and with whom?

The Tyranny of Structurelessness

by Joreen

During the years in which the women's liberation movement has been taking shape a great emphasis has been placed on what are called leaderless, structureless groups as the main—if not sole—organizational form of the movement. The source of this idea was a natural reaction against the overstructured society in which most of us found ourselves, the inevitable control this gave others over our lives, and the continual elitism of the Left and similar groups among those who were supposedly fighting this overstructuredness.

The idea of structurelessness, however, has moved from a healthy counter to these tendencies to becoming a goddess in its own right. The idea is as little examined as the term is much used, but it has become an intrinsic and unquestioned part of women's liberation ideology. For the early development of the movement this did not much matter. It early defined its main goal, and its main method, as consciousness-raising, and the "structureless" rap group was an excellent means to this end. The looseness and informality of it encouraged participation in discussion and its often supportive atmosphere elicited personal insight. If nothing more concrete than personal insight ever resulted from these groups, that did not much matter, because their purpose did not really extend beyond this.

The basic problems didn't appear until individual rap groups exhausted the virtues of consciousness-raising and decided they wanted to do something more specific. At this point they usually floundered because most groups were unwilling to change their structure when they changed their tasks. Women had thoroughly accepted the idea of "structurelessness" without realizing the limitations of its uses. People would try to use the "structureless" group and the informal conference for purposes for which they were unsuitable out of a blind belief that no other means could possibly be anything but oppressive.

If the movement is to grow beyond these elementary stages of development, it will have to disabuse itself of some of its prejudices about organization and structure. There is nothing inherently bad about either of these. They can and often are misused, but to reject them out of hand because they are misused is to deny ourselves the necessary tools to further development. We need to understand why "structurelessness" does not work.

Formal and Informal Structures

Contrary to what we would like to believe, there is no such thing as a structureless group. Any group of people of whatever nature that comes together for any length of time for any purpose will inevitably structure itself in some fashion. The structure may be flexible; it may vary over time; it may evenly or unevenly distribute tasks, power, and resources over the members of the group. But it will be formed regardless of the abilities, personalities, or intentions of the people involved. The very fact that we are individuals, with different talents, predispositions, and backgrounds makes this inevitable. Only if we refused to relate or interact on any basis whatsoever could we approximate structurelessness—and that is not the nature of a human group.

This means that to strive for a structureless group is as useful, and as deceptive, as to aim at an "objective" news story, "value-free" social science, or a "free" economy. A "laissez faire" group is about as realistic as a "laissez faire" society; the idea becomes a smoke screen for the strong or the lucky to establish unquestioned hegemony over others. This hegemony can be so easily established because the idea of "structurelessness" does not prevent the formation of informal structures, only formal ones. Similarly "laissez faire" philosophy did not prevent the economically powerful from establishing control over wages, prices, and distribution of goods; it only prevented the government from doing so. Thus structurelessness becomes a way of masking power, and within the women's movement is usually most strongly advocated by those who are the most powerful (whether they are conscious of their power or not). As long as the structure of the group is informal, the rules of how decisions are made are known only to a few and awareness of power is curtailed to those who know the rules. Those who do not know the rules and are not chosen for initiation must remain in confusion, or suffer from paranoid delusions that something is happening of which they are not quite aware.

For everyone to have the opportunity to be involved in a given group and to participate in its activities the structure must be explicit, not implicit. The rules of decision-making must be open and available to everyone, and this can happen only if they are formalized. This is not to say that formalization of a structure of a group will destroy the informal structure. It usually doesn't. But it does hinder the informal structure from having predominant control and make available some means of attacking it if the people involved are not at least responsible to the needs of the group at large. "Structurelessness" is organizationally impossible. We cannot decide whether to have a structured or structureless group; only whether or not to have a formally structured one. Therefore the word will not be used any longer except to refer to the idea it represents. *Unstructured* will refer to those groups which have not been deliberately structured in a particular manner. *Structured* will refer to those which have. A Structured group always has a *formal* structure, and may also have an informal one. An Unstructured group always has an informal, or covert, structure. It is this informal structure, particularly in Unstructured groups, which forms the basis for elites.

The Nature of Elitism

"Elitist" is probably the most abused word in the women's liberation movement. It is used as frequently, and for the same reasons, as "pinko" was used in the fifties. It is never used correctly. Within the movement it commonly refers to individuals, though the personal characteristics and activities of those to whom it is directed may differ widely. An individual, *as an individual,* can never be an elitist, because the only proper application of the term "elite" is to groups. Any individual, regardless of how well known that person may be, can never be an elite.

Correctly, an elite refers to a small group of people who have power over a larger group of which they are part, usually without direct responsibility to that larger group, and often without their knowledge or consent. A person becomes an elitist by being part of, or advocating the rule by, such a small group, whether or not that individual is well known or not known at all. Notoriety is not a definition of an elitist. The most insidious elites are usually run by people not known to the larger public at all. Intelligent elitists are usually smart enough not to allow themselves to become well known; when they become known, they are watched, and the mask over their power is no longer firmly lodged.

Because elites are informal does not mean they are invisible. At any small group meeting anyone with a sharp eye and an acute ear can tell who is influencing whom. The members of a friendship group will relate more to each other than to other people. They listen more attentively, and interrupt less. They repeat each other's points and give in amiably. The "outs" they tend to ignore or grapple with. The "outs' " approval is not necessary for making a decision, but it is necessary for the "outs" to stay on good terms with the "ins." Of course the lines are not as sharp as I have drawn them. They are nuances of interaction, not pre-written scripts. But they are discernible, and they do have their effect. Once one knows with whom it is important to check before a decision is made, and whose approval is the stamp of acceptance, one knows who is running things.

These friendship groups function as networks of communication outside any regular channels for such communication that may have been set up by a group. If no channels are set up, they function as the only networks of communication. Because people are friends, because they usually share the same values and orientations, because they talk to each other socially and consult with each other when common decisions have to be made, the people involved in these networks have more power in the group than those who don't. And it is a rare group that does not establish some informal networks of communication through the friends that are made in it.

Some groups, depending on their size, may have more than one such informal communications network. Networks may even overlap. When only one such network exists, it is the elite of an otherwise Unstructured group, whether the participants in it want to be elitists or not. If it is the only such network in a Structured group it may or may not be an elite depending on its composition and the nature of the formal Structure. If there are two or more such networks of friends, they may compete for power within the group, thus forming factions, or one may deliberately opt out of the competition, leaving the other as the elite. In a Structured group, two or more such friendship networks usually compete with each other for formal power. This is often the healthiest situation as the other members are in a position to arbitrate between the two competitors for power and thus to make demands on those to whom they give their temporary allegiance.

The inevitably elitist and exclusive nature of informal communication networks of friends is neither a new phenomenon characteristic of the women's movement nor a phenomenon new to women. Such informal relationships have excluded women for centuries from participating in integrated groups of which they were a part. In any profession or organization these networks have created the "locker room" mentality and the "old school" ties which have effectively prevented women as a group (as well as some men individually) from having equal access to the sources of power or social reward. Much of the energy of past women's movements has been directed to having the structures of decision-making and the selection processes *formalized* so that the exclusion of women could be confronted directly. As we well know, these efforts have not prevented the informal male-only networks from discriminating against women, but they have made it more difficult.

Elites are not conspiracies. Very seldom does a small group of people get together and deliberately try to take over a larger group for its own ends. Elites are nothing more, and nothing less, than groups of friends who also happen to participate in the same political activities. They would probably maintain their friendship whether or not they were involved in political activities; they would probably be involved in political activities whether or not they maintained their friendships. It is the coincidence of these two phenomena which creates elites in any group and makes them so difficult to break.

Since movement groups have made no concrete decisions about who shall exercise power within them, many different criteria are used around the country. Most criteria are along the lines of traditional female characteristics. For instance, in the early days of the movement, marriage was usually a prerequisite for participation in the informal elite. As women have been traditionally taught, married women relate primarily to each other, and look upon single women as being too threatening to have as close friends. In many cities, this criterion was further refined to include only those women married to New Left men. This standard had more than tradition behind it, however, because New Left men often had access to resources needed by the movement—such as mailing lists, printing presses, contacts and information—and women were used to getting what they needed through men rather than independently. As the movement has changed through time, marriage has become a less universal criterion for effective participation, but all informal elites establish standards by which only women who possess certain material or personal characteristics may join. They frequently include: middle-class background (despite all the rhetoric about relating to the working class); being married; not being married but living with someone; being or pretending to be a lesbian; being between the ages of twenty and thirty; being college educated or at least having some college background; being "hip"; not being too "hip"; holding a certain political line or identification as a "radical"; having children or at least liking them; not having children; having certain "feminine" personality characteristics such as being "nice"; dressing right (whether in the traditional style or the anti-traditional style); etc. There are also some characteristics which will almost always tag one as a "deviant" who should not be related to. They include: being too old; working full time, particularly if one is actively committed to a "career"; not being "nice"; and being avowedly single (i.e., neither actively heterosexual nor homosexual).

Other criteria could be included, but they all have common themes. The characteristics prerequisite for participating in the informal elites of the movement, and thus for exercising power, concern one's background, personality, or allocation of time. They do not include one's competence, dedication to feminism, talents, or potential contribution to the movement. The former are the criteria one usually uses in determining one's friends. The latter are what any movement or organization has to use if it is going to be politically effective.

The criteria of participation may differ from group to group, but the means of becoming a member of the informal elite if one meets those criteria are pretty much the same. The only main difference depends on whether one is in a group from the beginning, or joins it after it has begun. If involved from the beginning it is important to have as many of one's personal friends as possible also join. If no one knows anyone else very well, then one must deliberately form friendships with a select number and establish the informal interaction patterns crucial to the creation of an informal structure. Once the informal patterns are formed they act to maintain themselves, and one of the most successful tactics of maintenance is to continuously recruit new people who "fit in." One joins such an elite much the same way one pledges a sorority. If perceived as a potential addition, one is "rushed" by the members of the informal structure and eventually either dropped or initiated. If the sorority is not politically aware enough to actively engage in this process itself it can be started by the outsider pretty much the same way one joins any private club. Find a sponsor, i.e., pick some member of the elite who appears to be well respected within it and actively cultivate that person's friendship. Eventually, he will most likely bring you into the inner circle.

All of these procedures take time. So if one works full time or has a similar major commitment, it is usually impossible to join simply because there are not enough hours left to go to all the meetings and cultivate the personal relationships necessary to have a voice in the decision-making. That is why formal structures of decision-making are a boon to the overworked person. Having an established process for decision-making ensures that everyone can participate in it to some extent.

Although this dissection of the process of elite formation within small groups has been critical in perspective, it is not made in the belief that these informal structures are inevitably bad—merely inevitable. All groups create informal structures as a result of the interaction patterns among the members of the group. Such informal structures can do very useful things. But only Unstructured groups are totally governed by them. When informal elites are combined with a myth of "structurelessness," there can be no attempt to put limits on the use of power. It becomes capricious.

This has two potentially negative consequences of which we should be aware. The first is that the informal structure of decision-making will be much like a sorority—one in which people listen to others because they like them and not because they say significant things. As long as the movement does not do significant things this does not much matter. But if its development is not to be arrested at this preliminary stage, it will have to alter this trend. The second is that informal structures have no obligation to be responsible to the group at large. Their power was not given to them; it cannot be taken away. Their influence is not based on what they do for the group; therefore they cannot be directly influenced by the group. This does not necessarily make informal structures irresponsible. Those who are concerned with maintaining their influence will usually try to be responsible. The group simply cannot compel such responsibility; it is dependent on the interests of the elite.

The "Star" System

The idea of "structurelessness" has created the "star" system. We live in a society which expects political groups to make decisions and to select people to articulate those decisions to the public at large. The press and the public do not know how to listen seriously to individual women as women; they want to know how the group feels. Only three techniques have ever been developed for establishing mass group opinion: the vote or referendum, the public opinion survey questionnaire, and the selection of group spokespeople at an appropriate meeting. The women's liberation movement has used none of these to communicate with the public. Neither the movement as a whole nor most of the multitudinous groups within it have established a means of explaining their position on various issues. But the public is conditioned to look for spokespeople.

While it has consciously not chosen spokespeople, the movement has thrown up many women who have caught the public eye for varying reasons. These women represent no particular group or established opinion; they know this and usually say so. But because there are no official spokespeople nor any decision-making body the press can query when it wants to know the movement's position on a subject, these women are perceived as the spokespeople. Thus, whether they want to or not, whether the movement likes it or not, women of public note are put in the role of spokespeople by default.

This is one main source of the ire that is often felt toward the women who are labeled "stars." Because they were not selected by the women in the movement to represent the movement's views, they are resented when the press presumes that they speak for the movement. But as long as the movement does not select its own spokeswomen, such women will be placed in that role by the press and the public, regardless of their own desires.

This has several negative consequences for both the movement and the women labeled "stars." (1) Because the movement didn't put them in the role of spokesperson, the movement cannot remove them. The press put them there and only the press can choose not to listen. The press will continue to look to "stars" as spokeswomen as long as it has no official alternatives to go to for authoritative statements from the movement. The movement has no control in the selection of its representatives to the public as long as it believes that it should have no representatives at all. (2) Women put in this position often find themselves viciously attacked by their sisters. This achieves nothing for the movement and is painfully destructive of the individuals involved. Such attacks only result in either the woman leaving the movement entirely—often bitterly alienated—or in her ceasing to feel responsible to her "sisters." She may maintain some loyalty to the movement, vaguely defined, but she is no longer susceptible to pressures from other women in it. One cannot feel responsible to people who have been the source of such pain without being a masochist, and these women are usually too strong to bow to that kind of personal pressure. Thus the backlash to the "star" system in effect encourages the very kind of individualistic non-responsibility that the movement condemns. By purging a sister as a "star," the movement loses whatever control it may have had over the person, who then becomes free to commit all of the individualistic sins of which she has been accused.

Political Impotence

Unstructured groups may be very effective in getting women to talk about their lives; they aren't very good for getting things done. It is when people get tired of "just talking" and want to do something more that the groups, unless they change the nature of their operation, flounder. Because the larger movement in most cities is as Unstructured as individual rap groups, it is not too much more effective than the separate groups at specific tasks. The informal structure is rarely together enough or in touch enough with the people to be able to operate effectively. So the movement generates much motion and few results. Unfortunately, the consequences of all this motion are not as innocuous as the results, and their victim is the movement itself.

Some groups have turned themselves into local action projects if they do not involve many people and work in a small scale. But this form restricts movement activity to the local level; it cannot be done on the regional or national. Also, to function well the groups must usually pare themselves down to that informal group of friends who were running things in the first place. This excludes many women from participating. As long as the only way women can participate in the movement is through membership in a small group, the non-gregarious are at a distinct disadvantage. As long as friendship groups are the main means of organizational activity, elitism becomes institutionalized.

For those groups which cannot find a local project to which to devote themselves, the mere act of staying together becomes the reason for their staying together. When a group has no specific task (and consciousness-raising is a task), the people in it turn their energies to controlling others in the group. This is not done so much out of a malicious desire to manipulate others (though sometimes it is) as out of a lack of anything better to do with their talents. Able people with time on their hands and a need to justify their coming together put their efforts into personal control, and spend their time criticizing the personalities of the other members in the group. Infighting and personal power games rule the day. When a group is involved in a task, people learn to get along with others as they are and to subsume personal dislikes for the sake of the larger goal. There are limits placed on the compulsion to remold every person in our image of what they should be.

The end of consciousness-raising leaves people with no place to go and the lack of structure leaves them with no way of getting there. The women in the movement either turn in on themselves and their sisters or seek other alternatives of action. There are few that are available. Some women just "do their own thing." This can lead to a great deal of individual creativity, much of which is useful for the movement, but it is not a viable alternative for most women and certainly does not foster a spirit of cooperative group effort. Other women drift out of the movement entirely because they don't want to develop an individual project and they have found no way of discovering, joining, or starting group projects that interest them.

Many turn to other political organizations to give them the kind of structured, effective activity that they have not been able to find in the women's movement. Those political organizations which see women's liberation as only one of many issues to which women should devote their time thus find the movement a vast recruiting ground for new members. There is no needs for such organizations to "infiltrate" (though this is not precluded). The desire for meaningful political activity generated in women by their becoming part of the women's liberation movement is sufficient to make them eager to join other organizations when the movement itself provides no outlets for their new ideas and energies.

Those women who join other political organizations while remaining within the women's liberation movement, or who join women's liberation while remaining in other political organizations, in turn become the framework for new informal structures. These friendship networks are based upon their common nonfeminist politics rather than the characteristics discussed earlier, but operate in much the same way. Because these women share common values, ideas, and political orientations, they too become informal, unplanned, unselected, unresponsible elites—whether they intend to be so or not.

These new informal elites are often perceived as threats by the old informal elites previously developed within different movement groups. This is a correct perception. Such politically oriented networks are rarely willing to be merely "sororities" as many of the old ones were, and want to proselytize their political as well as their feminist ideas. This is only natural, but its implications for women's liberation have never been adequately discussed. The old elites are rarely willing to bring such differences of opinion out into the open because it would involve exposing the nature of the informal structure of the group. Many of these informal elites have been hiding under the banner of "anti-elitism" and "structurelessness." To effectively counter the competition from another informal structure, they would have to become "public" and this possibility is fraught with many dangerous implications. Thus, to maintain its own power, it is easier to rationalize the exclusion of the members of the other informal structure by such means as "red-baiting," "reformist-baiting," "lesbian-baiting," or "straight-baiting." The only other alternative is to formally structure the group in such a way that the original power structure is institutionalized. This is not always possible. If the informal elites have been well structured and have exercised a fair amount of power in the past, such a task is feasible. These groups have a history of being somewhat politically effective in the past, as the tightness of the informal structure has proven an adequate substitute for a formal structure. Becoming Structured does not alter their operation much, though the institutionalization of the power structure does open it to formal challenge. It is those groups which are in greatest need of structure that are often least capable of creating it. Their informal structures have not been too well formed and adherence to the ideology of "structurelessness" makes them reluctant to change tactics. The more Unstructured a group is, the more lacking it is in informal structures, and the more it adheres to an ideology of "structurelessness," the more vulnerable it is to being taken over by a group of political comrades.

Since the movement at large is just as Unstructured as most of its constituent groups, it is similarly susceptible to indirect influence. But the phenomenon manifests itself differently. On a local level most groups can operate autonomously; but the only groups that can organize a national activity are nationally organized groups. Thus, it is often the Structured feminist organizations that provide national direction for feminist activities, and this direction is determined by the priorities of these organizations. Such groups as NOW, WEAL, and some Left women's caucuses are simply the only organizations capable of mounting a national campaign. The multitude of Unstructured women's liberation groups can choose to support or not support the national campaigns, but are incapable of mounting their own. Thus their members become the troops under the leadership of the Structured organizations. The avowedly Unstructured groups have no way of drawing upon the movement's vast resources to support its priorities. It doesn't even have a way of deciding what they are.

The more Unstructured a movement is, the less control it has over the directions in which it develops and the political actions in which it engages. This does not mean that its ideas do not spread. Given a certain amount of interest by the media and the appropriateness of social conditions, the ideas will still be diffused widely. But diffusion of ideas does not mean they are implemented; it only means they are talked about. Insofar as they can be applied individually they may be acted on; insofar as they require coordinated political power to be implemented, they will not be.

As long as the women's liberation movement stays dedicated to a form of organization which stresses small, inactive discussion groups among friends, the worst problems of Unstructuredness will not be felt. But this style of organization has its limits; it is politically inefficacious, exclusive, and discriminatory against those women who are not or cannot be tied into the friendship networks. Those who do not fit into what already exists because of class, race, occupation, education, parental or marital status, personality, etc., will inevitably be discouraged from trying to participate. Those who do fit in will develop vested interests in maintaining things as they are.

The informal groups' vested interests will be sustained by the informal structures which exist, and the movement will have no way of determining who shall exercise power within it. If the movement continues to deliberately not select who shall exercise power, it does not thereby abolish power. All it does is abdicate the right to demand that those who do exercise power and influence be responsible for it. If the movement continues to keep power as diffuse as possible because it knows it cannot demand responsibility from those who have it, it does prevent any group or person from totally dominating. But it simultaneously insures that the movement is as ineffective as possible. Some middle ground between domination and ineffectiveness can and must be found.

These problems are coming to a head at this time because the nature of the movement is necessarily changing. Consciousness-raising as the main function of the women's liberation movement is becoming obsolete. Due to the intense press publicity of the last two years and the numerous overground books and articles now being circulated, women's liberation has become a household word. Its issues are discussed and informal rap groups are formed by people who have no explicit connection with any movement group. Purely educational work is no longer such an overwhelming need. The movement must go on to other tasks. It now needs to establish its priorities, articulate its goals, and pursue its objectives in a coordinated fashion. To do this it must get organized—locally, regionally, and nationally.

Principles of Democratic Structuring

Once the movement no longer clings tenaciously to the ideology of "structurelessness," it is free to develop those forms of organization best suited to its healthy functioning. This does not mean that we should go to the other extreme and blindly imitate the traditional forms of organization. But neither should we blindly reject them all. Some of the traditional techniques will prove useful, albeit not perfect; some will give us insights into what we should and should not do to obtain certain ends with minimal costs to the individuals in the movement. Mostly, we will have to experiment with different kinds of structuring and develop a variety of techniques to use for different situations. The Lot System is one such idea which has emerged from the movement. It is not applicable to all situations, but is useful in some. Other ideas for structuring are needed. But before we can proceed to experiment intelligently, we must accept the idea that there is nothing inherently bad about structure itself —only its excess use.

While engaging in this trial-and-error process, there are some principles we can keep in mind that are essential to democratic structuring which are also politically effective:

1. *Delegation* of specific authority to specific individuals for specific tasks by democratic procedures. Letting people assume jobs or tasks by default only means they are not dependably done. If people are selected to do a task, preferably after expressing an interest or willingness to do it, they have made a commitment which cannot so easily be ignored.

2. Requiring all those to whom authority has been delegated to be *responsible* to those who selected them. This is how the group has control over people in positions of authority. Individuals may exercise power, but it is the group that has ultimate say over how the power is exercised.

3. *Distribution* of authority among as many people as is reasonably possible. This prevents monopoly of power and requires those in positions of authority to consult with many others in the process of exercising it. It also gives many people the opportunity to have responsibility for specific tasks and thereby to learn different skills.

4. *Rotation* of tasks among individuals. Responsibilities which are held too long by one person, formally or informally, come to be seen as that person's "property" and are not easily relinquished or controlled by the group. Conversely, if tasks are rotated too frequently the individual does not have time to learn her job well and acquire the sense of satisfaction of doing a good job.

5. *Allocation* of tasks along rational criteria. Selecting someone for a position because they are liked by the group or giving them hard work because they are disliked serves neither the group nor the person in the long run. Ability, interest, and responsibility have got to be the major concerns in such selection. People should be given an opportunity to learn skills they do not have, but this is best done through some sort of "apprenticeship" program rather than the "sink or swim" method. Having a responsibility one can't handle well is demoralizing. Conversely, being blacklisted from doing what one can do well does not encourage one to develop one's skills. Women have been punished for being competent throughout most of human history; the movement does not need to repeat this process.

6. *Diffusion of information* to everyone as frequently as possible. Information is power. Access to information enhances one's power. When an informal network spreads new ideas and information among themselves outside the group, they are already engaged in the process of forming an opinion—without the group participating. The more one knows about how things work and what is happening, the more politically effective one can be.

7. *Equal access to resources* needed by the group. This is not always perfectly possible, but should be striven for. A member who maintains a monopoly over a needed resource (like a printing press owned by a husband, or a darkroom) can unduly influence the use of that resource. Skills and information are also resources. Members' skills can be equitably available only when members are willing to teach what they know to others.

When these principles are applied, they insure that whatever structures are developed by different movement groups will be controlled by and responsible to the group. The group of people in positions of authority will be diffuse, flexible, open and temporary. They will not be in such an easy position to institutionalize their power because ultimate decisions will be made by the group at large. The group will have the power to determine who shall exercise authority within it.

Editorial:
Notes From the Third Year

In its few years of existence, the feminist movement has grown at an extraordinary rate. We are no longer only a small collection of organized groups; the "women's movement" today is found as well in the myriad new women's studies programs; in job actions for better pay; in child care and abortion projects; in the wealth of new writing by feminist journalists and writers; in the speak-outs and teach-ins; in the legal suits challenging sexist laws; and in the changing consciousness of literally millions of individual women.

This explosion, rather than being a sign of disorganization or failure, is a sign of our success as a grass roots movement. The women's movement is thus not only an organized political force but a state of mind as well. The contents of *Notes From the Third Year* reflect this expansion. This year has seen fewer manifestoes and more work on specific issues such as prostitution, women's literature, rape, and lesbianism. It has been a period of intensive rather than extensive analysis.

But there are problems to solve if the feminist movement is to achieve its end of eliminating sex roles. A euphoric period of consciousness-raising has come to an end, and a more sober evaluation has replaced it. Women are beginning to see that consciousness-raising is meant as a stage of growth, not the ultimate stage of growth. It is limited as a tool. If we don't move on from consciousness-raising both as individuals and as groups, we face the danger of stagnation. Instead we must begin to use the knowledge gained to make both internal and external changes. Groups must move to analysis, small group actions and, most difficult, large collective actions and organization.

In moving from the small amorphous rap group toward a more outward-directed group, the problem of "structure" arises. The women's movement will need to work out for itself a satisfactory form which can avoid the typical pitfalls of authoritarian leadership or inflexible ideology which so many other movements have experienced. With so many women's present dislike for authoritarianism, perhaps one of the major achievements of feminism will be to work out new ways of organizing ourselves that will encourage responsibility in all members, but discourage elitism—a form which can encourage strength in all women rather than create followers. Our success in accomplishing this goal will in no small part depend upon our ability to be as actively supportive of each other's new strengths and achievements as before (especially during consciousness-raising) we have been supportive and compassionate of each other's failures.

Another important development in the women's movement over the past year has been the increased cross-fertilization between the so-called "women's rights" sector and the "women's liberation" sector. Feminists are discovering not only that moderate and radical feminists can be found in both camps (coming from the Left, for example, does not guarantee radical feminism), but also that they have a great deal more in common than was originally thought. Each sector makes important contributions to the larger feminist struggle; the "rights" sector's strong emphasis on legal changes, for example, must be united with the "liberation" sector's stress on internal changes. Together we can win important victories, always with the understanding that no one issue wins the whole fight, and that the final victory lies both in destroying the institutions of sexism and in the changed consciousness of all women.

December, 1971

Congress to Unite Women:

Report from the New York City Meeting
of November 21, 22, 23, 1969

The following notes are a collection of the resolutions brought to the general meeting on Sunday, November 23, from the various workshops held on Saturday, November 22, 1969. The notes are as complete as the editing group could make them. We hope we have not left anything out. They are preceded by the preamble to the news release issued to the press on Monday, November 24, and followed by a discussion of the continuing structure of the Congress.

The Congress to Unite Women is committed to the liberation of all women now. We know that only with power can we end the oppression of women. Together, in a united Congress, we will fight for what is good for women.

The Congress is a historic event in the unfinished revolution for women's liberation. Over 500 women from the eastern United States, from cities and campuses, from New York, Pittsburgh, Syracuse, Cornell University, Worcester, Boston, Baltimore, Princeton, Bryn Mawr, Clark University, Buffalo, Penn State University, Rutgers, and elsewhere, met in New York this weekend [21–23 November 1969] to set up a Congress to Unite Women.

The results of each of the 12 workshops that met on Saturday, November 22, are covered in the following order:

A Workshop title and original descriptive paragraph distributed to all Congress participants.

B Conclusions of each workshop (both sessions were available), and an indication of whether these conclusions were adopted, tabled, or rejected as Congress resolutions by the plenary session on Sunday, November 23.

A shorter version appeared in *Notes From the Second Year*.

C Text of the news release statement on each topic, issued at the Congress news conference Monday, November 24. These statements should not be taken as summaries of the Congress stand where fuller statements from the workshops exist.

[The reports of some workshops were not available, and some topics were not covered in the news release; these omissions are indicated where they apply.]

I Early Childhood: Care & Education

A More and better child care facilities are an absolutely urgent need, to make the liberation of women real. It is imperative we activate present laws in this area or find further possibilities for political action, immediately, for the benefit of: working mothers, non-working mothers, fathers, the changing family structure, equal partnership between men and women regardless of income, the growing needs of today's children, who live in a complex, pluralistic society. Do you agree or disagree?

B [Morning workshop:] We demand:

1 Free public nurseries and child-care centers for the working mothers and mothers who attend high school and college, mothers who are painters and writers, unmarried mothers, and unmarried mothers who are living with a man.
2 Planned parenthood centers available to any man or woman.
3 Legal abortions done in free and well-staffed clinics.
4 Summer camps for all children.
5 Reorganization of home industry by application of mass production methods.
6 Equal economic, social, and intellectual opportunities.
7 Fathers and mothers on four-hour days or shortened work weeks so that the fathers may regain their lost role and growth experiences with the children, as suggested by Ashley Montagu.
8 Payment of wages to mothers for the bearing and raising of children.

This last demand would give social recognition to women for the bearing and raising of children and remuneration for their labor as being just as important as any other form of labor. It would recognize the bearing of children as a part of the socially necessary labor in the production and reproduction of life. It would help to eliminate 'commodity' relations between people and establish relations based on personality and emotional needs instead. It would make strong self-confident men and women not suffering from the sicknesses and neuroses of exploitative relations. Men and women could consider each other as equal human beings with unequal development of potentialities—as persons instead of things. Middle class women should not exploit other women and make them do their dirty housework. ADOPTED.

[Afternoon workshop:] The afternoon report stressed the fact that although women must have alternatives, the whole matter was so complex that further study and discussion were needed.

ADOPTED.

C   We demand nationwide free 24-hour-a-day child care centers for all children from infancy to early adolescence regardless of their parents' income or marital status, with child-care practices decided by those using the centers. To encourage the breakdown of sex-role stereotypes, these centers must be staffed equally by women and men. Their wages should be equal to those of public-school teachers. Until these free child-care centers are established, we demand immediate national and state legislation for deduction of childcare expenses from income before taxes.

II   Education (with stress on secondary & higher)

A   To open the door to true equality for women today, we must equalize higher education opportunities across the board, in: aptitude evaluation; college entrance requirements; "women's studies" —substituting facts for mystiques and myths; course planning; study and vocational counseling; graduate school qualifications; loans and fellowships; professional training quotas; double-standard social regulations on campus; female role models; faculty nepotism rules; "continuing education" for women returning to work. Do you agree or disagree?

B 1   We will re-examine the entire structure of education.

2   Changes in curricula and materials:

We will urge changes in hygiene course curricula.

We will list good history texts and also list what areas not covered in existing texts need to be covered, and give these lists to schools. We will also press for history books to explain that oppression, not incapability, is the reason why women have not contributed as substantially as men to history to date, and we will seek to show how the writing of history is biased in favor of the things men have traditionally done.

We will write a literary anthology for high-school use. Alix Shulman has volunteered to help with this project. A college anthology is being done by Ann Scott. We hope to develop films and slides for high-school and college use.

3   Education about the problems of women:

Through publicity we will seek to convince people that discrimination does exist in education. We will cite the proportionately smaller number of degrees being granted to women and other such statistics to prove our point.

We will attempt to provide role models for high-school girls by visiting classes and assemblies as professional or otherwise accomplished women who do not fit the stereotypes, and by talking about our work.

We will try to get to counselors of high-school and college students through the American Personnel and Guidance Association and urge the restructuring of teachers' education courses, especially psychology. A manual is available through Joy Osofsky at Cornell, done by Carolyn Bratt, on teaching courses on women.

4   Tactics to initiate Women's Studies:

This would be a program we would seek to develop at least on the college level, and perhaps later on the high-school level. The courses would probably be interdisciplinary and coed.

We will contact all our Congress people in universities to start teach-ins, first developing a tactics sheet for them to use, and ask them to concentrate initially on psychology and sociology departments.

We will provide them with a list of available and qualified teachers so that if administrators say no one can teach women's studies, they will be prepared to refute the argument. We will not, however, try to force our listed people on any school.

We will compile materials and set up curricula to serve as samples so that our people trying to start women's studies programs will have materials to show educators and concrete proposals for how courses might be run. A curriculum has been done by Joy Osofsky at Cornell, and bibliographies are also available from several sources, including Joy.

We will contact by letter all women's groups and individuals on campuses to form a national coalition for the promotion of women's studies. Such a national group could also deal with related women's problems in education, such as equal parietal rules.

5   Other activities:

We will set up a clearing-house to provide materials, such as bibliographies and syllabi, which will be constantly updated through a newsletter. KNOW, Inc., 502 Bevington Road, Pittsburgh 15221, is already working on this project. The materials should be sent not only to libraries but to interested radical groups and to us.

We will create a speakers' bureau. People who have experience in speaking will be available to train others if they want help, and anybody willing will be encouraged to submit any speeches she has written to a pool so other people can use the same speeches.

We will survey attitude changes due to workshops and courses on women and publish the results.

We will publish and publicize new research or reinterpretations of older research, and widely advertise the news of any colleges establishing a program of women's studies.

C   In the field of education we are against the tracking system. We believe high-school and college guidance counseling must not restrict individuals to sex-determined roles. Home Economics, shop, and other vocational courses must be made available to all without regard to sex. History texts and anthologies of literature must be changed to represent fairly and correctly the achievements of women. Workshops on women's problems should be conducted for parents, teachers, and teachers-in-training, and included in adult and continuing education courses. Women, regardless of marital status or pregnancy, must be guaranteed the right to attend school.

We demand a women's studies section in all public libraries and school and university libraries.

We encourage the academic community to restructure language to reflect a society in which women have equal status with men.

Educational institutions must no longer be exempt from Title VII of the 1964 Civil Rights Act.

We demand elimination of nepotism rules from colleges and universities.

We demand that all educational institutions set up day-care centers for all students, faculties, and staff.

Women's studies programs should be established in all colleges and universities.

III Employment

A   Damaging inequality hits the working woman in: salaries, legal rights and restrictions, sexist typecasting, unwritten laws of behavior, authority, access to information, amount of work expected, time structuring, status, getting credit, value to employer and prospective employers, use of capabilities, growth potential, the ceiling on her aspirations. Do you agree or disagree?

B   [No workshop report was submitted.]

C   On the subject of employment, we demand that working hours be made flexible for both men and women.

We demand legal steps to open trade schools and unions to women.

We support ACLU Women's Rights Project, and intend to create dossiers analyzing individual companies and the per-cent of women hired in each job category.

Part-time employment must be made available for women who want it.

IV Family Structure

A   Central to family structure is the institution of marriage. We will examine how women are forced into marriage and how this institution constitutes legal slavery, as well as the myth that marriage and family structures benefit women. Also to be discussed will be the economic function of the family unit and its importance in maintaining male supremacy.

B   [No workshop report was submitted.]

C   [The news release did not cover this topic.]

V The "Feminine Image"

A   Our stereotyped image—most blatantly seen in the presentations of the mass media, academic fields, etc.—is in fact in everybody's head. Women did not create this set of stereotypes. Who produces and reinforces this image? Why? Who benefits? From our awareness that it is not to our advantage to perpetuate this "Feminine Image" we see the need to work together to create a new and fully-human concept of Woman.

B   [Morning workshop:] We have a 3-fold problem:
1   communication among ourselves;
2   the manner in which the media portray women;
3   the manner in which the media portray feminists.
We will:

a. establish a coalition newsletter with Media Women coordinating it, with no censorship;

b. as long as we do not have editing rights the media can and do make fools of us. We should cooperate with women reporters only, and on our own terms;

c. A committee will be formed out of those people who left their names at the Media Women desk for the newsletter. The newsletter will carry information on boycotts, etc.

[Afternoon workshop:]

1   Hold demonstrations covered by TV and the press, featuring humorous parodies of ads, plays, etc., which are derogatory to women.

2   Boycott Mattel Toys and flood the company and their advertising agency with protests, especially at the Christmas season.

3   Once a month, or however often the coalition newsletter comes out, choose an ad which is especially offensive to women. The address of the agency and company will be given in the newsletter, and the whole Congress, the individual member organizations, and individual persons will all be urged to send telegrams and letters or call the agency and company responsible for the ad.

4   Stickers saying "This ad is an insult to women" will be printed up and given to members to paste on ads at their own discretion.

C   We protest the derogatory image of women presented by the media. This Congress deplores the misrepresentation of the movement for women's liberation to the women of America.

VI How Women Are Divided: Class, Racial, Sexual, and Religious Differences

A If sisterhood between women were a fact, it would not be necessary to hold this conference. This workshop will explore the specific ways we are divided, with the hope that understanding this may help us to find out how we can work together and who and what is responsible for the division.

B [Morning workshop:] We will work with all women recognizing that the uniqueness of our revolution transcends economic, racial, generational, and political differences, and that these differences must be transcended in action, the common interest of our liberation, self-determination, and development of our political movement.   TABLED.

We support all women in their struggle for liberation, regardless of their sexual experiences, whether they be heterosexual, homosexual, celibate, married or single, mothers or not, because we recognize that women know best what situation they can best handle now in this male supremacist society; and because we feel that at this time in history there is no individual solution that in some way does not oppress another woman, this will only come about when there is not a male supremacist society.   TABLED.

C All women are oppressed as women and can unite on that basis; however, we acknowledge that there are differences among women, male-created—of economic and social privilege, race, education, etc.—and that these differences are real, not in our heads. Such divisions must be eliminated. They can only be eliminated by hard work and concrete action, not by rhetoric.   ADOPTED.

VII Love and Sex

A Tracing briefly the history of the concept of love, and the institution of heterosexual sex down through the ages—especially in western society; relationship between love in sex and love in religion; theories of sex and how they are used to degrade and exploit women; the semantics of love in sex; the concept of love as a reaction to, and defense against, oppression; female fantasies and media reinforcement of male fantasies; would women's liberation lead to the end of sex or to better sex?

B   [No workshop report was submitted.]

C   [The news release did not cover this topic.]

VIII   The Nature and Function of a Feminist Group

A   Why we need a group (the superiority of collective to individual action; the "consciousness" and "stability" of a group versus the "spontaneity" of a purely mass movement); structure—the ways in which a group organizes to insure a maximum of efficiency, to create power for itself, and to develop skills and abilities in each of its members. The ways in which individual responsibility and self-discipline are encouraged and utilized by the group. Equality and the lot system in a leaderless group. Resistance to the idea of a group.

B   [Morning workshop:] We are united here because each of us as a woman is oppressed within this society. Regardless of political, economic, social, cultural, religious, or age differences we share and agree upon basic issues of women's oppression where action must be taken. Therefore we propose:

1   Formation of a loose national women's coalition which will not subvert the objectives of individual organizations and groups but will provide communication and cooperation on issues where we must unite for strength and action. We propose establishing at least four regional offices which will collect and disseminate information and help coordinate collective action on single issues.

2   We propose that all resolutions that come out of this Congress be mimeographed and mailed to every participant.

[Afternoon workshop:] We support the statement of the morning group and re-emphasize the need for unity among the groups working for women's liberation and present the following proposals:

1   That the Congress to Unite Women hereby pledges that any attempt to take action against women for feminist activities will cause an appropriate response.

2   Because we support the morning statement we feel each area coalition should have as the first order of business the development of a system for collecting, using, and accounting for money.

3 The coordinating group in each area should organize all those interested in such fund-raising activities as designing and making things to sell, e.g., buttons, banners, posters, etc.

4 We believe it would be desirable to have a single symbol which would stand for our national coalition.

5 The national coalition should set up a permanent non-partisan unit which would have materials and information readily available for distribution on such topics as:

   a. how to organize neighborhood groups,

   b. literature and films covering all aspects of women's liberation as seen by each group,

   c. speakers' bureau on a regional basis.

6 We suggest that each area organize educational and/or organizational meetings with the purposes of:

   a. publicity to inform people—most importantly, women—of the concepts and means of women's liberation,

   b. education,

   c. exploring the problems of the area, making themselves and their existence known.

C [The news release did not cover this topic.]

IX   Political Power

A   The movement of women's liberation requires re-examination of all institutions, both political and those not now considered political, in terms of how they keep women politically powerless. The concept of individual liberation is an illusion. The goals of the women's liberation movement can only be achieved by means of a united political struggle.

B   [No workshop report was submitted.]

C   The Congress to Unite Women announces the formation of a women's political power bloc to fight for women's liberation. We now expand the definition of political to include women's "personal" lives, meaning both the structure of government in the present society and new alternatives on which women unite. While we demand representation on all such bodies in proportion to our numbers (presently 51%), we see this as only a means to an even larger end—the total liberation of women by every avenue available.

1   We will work against people in politically powerful positions who have demonstrated that they oppose our interest.

2   We are determined to get priority in political attention for our issues, particularly child care, abortion, civil rights, and the Equal Rights Amendment.

X   Reproduction and Its Control

A   This group will discuss: the freedom to choose whether to bear children as a woman's basic human right, and as a prerequisite to the exercise of the other freedoms she may win; elimination of all laws and practices that compel women to bear children against their will (professional practices, public and private attitudes, and legal barriers limiting access to contraception and abortion); research in extra-uterine gestation.

B   [Morning and afternoon workshops' joint report:]
The Congress to Unite Women, recognizing the basic human right to decide whether to have a child, and believing that it is a prerequisite to the exercise of the other freedoms women will win, opposes all attitudes, practices, and laws that would compel ANY woman to bear a child against her will. Specifically:

1   We support the phrase "birth control" and use it to mean both contraception (including voluntary sterilization) and abortion. We reject the phrases "family planning" and "planned parenthood" because of the strong social stereotypes they convey.

2   We demand the TOTAL removal NOW of all restrictions on free access to contraception and abortion.

    a. We condemn all so-called abortion "reform" bills—such as that sponsored by Albert Blumenthal in the New York State Assembly. Such restrictive bills are condescending and paternalistic, and reinforce the myth of woman's inability to make decisions about her life and her body.

    b. We also oppose abortion bills that call themselves "repeal" but in fact include unnecessary statutory requirements such as that abortions be available only in hospitals, or only from licensed doctors. Such proposals insure that the decision will be left to the doctor, rather than to the woman, despite technological advances that will soon make these restrictions obsolete. Women should be guaranteed their affirmative civil right to abortion performed by any person qualified to do so, including themselves when appropriate techniques are developed.

c. The Congress to Unite Women OPPOSES the 1970 Cook-Leichter abortion bill in New York State, because it adds statutory requirements that abortion MUST be performed by physicians. This hampers the development of new birth-control technologies, and—like the anti-abortion bill of 1828—binds both women and medicine to the techniques and attitudes of the past.

3 a. We demand legislation requiring that general hospitals receiving any public funding—which comes from the taxes of women—offer to everyone a choice among all safe and effective methods of birth control, as defined in part 1.

b. We demand legislation requiring the establishment of a network of local public clinics to offer these birth-control services at no charge, and requiring that the availability of these services be widely and continuously publicized.

c. We demand that these services be offered by all college health services.

d. We demand that Blue Cross, Blue Shield, and all other medical insurance plans be required to provide coverage to all policyholders regardless of marital status, for all pregnancy-related medical care—including contraception, sterilization, and abortion—desired by the policyholder.

4 We demand that medical and paramedical personnel be fully trained in the techniques necessary to provide these birth-control services.

5 a. We demand greatly expanded research NOW to develop new, safe, and effective methods of abortion, and of contraception for both sexes, as well as methods of extra-uterine gestation.

b. We demand greatly expanded access to existing contraceptive devices for both sexes, through such outlets as grocery stores and vending machines.

6 While we support voluntary birth control, we oppose contraception, sterilization, or abortion imposed under force or coercion—which is often used against women as a punishment.

7 We strongly support ALL possible efforts, whether through

the courts, the legislatures, or DIRECT ACTION, to rid this country of all anti-contraception and anti-abortion laws NOW.

8 We support all referral services that supply women with abortion "first aid," and urge women to set up many more such services as acts of sisterly aid and civil disobedience.

9 We support the teaching of sex education to people of all ages, and demand that this sex education include instruction in all aspects of birth control and EXCLUDE instruction in so-called "sex roles."

ALL ACCEPTED.

Resolved that a protest be made against the setup of the Congress to Unite Women that automatically excluded men because of sex.

REJECTED.

Resolved that the next Congress invite ALL PEOPLE who have an interest in women's liberation. REJECTED.

Resolved that the Congress support Bill Baird's effort in behalf of women's right to birth control information and devices regardless of marital status, and condemn his prison sentence for violating the Massachusetts state anti-contraception law. REJECTED. [This failed after a short discussion in which objections were raised on the grounds that other men had also contributed time and energy helping women and it was unfair to single out one particular man.]

C The Congress to Unite Women recognizes women's basic human right to decide whether to have children and opposes in the courts, the legislatures, and in direct action all attitudes, practices, and laws that would compel any woman to bear a child against her will. We not only demand the TOTAL repeal NOW of all laws restricting access to contraception, sterilization, and abortion and the free public provision of such birth-control services in all hospitals and clinics; but concomitantly we insist that appropriate safeguards be developed so that women are not coerced or in any way pressured into birth control [sic], sterilization, or abortion.

XI The Sex-Role System

A Despite technological advances, humanity has made no progress in interpersonal relationships. This workshop will explore the alternatives to the traditional female and male sex roles, and how to cope with the hostilities that one encounters when one dares to have an identity independent of those sex roles. We will attempt to re-define male and female roles—or, better yet, eliminate them alto-gether.

B   [No workshop report was submitted.]

C

1   We must proceed on the assumption that there are NO bio-logical bases for any sex-role differentiation beyond the basic re-productive functions. If we are truly free we will soon find out what differences there are, if any

2   Children should be given HUMAN models to emulate, not just MALE and FEMALE models.

3   We must each have the courage to fight to live out our own beliefs in undifferentiated sex roles.

XII   Women and the Law

A   Review of the bases of the Supreme Court decisions—as late as 1961—that women are not "persons" in the legal sense, with dis-cussion of what legislative measures are necessary to accomplish equal protection of the law, civil rights, and affirmative action pro-grams on behalf of women. Please bring ideas.

B   We resolve to direct attention to two issues now:

1   Civil Rights Act of 1964: includes sex in only Title VII (which covers employment). There is no provision for penalty against discrimination or for enforcement of the act. There is no money available for suits, which must be instituted at the expense of the plaintiff.

2   Equal Rights Amendment is essential. While the 14th Amend-ment guarantees equal protection under the law for all persons who are citizens, the Supreme Court has refused to rule on the issue of whether women are persons.

A mass demonstration in Washington to implement this was sug-gested and TABLED.

Suggestions for action: write congressman and senator every week; demonstrate. Demonstrate against Emanuel Celler, who said the equal rights amendment will only go through "over my dead body."

Amend each title of the 1964 Civil Rights Act to include references to sex: public accommodations, public facilities, public education, federally-assisted programs, and community-relation services.

Enforcement: add a section specifically providing for private rights of action or a section giving the EEOC a specific time in which to act after which time it should recognize private actions. Develop a special EEOC resource for women's rights. Get specific senators etc. to support this movement.

C   [The text of the news release is identical to 1 & 2 above.]

Plans to Set Up a Continuing Structure for the Congress, considered at the plenary session on Sunday, November 23, 1969

1   Continuing newsletter (Media Women volunteers)
2   Structure to decide how to put into action what happened here
3   Press conference: to announce this meeting to the public and announce women's unity

Motion made and seconded to have every group nominate one woman to form coalition group. ACCEPTED.

Motion to read report of the workshop discussing the Nature and Function of a Feminist Group. ACCEPTED. [See report 8.]

Discussion as to what women should be included in on-going committee: all women's groups, including such as the DAR; all liberation groups; just women represented at the Congress. The argument was between those who felt the most pressing need was for a tight effective organization for political action and those who wanted to broaden the base of the movement. Motion to direct the on-going committee to expand itself to include all other women's groups (amended to read liberation groups) as this became appropriate. ACCEPTED.

(It was previously moved and seconded that non-affiliated women elect four representatives to committee; REJECTED.)

Moved and seconded that each group present elect a representative to the committee to carry on work of the Congress as set forth in the report on the Nature and Function of a Feminist Group. ACCEPTED. Recess for this selection followed.

The following is a list—as complete as could be put together—of the groups that participated in the planning of the first meeting of the Congress to Unite Women:

Albany State Women's Liberation Front
Buffalo NOW
Columbia Women's Liberation
Daughters of Bilitis
Downtown Women's Liberation (New York City)
Female Liberation (Boston)
HIP Women (NYC)
Long Island NOW
Lower East Side Women (NYC)
Lower East Side Women's Liberation (NYC)
Media Women (NYC)
National NOW
New Democratic Coalition Women's Rights Group (NY)
New York NOW
New Yorkers for Abortion Law Repeal
Pittsburgh NOW
Princeton NOW
Radical Feminism (NYC)
Redstockings
Socialist Workers Party (NY)
Stanton-Anthony Brigade (NYC)
Student Homophile League
WITCH Resurrectus
Women Lawyers—Boston
Women's Liberation Club, Bronx High School of Science
Women's Liberation 55 (NYC)
Worcester NOW
Young Socialist Alliance

Women and
the Radical Movement

by Anne Koedt

Within the last year many radical women's groups have sprung up throughout the country. This was caused by the fact that movement women found themselves playing secondary roles on every level—be it in terms of leadership, or simply in terms of being listened to. They found themselves (and others) afraid to speak up because of self-doubts when in the presence of men. They ended up concentrating on food-making, typing, mimeographing, general assistance work, and serving as a sexual supply for their male comrades after hours.

As these problems began being discussed, it became clear that what had at first been assumed to be a personal problem was in fact a social and political one. We found strong parallels between the liberation of women and the black power struggle—we were both being oppressed by similar psychological/economic dynamics. And the deeper we analyzed the problem and realized that all women suffer from this kind of oppression, the more we realized that the problem was not just confined to movement women.

It became necessary to go to the root of the problem, rather than to become engaged in solving secondary problems arising out of that condition. Thus, for example, rather than storming the Penta-

Speech given at a city-wide meeting of radical women's groups at the Free University in New York City on February 17, 1968. First printed in *Notes From the First Year*, June, 1968. The speech is representative of the early attempts to define the relationship between the new left and the beginning feminist consciousness. The word feminist then was scarcely if ever used for fear that women's oppression would not be considered "radical." By 1971 the critique of the left was more sharply delineated, cf., *The Fourth World Manifesto*.

gon as women, or protesting the Democratic Convention as women, we must begin to expose and eliminate the *causes* of our oppression as women. Our job is not only to improve the conditions of movement women any more than it is only to improve the conditions of professional working women. Both acts are reformist if thought of only as ends in themselves; and such an approach ignores the broader concept that one cannot achieve equality for some members of one's group while the rest are not free.

In choosing to fight for women's liberation it is not enough, either, to explain it only in general terms of "the system." For the system oppresses many groups in many ways. Women must learn that the technique used to keep a *woman* oppressed is to convince her that she is at all times secondary to man, and that her life is defined in terms of him. We cannot speak of liberating ourselves until we free ourselves from this myth and accept ourselves as primary.

In our role as radical women we are confronted with the problem of assuring a female revolution within the general revolution. And we must begin to distinguish real from apparent freedoms.

Radical men may advocate certain freedoms for women when they overlap with their own interests, but these are not true freedoms unless they spring out of the concept of male and female equality and confront the issue of male supremacy. For example, men may want women to fight in the revolution because they need every able bodied person they can get. And they may need women to join the work force under a socialist economic system because they cannot afford, like capitalism, to have an unemployed (surplus) labor force not contributing work and being supported by the state. And men may therefore advocate state nurseries so that mothers are not kept from work. But has the fundamental concept of women changed? Do these changes mean that men have renounced the old supremacy relationship, wherein women must always be defined in terms of men? Has the basic domination changed?

It is important to analyze the history of revolutions in terms of special interest groups. The American Revolution was a white male bourgeois revolution. The issues were self-government and the right to make a profit without England's interference; the Declaration of Independence was specifically written to justify independence from

England. It was a document which guaranteed rights neither to blacks nor to women. Crispus Attucks, one of the first black men to lose his life for the revolution, was fighting in a vicarious revolution—the white revolution. Betsy Ross sewing the flag was participating vicariously in a male revolution. The rights gained were not for her.

It is always true of an oppressed group that the mere fact of their existence means that to a certain extent they have accepted their inferior-colonial-secondary status. Taught self-hatred, they identify instead with the oppressor. Thus such phenomena as blacks bleaching their skin and straightening their hair, and women responding with horror at the thought of a woman president.

The economic revolution—i.e., change from capitalism to socialism—can also be viewed in terms of male interest. Under capitalism, the majority of men were exploited and controlled by a few men who held the wealth and power. By changing the economic structure to socialism, this particular economic exploitation was largely eradicated. Women in the Soviet Union fought for and supported such a revolution. But whether out of a genuine hope that non-exploitation would be applied as liberally to them, or worse, out of a lack of even a minimum awareness that they themselves were important, the Soviet revolution remained a male power revolution, although many new benefits fell to women. The Soviet Union is still primarily male governed; women's integration into the labor force meant simply that she transferred her auxiliary, service relationship with men into the area of work. Soviet women are teachers, doctors, assistants, food handlers. And when they come home from work they are expected to continue in their submissive role to men and do the housework, cooking and take primary responsibility for child rearing.

It is important for radical women to learn from these events. The dominant/submissive relationship between men and women was not challenged. Not confronted. We were asked by them instead to equate our liberation with theirs—to blame our inferior conditions on the economic structure rather than confront the obvious male interest in keeping women "in their place." We never insisted upon as explicit a program for freeing women as men had demanded for freeing themselves from economic exploitation. We never confronted men and demanded that unless they give up their domination over us, we would not fight for their revolution, work in their revolution. We never fought the primary cause, hoping instead that changing the secondary characteristics would win us freedom. And we ended up with a revolution that simply transferred male supremacy, paternalism and male power to the new economy. A reformist revolution that only improved upon our privileges but did not change the basic structure causing our oppression.

A black male revolutionary today would not be satisfied knowing only that the economic structure went from private to collective control; he would want to know about racism. And you would have to show him how white power and supremacy would be eliminated in that revolution before he would join you.

Until we make such similar demands, revolution will pass us by.

The Fourth World Manifesto

by Barbara Burris

In agreement with Kathy Barry, Terry Moore, Joann DeLor, Joann Parent, Cate Stadelman.

Barbara Burris had an early involvement in the civil rights movement, the peace movement, and SDS. She became a feminist in 1966 and joined the women's movement in early 1967, where she became very active. She is currently "trying to find myself as a complete person—now writing and learning sculpture."

Background

The "Fourth World Manifesto" was originally written partly as a reply to the way in which a "women's liberation" conference was planned. We were upset at the dishonesty of the call for a "women's liberation" conference with Indochinese women in the spring of 1971.

The women who planned and worked on the conference defined themselves as anti-imperialist women. Some of them have also been active in the women's movement. While stating in one of their planning leaflets that it was necessary to be "upfront about our politics," they discussed, sometimes subtly and sometimes very blatantly, the use of the women's liberation movement to further their own political ends.

As we stated in the original "Manifesto," we do not concede to the women who planned the conference the title of "anti-imperialists." We feel they used a very narrow definition of imperialism taken without question from the male-dominated Left. We find it self-evident that women are a colonized group who have never—anywhere—been allowed self-determination. Therefore, all women who fight against their own oppression (colonized status) as females under male domination are anti-imperialist by definition. In the second part of this "Manifesto" is a detailed discussion of women as a colonized group.

It should go without saying that those of us connected with the "Fourth World Manifesto" are deeply opposed to the war in Indochina. As individuals all of us have strong commitments against this war. There are plenty of anti-war groups (however male-dominated) that women, as individuals, can relate to if they wish. But it would be disastrous to turn the independent feminist movement into simply another adjunct to the anti-war and anti-imperialist movements—with the same male-dominated perspective which those movements have.

The anti-imperialist women, like the rest of the anti-war and anti-imperialist Left movement, never question war and national imperialism as male-supremacist institutions. They ignore the roots of domination, aggression, imperialism, and war in male-supremacist society. Because they do not see imperialism and war in their deepest aspects as male-supremacist institutions in *all* societies, the anti-imperialist women are anxiously concerned that an "anti-imperialist consciousness" be injected into the women's movement. They make a strong effort to change the direction of the women's movement from independent feminist issues to anti-imperialist activities as these have been narrowly defined by the male Left.

The anti-imperialist women were less than honest in calling their conference a women's liberation conference with the Indochinese women. We would have had no objections to their conference if they had stated honestly that they were calling an anti-imperialist conference for women interested in anti-war work. It was the dishonesty of the anti-imperialist women's attempt to use and convert the women's liberation movement to their brand of anti-imperialist politics that roused our anger. We have experienced too much of this kind of manipulation of the women's movement by Left groups.

Most of our criticism of the conference was developed in the original "Manifesto." We do not want to go over the details of it here. However, we do feel that it is crucial to open up a discussion of the emotional and ideological reasons underlying attempts to co-opt the women's movement into other "more important" struggles.

In an expanded edition of the "Manifesto" we have worked out a deeper analysis of the emotional, psychological, and social assumptions underlying the attitude that women's liberation is less important than black liberation, anti-imperialism, anti-capitalism, etc. In the expanded "Manifesto" we criticize the male definition of oppression which does not recognize the unique position of females as a subjugated group.

But we feel it is necessary in this limited space to focus strongly on the male-dominated Left. The anti-imperialist women are criticized here only as they are one of the most recent examples in a series of attempts to re-direct the women's movement into male Left-dominated priorities.

Now that the women's movement (thanks to independent women) has become a force to be reckoned with in society, there are many Left groups trying to get a finger in the women's movement pie. Over the last year and a half the SWP-YSA (Socialist Workers Party-Young Socialist Alliance) has made a nationally coordinated attempt to infiltrate and take over women's centers and organize women's liberation groups (which they hope to mold to their "single issue" approach and subordinate to their organizational aims). This "Manifesto" is not simply directed at the "anti-imperialist" women. What is said of the anti-imperialist women's manipulation of the women's movement applies equally well to every other Left group— the Communist Party, Socialist Workers Party, Young Socialist Alliance, International Socialists, Students for a Democratic Society, Progressive Labor, Youth Against War and Fascism, etc. The criticisms we make of the anti-imperialist women apply equally to all of the male Left and the women in the male-dominated Left.

The Invisible Audience

In an honest article in the February issue of *Radical America*, Marlene Dixon described the pressures on women radicals to conform to a male-dominated movement.

In discussing the First National Conference of Women's Liberation near Chicago in 1968, she says:

> The Invisible Audience at the Chicago Conference were the very "male heavies" who had done so much to bring about the existence of a radical Women's Female Liberation Movement. [p. 27]
>
> The radical women were decimated by the invisible male audience. Thus the real split among the women hinged upon the sig-

nificant audience that women addressed: other women, or Movement men. [p. 28]

But why were these women so super-conscious of a "male presence" at an all-women conference of women's liberationists at a camp near Chicago—with no Left males for miles around?

> Because women had learned from 1964 to 1968 that to fight for or even sympathize with Women's Liberation was to pay a terrible price: what little credit a woman might have earned in one of the Left organizations was wiped out in a storm of contempt and abuse. [p. 27]

But perhaps becoming a "success" in the male Left is not the highest of all possible goals for a woman—or for anyone.

> Women must face facts. Men will never, until forced by circumstances, place first, or even urgent, priority upon a struggle against the oppression of women. Witness the fact that there is not one male dominated organization, from the Left-liberal New University Conference to the radical Youth Movement, that has been willing to place top priority upon the women's struggle. Indeed the idea is so repugnant to many men that they cannot tolerate a woman who refuses male leadership in order to address her energies primarily to the liberation of her sisters. [p. 33]

Women who still are acting for the Left male invisible audience but who now form women's collectives to organize women in relation to the priorities set up by a male Left are little more independent than they were working with the males. They are somewhere between fear and open rebellion. They fear to work on their own definition of women and women's issues and so still relate primarily to the invisible audience of "male heavies."

What a difference it would make—in terms of male approval—if the women working in "anti-imperialist" collectives or on "anti-imperialist" issues were working on their own women's issues.—If they themselves developed a perspective on how women are a colonized group in relation to men all over the world, in all classes and races, including the Third World. With that perspective they would no longer be a part of the male Left. But it doesn't even seem to occur to the "anti-imperialist" women that the male definition of imperialism may be extended and perhaps truly was originally applicable to women.

The "anti-imperialist" women are trying to get women to work on "anti-imperialist" issues in a certain way in which they are defined by the male Left. We quote an article describing the last planning meeting that was held in Baltimore (October 24–25). "In order to spread the word about the Conferences [planning] more widely and to get women involved in anti-war activities, a series of actions are being planned as part of a whole anti-imperialist offensive of women." (From "Battle Acts," published by Women of Youth Against War and Fascism.)

It is one thing to be against the Vietnam War and all wars and quite another for a group of women to try to draw women working in their own Movement away from it into the male-dominated, very narrowly defined anti-war and anti-imperialist movements. The same mistake happened at one point (there's always something more "important" than female liberation) when a large segment of the earlier Feminist Movement went into the Women's International League for Peace and Freedom and fizzled out as a threatening force in the society.

The demand for an end to sex roles and male imperialist domination is a real attack on the masculine citadel of war. After all, women don't declare or fight in offensive wars. War is a male institution—as are all other institutions in the society—and war is simply an extension of the colonial policy of the subjection of the female culture and "weaker" male cultures, i.e., "weaker" national cultures. Women, who have nothing to say about running the country or fighting in the war, will never end war except by attacking and ending male domination and the sex roles where men learn their war mentality. The women who went into WILPF took the safest and therefore totally ineffective and reactionary (for women) way out. They opted to reinforce the split between male and female and to use their "feminine myths" to act as adjuncts to the male peace movement and claim that women's voice was needed (in the same old role, of course) to save men from themselves—their own self-imposed slaughter. The oppressed are going to "save" with their oppressed "virtues" (defined by males and unsifted and unquestioned) their own oppressors.

The anti-imperialist women, in a new refrain to an old song, are in essence asking that women in the independent Women's Movement focus their energies on "anti-imperialism" as the male Left defines it. This is like asking the Women's Movement to move from a position of independence to a position of subservience to the male-dominated Left.

But the Women's Liberation Movement started out from the Civil Rights Freedom Movement, Student Movement, and Anti-War Movement. Women got the notion working in these movements that the idea of freedom should apply to women too. But the males in these movements never intended the freedom struggle to extend to women. It is still too subversive an idea for any of these movements to tolerate on any real level. So many women who got the freedom bug too bad left to relate to women in a Female Movement.

And just as the freedom and anti-war struggle never applied to women, so neither does the present Left anti-imperialist movement. Is there *any* analysis about imperialism against women? Is there any recognition in writing or action that women are a colonized group, brutally exploited by their colonizers—men—and that this is a primary fact of women's existence? No. And this kind of analysis will never happen in the male-dominated Left or its periphery because males are the colonizers. And the colonizer has never yet defined his privileges out of existence—only the colonized will.

The male Left has absolutely no interest in a female revolution. Rather, the male Left has a direct interest in perpetuating the status quo, i.e., male privileges, and preventing any real threats to male supremacy from both within the Left and without it.

A Specter is Haunting the Left—
The Specter of Feminism

The only real threat to male supremacy is the independent Women's Movement. Therefore the male Left has done a great deal to impede the development of independent Women's Liberation and tried in numerous ways to co-opt the energies of women away from working independently with other women on women's issues. There have been numerous devices used by the Left to this end depending on the situation and the consciousness of the women involved.

The first tactic in reaction to Women's Liberation was laughter. But that didn't stop some women—in fact it made some of them so furious they left and began "organizing" other women. The next tactic was anger. "You castrating bitches." "What do you women want anyway?" And that didn't work either—even more women left to join the newly emerging independent Women's Movement.

Then the men began to get really nervous—after all women were leaving the Left in increasing numbers—and the men began to play guilt games. "So what makes *you* think *you're* oppressed, you white middle-class chick?" (Notice the order of the defining words the male Left uses—"chick" is last.) That tactic made some women even madder but it began to cut deep into many women. And this tactic began to work on some of the less strong women—those who were still full of white male-imposed guilt and self-hatred. The Left males realized that they had struck a tender nerve. And they began to manipulate women's guilt and started becoming very liberal toward the Women's Liberation Movement—that is, when they weren't chuckling about those "frustrated bitches" in male-only company. And they had to be liberal anyway because that God-damned Women's Liberation Movement composed only of females was putting the heat on them and they might lose "their" women to it if they didn't play it cool. So they put up with the discomfort of women's caucuses rather than lose all "their" women to the independent Women's Movement. At first it was pretty rough and more than one male Left organization folded under the pressures of the women's caucuses.

But then the Left males began to see that the women's caucuses could have some real value for their organizations. They could be used as important organizing tools for recruiting new members and for working with women associated with the males whose problems the Left organization was concerned with. Such as having the women work with GI wives while the men worked at "organizing" the GI's in the army. Women in the caucuses express best the male attitudes of the organization toward "women's issues" and women's struggle for liberation. We give only two examples out of many. One is a leaflet passed out by PAR (People Against Racism) women at a women's liberation conference in Detroit in 1968. They list as one of their concerns something which reveals the manipulative way in which the Women's Movement is viewed: They wish to use Women's Liberation "as an organizing tactic for broader political movement."

Bernadine Dohrn's equally blatant statement in the *New Left Notes* special issue on women is every bit as revealing. She says, "Everywhere around us there are concentrations of women: dorms, women's schools, education and home economics departments, high schools, jobs—women can be mobilized to fight against imperialism and racism." Maybe women's caucuses were really a boon to the male Left and not the threat they had expected them to be and which they were at first.

So a pattern was generally established throughout the male Left that women could stay in the caucuses and organize other women into the Left male-dominated Movement as long as they concentrated on:

(1) Raising women's issues mainly as they related to the structure of the male-dominated organization which the women remained working for;

(2) Raising women's issues on the periphery of the male-defined "important" issues of the organization;

(3) Relating to the Women's Liberation Movement as caucus members only of the primary male organization to "raise" the issues of the male organization in the Women's Movement, and, if possible, get its focus off independent women's struggle and onto how women can relate to male-defined Left issues.

Women's collectives, unless they are truly autonomous women's collectives working from their own analysis on women's issues, can be and are used in much the same manner as the Left women's caucuses. Because they too relate primarily to the male Left Movement and only secondarily as females to female liberation issues. They are one step ahead of the women's caucuses if only because they know they can no longer work with the males in the organization—but they still remain working *for* them even though now working in women's collectives. Also, "women's collectives" is now being used by a number of women as synonymous with caucus group —but a more "hip" term than caucus.

The Myth of the White Middle-Class Woman

The male Left tries to intimidate Left women into not taking a strong and independent stand on the female liberation struggle with the "abusive" statement, "They're only a bunch of white, middle-class women." It would take another long article to refute this statement, but we will do it in a very cursory manner here.

White is the first defining word of "white middle-class women."

This implies that the primary position of women in the society is due to white privileges. *If* this is so, then *all* whites must have the same privileges, i.e., *all* whites must control the institutions, make the laws, control the army and police, control the government, the religion, education, and business, and have the very best positions in jobs, etc. But it is white males only who are in positions of power and control in all of the institutions of the society. Women are excluded from control and decision-making, are discriminated against in jobs more than any other group, get the lowest pay, are defined as inferiors and as a sexual caste, etc. Also, women were the first group to be subjected as a caste all over the world, thousands of years ago—long before blacks were subjected to whites in America or anywhere else. Obviously whiteness does not overcome the caste position of being a woman in this society. There are some incidental advantages to being white for a woman who is white, but there are also advantages for black males in being males in this society. But the incidental advantages—which are meaningless in terms of woman's true caste position as a sex—come to her mainly in her affiliation with a dominant white male.

The Left very shallowly sees women associating and living with white males and therefore assumes that women share white male privileges. This is false. Being integrated *as subordinates* does not mean that women share the privileges of the ruling caste—white males. Women get the crumbs. In fact, as the black liberation struggle found out, there are distinct disadvantages to being "integrated" with your oppressor, especially when he still has all the power. The control over the oppressed is just that much more complete.

The second defining word in the series, "white middle-class women," is middle-class. If class defines women before her sex does, then she should be able to compete with any male for any job on an equal level. But this is not the case. Women are almost in a different labor market than men because of the extremely rigid female caste labor role. The discrimination against females in the economy is the most intense of any group. Female labor is the lowest paid. Doesn't everyone know the statistics by now? In 1966, the median income for a white man was $7,164; for a nonwhite man, $4,528; a white woman, $4,152; a nonwhite woman, $2,949 (full-time year-round labor). In 1955, the median wage of women working full time was 64 percent of that of men; in 1967, it was down to 60 percent. Things are getting worse and we could go on and on quoting statistics you have probably already heard. But it is clear that the white male and the black male get paid more and the white female and the black female get paid less. The black female is doubly disadvantaged as a female and black, and has the lowest pay level of all. That "female" work is the lowest and the caste lines of labor are most rigid in terms of sex can be proved by the fact that black males—while demanding integration in jobs in male fields, i.e., better paying jobs—have never demanded to integrate (sexually, that is) as secretaries, waitresses, salesgirls, etc. When black males integrate into a female job (which is rare) such as nursing, they are paid more than the females doing the same job.

A woman's class is almost always determined by the man she is living with. From her father's house to her husband's house, his income determines her class. Her income and job are only "extra." In fact, if all women were to be put out of all their men's houses and had to depend on their own earning power, almost all of them would be lower or working class—no matter what their class positions were when living with the man. They would be lower or working class because of women's sexual caste position in the economy. Class is therefore basically a distinction between males, while the female is defined by her sexual caste status.

So we have only the last word left in the "taunt" of "white middle-class women." And woman—a sexual caste subordinated to the dominant ruling sex, man—is defined primarily by that relationship.

But it is true that women—through self-hatred and manipulation by male culture (as evidenced by the male Left example above)—do not necessarily identify with their true caste position as women. She often identifies with her oppressor's privileges as white or middle or upper class or even as male. But the Left, which is so upset about her identification with whiteness and class, does not have a comparable critique of black and Third World male identification with male supremacy and privileges (humorously referred to as "foreskin privileges"). This is because the identification with male privileges by black and Third World males—even in their movements—fits in with white male movement domination.

But as women, we are upset about any inequality—any identification with privileges—between women or within the Women's Movement. We have tremendous barriers to overcome. As the Female Liberation Movement must cut across all (male-imposed) class, race, and national lines, any false identification of women with privileges that are really male (such as whiteness or class, etc.) will be fatal to our Movement. Any identification with privileges will destroy the basis of communication which we females share as a suppressed caste and will divide us up as enemies where we should be friends and equals. And the male Right and the male Left movements will manipulate these differences among women to prevent women from overcoming the barriers that keep us apart and therefore unable to effectively change our sexual caste position as females.

Many women do identify with white and class privileges. Our task as women is not, as the male Left does, to write them off as white bourgeois but to patiently discuss and communicate with women, as sisters, what our true caste position in society is. Once we really understand our suppressed caste status and begin to move to free ourselves from it, we women can then understand other groups' oppression—but not before. But it is not an automatic result. People can see their own oppression clearly and be blind to others' oppression. So the understanding of the oppression of other groups needs to be a very conscious and important part of the Women's Liberation Movement, but only from the basis of an understanding and struggle for our own freedom as females—not as an imposed lecture by some "movement organizers" who will "raise our consciousness" about oppression, and try to impose their white male guilt on us.

The male Left tries, through guilt, to play one oppressed group off against another oppressed group in much the same way the Establishment plays one against the other. They are always going in circles with the "who's most oppressed" musical chairs. How does one decide who is "most oppressed"? Surely the male white Left—as oppressors—cannot decide this. But they do and try to impose their decision on everyone, especially women. And women are—of course—defined as "least oppressed" by the male-dominated Left.

Let us suppose, for a moment, that we are in a male Left meeting and they are trying to decide who is "most oppressed," therefore who most deserves their solicitous attentions and rhetoric. First of all they decide that blacks are most oppressed. But then someone says that black females are more oppressed than black males. Someone else counters that black females in Third World countries are even more oppressed than are black females in the U.S. Then another person realizes that a black female in the Third World who is in the working class is more oppressed. But someone else says that a black female in the Third World country who is in the working class and under eighteen years of age is even *more* oppressed. But the *most* oppressed, and therefore logically and morally the only people they should try to "organize" and work with, are black females in Third World countries, in the working class, under eighteen years of age, pregnant, and culturally defined as ugly.

Such is the "logic" of the "most oppressed." But we can take one last look at it from another angle.

A Dramatic Meeting of Two Oppressed/Oppressors, or "Who is More Guilty?"

A black man meets a white woman on the street. He is oppressed because he's black and so need feel no guilt toward her. She feels guilty because she's white. But then the balance shifts as she realizes she's a woman and therefore oppressed and needn't feel guilt. But then he feels guilty because he's a male. Then she begins to feel guilty because she's middle class. Then he feels free of guilt because he's working class. But he begins to feel guilty because he's older and she's very young and oppressed. She feels oppressed as a youth and therefore doesn't feel guilty . . . *ad infinitum.*

The fact that has to be faced by the male Left at some point is that *everyone* in the society—including the white male—is both oppressor and oppressed. Psychologically this could be a revolutionary concept for the Left. If we can only identify with our oppression and not see how we also oppress others we are fooling ourselves. If we feel only guilty about being oppressors we are also fooling ourselves.

The male Left is in a vicious circle of guilt and righteousness, because people in the male Left refuse to go deep enough into their own personal processes of guilt and anger at their own oppression, which becomes a confused mixture of violence and revenge. The male Left has become so hung-up on guilt and "who's most oppressed" that they have lost an elemental sense of justice for *all* human beings.

We, as women, do not want males to feel guilty. We don't care about guilt; what we want is change. All we demand is justice for our sisters, and that cannot come from a guilt-ridden movement which has defined half of humanity's freedom as a "side effect" of the "real" revolution which will be made by other "vanguard," "more oppressed" groups.

The males in the Left continue, through control of leadership, control of the Left organizations, control of writing and publishing, to define the issues which Left workers will concentrate on. This often goes in fads. The latest one is anti-imperialism. (Which is not to negate the importance of imperialism but to say it has been taken up in a shallow and faddish manner and as an escape from the realities of American society.) The definition of imperialism is carefully male-controlled and does not include women's colonial status.

The women who are organizing this "women's" Conference have accepted the male Left priorities and their definition of "anti-imperialism," which excludes women's movements for self-determination.

The women who call themselves anti-imperialists made this statement in their planning leaflet:

> Discussions followed concerning the level of anti-imperialist consciousness within the Women's Liberation Movement in the various cities represented. It was evident that although there was both a high degree of women's consciousness and of anti-imperialist consciousness in various parts of the Movement, the relation between the two has not been made clear to most women in the Movement. [p. 3]

Let us explain to the "anti-imperialist" women what imperialism and anti-imperialism really are to women.

There are two definitions of imperialism. The Webster dictionary states that imperialism is:

> ... the policy and practices of forming and maintaining an empire; in modern times, it is characterized by a struggle for the control of raw materials and world markets, the subjugation and control of territories, the establishment of colonies, etc.

The imperialist is defined by Webster's as a person favoring imperialism.

Fanon and the whole black liberation struggle have recently extended the dictionary definition of imperialism or colonialism to mean a group which is prevented from self-determination by another group—whether it has a national territory or not. The psychological and cultural mutilation is particularly intense and the colonialism more brutal when the group that colonizes and the group colonized have different defining physical characteristics that set them clearly apart.

All of the above definitions apply to the subjection of women, as a sex.

The dictionary definition of imperialism included "the subjection and control of territories . . . ." Women, set apart by physical differences between them and men, were the first colonized group. And the territory colonized was and remains our women's bodies.

Our bodies were first turned into property of the males. Men considered female bodies as territory over which they fought for absolute ownership and control. Consider the imperialist implications of the language: He related his sexual "conquests," she "surrendered" to him, he "took her," etc. Marriage (exclusive of property rights) and the patriarchal family system are colonial institutions created and controlled by males for the subjugation of females.

Our bodies are free territory to other male colonizers when not "protected" by an individual male colonist. What is rape but an imperialist act upon the territory of our bodies?

There are two forms of the colonization of our bodies (territories) by males. Most males have an individual colonial relationship to an individual female and most males identify with and act on the group colonization of women. For instance, rape is an individual male imperialist act against an individual woman while the abortion laws are male group control over their collective female territories. (We realize that we are generalizing here about males and that some of them do not perceive women simply as open territory for conquest. But unfortunately, there are too few males who perceive females as equal human beings to change the generalization much at this point.)

Another example of group colonization of women is the way our bodies are defined as open territory for exploitation (compare the exploitation for sexual satisfaction of the male colonizer to exploitation for raw materials—female bodies are the raw materials). In all forms of the dominant male culture—advertising, pornography, the underground press, literature, art, etc.—female bodies are exploited as territory to demean, subject, control, and mock.

The fact that each male petty colonialist has an individual interest in perpetuating the subjection of his individual territory, i.e., woman, makes the colonization of women more complete than that of any other group. The colonial rule is more intense for females as we have no escape into a ghetto and at all times are under the watchful eye of the male colonizers, from father to lover to husband. Therefore our suppression as a group (culture) and as individuals has been more complete as has been our identification with our masters' interests (much like the proverbial house nigger).

Fanon shows that it is not enough for the colonizer to control the territory and subject the inhabitants of it to his rule. The colonizer must destroy the culture and self-respect of the colonized. And colonialism's condemnation of the colonized's culture transcends any national boundaries, for it is the essence of the colonized physical and cultural differences that threaten the colonizer.

Fanon says in *The Wretched of the Earth* that "Colonialism . . . turns to the past of the oppressed people, and distorts, disfigures and destroys it." [p. 210] He says that the colonized (in his book, speaking of blacks) "must demonstrate that a Negro culture exists."

The great mass of women have been totally ignored in history except where they appear as adjuncts to men. And the history of Female Liberation Movements has been distorted and almost completely censored. Through the almost complete censorship of the realities of women's condition throughout history, women have been robbed of the means to knowledge about the origins and extent of their subjugation. History (of art, politics, literature, etc.) as related by males has engraved upon women's minds a male image of the world.

Women Are Now in the Process of Having to Prove that a Female Culture Exists.

Culture is defined by Webster's as the "concepts, habits, skills, art, instruments, institutions, etc. of a given people in a given period." We will show that the concepts, habits, skills, art, and instruments of women in any period have been different from men's and have been ridiculed and/or suppressed by them. We will show that in all the major institutions of society women receive unequal treatment and the appearance that these institutions are the same for men and women is false.

A female culture exists.

We also hold that female and male culture began with the definition of females as embodying all those human attributes which
males as dominators could not reconcile with their own self-image
and therefore projected onto females, thus causing a schizophrenic
split of personality into masculine and feminine. —That women,
defined by these attributes (such as emotional, intuitive, etc.) by
males and further limited by their physical position in society as to
work and tools, developed a female or "feminine" culture, and a
culture of resistance to male domination. Although the concept of
the "feminine" was imposed upon women, we have, through the
centuries, developed and created within the confines of the feminine,
a female culture.

Female and Male Culture

What do most people imagine when they think of differences in
culture? They most often think of strange customs and a different
language. The traveler to a foreign culture will notice women carrying pails of water on their heads or men riding donkeys, different
and strange costumes and white-washed houses. In another culture
she will notice people riding bicycles, small towns, sidewalk cafés,
small shops, more chic dress, different foods, etc. Especially will the
traveler notice the difference in language if there is one.

Although these are just a few of the differences of national culture that distinguish the lives that both women and men lead, and
we respect these differences, they are the superficialities that cover
up the fundamental similarity of all national cultures the world over.
This fundamental similarity is the split between male culture and
female culture.

Let us go back to some of those superficial differences that the
traveler noticed. In the first culture, the women were carrying pails
of water on their heads and the men riding donkeys to market. What
was seen as one whole is now divided up by sexual work role. The
different costumes which were seen as a whole unit are now divided
up into male costumes and female costumes. The small shops noticed
are owned by men and sometimes staffed by women. A split is now
seen between male ownership and female workers. The cafes are
served by women, if cheap, and staffed by male waiters if more
expensive. A difference in value of work and pay between male and

female is perceived. The food production in agriculture is done primarily by males but prepared in each home by females. What was seen as culinary differences now reminds the traveler of the role of women in the home and woman's caste work roles all over the world. The traveler in this second look at the culture begins to notice the basic sameness of the male-female cultural split under the superficial differences that were so striking to her at first.

The problem is that the split is so obvious and taken for granted that practically nobody can see it. Things which are conceived of as "natural" cannot ordinarily be perceived. But the emperor had no clothes in spite of what everybody "saw," and a female culture exists whether or not most people will acknowledge the facts of its existence.

Let us again take up those things (habits, skills, art, concepts, and institutions) which distinguish one culture from another according to Webster's definition. Part of the customs of a culture are its habits. Habits here means what people do in their daily lives. It can also include how they go about doing these things. It is clear that women and men have very different daily habits. Women in practically all parts of the world, whether they are working outside the home or not, have responsibility for the cooking, cleaning, and child "raising" chores of the society. This means that most women spend their time with children. This in itself is a cultural split, as men go out and mix mainly with other males in the male world outside the home. Generally males do not do any of the work designated as "female work." Women, mainly in the company of other women and children, organize their time and routines and socializing on an entirely different basis than males. Female work, being so completely caste labor, is organized and done by women in ways peculiar to the female view of things (which is very much determined by woman's secluded work place, i.e., the home and its environs). The whole daily routine of a man and a woman is totally different.

The woman develops skills associated with her work role. Her skills are usually entirely different than the male's. She usually knows a lot about cooking, child care, washing, sewing, colors, decorating, and cleaning, while he knows mechanical or carpentry skills and anything he may learn as a skill at his job. The instruments or tools a woman uses are defined by the work and skills she is allowed.

If the woman goes out to "work" she will have all the home

chores in addition to her outside "job." But women's skills outside the home are limited by what the male-run economy will train her for or let her do. She usually fills "service" roles which utilize the "skills" she has learned in her role as wife and mother. She is allowed limited acquisition of physical skills in such things as typing and small tedious work. She fills completely different job roles than males in the male-dominated economy and is segregated into "female jobs" almost completely. Males do almost all the specialized skillful work—for higher pay.

At one time in the process of the cultures, women did almost everything and men did nothing but hunt and make weapons and war. As men had free time due to women's performing all the drudge work for them (as slave labor, really), they began to develop skills in certain things. As a skill developed, women were no longer allowed to perform the task and it was passed on from father to son. As specialization increased women had more of the skills and trades taken away from them and were left only with the drudge chores of cleaning, washing, cooking, "raising" children, etc. This culminated in Europe in the all-male guilds of feudal times.

When the feudal guild system broke down with the onset of industrialism, cheap unskilled labor was needed and women were used again—sewing, weaving, mining, working metal in factories, etc. It was on the backs of cheap "unskilled" female labor (and child labor) that the grotesque edifice of Western industrialism was built. Female slave labor in the cotton mills and black slave labor in the cotton fields produced industrialism for the white male Western world.

And when industrialism was achieved, hordes of women were sent back home and men replaced them in the factories. So that now we have a small body of lowest-paid female labor in the factories but almost totally female personnel in sales and service roles (typing, nursing) which were once male "skills" but are now just very low-paying drudge work.

The final three parts of Webster's definition of culture are the art, concepts, and institutions of a people.

Women have been excluded from contributing to the art, philosophy, and science of all national cultures. These things are in tight male control. The male culture, which is the dominant culture in every nation, i.e., is synonymous with the national culture, cannot accept a female view of things as expressed by female writers, artists, and philosophers. When some women break through male prejudice to create truly great art—which is often very sensitive to the female culture and values—they are not given the recognition they deserve, because males, looking through their own culturally distorted view of the world, cannot give any credence to an art that expresses the female view. In fact, most males cannot understand what is going on in female culture and art. The worth of female art is thoroughly suppressed in a male-dominated society.

The female soul, suppressed and most often stereotyped in male art, is defined by negative comparisons to the male. The eternal feminine is seen as a passive, earthy, malleable, mysterious, unthinking, emotional, subjective, intuitive, practical, unimaginative, unspiritual, worldly, evil, lustful, super-sexual, virginal, forever waiting, pain-enduring, self-sacrificing, calculating, narcissistic, contradictory, helpless, quivering mass of flesh.

The fact that women live under the power of belief in these characterizations causes a certain outlook which molds the female culture. Woman's position in society, her economic and psychological dependence, reinforce the female stereotypes. Because of the belief in these attributes and woman's position in society—not because of our inherent "female nature"—women's concepts of the world are much different than men's.

Almost everything that has been defined as a male view of the world has its opposite in a female view. Because of the child raising role and the emphasis on personal relationships, women have a more personal, subjective view of things. Because of our subjection, women have a more fatalistic, passive view of the world. We are more in touch with our emotions and often find it necessary to use emotions in manipulating men. Through the imposition of a servant status on women, the female culture has elaborated a whole servile ethic of "self-sacrifice." As the major ethic of the female culture, self-sacrifice has been one of the most effective psychological blocks to women's open rebellion and demand for self-determination. It has also been a major tool of male manipulation of females.

The institutions of a people are an essential part of their culture. The major institutions of every culture are the same: the family, religion, government, army, and economy. Men and women have a completely different relationship to the institutions of "their" culture. In fact there are two cultures hidden by the appearance of one culture under one set of institutions.

Women are excluded, except sometimes in token numbers and in the lowest working ranks, from participation in government, the army, and religion. There are basically two economic institutions of a society: the substructure or family and the superstructure or outside world of work. Women are limited to an economic dependence in "their" caste work in the family. In work outside the family, women are caste laborers in the lowest-paid drudge work. Women are kept from management or decision-making in work outside the home.

Though it appears that both men and women live together within the institutions of a society, men really define and control the institutions while women live under their rule. The government, army, religion, economy, and family are institutions of the male culture's colonial rule over the female.

A FEMALE CULTURE EXISTS. IT IS A CULTURE THAT IS SUBORDINATED AND UNDER MALE CULTURE'S COLONIAL, IMPERIALIST RULE ALL OVER THE WORLD. UNDERNEATH THE SURFACE OF EVERY NATIONAL, ETHNIC, OR RACIAL CULTURE IS THE SPLIT BETWEEN THE TWO PRIMARY CULTURES OF THE WORLD—THE FEMALE CULTURE AND THE MALE CULTURE.

National cultures vary greatly according to the degree of the suppression of the female culture. The veil and seclusion of women and their almost total segregation in Arab culture make for differences between them and, for example, Swedish women. A Swedish woman may not be able to tolerate the suppressed life of Arab women but she also, if she is sensitive, may not be able to tolerate her suppression as a female in Sweden. Crossing national boundaries often awakens a woman's understanding of her position in society. We cannot, like James Baldwin, even temporarily escape from our caste role to Paris or another country. It is everywhere; there is no place to escape.

The repression of female culture is only a question of degree all over the world; the underlying reality is basically the same: the denial of self-determination for women. Women traveling to a foreign country can readily communicate and understand other women in that country because female work and roles (culture) are basically the same all over the world. But it too often happens that women falsely identify with "their" country's dominant male culture and so cannot communicate with their sisters in subjection in other lands or in other races. This female identification with male cultural supremacy must be overcome if the Women's Movement is to be a truly liberating force.

Most males all over the world perceive and compare females as a caste group. A male of any culture perceives a woman as a woman first and only secondly as "representing" a national or ethnic culture. And he treats every woman as females as a caste are treated. The "Miss World" and "Miss Universe" etc. female flesh auctions, comparing various nationalities of female flesh, are only one example of many. The best way for any woman to find out the truth of this statement is to do some traveling to different countries.

"National" Culture is the Dominant Male Culture

Whoever defines and controls the institutions of a society controls that society. Males define and control all the institutions of all "national" cultures—including every purportedly socialist nation that has ever existed.

Because the male culture is dominant and in control in every nation, the "national" culture becomes synonymous with, and in fact is, the male culture. The female culture exists "invisibly," in subjection to the male-defined "national" culture.

What appears as one national culture, due to male propaganda, is in reality the male culture setting itself up as *the* national culture through subordination of the female. The male army, the male government, the male religion, the male-run economy, the male-defined institution of the family, along with the male culture in the "narrower" sense—i.e., the male arts, sciences, philosophy, and technology—are defined as *the* national culture when in fact they represent nothing but the male view and male interests.

One national culture vs. another national culture is simply one male-dominated society vs. another male-dominated society, with women carried along or used outside their subservient role temporarily if this is necessary for victory of the male national culture. Women are obviously hurt doubly by the imposition on them of two male-dominated cultures—one "their" own males', the other the foreign males'. But the confusion comes when "our" own males, who dominate and define the female culture, refuse to recognize that for women it is simply two dominant male cultures that have to be resisted. "Our" own male dominators always want us *only* to resist the *other* males' domination in the guise of fending off the destruction of "our common culture"—which they have always excluded us from and subordinated us to.

Because of this identification of the male culture with the national, ethnic, racial, or revolutionary culture, some very oppressive male-supremacist attitudes are widespread in national and racial liberation movements. For this reason it is extremely important to make a clear distinction between national or racial liberation and female liberation, although the basis is the same: self-determination. Fanon, for example, in the chapter called "Algeria Unveiled" in *A Dying Colonialism*, makes the mistake of confusing the two and exposes his own identification with male cultural supremacy. Fanon takes the veil as the symbol of Arab and Algerian culture:

> The veil worn by the women appears with such constancy that it generally suffices to characterize Arab society. . . . The way people clothe themselves, together with the tradition of dress and finery that custom implies, constitutes the most distinctive form of a society's uniqueness. . . . [p. 35]

Now the veil can be seen as a distinctly Arabian cultural trait or a national cultural trait. We have shown that the national culture is synonomous with the male culture. In this case the male Arab culture has a unified way of defining and limiting the female through the veil. The female cultural suppression is symbolically represented by the veil, which must be worn by females from the age of puberty on.

Fanon is correct in saying that the French tried to destroy Algerian (male) culture and that this is a typical colonial tactic of one male culture vs. another colonized male culture. But Fanon shows a typical male inability to see the brutal colonization of females by males. In his use of the veil as a symbol of Algerian culture that the French were trying to destroy, he oversimplifies in order to avoid a recognition of his own male guilt and the Algerian males' culpability toward the Algerian females' repressed and demeaned culture.

If Fanon were more honest he would recognize that the French, as a male culture, had no more interest in the Algerian woman's freedom than the Algerian male had. But Fanon, who has such passionate anger against the French colonizers, does not extend his vision to demand justice for the Algerian female. In fact he pooh-poohs the idea that Algerian women are oppressed at all. Nowhere, except in what he reveals unknowingly, does he admit the fact of female oppression by the male in Algeria. (We will later quote an Algerian woman who, for obvious reasons, does not share his bigoted blindness on the colonized status of women in Algeria.) Fanon says:

> To begin with there is the much-discussed status of the Algerian woman—her alleged confinement, her lack of importance, her humility, her silent existence bordering on quasi-absence. And "Moslem society" had made no place for her, amputating her personality, allowing her neither development nor maturity, maintaining her in a perpetual infantilism. . . . Such affirmations, illuminated by "scientific works," are today receiving the only valid challenge: the experience of revolution. [pp. 65, 66]

For one who is so concerned with the psychological mutilation of the colonized group, this statement shows a callousness equaled only by colonial French statements about the "non-oppression" of French rule. Compare this to a statement Fanon made about the mutilation of the Algerian personality by the French:

> French colonialism has settled itself in the very center of the Algerian individual and has undertaken a sustained work of cleanup, of expulsion of self, of rationally pursued mutilation. [p. 65]

But not only does Fanon deny the existence of female oppression in Algeria, like any other colonizer he must justify it as chosen by the colonized:

> The Algerian woman's ardent love of the home is not a limitation imposed by the universe [no, it was imposed by males]. It is not flight from the world. The Algerian woman, in *imposing such a restriction on herself* [in not taking off the veil, and staying home], in *choosing* a form of existence limited in scope, was deepening her consciousness of struggle and preparing for combat. [p. 66]

In this a typical male-supremacist attitude emerges. Women who give up their own struggle for freedom are the most "conscious" women if they are then prepared to fight alongside their male oppressors. Fanon says: "What was most essential was that the occupier should come up against a united front." [p. 66] And a united front means women must give up their "silly, trivial" ideas of a female anti-colonial movement and fight in the male-dominated "anti-"colonial revolution.

Fanon shows that the Algerian national liberation struggle was a male struggle and that when, out of necessity, women were included, they were under male leadership and control.

> Until 1955, the combat was waged exclusively by the men. The revolutionary characteristics of this combat, the necessity for absolute secrecy, obliged the militant to keep his woman in absolute ignorance [p. 48]

Fanon never questions what made possible the male's position of fighting and the female's of being kept in ignorance. He never questions male control of the revolution. He states: "As the enemy gradually adapted himself to the forms of combat, new difficulties appeared which required original solutions." [p. 48] Among the "original solutions" was the possibility of including women in the fighting—but not really in the revolution, because women were not to be freed by it. The excuse given before was male chivalry: after all, women might get tortured and killed. But when it was necessary to use women the chivalry arguments were conveniently forgotten.

The decision to involve women was made wholly by males. "The decision to involve women as active elements of the Algerian Revolution was not reached lightly." [p. 48] But before it was decided to include women in the revolution, the male revolutionists came up against the effects of their own colonization of women. They pondered how the Algerian woman's colonized status in relation to Algerian males might interfere with her "use" in the revolution. Fanon never says it occurred to the Algerian males that Algerian women needed to engage in an anti-colonial resistance to Algerian male domination. Women's colonized status was seen simply as an obstacle to her "use."

> Having been accustomed to confinement, her body did not have the normal mobility before a limitless horizon of avenues, of unfolded sidewalks, of houses, of people dodged or bumped into. This relatively cloistered [i.e. slave] life, with its known, categorized, regulated [by males] comings and goings, made an immediate revolution seem a dubious proposition. The political leaders were perfectly familiar with these problems [i.e., with the

suppressed status of Algerian females], and their hesitations expressed their consciousness of their responsibilities. They were
entitled to doubt the success of this measure. Would not such a
decision [to involve Algerian women] have catastrophic consequences for the progress of the Revolution? [p. 49]

Here the revolution is defined as male and women are to be used;
but female liberation is never considered. In fact, the idea is how
to use women without too much upsetting their colonial status.

In the final decision to "admit" them to the revolution, women,
naturally, were not consulted:

After a final series of meetings among leaders, *and especially in
view of the urgency of the daily problems that the Revolution
faced*, the decision to concretely involve women in the national
struggle was reached. [p. 51; emphasis added]

Fanon waxes euphoric in discussing Algerian womanhood's role in
the revolution. Even though woman's position in Algerian society
did not change during or after the revolution, he continues to state
that women fought as sisters alongside the Algerian brothers and
this proves that the Algerian women are not slaves of the Algerian
men. In fact it only shows that the Algerian men needed them and
were able to tolerate them outside of their traditional role in order
to win the revolutionary battle. There are many quotes from Fanon
to show that women within the revolution had a subservient role. He
makes some incredibly paternalistic remarks about "accepting"
women's "support" in the revolution. This seems to show a subconscious understanding on his part that it was a revolution made
by and for the Algerian males. He says:

The married women whose husbands were militants were the first
to be chosen. Later, widows or divorced women were designated.
In any case, there were never any unmarried girls—first of all,
because a girl of even twenty or twenty-three hardly ever has
occasion to leave the family domicile unaccompanied. But the
woman's duties as mother and spouse, the desire to limit to the
minimum the possible consequences of her arrest and her death,
and also the more and more numerous volunteering of unmarried
girls, led the political leaders [male] to make another leap, to
remove all restrictions, to accept indiscriminately the support of
all Algerian women. [p. 51]

Notice that he said "support" instead of "equal participation."

The Algerian woman's role was limited and defined by the males in spite of Fanon's glowing rhetoric about her equality in the revolution and how this gave the lie to accusations of Algerian male unfairness to her.

> ... the Algerian woman assumes all the tasks entrusted to her. Among the tasks entrusted to the Algerian woman is the bearing of messages or complicated verbal orders learned by heart, sometimes despite complete absence of schooling. But she is also called upon to stand watch for an hour and often more, before a house where district leaders are conferring. [p. 53]

That the district and revolutionary leaders are all male and do not include women in the decision-making is evident from a number of statements (emphasis is added):

> During those interminable minutes when she must avoid standing still, so as not to attract attention, and avoid venturing too far since she is responsible for the safety of the *brothers* within, incidents that are at once funny and pathetic are not infrequent. [p. 53]
> Meanwhile the woman who might be acting as a liaison agent, as a bearer of tracts, as she walked some hundred or two hundred meters ahead of the *man under whose orders she was working,* still wore a veil.... [p. 51]

Fanon reveals the hypocrisy of the male Third World when he mocks the "allegations" that the Algerian female is oppressed. His defense of Algerian male culture is every bit as smooth as the French justification of colonial rule. And he denies female oppression under the guise of defending the Algerian national culture from vulture-like attacks by the French. No one will doubt that the French were brutal colonizers of the Algerians, but that does not either deny or excuse the equally brutal colonization of Algerian females by Algerian males. Fanon says:

> ... the dominant administration solemnly undertook to defend this woman, pictured as humiliated, sequestered, cloistered.... It described the immense possibilities of woman, unfortunately transformed by the Algerian man into an inert, demonetized, indeed dehumanized object. The behavior of the Algerian was very firmly denounced and described as medieval and barbaric.
>
> Lamentations were organized. "We want to make the Algerian ashamed of the fate that he metes out to women." Algerian women were invited to play a "functional, capital role" in the transforma-

tion of their lot. They were pressed to say no to a centuries-old subjection.

After it had been posited that the woman constituted the pivot of Algerian society, all efforts were made to obtain control over her. [p. 38]

Never once does Fanon see the Algerian woman simply as a pawn of both the French male-supremacist culture and the Algerian males, neither of whom were interested in her humanity. What he does instead is to deny her oppression and then to sympathize with Algerian male colonists who used her oppression as a symbol of their manhood and Algerian culture. In fact he is terribly moved by the plight of the Algerian male in his fight to retain control over "his woman." The Algerian male has his manhood (synonymous with male culture and control) destroyed by any attempts to "free" the Algerian woman. So he clings more tenaciously to his dominance, which he equates with his culture.

Converting the woman ... wrenching her free from her status, was at the same time achieving a real power over the man and attaining a practical effective means of destructuring Algerian culture.

The Algerian men, for their part, are a target of criticism for their European comrades, or more officially for their bosses. "Does your wife wear the veil? Why don't you take your wife to the movies, to the fights, or to the cafe? ... The boss will invite the Algerian employee and his wife. Before this formal summons, the Algerian sometimes experiences moments of difficulty. If he comes with his wife, it means admitting defeat, it means prostituting his wife, exhibiting her, abandoning a mode of resistance.... [There are] traps set by the European in order to bring the Algerian to expose himself, to declare: "My wife wears a veil, she shall not go out," or else to betray: "Since you want to see her, here she is," would bring out the sadistic and perverse character of these contacts and relationships and would show in microcosm the tragedy of the colonial situation on the psychological level, the way the two systems directly confront each other, the epic of the colonized society, with its specific ways of existing, in the face of the colonialist hydra. [pp. 39, 40]

It seems never to occur to Fanon that the "sadistic and perverse character of these contacts and relationships" between the male and female in Algerian culture shows also the "tragedy of the colonial situation" of females "on the psychological level." Fanon, for all his justified bitterness and hatred of the French and European colonizer, does not have a corresponding sense of justice for the plight of the colonized Algerian female.

Perhaps it would be too difficult, psychologically, to admit that the Algerian males have been doing to the Algerian females for many centuries what has been done to Algeria for 130 years by the French. Perhaps it would not be so easy to appear the "innocent" oppressed if the Algerian males had also to admit their own colonial rule of Algerian females. Because the Algerian male then might have to identify consciously with his own French oppressor to see his own role in relation to "his" women. This is why Fanon reacts so vehemently against the idea—the actual facts—of female domination by the Algerian male. And this is probably why the French male colonizers knew they could cut so deep on this issue.

But there is such a thing as justice, whether our own personal guilt is touched or not. And if, as Fanon so passionately argued, anything necessary to win freedom for the oppressed colonial culture is to be done, then he should honestly accept that principle for the colonial oppression of women. Otherwise he should reconsider whether he himself as a male does not have a strong interest in and identification with being a colonial oppressor. Perhaps he should then consider what this means in terms of his philosophy of violence and terrorism for the "unredeemable" oppressor. Perhaps women too can achieve catharsis through terrorism against the colonial male culture. But does Fanon want that? Does any male "revolutionary" want that?

The Betrayal of Female Culture in the Anti-Imperialist Revolution

All of Fanon's emotional sympathy is wrapped up with the male Algerian wherever it is a question of two male cultures—European and Algerian—clashing over who will control the colonized status of the female Algerian. But a female has a different view of things —that is, a female who can see through both the European and Algerian colonial male cultures.

A few years after Algeria won its independence, Fadela M'Rabet, an Algerian woman, wrote a book entitled *La Femme Algérienne* (published by Maspero). In it she charged that the women who fought in the Resistance were used in the Algerian nationalist revolution only to be returned to their former subservience after "independence" was gained. She said that not very many women participated in the struggle and their lives were never affected in any way. She compared the position of women in Algeria before and after the "revolution" to the position of black Africans in South Africa, and cites case after case of the oppression of women in "liberated" Algeria. She says:

> In order to understand the situation of the woman (and her reactions) it is necessary to start with the man; if she submits or revolts, if she accepts her condition or does not, the Algerian woman has evolved in a world which is made by men, for men, and at his advantage only. The Constitution, without doubt, and the resolutions of the Congress proclaim the equality of all citizens; but the gap is such between the texts and the facts that all is as if the texts did not exist.
>
> Socially the most honorable, the state of the married woman is, *in fact,* as degrading as that of the concubine. . . . The mother, the wife; there is for the Algerian man a third category of women— the sister. And if it is not very comfortable to be the mistress or the wife of an Algerian man, it is nearly a calamity to be his sister . . . it is allowed to him to completely dominate her.

Let us listen to another Algerian woman concerning the "cultural symbol" of the Arab culture, the veil. Claudine, in an interview in a *New York Times Magazine* article (October, 1967) after Algerian independence was won, said that she was lucky that her father allowed her to go to school and not wear the veil. Most Algerian girls get no schooling—even after the revolution—because, as Fadela M'Rabet has said, too much schooling for a girl is considered very dangerous by the male society. But the local Mufti intervened when Claudine was sixteen. By that time there were only two other girls in her class at the lycée, and twenty-five boys. The other girls went veiled. The Mufti insisted that Claudine do the same or quit school; her father would be banned from the Mosque if she refused. She says:

> . . . so I had to agree. The Mufti still complained though. When I rode to school, he always stood watching for me, and I had to get down off my bicycle and kiss his hand on my way to and from school. It wasn't easy because in Constantine they don't use the nose veil. There is just a great big square you wrap all around

you, covering everything except one eye. You have to hold it closed with your teeth and your hands. . . .

It is also interesting to note that Ben Bella in 1964—two years after independence—did not share Fanon's opinion that women's oppression was a fabrication of the French colonialists. Ben Bella said at this time:

> There are in our country five million women who submit to a servitude unworthy of Socialist and Moslem Algeria. The liberation of the woman is not a secondary aspect which is to be put under our other objectives: it is a problem, the solution of which is a preliminary to the whole nature of socialism [quoted in *La Femme Algérienne*]

But Fadela M'Rabet lays the blame for women's oppression on the Moslem tradition of male privilege in the home, separation of the sexes in school, and perpetuation of a racist notion that women are objects worthy only of disdain. She says, "If we really want to end our underdeveloped status, then let's not wait. Let's ban apartheid." She argues eloquently for a female revolution now.

> Must we wait several generations under the pretext that our society is not "ready"? We [Algeria] are the product of 130 years of colonialism. *But how many centuries of exploitation have women lived under: Their colonizers have been the men.* [Emphasis added]

We use the example of Algeria only to show that a nationalist, anti-imperialist revolution does not free women because the dominant male culture is identified as the national culture and male supremacy is never attacked.

Women have always been used and abused in male revolutions because the male revolutionists are colonialist imperialists in relation to females. It is as if the Algerians fighting with the French in World War II expected the French to liberate Algeria. The French didn't want to be dominated by another country but they wanted to continue their own domination of Algeria. Males don't want to be dominated by other males or another male culture, but they have no intention of discontinuing their domination of the female culture.

No anti-capitalist, working-class, Third World, anti-imperialist etc. movement will ever free women. There is too much at stake for the male colonialists to ever give up their privileges without a struggle. And they control all of those movements as they control all the national cultures.

The female culture will continue to be betrayed by the ruling male culture and by male revolutionaries whose primary identification is with male culture.

The anti-imperialist movement as it is defined by males is a dead end for women. Males, as members of the dominant male culture in the Third World as well as in the imperialist countries, are equally concerned with maintaining male dominance though they may be in a death struggle between themselves.

Oppressed Groups and the Feminine

There have been a great deal of comparisons of woman's position with the position of minority groups in feminist literature. Particularly, there have been comparisons between stereotypes of black people and women. Women are described as fitting the typical Negro stereotype and comparisons are made between black oppression and female oppression to prove that females are in fact an oppressed group.

But really the analogy should go the other way around. One should compare the stereotypes of blacks and other minority groups and suppressed cultures to the female stereotypes.

Woman was the first group to be oppressed and subordinated as a caste to another group—men. Without going into all the reasons for this subordination, we can still discuss the psychological and cultural results. A schizophrenic split developed when the dominating males projected onto women all of their emotions which they could not reconcile with their self-image and role as dominators, and which they were afraid of and would not allow themselves to be "weakened" by.

This schizophrenic split made female and male definitions into opposites. Generally, since males are defined as the human norm, females are defined as their subhuman negatives. Yin and Yang define the male and female stereotypes as opposites, with females getting the negative characteristics. Men are seen as "day," positive, forceful, aggressive, dominant, objective, strong, intellective, etc. Women have been defined for thousands of years as weak, "night," passive, emotional, intuitive, mysterious, unresponsible, quarrelsome, childish, dependent, evil, submissive, etc.

(A study was done at Worcester State Hospital in Massachusetts using a sex-role questionnaire with over a hundred polar items, one pole being stereotypically male and the other stereotypically female. The subjects, a group of clinical professionals, assigned a mentally healthy adult and a mentally healthy male the same characteristics. But a mentally healthy female was seen as passive, emotional, dependent, less competitive, non-objective, submissive, and more easily influenced. —*Psychology Today*, September, 1970, p. 53.)

As females were the first colonized group and the first to be stereotyped as a caste, male culture, when it extended its boundaries and subjected other males or male cultures to its rule, defined them as inferior by assigning them female characteristics. Female characteristics were the only negative characteristics the male culture knew.

A male as a male in relation to females is defined by all the masculine stereotypes, but that same male in subjection to another male is defined as inferior through having female qualities. He is then "effeminate" or passive, or weak—all of which are female stereotypes. This idea can be extended to a culture. One male culture which dominates and controls another male culture defines the subservient males and their culture as feminine, i.e., all the female stereotypes become the minority stereotypes for the subjected males. They are defined, by being subservient, as mysterious, emotional, intuitive, personal, childlike, evil, irresponsible, quarrelsome, passive, dependent, etc. This holds for all subjected male national cultures and racial cultures.

But the female within the subjected male national or racial culture is defined twice as female. In other words, her definition as a female is her primary definition. For example a black woman is defined as a woman by all the female stereotypes—as passive, emotional, intuitive, personal, mysterious, quarrelsome, irresponsible, dependent, etc. The imposition of these stereotypes on her again in the form of racial stereotypes is unnecessary as they are basically the imposition of female stereotypes on the males of the race. And when the racial battle is won and her race is free, she will realize that the stereotypes—though they no longer oppress her man—are still her defining stereotypes as a woman. He now has his manhood back (defined as opposites of female stereotypes), but she continues to be defined by her womanhood as inferior.

The problem of male supremacy comes in again when national

(male) and racial (male) cultures repudiate the female characterizations and stereotypes assigned to them in revolting against
their male dominators. What happens is that they assert their manhood, i.e., male dominance stereotypes, against the female stereotypes which they have come to loathe as depriving them of virility
and their "natural" "birthright" as dominators, i.e. males. They
make a super-identification with the male culture in reaction to the
female. They try to become tough super-males in reaction to the
imposition of female stereotypes upon them. Then we have the
"don't deprive me of my manhood, i.e. balls" and "stand behind
me, woman, where you belong" syndrome. Often there is such a
strong open reaction against the female culture that the females of
the suppressed national or racial group are threatened and defined
as castrating females if they don't become invisible and get where
they belong—in the subservient female culture, into silence, and
"prone" as Stokely Carmichael once said.

The males of the suppressed national or racial group never question the values of the male culture which impinges upon them and
which they impose upon "their" women. They accept the right of a
male to dominate but feel it should be limited to females and revolt
to overthrow the dominant male culture's rule over them.

The problem is that the original split between the stereotypes of
male and female which started this whole mess will never be resolved by the suppressed male national or racial culture, as the
suppressed males are too busy trying to prove they are super-males
and that they don't have female characteristics in any way. They
loathe the female principle as having defined them as inferiors—
with its symbolic castration.

Up With the Female Principle

Only the suppressed female culture in all races, in all lands, can
be proud of the female principle. For females need not prove their
"manhood," as they can never be males or a part of the dominant
male world culture. Therefore women will be forced, by the very
fact of being female, to defend and raise the banner of the female
principle.

All of the female culture traits are defined as negatives by the
dominant world culture. We do not believe them to be so (except

all those that keep us subservient, such as passivity, self-sacrifice, etc.).

We are proud of the female culture of emotion, intuition, love, personal relationships, etc., as the most essential human characteristics. It is our male colonizers—it is the male culture—who have defined essential humanity out of their identity and who are "culturally deprived."

We are also proud as females of our heritage of known and unknown resisters to male colonial domination and values.

We are proud of the female principle and will not deny it to gain our freedom.

It is only by asserting the long suppressed and ridiculed female principle that a truly human society will come about. For the split between the male and the female will only be bridged and a fully human identity developed—encompassing in each person all human characteristics which were previously split up into male and female —when the female principle and culture is no longer suppressed and male domination is ended forever.

We identify with all women of all races, classes, and countries all over the world. The female culture is the Fourth World.

Author's Postscript

The female culture and the male culture are not natural; they are artificial creations of a male-dominated world. The artificial split between what has been defined as female and what has been defined as male has nothing to do with the inherent nature or potential of females or males. The definitions of the male principle and female principle and the female and male cultures are social definitions only. They are abstractions of a primal abstraction—the splitting up of the whole human personality into the caricatures known as male and female, masculine and feminine.

This "Manifesto" was never intended to be a glorification of the female principle and culture. It was never intended to imply that women have more "soul" than men or that women are inherently more human than men. It is simply a truth that there is a split between the female and male and that the female half of life has been suppressed by the male half of life. Those things which have been socially defined as female have been suppressed in males and suppressed in society through the oppression of females.

If one is born a male one is taught to repress one's "female" self and to develop only those things which will make one a true "man" and a part of the male culture. If one is born a female one is taught to repress that part of oneself which is "male" and to develop only those parts of the self which will make one a "true woman" and able to fit into the submissive female culture.

The extreme of the male culture has become a grotesque carica-ture of part of the potential inherent in every human being, whether female or male. Why are so many blind to the grotesqueness of the tough, hard, super-balls, insensitive, unemotional male image in John Wayne, James Bond, the Marines, etc.? Or so blind to the grotesqueness of the super-mind, intellect, reasoning, and abstrac-tion removed from any connection with life in the "think tanks" of the Rand Corporation, the academy, the corporations, the Army Corps of Engineers, most scientific research, war games strategies, etc.?

The extreme of the female culture has also become a grotesque caricature of the potential inherent in every human being. Why are so many blind to the grotesqueness of the super-sex goddesses, the sex-object removed from mind and emotion, the motherhood myth, the pettily personal existence which is not allowed to transcend itself into the individual autonomous existence, the enforced delicacy without full feeling and intensity, the sentiment turned into bathos because removed from direct sexual or creative expression, etc.?

The abstractions of male and female are extreme and many people are not molded wholly into either category—there is a great deal of overlap. But no one in the society is allowed to be a whole human being as long as the tyranny of the male and female culture or sex role split exists.

Recently there has been an unfortunate reaction among some women's liberationists and feminists. Some women have begun to call anything which they do not like "male." They seem to think that anything that has been defined as a "male quality" is inherently bad. A woman who is strong or takes initiative is told that she is "acting like a man" or "talking like a man." The crushing of initia-tive and strength and self-expression in women is now being done by other women in the movement under the guise of "anti-elitism," "anti-male-identification," and "collective self-suppression." It would be a tragedy if women were to make our oppressed state into a virtue and a model of humanity and the new society. We need to sift out what is good in our imposed definition as females and to honestly examine what is stupid and self-destructive. We need also to sift out what is good in what has been defined as male and therefore denied expression in us. We need no more glorification of the oppressed and their "super-soul" and "superior" culture, for that will blind us to our weaknesses and only lead us back into the same mire from which we have been trying to free ourselves.

Neither the male culture nor the female culture is a model for a human society.

It is true that women have no recourse other than to rise up in a strong feminist movement to end male domination. We must have our own independent women's movement free from male interference and domination. But we should not lose sight of our ultimate goals. There is a danger that the women's movement will help destroy its own ends if the split between the female and male is made into a new feminist orthodoxy. The women's movement has to be free enough to explore and change the entire range of human relationships and it must be open enough to heal the split between the female and male and draw out the total human potential of every person. If we want to be free as female human beings, we must really be willing to end the split of the human personality that has cut men off from a part of themselves and which has caused untold suffering to women.

The Selling of a Feminist

by Claudia Dreifus

Claudia Dreifus is a former union organizer and a founder of Media Women, in which she is currently active. She's a free-lance writer who has contributed to Nation, Evergreen, McCalls, Social Policy, Realist, and Cosmopolitan, and is the author of Radical Lifestyles published by Lancer. She is currently at work on a book on consciousness raising.

(Review of THE FEMALE EUNUCH by Germaine Greer)

Early last year, when the high priests of publishing began to discover that their female readers were insatiably curious about the women's liberation idea, there was much discussion as to which of the bountiful crop of feminist authors would become the big femme lib superstar. Betty Friedan had no appeal for the literary lions— she was too old, too bourgeoise, too organization-conscious. Shulamith Firestone, the author of *The Dialectic of Sex* and organizer of New York Radical Feminists, was strikingly attractive; but alas, anti-love, perhaps even anti-men. Ti-Grace Atkinson, an advocate of extra-uterine birth, was considered too far out for a whirl through the major networks. For a while it seemed as if the brilliant and beautiful Kate Millett, whose *Sexual Politics* was for a short time on the best-seller list, might be star material. But she made the mistake of openly asserting her bisexuality. *Time* took due note of this state of affairs, and that finished Millett. So who was left to launch on the Dick Cavett-Johnny Carson-Virginia Graham-*Time-Life* circuit? American feminists, with their dogged determination to be themselves, were a publicity man's nightmare. Someone more palatable would have to be found.

Or even imported. On a warm spring day, Germaine Greer, the

author of the English best seller, *The Female Eunuch*, jetted into New York from London. Miss Greer was everything those messy American feminists were not: pretty, predictable, aggressively heterosexual, media-wise, clever, foreign, and exotic. Her background was fascinating. At thirty-two, she was an accomplished actress, a Ph.D. who lectured in Shakespeare at Warwick University, editor of the European pornographic journal, *Suck*, and contributor to various London underground newspapers. Her philosophy, as outlined in *The Female Eunuch*, could be expected to appeal to men: women's liberation means that women will be sexually liberated; feminism equals free love. Here was a libbie a man could like.

Full-page ads announced that Miss Greer had written the women's liberation book of the year, and that despite this achievement, she was "a feminist leader who admittedly loves men." Six feet tall, fashion-model beautiful, Miss Greer was the toast of *The Tonight Show*. Dick Cavett was enthusiastic about her. Norman Mailer suggested that her book was worth reading.

There is a catch to this fairy tale. Germaine Greer is not the feminist leader she is advertised to be. Back home in London she has no active connections with any women's liberation group. And the book she has written is hardly feminist. True, *The Female Eunuch* does contain an obligatory enumeration of the many economic and psychological horrors that women are subjected to. But Miss Greer's information is hardly new, and could be gleaned from a half-dozen other books. What's more, the whole tone of *The Female Eunuch* is shallow, anti-woman, regressive, three steps backward to the world of false sexual liberation from which so many young women have fled.

Miss Greer quite rightly asks women to abandon the institution of marriage, but she means to replace it simply with the dehumanizing, anonymous, and spiritually debilitating thrusting that men call sex. In her view, sex is something to be collected—like money. The more of it you get, the richer you are. The difficulty is that many feminists have been to that movie before. Many of the younger women in the movement recall a period, four or five years ago, when in order to qualify as hip, emancipated females, their alternate-culture brothers insisted they perform as sexual gymnasts. Resentment at this treatment is one powerful motive for the current women's movement.

The author's insistence that "sexual liberation" is the prerequisite for women's liberation has a lot to do with the fact that she thinks like a man. She has done very well in the male world, and she has yet to identify herself with the essential condition of women. From her book, one learns that Germaine Greer has rarely (except during a miserable youth) had to suffer the kinds of misfortune that most women endure. She was always accepted in the world of men. She was always treated as an equal. That good fortune just about disqualifies her for writing a feminist book. She has had no experience of what it means to be adult and female in the world inhabited by most women, and she does not have the gift of imagination that could make up for that lack. Indeed, she consistently takes a viewpoint that is not merely male but inimical to women. Her book is littered with unkind and unfeminist snipes at her sisters. Most of the women in her book are described as whiny, simpy, and boring. "As a female lecturer at a provincial university," she complains in a typical passage, "I have to tolerate the antics of faculty wives, but they are strikingly easy to ignore." What separates Germaine Greer from women's liberationists is that a sensitive feminist would regard a faculty wife's failings as the end product of a useless, oppressive, and unfulfilling life. A feminist would feel sisterly sympathy for the faculty wife, and be interested in working with her to help change her condition.

Aside from the author's obvious misogyny, she exhibits very little respect for those women who are organizing against sexual oppression. Her chapters on "Rebellion" and "Revolution" are packed with contradictory ranting about how the women's revolution must be part of The Bigger Revolution, how the feminist movement is not militant enough, how the movement is too middle class. On the one hand, she exhorts the women's liberationists to be more militant in their fight against sexism. On the other, she suggests that women make love, not war. "Women cannot be liberated from their impotence by the gun . . . . The process has to be the opposite: women must humanize the penis, take the steel out of it and make it flesh again."

If Miss Greer has no patience with the state of the feminist movement, she has even less love for the literary women who have aligned themselves with it. Betty Friedan is described as middle class and boring. Kate Millett "persists in assuming that [Norman] Mailer is a cretin." Anne Koedt, author of the important Women's

Liberation pamphlet, "The Myth of the Vaginal Orgasm," is dismissed this way: "One wonders just whom Miss Koedt has gone to bed with."

On the whole, *The Female Eunuch* is a grossly inconsistent book. Yes, Germaine Greer says all the right things about the economics of sexism. Yes, she is extraordinarily observant about some of the physiological results of our sexual conventions. Her chapters on female anatomy are brilliant. Where she falls down is in her inveterate dislike of women, her idiotic exhortations to revolution and nonviolence alike, and her passionate identification with all things male.

Throughout history there have always been a few women who have been able to fight and seduce their way to the top of the patriarchy. In pre-revolutionary France, these women were highly educated, highly cultivated courtesans who provided intellectual and sexual stimulation for the male nobility. (What self-respecting noble would try to carry on an intelligent discussion with his wife?) Germaine Greer is the closest thing we have to this old-world, old-style courtesan. Nor would she be offended by this description. By her own admission, she is a groupie, a supergroupie—which means that she is a sexual and intellectual consort to the royalty of rock music. On television programs she has made comments like: "I'm really just an intellectual superwhore!"

The Female Eunuch is designed to provide intellectual and sexual thrills to those men who would like to see a feminist revolution because it would take that *one* woman off their back and make a lot more women available to them. How nice to be told that women's liberation will mean the liberation of more women for bed service! One reading of *The Female Eunuch* suggested to me that it had been written to assuage the fears of jittery male chauvinists. A second reading convinced me that if Germaine Greer didn't exist, Norman Mailer would have had to invent her.

Manifestos

Sexual Politics:
A Manifesto for Revolution

by Kate Millett

Kate Millett is a writer, film maker, sculptor and active feminist. She is the author of Sexual Politics and The Prostitution Papers. This manifesto was written in 1968 in connection with the organizational meeting of the first women's liberation group at Columbia University. Both The Columbia Spectator and the Columbia Radio Station refused to publish or broadcast it, even though it was written by a faculty member to whom they had promised the space and time.

When one group rules another, the relationship between the two is political. When such an arrangement is carried out over a long period of time it develops an ideology (feudalism, racism, etc.). All historical civilizations are patriarchies: their ideology is male supremacy.

Oppressed groups are denied education, economic independence, the power of office, representation, an image of dignity and self-respect, equality of status, and recognition as human beings. Throughout history women have been consistently denied all of these, and their denial today, while attenuated and partial, is nevertheless consistent. The education allowed them is deliberately designed to be inferior, and they are systematically programmed out of and excluded from the knowledge where power lies today—e.g., in science and technology. They are confined to conditions of economic dependence based on the sale of their sexuality in marriage, or a variety of prostitutions. Work on a basis of economic independence allows them only a subsistence level of life—often not even that. They do not hold office, are represented in no positions of power, and authority is forbidden them. The image of women fostered by cultural media, high and low, then and now, is a marginal and demeaning existence, and one outside the human condition—which is defined as the prerogative of man, the male.

Government is upheld by power, which is supported through consent (social opinion), or imposed by violence. Conditioning to an ideology amounts to the former. But there may be a resort to the latter at any moment when consent is withdrawn—rape, attack, sequestration, beatings, murder. Sexual politics obtains consent through the "socialization" of both sexes to patriarchal policies. They consist of the following:

1) the formation of human personality along stereotyped lines of sexual category, based on the needs and values of the master class and dictated by what he would cherish in himself and find convenient in an underclass: aggression, intellectuality, force and efficiency for the male; passivity, ignorance, docility, "virtue," and ineffectuality for the female.

2) the concept of sex role, which assigns domestic service and attendance upon infants to all females and the rest of human interest, achievement and ambition to the male; the charge of leader at all times and places to the male, and the duty of follower, with equal uniformity, to the female.

3) the imposition of male rule through institutions: patriarchal religion, the proprietary family, marriage, "The Home," masculine oriented culture, and a pervasive doctrine of male superiority.

A Sexual Revolution would bring about the following conditions, desirable upon rational, moral and humanistic grounds:

1) the end of sexual repression—freedom of expression and of sexual mores (sexual freedom has been partially attained, but it is now being subverted beyond freedom into exploitative license for patriarchal and reactionary ends).

2) Unisex, or the end of separatist character-structure, temperament and behavior, so that each individual may develop an entire—rather than a partial, limited, and conformist—personality.

3) re-examination of traits categorized into "masculine" and "feminine," with a total reassessment as to their human usefulness and advisability in both sexes. Thus if "masculine" violence is undesirable, it is so for both sexes; "feminine" dumb-cow passivity

likewise. If "masculine" intelligence or efficiency is valuable, it is so for both sexes equally, and the same must be true for "feminine" tenderness or consideration.

4) the end of sex role and sex status, the patriarchy and the male supremacist ethic, attitude and ideology—in all areas of endeavor, experience, and behavior.

5) the end of the ancient oppression of the young under the patriarchal proprietary family, their chattel status, the attainment of the human rights presently denied them, the professionalization and therefore improvement of their care, and the guarantee that when they enter the world, they are desired, planned for, and provided with equal opportunities.

6) Bisex, or the end of enforced perverse heterosexuality, so that the sex act ceases to be arbitrarily polarized into male and female, to the exclusion of sexual expression between members of the same sex.

7) the end of sexuality in the forms in which it has existed historically—brutality, violence, capitalism, exploitation, and warfare —that it may cease to be hatred and become love.

8) the attainment of the female sex to freedom and full human status after millennia of deprivation and oppression, and of both sexes to a viable humanity.

The Feminists:
A Political Organization
to Annihilate Sex Roles

The following represents the thought of THE FEMINISTS as of the dates attached. Since that time the analysis of the group has undergone considerable change. Specifically, THE FEMINISTS has discarded the notion generally accepted by popular feminism that the sex-role system defines the oppression of women or that our enemy is the male role. The inadequacy of the sex-role theory of oppression becomes obvious when one considers its implication: that both men and women are oppressed by their respective sex-roles. Which is comparable to: both slaves and masters are oppressed by the slave system. By adopting this theory the women's movement has managed to skirt the issue of power and its relationship to oppression. Our present theory, The Function-Activity Theory, relates oppression and power by defining oppression in terms of confinement to *inherently* powerless activities. An explanation of this interpretation as well as a criticism of the sex-role theory can be obtained from THE FEMINISTS, 120 Liberty Street, New York.

History

On October 17, 1968, New York City, a group of feminists decided to begin a new kind of feminist movement: radical feminism. Most of us had been crossing organizational lines during the past year in the attempt to formulate an adequate solution to the persecution of women. But it had finally become evident that what we were groping for was not the sum of current ideas on women, but

This article first appeared in *Notes From the Second Year.*

an approach altogether new not only to feminism but to political theory as well.

We decided to operate under the transitional name of the day of our beginning, *October 17th,* until we were prepared to outline our analysis of the class condition of women and its implications and to present our program for the elimination of that class condition. We are now ready to present our analysis and plan and, therefore, announce the formation of our organization: THE FEMINISTS.

June 13, 1969

I. Conceptual Analysis

The class separation between men and women is a political division. It is in the interests of those individuals who assume the powerful role and against the interests of those assigned the powerless role. The role (or class) system must be destroyed.

The role system is neither necessary to nor in the interests of society. It distorts the humanity of the Oppressor and denies the humanity of the Oppressed. The members of the powerful class substitute the appropriation of others to extend the significance of their own existence as an alternative to individual self-creativity. The members of the powerless class are thereby prevented from individual self-creativity. The role system is an attempt to justify living for those who believe there is no possible justification for life in and of itself.

Women, or "females," were the first class to be separated out from humanity and thus denied their humanity. While men performed this expulsion, it is the male role or the role of the Oppressor that must be annihilated—not necessarily those individuals who presently claim the role. Men, as the only possible embodiment of the male role and as the first embodiment of the Oppressor role, are the enemies and the Oppressors of women. The female role is the product of the male role: it is the female's self-defense against the external coercions imposed by the male role. But because the female role is the internal adjustment of the female to the male role, the female role stabilizes the role system. Both the male role and the female role must be annihilated.

It is clear that, in addition to the role system, all those institutions which reinforce these humanly restrictive definitions must be eliminated. But we are not sure yet how many forms in human culture are patterned on the role system. Certainly all those institutions which were designed on the assumption and for the reinforcement of the male and female role system such as the family (and its sub-institution, marriage), sex, and love must be destroyed. In order to annihilate these institutions, we must clearly understand the dynamics *within* them. Until we fully understand these dynamics, we cannot know everything that must be eliminated nor the desirable form of our alternative.

All political classes grew out of the male-female role system, were modeled on it, and are rationalized by it and its premises. Once a new class system is established on the basis of this initial one, the new class is then used to reinforce the male-female system. It is necessary for the members of all classes to understand and root out of our value system those principles and justifications for classifying any individual out of humanity.

The pathology of oppression can only be fully comprehended in its primary development: the male-female division. Because the male-female system is primary, the freedom of every oppressed individual depends upon the freeing of every individual from every aspect of the male-female system. The sex roles themselves must be destroyed. If any part of these role definitions is left, the disease of oppression remains and will reassert itself again in new, or the same old, variations throughout society.

In addition, we must propose a moral alternative for the self-justification of life to our present system of the appropriation and denial of other individuals' humanity. We need a new premise for society: that the most basic right of every individual is to create the terms of its own definition.

July 15, 1969

II. Organizational Principles and Structure

THE FEMINISTS is a group of radical feminists committed to intense study of the persecution of women and direct action to eradicate this persecution.

The group is open only to women who accept our principles as recorded in these FEMINISTS papers. Membership must be a primary commitment and responsibility; no other activity may supersede work for the group.

THE FEMINISTS is an action group. The theoretical work we do is aimed directly at studying the means by which women are oppressed so that we may effectively plan positions and actions to fight our oppression. Outside study, participation in discussions, completion of individual assignments *and* attendance at actions are all equally important and compulsory.

In order to achieve the goal of freeing women, the group must maintain discipline. Any member who consistently disrupts or interferes with our discussions or activities may be expelled. A single action which goes against the will of the group, constitutes an exploitation of the group, or seriously endangers its work or survival, is grounds for expulsion. Expulsion of a member requires a two-thirds majority decision of all members present at a meeting about which notification has been sent to all members at least ten days in advance.

Since infiltration of the group is not unlikely, if a member suspects another of being an infiltrator, that member should confront her before a meeting of the group. When the act of infiltration is established to the satisfaction of the group, the agent(s) will be expelled immediately.

THE FEMINISTS is an organization without officers which divides work according to the principle of participation by lot. Our goal is a just society all of whose members are equal. Therefore, we aim to develop knowledge and skills in all members and prevent any one member or small group from hoarding information or abilities.

Traditionally official posts such as the chair of the meeting and the secretary are determined by lot and change with each meeting. The treasurer is chosen by lot to function for one month.

Assignments may be menial or beyond the experience of a member. To assign a member work she is not experienced in may involve an initial loss of efficiency but fosters equality and allows all members to acquire the skills necessary for revolutionary work. When a member draws a task beyond her experience she may call on the knowledge of other members, but her own input and development are of primary importance. The group has the responsibility to support a member's efforts, as long as the group believes that member to be working in good faith. A member has the duty to submit her work for the group—such as articles and speeches—to the group for correction and approval.

In order to make efficient use of all opportunities for writing and speaking, in order to develop members without experience in these areas, members who are experienced in them are urged to withdraw their names from a lot assigning those tasks. Also those members, experienced or inexperienced, who have once drawn a lot to write or speak must withdraw their names until all members have had a turn.

The system of the lot encourages growth by maximizing the sharing of tasks, but the responsibility for contributions rests ultimately with the individual. One's growth develops in proportion to one's contributions.

August 22, 1969

III. Membership Requirements and Benefits

One of the characteristics that distinguishes THE FEMINISTS from other feminist groups is its concern for the human development of each individual in the group. Three assumptions underlie this concern of THE FEMINISTS: (1) that women are deprived of their individuality as human beings, and therefore are entitled to expect from a feminist group every aid in achieving this human right, (2) that groups with leaders are hierarchical, and hierarchy necessarily suppresses the initiative of at least the majority of the membership, and (3) furthermore, as leaderless groups are dependent upon the strength of each member, an equal share in responsibility and creativity to oneself and to the group is necessary. With this concern in mind, the group has constructed the following mechanism for achieving the introduction and integration of new members to confident, creative, and responsible participation in the group.

There are three prerequisites for membership in THE FEMINISTS:

1. Basic agreement with THE FEMINISTS' policy statements.
2. A minimal familiarity with the issues of feminism. It is necessary for each member to develop a working knowledge of the

concepts, the statistics, and the history of feminism, to feel at ease within and to contribute to the group.*

3. Two special orientation meetings concerning THE FEMI-NISTS.† All new members have questions about the history or ideology of a group that should be answered but that would not be profitable for the group as a whole to review. For this reason we have two meetings: (a) for a discussion of personal experiences and issues relevant to feminism; (b) for the clarification of our policy statements.

While THE FEMINISTS requires a certain preparation for membership, it is very interested in what a feminist group can offer its members, both as initiates and as members.‡ The self-development of each individual, relevant to the group, is considered in two of its aspects: self-perception and confidence. At least three concepts within the group were motivated by this concern for individual self-development:

1. Each member through the meetings should develop an awareness and constructive understanding of the particular ways in which feminist analyses are relevant to each member's personality and circumstances.

2. Each member can expect the encouragement of, and should give that encouragement to, the other members to develop each member's areas of special interest(s) relevant to feminism through some medium, e.g., writing, acting, design, radio.

3. Each member is guaranteed, and in return is responsible for, equal development on all levels by the lot system and is expected to participate in equal amounts, both as to tasks and hours, with all other members in all the activities of the group. The lot system adds dimension to the types of experience within each individual's repertoire, and the individual thus gains a sense of self-sufficiency and group spirit.

---

* One method of quickly surveying this material might be to read such books as *The Second Sex*, Simone de Beauvoir; *The Century of Struggle*, Eleanor Flexner; the latest publications from the President's Citizens' Advisory Council on the Status of Women, 1968.

† These meetings may be scheduled together.

‡ Each week, the two individuals who chaired the meeting that week will be available to answer new members' questions outside of meeting time.

1. (a) Because THE FEMINISTS considers each member to have equal responsibility to the group in accordance with the best of that member's abilities at all given times, and

   (b) Because consistent attendance at meetings is considered a minimal ability and responsibility of all members, and

   (c) Because consistent attendance is essential for knowledgeable, i.e., responsible, voting,

ANY MEMBER MISSING MORE THAN ONE-QUARTER OF THE MEETINGS IN ANY GIVEN MONTH FORFEITS VOTING PRIVILEGES UNTIL THE THIRD CONSECUTIVE MEETING OF THAT INDIVIDUAL'S RENEWED ATTENDANCE.

SHOULD THIS OCCUR THREE TIMES IN A THREE MONTH PERIOD WITHOUT A VALID EXCUSE (E.G., EMPLOYMENT OR ILLNESS), THE PERSON INVOLVED IS NO LONGER A MEMBER OF THE FEMINISTS. SHE CAN REAPPLY FOR MEMBERSHIP IF SHE WISHES.

2. (a) Because THE FEMINISTS considers the institution of marriage inherently inequitable, both in its formal (legal) and informal (social) aspects, and

   (b) Because we consider this institution a primary formalization of the persecution of women, and

   (c) Because we consider the rejection of this institution both in theory *and in practice* a primary mark of the radical feminist,

WE HAVE A MEMBERSHIP QUOTA: THAT NO MORE THAN ONE-THIRD OF OUR MEMBERSHIP CAN BE PARTICIPANTS IN EITHER A FORMAL (WITH LEGAL CONTRACT) OR INFORMAL (E.G., LIVING WITH A MAN) INSTANCE OF THE INSTITUTION OF MARRIAGE.

August 8, 1969

IV. Programmatic Analysis

The political class of women consists of all those individuals assigned to the female role—all females. The male-female role system is political because the roles are defined by one group (men); men are the powerful class and women the powerless class; men exert their control by way of institutions—the tools of the male role—which, taken together, form the system which ossifies the female role. All male-female institutions stem from the male-female role system and all are oppressive because (1) they are not only the expressions of this role system but perpetuate this system as well; (2) they are rigid and destroy individuality; (3) they divide (cause competition between) and isolate the oppressed.

In the female role women are defined by their child-bearing capacity which is interpreted as their function. The maternal instinct—desire to bear and raise children—is attributed to women. The concept "maternal instinct"—meaning passivity, unconditional giving, sacrificing, suffering—is used to define woman's so-called "nature," thus it creates the context for her exploitation by men.

We seek the self-development of every individual woman. To accomplish this we must eliminate the institutions built on the myth of maternal instinct which prevent her self-development, i.e., those institutions which enforce the female role.

We must destroy love (an institution by definition), which is generally recognized as approval and acceptance. Love promotes vulnerability, dependence, possessiveness, susceptibility to pain, and prevents the full development of woman's human potential by directing all her energies outward in the interests of others. The family depends for its maintenance on the identification by the woman of her own desires and needs with the desires and needs of the others. Motherhood provides blind approval as a bribe in return for which the mother expects to live vicariously through the child. Between husband and wife love is a delusion in the female that she is both a giver and a receiver, i.e., she sacrifices to get approval from the male. Love is a self-defense developed by the female to prevent her from seeing her powerless situation; it arises from fear when contact with reality provides no alternative to powerlessness. It is protection from the violence of violations by other men. Heterosexual love is a delusion in yet another sense: it is a means of escape from the role system by way of approval from and identification with the man, who has defined himself as humanity (beyond role)—she desires to be him. The identification of each woman's interests with those of a man prevents her from uniting with other women and seeing herself as a member of the class of women.

All contributions to society which do not add to the individual's unique development must be shared equally, e.g., all "wifely" and "motherly" duties. Child-rearing to the extent to which it is necessary is the responsibility of all; children are part of society but they should not be possessed by anyone. Extra-uterine means of reproduction should be developed because the elimination of pain is a humane goal. Marriage and the family must be eliminated.

Friendship between men and women, under the present conditions of inequality, is the pretense that equality and mutual respect exist. So long as the male role exists, men have the option of assuming it; therefore, the relationship is one of jeopardy to women. In actuality, friendship serves to reinforce the female role need for approval and support. True friendship between men and women necessarily presupposes the giving up of all male privileges and the active combatting on the part of the man of male supremacy. Only then can we extend to all a mode of appreciating and understanding each other as unique human beings. This mode must account for free choice, non-dependence, and non-appropriation of others.

We must destroy the institution of heterosexual sex which is a manifestation of the male-female role. Since physical pleasure can be achieved in both sexes by auto-erotic acts, sex as a social act is psychological in nature; at present its psychology is dominance-passivity. One of the ways the female is coerced into sexual relations with the male is by means of satisfying her supposed need to bear children. When reproduction had to be controlled, the myth of vaginal orgasm was created so that the female would remain sexually dependent on the male. The myth of vaginal orgasm stresses intercourse as a primary means of sexual gratification and this emphasis on the genital area and the vagina in particular reinforces the definition of the female as child-bearer even when contraceptives are used to avoid pregnancy.

It is in the interest of the male in the sexual act to emphasize the organ of reproduction in the female because it is the institution of motherhood, in which the mother *serves* the child, which forms the pattern (submission of her will to the other) for her relationship to the male.

If sexual relations were not programmed to support political ends —that is, male oppression of the female—then the way would be clear for individuals to enter into physical relations not defined by roles, nor involving exploitation. Physical relations (heterosexual and homosexual) would be an extension of communication between individuals and would not necessarily have a genital emphasis.

Rape is the simplest and most blatant form of the male wantonly forcing his will on the female. Rape occurs whenever a woman unwillingly submits to the sexual advances of a man. In courtship and marriage, rape is legalized because sexual relations are part of the marriage contract.

Prostitution was created by men as the terrifying alternative to the institution of marriage. The other so-called "alternatives" devised by men are modeled on the principles of prostitution—the principles of debasement and deprivation. Thus, the essence of the female (by male definition) is seen to be that of a sexual object, and is the only means through which she can survive. No female is permitted to maintain existence outside her sex-object/motherhood definition. All work for women in the public area must involve only attitudes and skills applicable to her home functions.

Political institutions such as religion, because they are based on philosophies of hierarchical orders and reinforce male oppression of females, must be destroyed.

The elimination of these institutions requires a program understood in terms of stages. Each stage takes into account the interrelationship of all the institutions and therefore calls for simultaneous attacks on all of them. The strategy requires that all avenues of escape from our destruction of the male role and role system be closed. The web of institutions which must be dealt with are: marriage (and the family—child-bearing and child-rearing), the destruction of which requires the simultaneous destruction of prostitution (and "free" love) and exclusively heterosexual sex; the provision for a real alternative for the female (e.g., guaranteed equal annual income); and a program of reparations (e.g., preferential education and employment).

August 15, 1969

V. Alliances with Other Groups

THE FEMINISTS will not form alliances with other groups except on clearly feminist issues. In addition, the focus of the issues must be consistent with our program. The degree of our involvement (in terms of group time) will be in proportion to how essential it is to our program.

    1. Support—If another group plans an action directly related to a feminist issue, we may give our group support.

2. Cooperation—We will join with another group(s) to plan and execute a single short- or long-term action.
3. Coalition—In this instance we may join with another group(s) in a long-term multifaceted association.

August 26, 1969

THE FEMINISTS
120 Liberty St.
New York, N.Y. 10006
212-344-7750

Politics of the Ego:
A Manifesto For
N.Y. Radical Feminists

Radical feminism recognizes the oppression of women as a fundamental political oppression wherein women are categorized as an
inferior class based upon their sex. It is the aim of radical feminism
to organize politically to destroy this sex class system.

As radical feminists we recognize that we are engaged in a power
struggle with men, and that the agent of our oppression is man
insofar as he identifies with and carries out the supremacy privileges
of the male role. For while we realize that the liberation of women
will ultimately mean the liberation of men from their destructive
role as oppressor, we have no illusion that men will welcome this
liberation without a struggle.

Radical feminism is political because it recognizes that a group
of individuals (men) have organized together for power over
women, and that they have set up institutions throughout society
to maintain this power.

A political power institution is set up for a purpose. We believe
that the purpose of male chauvinism is primarily to obtain psychological ego satisfaction, and that only secondarily does this manifest
itself in economic relationships. For this reason we do not believe
that capitalism, or any other economic system, is the cause of female oppression, nor do we believe that female oppression will
disappear as a result of a purely economic revolution. The political
oppression of women has its own class dynamic; and that dynamic
must be understood in terms previously called "non-political"—
namely the politics of the ego.†

Manifesto adopted by N.Y. Radical Feminists at its founding meeting
December, 1969. First published in *Notes From the Second Year*.
†Ego: We are using the classical definition rather than the Freudian:
that is, the sense of individual self as distinct from others.

Thus the purpose of the male power group is to fulfill a need. That need is psychological, and derives from the supremacist assumptions of the male identity—namely that the male identity be sustained through its ability to have power over the female ego. Man establishes his "manhood" in direct proportion to his ability to have his ego override woman's, and derives his strength and self-esteem through this process. This male need, though destructive, is in that sense impersonal. It is not out of a desire to hurt the woman that man dominates and destroys her; it is out of a need for a sense of power that he necessarily must destroy her ego and make it subservient to his. Hostility to women is a secondary effect, to the degree that a man is not fulfilling his own assumptions of male power he hates women. Similarly, a man's failure to establish himself supreme among other males (as for example a poor white male) may make him channel his hostility into his relationship with women, since they are one of the few political groups over which he can still exercise power.

As women we are living in a male power structure, and our roles become necessarily a function of men. The services we supply are services to the male ego. We are rewarded according to how well we perform these services. Our skill—our profession—is our ability to be feminine—that is, dainty, sweet, passive, helpless, ever-giving and sexy. In other words, everything to help reassure man that he is primary. If we perform successfully, our skills are rewarded. We "marry well"; we are treated with benevolent paternalism; we are deemed successful women, and may even make the "women's pages."

If we do not choose to perform these ego services, but instead assert ourselves as primary to ourselves, we are denied the necessary access to alternatives to express our self-assertion. Decision-making positions in the various job fields are closed to us; politics (left, right or liberal) are barred in other than auxiliary roles; our creative efforts are *a priori* judged not serious because we are females; our day-to-day lives are judged failures because we have not become "real women."

Rejection is economic in that women's work is underpaid. It is emotional in that we are cut off from human relationships because we choose to reject the submissive female role. We are trapped in an alien system, just as the worker under capitalism is forced to sell his economic services in a system which is set up against his self-interest.

Sexual Institutions

The oppression of women is manifested in particular institutions, constructed and maintained to keep women in their place. Among these are the institutions of marriage, motherhood, love, and sexual intercourse (the family unit is incorporated by the above). Through these institutions the woman is taught to confuse her biological sexual differences with her total human potential. Biology is destiny, she is told. Because she has childbearing capacity, she is told that motherhood and child rearing is her function, not her option. Because she has childbearing capacity she is told that it is her function to marry and have the man economically maintain her and "make the decisions." Because she has the physical capacity for sexual intercourse, she is told that sexual intercourse too is her function, rather than just a voluntary act which she may engage in as an expression of her general humanity.

In each case *her* sexual difference is rationalized to trap her within it, while the male sexual difference is rationalized to imply an access to all areas of human activity.

Love, in the context of an oppressive male-female relationship, becomes an emotional cement to justify the dominant-submissive relationship. The man "loves" the woman who fulfills her submissive ego-boosting role. The woman "loves" the man she is submitting to—that is, after all, why she "lives for him." LOVE, magical and systematically unanalyzed, becomes the emotional rationale for the submission of one ego to the other. And it is deemed every woman's natural function to love.

Radical feminism believes that the popularized version of love has thus been used politically to cloud and justify an oppressive relationship between men and women, and that in reality there can be no genuine love until the need to *control* the growth of another is replaced by love *for* the growth of another.

Learning to Become Feminine

The process of training women for their female role begins as far back as birth, when a boy child is preferred over a girl child. In her early years, when the basic patterns of her identity are being established, it is reinforced in her that her female role is not a choice but a fact. Her future will be spent performing the same basic functions as her mother and women before her. Her life is already determined. She is not given the choice of exploring activity toys. Her brothers play astronaut, doctor, scientist, race-car driver. She plays little homemaker, future mother (dolls), and nurse (doctor's helper). Her brothers are given activity toys; the world is their future. She is given service toys. She is already learning that her future will be in the maintenance of others. Her ego is repressed at all times to prepare her for this future submissiveness. She must dress prettily and be clean; speak politely; seek approval; please. Her brothers are allowed to fight, get dirty, be aggressive and be self-assertive.

As she goes through school she learns that subjects which teach mastery and control over the world, such as science and math, are male subjects; while subjects which teach appearance, maintenance, or sentiment, such as home economics or literature, are female subjects. School counselors will recommend nursing for girls, while they will encourage boys to be doctors. Most of the best colleges will accept only a token sprinkling of women (quota system), regardless of academic abilities.

By the time she is of marrying age she has been prepared on two levels. One, she will realize that alternatives to the traditional female role are both prohibitive and prohibited; two, she will herself have accepted on some levels the assumptions about her female role.

Internalization

It is not only through denying women human alternatives that men are able to maintain their positions of power. It is politically necessary for any oppressive group to convince the oppressed that they are in fact inferior, and therefore deserve their situation. For it is precisely through the destruction of women's egos that they are robbed of their ability to resist.

For the sake of our own liberation, we must learn to overcome this damage to ourselves through internalization. We must begin to destroy the notion that we are indeed only servants to the male ego, and must begin to reverse the systematic crushing of women's egos by constructing alternate selves that are healthy, independent and self-assertive. We must, in short, help each other to transfer the ultimate power of judgment about the value of our lives from men to ourselves.

It remains for us as women to fully develop a new dialectic of sex class—an analysis of the way in which sexual identity and institutions reinforce one another.

A. K./December, 1969.

Westchester
Radical Feminists

"Radical feminism recognizes the oppression of women as a fundamental political oppression wherein women are categorized as an inferior class based on their sex. . . .

Radical feminism is political because it recognizes that a group of individuals (men) have organized together for power over women and that they have set up institutions throughout society to maintain this power. . . .

The oppression of women is manifested in particular institutions . . . . among these are marriage, motherhood, love, sexual intercourse, (psychiatry and consumerism)*. Through these institutions a woman is taught to confuse her biological sexual differences with her total human potential. . . .

In each case her sexual difference is rationalized to trap her within (the institution)* . . . ."

Statement of Purpose

Suburban women, in common with all women, have lived in intimacy with and dependence on our oppressor. In isolation and tightly bound to our families, we have viewed the world and our condition from the level of patriarchal ideas of money and power. We now recognize that these patriarchal concepts have and still do dominate and control our lives, but our thinking, hopes and aspirations are changing. We are analyzing our past, present and future according to new feminist concepts and are beginning to discover that there can be new ways of dealing with our problems and our lives.

As suburban women, we recognize that many of us live in more economic and material comfort than our urban sisters, but we have

* Our addition
Politics of the Ego: A Manifesto For New York Radical Feminists

come to realize through the woman's movement, feminist ideas and consciousness raising, that this comfort only hides our essential powerlessness and oppression. We live in comfort only to the extent that our homes, clothing and the services we receive feed and prop the status and egos of the men who support us. Like dogs on a leash, our own status and power will reach as far as our husbands and their income and prestige will allow. As human beings, as individuals, we, in fact, own very little and should our husbands leave us or us them, we will find ourselves with the care and responsibility of children and without money, jobs, credit or power. For this questionable condition, we have paid the price of isolation and exploitation by the institutions of marriage, motherhood, psychiatry and consumerism. Although our life styles may appear materially better, we are, as all women, dominated by men at home, in bed and on the job; emotionally, sexually, domestically and financially.

Traditionally, as women and suburban women, we have put the cause of others before our own and are now determined to uphold our rights as top priority. Because we are convinced that all oppression stems from the fundamental oppression of women by men, it will follow that men will benefit from our liberation even though they may fight, resist and not welcome the change. We want to be identified as female liberationists and not as human liberators. Those men who agree with our cause will find a way to support us and we will welcome them, but it is not our job to convince, care for or teach men what we know to be right.

Although we are, as women, united on the basis of our common feelings and experiences, we are also individuals with varied ideas, preferences and goals. These differences are not antagonistic but are an indication of the richness and variety of our ideas and contributions. We, therefore, hope to remain loosely organized to allow individual expression and freedom to work and struggle through thoughts, feelings and ideas. Total agreement is not our goal but self realization, self initiative, mutual respect and a large variety of alternatives and choices are essentially what we hope to achieve.

We believe that:

1. The notion of fixed sex roles is arbitrary and unjust.
2. That suburbia is a wasteland; a human ghetto for women minimizing their opportunity for growth.

3. That diverse forms of sexual relationships based on mutual consent are a matter of individual choice and right.
4. The institution of marriage presumes and establishes the life-long servitude of women.
5. All economic institutions subject and deprive the suburban women, as well as all women, of economic power; even her power as a consumer is a myth since she spends and buys no more than her husband will allow.
6. Women are no more inherently suited to child rearing than men and men must be held responsible also for the emotional, educational and physical development of children.
7. The mutual dependence of mothers and children is in essence an act of tyranny which serves to thwart, retard and immobilize both mother and children.
8. The adjustment theories adhered to by most psychologists and psychiatrists and their institutions perpetuate destructive attitudes towards women, undermine their self value and self esteem and are generally harmful to the wholesome development and welfare of women.
9. The fact that we live with and even support some of these institutions which are sexist does not in any way alter our basic beliefs. We presently live the way we do because there are no good alternatives.
10. Women's liberation is not human liberation and we place the cause of women above all other causes.
11. We are committed to the understanding of our condition as women so that we may create and invent new ways to live and to find both collective and individual realization and strength.

A group of 15 Westchester women
May, 1972

. . .

The WESTCHESTER RADICAL FEMINISTS is currently involved in:
1. Consciousness raising.
2. Analyzing our condition in the institutions of psychiatry, marriage, motherhood.
3. Writing about the problems of suburban women.
4. Actively supporting abortion legislation.

5. Engaging in self-help supportive counseling.
6. Attacking sexist practices in local institutions such as schools, town clubs, local governments.
7. Each woman is encouraged to find or organize an action which interests her.

.   .   .

For further information contact:

Westchester Radical Feminists
c/o Helene Silverstein
820 Claflin Avenue
Mamaroneck, New York 10543

The Arts

Women Writers and the Female Experience

by Elaine Showalter

Elaine Showalter has been active in women's liberation for three years. At the first Congress to Unite Women in New York, she met two academic women working on women's studies and discrimination; they encouraged each other to get women's studies going in several universities. Since then she has taught courses in women's studies at Douglass College and done research on women writers. Currently she is a member of the Modern Language Association Commission on the Status of Women and the Rutgers University Committee on the Status of Women. She has published several articles and edited a book on women's liberation and literature. The following was given as a speech in 1971.

You might expect that women writers would be the most emancipated women in the world for a number of reasons. First of all, they have been allowed to practice their profession since the end of the eighteenth century: writing was a cheap hobby for daughters, and also a harmless one. Virginia Woolf, for example, recalls her father approving of the cheapness of paper and ink. Also, unlike many professional women, women writers could work at home. And this meant that they could work while they were baking the bread, which is what Emily Brontë did. And also that they could work at odd hours while the rest of the family was asleep. There have been many women writers like Frances Trollope, the mother of the Victorian novelist Anthony Trollope, who habitually got up at 4 A.M. and wrote a chapter before the baby woke up.

You might also expect that the length and breadth of the feminine experience would be recorded in the novels and poems and plays of women writers, because they couldn't have described anything else. After all, they didn't go to the university, they didn't go to the office, and they didn't go to war. Nonetheless, these expectations would be false, for the truth is that women writers, who are the second oldest of the female professions, have neither escaped the hostile stereotypes and repressive practices which have bound them from the beginning in their literary undertakings, nor have they succeeded in defining for the world the experience of their half of the human population.

We need not go back to 1850 to find hostile male criticism of female writers. Let me give you some recent examples. From the *New York Review of Books* in June, 1965, Bernard Bergonzi writes:

> Women novelists, we have learned to assume, like to keep their focus narrow. The female observer is happy with fewer properties; between one and four persons with bruised lives and fine understandings. I have an idea that female writers, in a fervor of emancipated zeal, have accepted too eagerly one of the major premises of modern—or at least post-Freudian—fiction, namely that sex is more important than money.

Taking an opposing viewpoint on this question, John Hollander wrote a double dactyl on the subject of sexual equality in literature, which goes as follows:*

> *Higgledy piggledy,*
> *Dorothy Richardson*
> *Wrote a huge book with her delicate muse,*
> *Where, though I hate to be*
> *uncomplimentary,*
> *Nothing much happens and nobody screws.*

Or, in the *New York Times* in May, 1970, the young male novelist, L. Woiwode, writing in review of female novelist Joanna Ostrow, said in praise, "Simon is one of the most four-square, full-bodied persons I've met in recent fiction. Everything about him rings true,

---

* By John Hollander from *JIGGERY-POKERY: A Compendium of Double Dactyls*, edited by Anthony Hecht and John Hollander. Copyright © 1966 by Anthony Hecht and John Hollander. Reprinted by permission of John Hollander and Atheneum Publishers.

and I find it almost inconceivable that he was created by a woman."

And, of course, the champion at this kind of thing, our archetypal male chauvinist, Norman Mailer, who has said about women writers:

> The sniffs I get from the ink of the women are always fey, old hat, quaintsy, goysy, tiny, too dikily psychotic, crippled, creepish, fashionable, frigid, outer-baroque, maquillé in manniquins whimsey, or else bright and stillborn.

And he concludes here, in a sentence, "In short, a novelist can do without everything but the remnants of his balls."[1] You don't have to be an expert in syllogistic reasoning to understand that this effectively excludes women. More recently, in *The Prisoner of Sex,* Mailer has made some concessions about women writers: now, he says, they're writing like "tough faggots."

But even very conservative and very orthodox twentieth-century critics have treated women writers as an inferior group of artists who are inherently limited by their sex and easily identifiable in their language and style. For example, Ernest Baker, who has written a classic ten-volume history of the novel, devotes a separate chapter to women writers, and defends himself by saying:

> The woman of letters has peculiarities of race or ancestral tradition. Whatever variety of talent, outlook or personal disposition may be discernible in any dozen women writers taken at random, it will be matched and probably outweighed by resemblances distinctively feminine.

Whether there are, in fact, these resemblances which are distinctly feminine is a question I'm going to try to discuss, because it is my experience, first of all, that the term "feminine" as it is used by literary critics is a pejorative. For example, Katherine Anne Porter said in an interview in the *Paris Review* a few years ago,

> If I show wisdom, the critics say I have a masculine mind. If I'm silly and irrelevant—and Edmund Wilson says I often am—then they say I have a typically feminine mind.

And in a very witty book about female stereotypes, *Thinking About Women,* Mary Ellmann says that with regard to literature, "femininity" means formlessness, passivity, instability, piety, materiality, and compliancy.

If it is true that women share literary traits, I think we're not in a society free enough to discover them. But we can say and agree that women have experiences in common—the experiences of daughterhood, adolescence, sexual initiation, marriage, and childbirth. In addition to these, women writers have their own individual experiences of life, and particularly their experiences as artists. It is my contention that these feminine experiences have not been fully explored, or honestly expressed by women writers, and that women have, in fact, been kept from their own experience by a double critical standard, by a double social standard, by external censorship, and, most dangerous, by self-censorship—which is sometimes exercised in self-defense, more frequently in self-hatred.

In order to demonstrate what I consider the longevity and the universality of these problems, I would like to focus on four books, by four different women: Charlotte Brontë's *Jane Eyre*, published in 1847; George Eliot's *Adam Bede*, 1859; Kate Chopin's *The Awakening*, 1899; and Mary McCarthy's *The Group*, 1963. The first two of these are by British women; the last two by American women.

First, Charlotte Brontë I think is a particularly good example of the double critical standard, because she published *Jane Eyre* under a masculine pseudonym. She used the name Currer Bell, and her two sisters used the names Ellis and Acton Bell, because, as she wrote:

> Without at the time suspecting that our mode of writing and thinking was not what was called feminine, we had a vague impression that authoresses are liable to be looked on with prejudice. We notice how sometimes critics use for their chastisement the weapon of personality, and for their reward a flattery which is not true praise.[2]

In 1847 the stereotypes for male and female writers were very rigid. Critics expected from a male writer strength, passion, and intellect, and from a woman writer they expected tact, refinement, and piety. They depended on these stereotypes so much, in fact, that they really didn't know how to proceed, what to say, or what to look for in a book if they were unsure of the author's sex.

So *Jane Eyre* created a tremendous sensation, and it was a problem for the Brontës. The name Currer Bell could be that of either a man or a woman and the narrator of *Jane Eyre* is Jane herself. The book is told as an autobiography. These things suggested that the author might have been a woman. On the other hand, the novel was considered to be excellent, strong, intelligent and, most of all, passionate. And therefore, the critics reasoned, it could not be written by a woman, and if it turned out that it was written by a woman, she had to be unnatural and perverted.

The reason for this is that the Victorians believed that decent women had no sexual feelings whatsoever—that they had sexual anesthesia. Therefore, when Jane says about Rochester that his touch "made her veins run fire, and her heart beat faster than she could count its throbs," the critics assumed this was a man writing about his sexual fantasies. If a woman was the author, then presumably she was writing from her own experience, and that was disgusting. In this case we can clearly see how women were not permitted the authority of their own experience if it happened to contradict the cultural stereotype.

But even more shocking than this to the Victorians was Jane's reply to Rochester, a very famous passage in the novel. He has told her he is going to marry another woman, an heiress, but that she can stay on as a servant. Jane answers him thus:

> "I tell you I must go," I retorted, roused to something like passion. "Do you think I can stay to become nothing to you? Do you think I am an automaton, a machine without feeling and can bear to have my morsel of bread snatched from my lips and my drop of living water dashed from my cup? Do you think because I am poor, obscure, plain and little, I'm soulless and heartless? You think wrong. I have as much soul as you and full as much heart. And if God had gifted me with some beauty and much wealth, I should've made it as hard for you to leave me as it is now for me to leave you. I am not talking to you now through the medium of custom, conventionality, nor even of mortal flesh. It is my spirit that addresses your spirit, just as if both had passed through the grave and we stood at God's feet equal—as we are."

This splendid assertion violated not only the standards of sexual submission, which were believed to be women's duty and their punishment for Eve's crime, but it also went against standards of class submission, and obviously against religion. And this sort of rebellion was not feminine at all.

The reviews of *Jane Eyre* in 1847 and 1848 show how confused the critics were. Some of them said Currer Bell was a man. Some of them, including Thackeray, said a woman. One man, an American critic named Edgar Percy Whipple, said the Bells were a team, that Currer Bell was a woman who did the dainty parts of the book and brother Acton the rough parts. All kinds of circumstantial evidence were adduced to solve this problem, such as the details of housekeeping. Harriet Martineau said the book had to be the work of a woman or an upholsterer. And Lady Eastlake, who was a reviewer for one of the most prestigious journals, said it couldn't be a woman because no woman would dress her heroines in such outlandish clothes.

Eventually Charlotte Brontë revealed her identity, and then these attacks which had been general became personal. People introduced her as the author of a naughty book; they gossiped that she was Thackeray's mistress. They speculated on the causes of what they called "her alien and sour perspective on women." She felt during her entire short life that she was judged always on the basis of what was becoming in femininity and not as an artist.

When she died—ironically enough, from complications of pregnancy at the age of thirty-nine—her close friend and sister novelist, Elizabeth Gaskell, wrote a biography, in part to defend Charlotte Brontë's reputation against the implications of being unladylike and unwomanly. The effect of this biography, though certainly not its intention, was to provide those critics who had never been able to accept the idea of female genius with a theory which explained things for them. The Brontës had a brother, Branwell, who was an alcoholic and an opium addict; he died at thirty-one. The theory was that Branwell had written not only *Jane Eyre* but also *Wuthering Heights*. Branwell was sick, violent, and weak, but at least he was a man, and occasionally one finds articles and tracts claiming his genius even today.

George Eliot had a confrontation with Victorian society which was even more explosive than Charlotte Brontë's. Her use of the male pseudonym—her real name was Mary Anne Evans—was not merely to avoid unjust criticism because she was a woman, although that was what she claimed. She *had* to use a pseudonym because she was living with a married man, George Henry Lewes, in defiance of all the codes of Victorian society, and her publishers were really in fear that moral outrage at her life style would affect the review and sales of her books.

Her first novel, *Adam Bede*, was published in 1859. It contained an episode which deals with the plight of an unwed mother, an ignorant dairymaid named Hetty, who gives birth to her child under tragic circumstances and subsequently murders it. This plot had been used previously by Sir Walter Scott in *The Heart of Midlothian,* but Scott was a stern moralist. George Eliot, on the other hand, views the incident from the point of view of the girl herself: a girl who is young and naive and terrified. She presents with sympathy the torment of this trapped creature, who also has a rather limited intelligence.

George Eliot's publishers were highly alarmed by this aspect of the book, not because Hetty murders the child but because she is said to be pregnant at all. To be on the safe side, the publishers sent the manuscript to the head physician in charge of obstetrics at the University of Edinburgh, who was to make sure that it was all decent. He did give it his seal of approval and sent it back, but they were still very anxious.

In spite of their fears, *Adam Bede* was an instant success; everyone acclaimed it, and virtually everyone took for granted this time that the author was a man. As the *Saturday Review* wrote, the book was thought "too good for a woman's story."[3] The *Westminster Review,* another Victorian journal, wrote that there wasn't a woman in England capable of the intellectual profundity of *Adam Bede.* This comment was particularly ironic because George Eliot had edited the *Westminster Review* for three years. (Of course, she did it behind the scenes: she didn't get paid, she didn't get the credit— she let her lover take both of those.)

But *Adam Bede* was so good that people had to find the author . . . they had to find George Eliot. They went out to look for him using various clues in the book. And before long, they actually found him. A man named Joseph Liggins who lived near Nuneaton, George Eliot's home town, admitted very modestly that he had written *Adam Bede* and that he had also written the book of stories by George Eliot which had preceded it. Liggins, who was obviously a lunatic, received pilgrims at his home, where he would discourse on the art of fiction.

The real George Eliot had some difficulty claiming that she actually had written the book. She wrote letters to *The London Times,* for example, but ultimately it was necessary for her to drop her pseudonym and to reveal her identity in order to scotch the rumors.

So about 1860 people knew that George Eliot was, in fact, a woman.

And then what happened to *Adam Bede?* Some critics went back and read it again. And this time they discovered that it was really not as distinguished a book as they had first believed. The editor of *The Athenaeum,* for example, wrote:

> It is time to end this pother about the authorship of *Adam Bede.* The writer is in no sense a great unknown. The tale, though bright in parts, and such as a clever woman with an observant eye and an unschooled moral nature might have written, has no great quality of any kind.[4]

Also in 1860, George Eliot's second novel, *The Mill on the Floss,* appeared. This time, knowing that the author was a woman, the critics preached long sermons in their reviews on the indecency of the book. The indecency consists of the heroine, Maggie Tulliver, awakening to a physical passion for a man who is engaged to her cousin. She knows she has to resist this passion and ultimately she does and is drowned at the end of the book.

Critics couldn't deny the truth of what she wrote; *The Mill on the Floss* contains a woman's very modest acknowledgement of sexual feeling. The most daring scene involves a kiss on the arm. Critics did, however, object to sexual knowledge of any sort on the part of a woman, and particularly if it was accurate. The *Saturday Review,* for example, wondered if women ought to even *think* about sex:

> We are not sure that it is quite consistent with feminine delicacy to lay so much stress on the bodily feeling for the other sex. George Eliot lets her fancy run to things which are not wrong, but are better omitted from the scope of female meditation. Perhaps we may go further and say that the whole delineation of passionate love as painted by modern female novelists is open to very serious criticism.[5]

After this novel, George Eliot virtually dropped the autobiographical and personal element in her fiction and turned to historical and political modes. Her real experience—her life experience as a woman defying social convention—could not be used in any explicit or even subtle way in her novels without risking her private happiness. For example, although her whole life was affected by the British divorce laws—or rather the lack of British divorce laws—she could not have protested them in her books without incurring serious scandal.

What happened then to women who actually tried to write, using their own names, about feminine experience? Kate Chopin did try this in *The Awakening,* a novel about a young mother, Edna Pontellier, in New Orleans at the turn of the century, married to a very rich, adoring and demanding husband. She has stifled, more from inertia than from will, a real sense of herself, of her abilities, her needs, her wishes. In the course of the book she is awakened sexually by falling in love with a young man, and this sudden understanding of her physical nature awakens her entire individuality.

This awakening is tragic for her. She can't fit into her society once she is awake. She gives up her social obligations; she tries to become a painter but she is not really a genius—she doesn't have that kind of discipline. She moves out of her home, she offers to get a divorce, but of course her lover won't marry her because he is going to protect her reputation. And so, in the last chapter of the book, there is nothing left for Edna and in a kind of hazy and sensual trance, she walks into the sea and drowns.

The book has recently been compared to *Madame Bovary,* and to the novels of D. H. Lawrence. It has been called "the most important piece of fiction about the sexual life of a woman written to date in America." So why have we never heard of it?

The Awakening was published in April, 1899. It was first reviewed in St. Louis because Chopin was a local author. Within twelve days it had been condemned by every critic in St. Louis; they said it was poisonous. One critic said that it was unacceptable that a real American lady should be allowed to disrupt "the sacred institution of marriage and American womanhood, and to disregard moral concepts without repenting it."[6]

The book was banned first in St. Louis and then nationally from Boston to Los Angeles. By the time Chopin had written a kind of ironic half-defense—not an apology, but a kind of grudging statement—the book had disappeared. Subsequently Kate Chopin discovered she could no longer get her short stories accepted for publication; even a collection which had previously been accepted for publication was returned. She lost confidence in her ability as a writer and, probably coincidentally, died shortly thereafter in 1904.

The Awakening is certainly not obscene. Male writers in the same period had published works which were equally frank and much more perverse: Strindberg, for example; Zola, Dreiser. But what was shocking in this was the insistence of the author, a woman, on defining the shape of her own experience. Even more disturbing was her rejection of the myth of domestic fulfillment.

Edna says to her best friend, "I would give up the unessential; I would give my money; I would give my life for my children, but I wouldn't give myself." She loves her children, but they don't fulfill her. Without being militant in any sense, she is also not apologetic. She simply seeks an authentic life for herself, however tragically and unsuccessfully, as a human being, with a kind of steadiness and quiet purpose.

It may appear that these are all ancient cases, that today women writers are free from this kind of Victorian prudery and sexual stereotyping. So I would like to consider, finally, the case of Mary McCarthy.

Mary McCarthy is, first of all, the only one of these four women who had a university education: she went to Vassar. She and Kate Chopin had children, the others did not. This, again, is not coincidental. Women writers—women artists in general—have always operated in a tradition where creativity for women meant childbearing, and where there is a kind of assumption that biological and literary creativity are mutually exclusive.

Like many American writers, Mary McCarthy has used her life as the basis for her fiction. Many men have done this: Fitzgerald not only used his life but Zelda's. As Nancy Mitford's recent biography of Zelda tells us, when she wrote her own autobiographical novel, he insisted that she cut parts of it out because he was the great writer in the family and her life was his material. Philip Roth, for another example, has used so many incidents from his teaching experience at the University of Chicago in his novel, *Letting Go*, that Chicago people call this book "The Gripes of Roth."

But when the artist is a man, we make allowances for this. We don't criticize or tax these writers for their lack of personal loyalty, but rather we admire their daring, their honesty, and their ruthless appropriation of life for their art. But with women the case is something different. With Mary McCarthy, a very similar kind of artistic pattern has earned her the title (from *Life* magazine) of "The Lady with the Switchblade," or the title (from critics): "The Modern American Bitch."

In fact, up until 1963, when Mary McCarthy published *The*

Group, she had been a good girl—as men define a good girl. She wrote her first short stories because her husband, Edmund Wilson, ordered her to produce fiction. As she describes it in an interview in the *Paris Review,* "He put me in a little room. He didn't literally lock the door, but he said 'Stay there.'" And so she wrote her stories. Her story is something like *Rumpelstiltskin:* the princess shut up to spin flax into gold; and I think this experience probably contributed to her continuing vision of her heroines as fairy tale princesses. The girls in *The Group* live in a tower; Polly is later described as living like Snow White surrounded by little dwarfs. It is generally one way of looking at women in her fiction.

But other aspects of her early career also show that she was accepting pretty much the work men gave her to do, and the view that they had of her. She said about her first job, which was as a theater critic for the *Partisan Review:*

> I was sort of a gay, good-time girl from their point of view. They were men of the thirties—very serious. That's why my position was so insecure on *Partisan Review.* It wasn't exactly insecure, but lowly. That was why they let me write about the theater. Because they thought the theater was of absolutely no consequence.[7]

But in *The Group* she said goodbye to all of that and struck out on her own. First of all, she was writing about feminine experience: the loss of virginity, buying a diaphragm, pregnancy, maternity, nursing a baby, marriage, adultery, masturbation, lesbianism. These are not themes likely to please male critics: they're feminine themes, and therefore trivial.

Reading the reviews of *The Group* which came out around 1963 and 1964, one senses the delight of male critics that they were at last able to convict her of writing a female book. Norman Podhoretz wrote, for example, that *The Group* was "a trivial lady writer's book." And, of course, Norman Mailer went wild. He wrote a very lengthy essay called "The Case Against McCarthy." In this essay he raves against the detail of *The Group,* seeing in it what he calls "the profound materiality of women." In a classical Freudian equation, Mailer describes this detail as "the cold lava of anality which becomes the truest part of her group, her glop, her impacted mass."

In short, his theory of Mary McCarthy is that as a writer she is constipated, and her characters are shit. He can, in fact, see to a limited degree what she is trying to do in this book; but he can't understand why. He can see in some way that she is writing about the inexorable socialization of women into roles they never intended to choose; that these women wind up as what he calls "these piss-out characters with their cultivated banalities, their lack of variety or ambition."[8]

But although Mailer thinks of himself as the guru of good sex, he can't see that one of the most famous sex scenes in the book—Dotty's sexual initiation—features the good old Freudian orgasm: one vaginal, one clitoral—with Dotty, who is obedient and brainwashed, feeling exactly what her college textbooks have told her to feel. Dotty evaluates her experience in the terms which she has been taught:

> This second climax, which she now recognized from the first one, though it was different, left her jumpy and disconcerted. It was something less thrilling and more like being tickled relentlessly or having to go to the bathroom. "Didn't you like that?" he demanded. Slowly Dotty opened her eyes and resolved to tell the truth. "Not quite so much as the other, Dick." Dick laughed. "A nice, normal girl. Some of your sex prefer that." Dotty shivered. She could not deny that it had been exciting, but it seemed to her almost perverted.

She is describing the clitoral orgasm, and recalling the "vaginal" one.

All of the women in *The Group*, I think, are similarly alienated from their own experience. They feel what they have been programmed to feel. In this sense, *The Group* is really a subversive novel about women's roles, and about marriage. It is not an accident that the most liberated woman in this book is a lesbian, and that she challenges Harold on his own territory, which is the bed. She suggests to him on their way to bury Kay, the heroine, that she has been there before him, that she has seduced Kay, and this suggestion defeats him totally. It is clear why Mailer hated this book.

Other male critics, like Brock Bower, took a different approach to Mary McCarthy. They treated her with chivalry, with charming condescension. Brower's profile of Mary McCarthy for *Esquire*, for example, doesn't say very much about her art; he doesn't talk about her particularly as a writer. But he starts with the description of her beautiful smile, and he ends with a lengthy account of her in the kitchen blissfully whipping up her famous cassoulet.

Where are women writers going to go from here? In the past, feminine experience has probably been more of a hindrance to women writers than a help. Katherine Anne Porter, for example, said it took her twenty years to write *Ship of Fools,*

> ... because you're brought up with the notion of feminine availability in all spiritual ways, and in giving service to anyone who demands it. And I suppose that's why it's taken me twenty years to write this novel. It's been interrupted by just anyone who could jimmy his way into my life.

There are some women who have made money out of the domestic cage that keeps other women from finding the time or the peace to write: Jean Kerr and Phyllis McGinley, for example, selling their housewives' trials, or Pearl Buck who advertises the Famous Writers' School as a service to homemaker shut-ins.

But in the future, women artists are going to have to be encouraged to take themselves seriously and perhaps even selfishly ... selfishly enough to make their work come first. More important, I think, women have been taught always to regard their experience as dull and minor and tame, which is, of course, what "domestic" means. As Hortense Calisher says, "We've been taught that a man's role is to hunt experience, a woman's to let it come upon us."[9] And Elizabeth Hardwick writes: "Women have much less experience of life than a man, as everybody knows."[10] But I suggest that no one has less experience of life than somebody else. We have different kinds of experience. We don't want now to have female versions of men's books; we don't want the female version of *Portnoy's Complaint.*

But women have always been overshadowed by the literary tradition which is masculine and splendid. Like the Romans inheriting Greek culture, we are not going to find our own originality as women by copying such a powerful past. If women artists are to liberate themselves from this past and discover their own originality, they are going to have to turn within and to explore the rich dowry of feminine experience which they all possess.

I think that this is taking place now. Some of the women writing today are engaged in this kind of search and exploration, coming into a kind of furious encounter with the fact of being female—the experience of being female—and I can give only a very brief sampling of what some of this new literature is like.

It is not feminine in any sense of that stereotype, but it is female. As Alicia Ostriker, a poet, writes in her long poem about pregnancy, "Once More Out of Darkness"* (which is written in nine parts and a post-partum):

> *What I have said and what I will say*
> *is female, not feminine.*
> *Yes, I said yes,*
> *not analytical, not romantic,*
> *but the book of practical facts.*

Women's poetry is extremely varied. There are some women poets like Elizabeth Sargent who are now trying erotic verse, enjoying the freedom to use sexual metaphors which were formerly taboo or reserved only to men.

There are others who are writing about the cages of sex roles. This is Anne Sexton's poem, "Housewife":*

> *Some women marry houses.*
> *It's another kind of skin; it has a heart*
> *a mouth a liver and bowel movements*
> *The walls are permanent and pink*
> *See how she sits on her knees all day*
> *faithfully washing herself down*
> *Men enter by force, drawn back like Jonah*
> *into their fleshy mothers*
> *A woman is her mother*
> *That's the main thing.*

She wants you to think about the title of the poem—"Housewife," the wife of the house. Many more women, like Adrienne Rich, Muriel Rukeyser, and Denise Levertov, are writing frequently about the cultural exchanges between men and women that we call love.

Less well known right now than the poets, but extremely exciting, are the new women writers who are working with fiction. Margaret

---

* Reprinted from *The Smith*, by permission of the author and publisher.
* Reprinted from *All My Pretty Ones*, Houghton Mifflin, by permission of the Sterling Lord Agency, Inc.

Atwood, a Canadian novelist, has written a funny, scary book called *The Edible Woman*. It is a kind of satire about a woman who is engaged and who suddenly feels: (a) that she is being consumed as a person, particularly by her fiancé, and (b) that she can't eat any more. First she can't eat steak and then she can't eat pork, and then she can't eat chicken and then she can't eat eggs, and then she can't eat rice pudding, and she is finally subsisting on vitamins. At the end of the novel, in a terrible crisis at an engagement party, she rushes home and bakes a cake in the shape of a woman, and frosts it and decorates it to look like herself. Then she calls up her fiancé and tells him to eat the cake and to leave her life alone.

In a more serious mode, a novel that seems part of the new wave of what women are doing as writers is British writer Margaret Drabble's *The Waterfall*, published in this country by Knopf. The novel begins with a childbirth scene: a woman is alone in a house; her husband has left her. She has moved into one bedroom, the only room that has heat, and she gives birth to a daughter during a snowstorm, with only a midwife present. The book begins with the mystery and beauty of the heroine in this warm, hidden place with the child. While she is still convalescing from childbirth, she begins an affair with the husband of her cousin, who has come to be with her in her isolation. He is somehow captivated and seduced by the state of the mother and child. Most of what follows is about their love affair and about the heroine's sense of her life, for which the waterfall is a metaphor. At one point, the heroine, considering her life—a typical woman's aimless life—tries to compare it to the past and particularly to heroines of fiction, all the sad sisterhood of fiction:

> Sometimes, once a week or so, I would get myself into a total panic about the extent of my subjugation, and I even went so far as to look it up in a sexual textbook, an old-fashioned one, Havelock Ellis, where I found the word "bondage," which seemed quite elegantly to describe my condition. I was in bondage. Having discovered this, I flipped through the rest of the book, gazing in amazement at all those curious masculine perversions, wishing I could attach myself to something more easily attainable than a living man. Perversions are cruel, but surely love is as cruel. It is too relative, too exclusive, too desperately mortal.
>
> There didn't seem to be very many female perversions in that book. Perhaps that was because it was old. Perhaps women have developed these things more recently as a result of emancipation.

But love is nothing new. Even women have suffered from it in history. It is a classic malady and commonly it requires participants of both sexes. Perhaps I'll go mad with guilt like Sue Bridehead, or drown myself in an effort to reclaim lost renunciations like Maggie Tulliver.

Those fictional heroines, how they haunt me. Maggie Tulliver had a cousin called Lucy, as I have, and like me she fell in love with her cousin's man. She drifted off down the river with him, abandoning herself to the water, but in the end she lost him. She let him go. Nobly she regained her ruined honor and, ahh, we admire her for it, all that superego gathered together in a last effort to prove that she loved the brother more than the man.

She should have . . . well, what should she not have done? Since Freud we guess dimly at our own passions, stripped of hope, abandoned forever to that relentless current. It gets us in the end; sticks, twigs, dry leaves, paper cartons, cigarette ends, orange peels, flower petals, silver fishes. Maggie Tulliver never slept with her man. She did all the damage there was to be done to Lucy, to herself, to the two men who loved her, and then, like a woman of another age, she refrained. In this age what is to be done? We drown in the first chapter.

In 1923, the poet Louise Bogan wrote, "Women have no wildness in them." She was wrong. Feminine experience is the wildness which women writers have only started to chart.

Footnotes

[1] Norman Mailer, "Evaluations—Quick and Expensive Comments on the Talent in the Room," in *Advertisements for Myself*, 1959.

[2] Biographical Notice of Anne and Emily Brontë, prefaced to 1850 edition of *Wuthering Heights* and *Agnes Grey*.

[3] *Saturday Review*, Vol. IX (1860), p. 470.

[4] See Gordon S. Haight, *George Eliot: A Biography*, New York, 1968, pp. 290–291.

[5] *Saturday Review*, p. 471.

[6] See Per Seyersted, *Kate Chopin: A Critical Biography*, University of Louisiana Press, 1969, for details of the critical reception of *The Awakening*.

[7] *Paris Review*, Vol. XXVII (1962), pp. 72, 74.

[8] Norman Mailer, "The Case Against McCarthy," in *Cannibals and Christians*, 1966.

[9] Hortense Calisher, "No Important Woman Writer," reprinted in *Woman's Liberation and Literature*, edited by Elaine Showalter.

[10] Elizabeth Hardwick, "The Subjection of Women," in *Woman's Liberation and Literature*, p. 209.

The Body is the Role: Sylvia Plath

Anita Rapone

Anita Rapone is a potter and graduate student in American Civilization. She has been active in the women's movement, worked with Notes From the Second Year, *and is an editor of* Notes From the Third Year.

In the past few years there has been increasing interest in the work of Sylvia Plath. In the environment of a growing feminist consciousness, it is clear why. Sylvia Plath's poetry is political not because it is ideological but because it presents our experience. The poems delineate the psychological and emotional horror of a woman living in a society that keeps women down. As such, they are our lives.

Sylvia Plath's poetry, particularly the collection *Ariel,* is the articulation of female pain in a world which denies a woman full value as a human being. The poetry constructs the coherent world-view of a single passive persona, and as such, in the voice of one woman, speaks to all women. In the world which emerges from her work, the female is reduced to biological and social functions which she can neither reject nor transcend. These roles conspire to lock her into a mere physical presence. Thus limited to her body, she is especially threatened by decay and destruction. And she is subject to physical and psychological control by others. Her body is her vulnerability. This absence of self-determination and autonomy results in self-hatred and alienation from both herself and others.

Sylvia Plath has written three volumes of poetry which show a

407

progressive concentration on the particularities of being female. The first volume, *Colossus,* has occasional signs of sex-role tension and polarization. In *Crossing the Water: Transitional Poems,* she begins to treat the female situation more directly. By using a persona—a single voice—she focuses on the alienating experience of being female, especially physically female. In "Face Lift," for instance, there is self-objectification in the persona imagining her discarded face, "the dewlapped lady/ . . . trapped . . . in some laboratory jar." In other poems, the persona describes her sense of occupying a body, of internal struggle. In "Witch Burning" she says: "I inhabit/ The wax image of myself, a doll's body./ Sickness begins here." To save itself, the ego is forced to flee from the body.

In *Ariel,* the last volume before her death, Sylvia Plath describes the biological predicament as a social predicament. Here she treats a fuller range of experience with the added dimension of social consciousness. Caught between reflecting social values and rebelling against them, the persona has conflicting attitudes toward the female biological role of reproduction. This conflict and preoccupation is displayed through her choice of recurrent images. A few poems connect worth with fertility through the image of the moon. In "Munich Mannequins," for example, the round complete, self-sufficient moon is associated with menstruation, a lost opportunity for reproduction.

> *(perfection) tamps the womb*
> *Where the yew trees blow like hydras,*
> *The tree of life and the tree of life*
> *Unloosing their moons, month after month, to no purpose.*

In "Elm," the moon is described as "Diminished and flat, as after radical surgery." Flatness, the result of mastectomy, lessens her value. In other poems, flatness itself means superficiality, removal from life, deadness.

Rebellion against the reproductive role is articulated in poems whose central image is the bee colony. This image makes connections between the reproductive function and its social enforcement. On the most simple literal level, "The Bee Meeting" is about a group of villagers who are removing the virgin bees from an old hive in order to start new hives. This activity becomes, on another level, a ceremony preparing the persona for marriage and mother-hood. The villagers—the rector, the midwife, and sexton, among others—first dress her in a white smock and straw hat with a significantly black veil. As they walk through the bean field, she notices flowers, "blood clots . . . that will one day be edible." The image connects the phases of the reproductive process.

As the poem develops, the tension of the persona increases. She becomes aware of the possibility for rebellion, which she is incapable of choosing, even though ceremonial acquiescence means self-destruction. She says:

> *I cannot run, I am rooted, and the gorse hurts me*
> *With its yellow purses, its spiky armoury.*
> *I could not run without having to run forever.*

The sexual references throughout the poem create the sense of the oppressiveness of the reproductive role. The hive, a "virgin" who has sealed "off her brood cells," is being raped.

A similar theme is developed in "Stings," a poem which describes the removing of honey from the hive. The persona identifies herself with the queen bee, whose life and value is determined by her biological function in the hive. Although in "The Bee Meeting" she was unable to defend herself, here she threatens a retaliatory return:

> *More terrible than she ever was, red*
> *Scar in the sky, red comet*
> *Over the engine that killed her—*
> *The mausoleum, the wax house.*

The conflicting attitudes of the persona toward the biological role depends upon whether she is considering it for other women or herself. While she makes accusations against others who do not fulfill their reproductive function, the persona senses the inherent threat to herself in this definition. She identifies with the prodded queen and virgin bees.

The reproductive role is only half of the definition externally imposed upon the persona. She is also assigned the role of wife. She sees this role as one in which her needs as a human being are secondary to her husband's. She must be constantly adapting to his varying needs, be they sexual, physical or emotional. This role is bitterly satirized in "The Applicant," where a fast talker is selling a living doll that not only cooks and sews, but talks.

While "The Applicant" is a functional description of the wife role, the pain of the lived experience comes through when the persona speaks directly, in poems such as "Lesbos." In this poem, the male-female relationship is so destructive to her that it affects all other relationships. Husbands are parasites on the emotional and sexual energies of their wives. The opening description of traditionally female territory, the kitchen, uses the metaphor of a Hollywood stage set, the appropriate home for a "living doll." The mood is repressed rebellion. The male-female relationship is presented in the image of female sexuality and male impotency. His needs and dependencies are such that they exhaust and limit her. Everyday, she must "fill him with soul-stuff, like a pitcher." This self-denial for the needs of the husband turns into self-hatred.

The ultimate destructiveness of this role system is dramatized by the inability of the persona in "Lesbos" to establish a meaningful relationship with the woman to whom she is speaking. Locked in their respective kitchens, they are kept apart by their own self-hatred. The poem conveys the feeling that they can change neither themselves nor the situation. Instead, they perpetuate the cycle by projecting their own self-hatred onto the girl-child. She is described as an "unstrung puppet, kicking to disappear," a girl who will "cut her throat at ten if she's mad at two." She indicates a special female insanity that comes from accepting an unacceptably limiting situation.

These poems, then, present a world in which the female is defined by two overlapping functions that focus her meaning in her body. When the definition of self is limited to the body in this way, it leads to an obsessive emphasis on physical vulnerability. The body is threatened by natural elements, such as the sun which gives ulcers, or the wind which gives T.B. It is subject to decay from within, such as in "Contusion," where a bruise is the first step to death. Fumes threaten to choke the body like Isadora's scarves. The body can be hurt by man-made implements such as axes and knives. The awareness of the body's vulnerability can become so heightened that ordinarily neutral or life-affirming things can threaten annihilation. In "Tulips," the red flowers watch her, use up her oxygen, and become "red lead sinkers round (her) neck."

The body is also the means through which she is controlled by others. One frequent image for this theme is the health care/patient relationship. In the poem "Tulips" the persona is hospitalized. She is merely an object in the bureaucratic mechanics of the hospital, "a pebble to them." Reducing her body to an object for tending, the hospital staff affects her psyche as well. She says, "They have swabbed me clear of my loving associations." In this situation her defense is passive withdrawal.

> *I am nobody ...*
> *I have given my name and my day-clothes up to the nurses*
> *And my history to the anaesthetist and my body to surgeons.*

In "Tulips" the situation is impersonal and functional; but, in poems such as "Lady Lazarus," she imputes malevolent motivation to the health deliverers. The doctor becomes "Herr Doktor, ... Herr Enemy." She is his "opus," his "valuable,/The pure gold baby." The poem is a cry of hatred, ending in a threat to return as something terrible which will "eat men like air." However, even in those few poems where she personalizes the situation, thus focusing her anger on a particular target, she cannot overcome her passivity. She can only go as far as threatening a menacing comeback, the "red scar in the sky." But the future does not materially change the present, and the battle on the physical plane is lost.

The experience of being controlled by another person and the hatred it creates overflows in "Daddy." The persona and her father move through a series of images in which their identities change, but the relationship between them remains constant. In this way, the poem explores several dimensions of the dominance-submission dynamic. In the first image she is a white foot totally contained by a black shoe. The black shoe grows into the Nazi, and the persona becomes first the Jew, then the gypsy, then the masochistic woman. The image then changes to the teacher-child, the teacher cleft-chinned, a devil, who then becomes the vampire finally killed by a stake in his heart.

Ariel is the presentation of a persona caught in a world which denies her humanity by defining her sexually. As a female, she has no substantial freedom or self-definition. The poems are studies of the resulting states of mind; we experience how she feels. Descriptions of scenery, for example, tell us not so much how the world looks, as how the world symbolizes her feelings. Not surprisingly, images concerned with the body recur throughout *Ariel*. On one level, the body can be directly affected by others, as in the doctor-patient images. Control is so complete that a doctor can obstruct her desire to die; he can force her to live. On another level, psychological and emotional oppression are physically rooted. The photograph of her husband and child are "smiles that catch onto my skin, little smiling hooks." Hooks, vampires, blood-suckers are images that recur throughout the poems.

Because the world gets to her by attacking her body, she has strong desires for self-dissolvement into amorphism. Escape into death becomes rarefaction into air, or dissolution into water. The call of the elements is the release from painful solidity. As the body unlocks, the spirit is released.

Finally, *Ariel* gives us the world in which destructive feelings and pain are grounded in real causes. As the poetry develops, the treatment of these themes becomes explicit, and is rooted in women's place in a woman-hostile world. The biological prison, the preoccupation with physical pain and deadness, are intimate consequences of a pre-eminently social ordeal. Inexorably trapped, the persona sharpens, narrows. Her defensive passivity, her search for dissolution into primordial sea and air, lead her forward to a single answer, a single way out.

Women's Private Writings: Anaïs Nin

Ann Snitow

Ann Snitow has been active in the New York Radical Feminists and the Abortion Project, and has done feminist reviews for WBAI's radio program Womankind. She is presently teaching English and women's studies at Livingston College, Rutgers University.

The following article is a radio talk, one of a series by Ann Snitow on women's diaries and letters to be heard on Nanette Rainone's Womankind *program, WBAI-FM, and reproduced with her permission.*

When I began this radio series on women's diaries and letters I had several goals. The first was to show how much women have written, and how well. The second was to show how hampered they have been by the necessity to think of their writing as largely a left-handed or private matter, not destined to be read by a large audience. However, out of this privacy came new subject matter and new forms. My third goal, then, was to explore what was unique about women's private writing which can and will become a part of the growth of our literature as a whole.

Until recently woman's subject matter has been a synonym for the trivial: Women are repetitive; women are subjective; women are gossips. All these qualities have a hard name in our culture. Women are frequently reminded of their ignorance of the world and their limitations are constantly being thrown in their faces. But the confined life most women have led is an historical fact, not an aesthetic judgment. Depth of experience is possible anywhere. Women do need a larger world, but the lack of one has not always doomed them to the inconsequence of which they are so often accused. Women are not without a subject matter; they are without respect for their subject matter. Nevertheless, the limitations placed on women have been, and continue to be, crippling. We, and our subject matter, must change.

Finally, my goal for the series has been to say to women that our writing in diaries or in letters is serious and potentially a public form, and to stimulate all women to write in this way. When you have written something in a diary, it becomes permanent, like any form of art, while your life begins instantly to diverge from what it was at the moment of writing. Having a record of an earlier state of mind is both a satisfaction in itself, and a gesture toward the future. The desire to make such a record is at the source of *all* writing.

If you are keeping a diary or spend energy writing long letters to friends, please write to *Womankind* about your experience. Maybe other women will be moved by something you say to start writing themselves. Write to: DIARY, c/o Womankind, 359 East 62nd Street, New York, N.Y. 10021.

Anaïs Nin began her diary when she was thirteen and there are now about 150 volumes of it stored in bank vaults. The small portion of this vast work available in print has become a kind of cult book for the feminist movement and I've been asking myself why this should be.

It's puzzling at first, because it's fairly plain Anaïs Nin isn't a conscious feminist as we understand the term now. For example, her closest friend in Paris in the Thirties was Henry Miller, who took incredible advantage of her energy and devotion. June Miller, his wife, Anaïs turns into a myth-like image of woman in the diary, and Anaïs's psychiatrist—Freud's famous disciple, Otto Rank—often gave her the kind of advice that would be intolerable to a feminist today. For example, he once told her that when neurotic men get cured, they become artists; when neurotic women get cured, they become—Woman.

It seems that then as now, psychiatrists were particularly bad offenders against women, and Anaïs Nin seems to be unaware of their treachery. Here, for example, is an exchange between her and the psychiatrist she went to before finding Otto Rank:

> Anaïs. I am analyzing what you said, and I do not agree with your interpretations.
>
> Dr. Allendy: You are doing *my* work, you are trying to be the analyst, to identify with me. Have you ever wished to surpass men in their own work, to have more success?
>
> Anaïs: Indeed not. I protected and sacrificed much for my brother's musical career, made it possible. I am now helping Henry [Miller] and giving him all I can, to do his own work. I gave Henry my typewriter. There I think you are very wrong.
>
> Dr. Allendy: Perhaps you are one of those women who are a friend, not an enemy of man.
>
> Anaïs: More than that, I wanted to be married to an artist rather than be one, to collaborate with him.

The lack of feminist consciousness in the passage is staggering, especially when in a later episode Anaïs mentions quite casually that Henry Miller took that precious typewriter she gave him and pawned it to buy drinks. But this is the painful truth of her diary. After all, she doesn't care about a mere typewriter. She is forgiving and compassionate about Henry Miller's weaknesses, his limitations. She loves him, is inspired by him, learns from him, and teaches him, and she is the one who can tell us the things that are wrong with him, and with herself, living through him. The portrait of Henry Miller in these pages is devastating, and every stroke of it laid on with love.

Anaïs Nin was the mediator between Miller and his wife June. With a confused kind of bisexuality she adored them both and understood them both. Henry was the artist, selfish but full of life. June was the model, unsure of her own existence, a victim of Henry's portrait of her in his books. Anaïs was the androgynous go-between who wanted to play the man to June, and play the male companion, the fellow artist, to Henry.

The diary explores this painful kind of bisexuality—so unlike the kind feminists dream of—in which, to create, you must in some way become a man, but to live in a human way, you must support men, give them your typewriter, and sacrifice those things in you the world calls masculine.

This is the great conflict of the diary. On the one hand, Anaïs Nin wants to be, in her psychiatrist's dreadful phrase, "A friend, not an enemy of man." On the other hand, she wants to live.

It is interesting that in her novels she tries to be true to Art, which to her, and to all her psychiatrists, is primarily a male principle. These novels are abstract, poetic, and literally disembodied. We began this series on women's private writings partly to raise the question, "Why do women crave anonymity so much that they can only write if they think no one, or almost no one, will ever see what they have said?" Why is it that Anaïs Nin's diary is full-blooded and complete while what she calls her Art is pale, fragmented, over-conscious? Henry Miller was always nagging Anaïs Nin with a related question: "Why," he kept asking her, "do women lie?"

There are all kinds of answers in the diary:

> I only regret that everyone wants to deprive me of the journal, which is the only steadfast friend I have, the only one which makes my life bearable; because my happiness with human beings is so precarious, my confiding moods rare, and the least sign of non-interest is enough to silence me. In the journal I am at ease.
>
> Playing so many roles, dutiful daughter, devoted sister, mistress, protector, my father's new found illusion, Henry's needed, all-purpose friend, I had to find one place of truth, one dialogue without falsity. This is the role of the diary.

So the diary is the place where a woman can speak the truth without hurting all those people she is supposed to protect and support. Women can't tell all, like Portnoy, since so much of what they feel would damn them in men's eyes. They are too dependent on men to be able to afford this luxury of self-revelation.

Here is the diary again:

> Dear diary, you have hampered me as an artist. But at the same time you have kept me alive as a human being. I created you because I needed a friend, and talking to this friend, I have, perhaps, wasted my life.
>
> Today I begin to work. Writing for a hostile world discouraged me. Writing for you gave me the illusion of a warm ambience I needed to flower in. But I must divorce you from my work. Not abandon you. No, I need your companionship. . . .
>
> Never have I seen as clearly as tonight that my diary writing is a vice. I came home worn out by magnificent talks with Henry at the cafe; I glided into my bedroom, closed the curtains, threw a log into the fire, lit a cigarette, pulled the diary out of its last hiding place under my dressing table, threw it on the ivory silk

quilt, and prepared for bed. I had the feeling that this is the way an opium smoker prepares for his opium pipe. For this is the moment when I relive my life in terms of a dream, a myth, an endless story.

This should perhaps prompt us to examine the opium content of our own private writings. To what extent are we cutting ourselves off, both from danger and each other? Certainly we need new forms of writing—women's forms—and a diary like this one offers another whole way of working and of thinking about our daily lives. But this private, complex, flowing kind of writing must be published, as only an inadequate portion of Anaïs Nin's diary has been thus far. Her friends and relatives are evidently resisting publication of certain parts of the diary. Out of deference to them, Anaïs Nin cuts herself off from the response of an audience.

People kept trying to get Anaïs Nin to stop writing the diary.

> Is Henry right? He does not want me to write a diary any more. He thinks it is a malady, an outgrowth of loneliness. I don't know. It has also become the notebook of my extroversion, a travel sketchbook: it is full of others. It has changed its aspect. I cannot abandon it, definitely. Henry says: "Lock up the journal, and swim. What I would like you to do is to live without the journal, and you would write other things."
>
> I would feel like a snail without its shell. Everyone has always stood in the way of the journal. My mother always urged me to go out and play. My brothers teased me, stole it, and made fun of it. It was a secret from my girl friends in school. Everyone said I would outgrow it. In Havana my aunt said it would spoil my eyes, frighten the boys away.

Otto Rank wanted her to give up the diary, too. "The diary is your last defense against analysis," he told her. "It is like a traffic island you want to stand on. If I am going to help you, I do not want you to have a traffic island from which you will survey the analysis, keep control of it. I do not want you to analyze the analysis. Do you understand?" For a time during the analysis, Anaïs Nin gave up the diary opium habit. Otto Rank comforted her during her withdrawal symptoms by saying, "Perhaps you may discover now what you want—to be a woman or an artist."

It is our good fortune Anaïs Nin never had the strength to make this absurd choice. Her strength lies elsewhere, in the diary itself. It was her traffic island, from which she judged them all.

In the diary she ceases to be a mirror for other people like Miller and Rank, and tries to become herself. But this is a terrible struggle. "... No one has ever loved an adventurous woman as they have loved adventurous men." So annihilating is this difference that the very images by which she expresses it are, of necessity, male:

> This struggle to live by my own truth is so difficult, so wearing. A terrible algebra, always. I am like the adventurer who leaves all those he loves, and returns with his arms full of gold; and then they are happy and they forget how they tried to keep this adventurer from exploring, from his voyage and his search.

A Woman's Place is in the Oven

by Sherry Sonnett Trumbo

Sherry Sonnett Trumbo is a writer who lives in California

One of the most valuable qualities of television is its ability to keep us in touch with the past. Tune in any time and there, in the form of countless old movies, the American past, unadorned and without comment, unwinds before our eyes. The movies of the past forty years provide a history of what this country was thinking, feeling, valuing, admiring, and condemning at any given time. The message may not be at all what was intended, since time has a way of distilling intentions until only actualities remain. But intended or not, the message is there and it is ours if we sit back and bear with the commercial interruptions.

The other night I watched a movie called "The Bachelor Party." Made in the middle 1950s, it's about a young married couple in New York. He works as a bookkeeper during the day and attends school four nights a week to qualify as a CPA. She discovers she's pregnant and that means *of course* she'll have to stop working (her job is so inconsequential that we never learn what it is), which is a blow both to the current finances and their future plans.

The wife, upset at first, quickly adjusts to the idea of parenthood and looks forward to it. The prospect of fatherhood, however, throws the husband into a crisis. Does he love his wife, does he want to be a CPA, is it all worth it?—"it all" meaning the emptiness, the boredom, the fatigue. In the course of a single night, he works it out with the help of assorted neurotics, including the standard nympho ("Just say you love me!"). In the end, he returns to his own bed and board, reaffirmed in his love for his wife, his desire for the baby, and the rightness of the course of his life. Somehow, the film seems to inform us, he has come through, he has grown up, he has accepted responsibility.

Well, what can you expect? The movie was made in the Fifties, right? And things have changed: if the movie was made now, the young man would see it's all hype—empty, pointless—and he would split, searching out who knows what, but at least free and together. Progress, right? May I now draw your attention to the little woman?

In both the actual and hypothetical versions of this story, it is the woman who represents home, family, and duty. Whether this is seen as security hence good, or security hence stultifying, the woman's role and position have not actually changed. In spite of all the progress we are eager to tell ourselves has been made in the last few years, we can count on the depiction of woman's place to be pretty much the same. ("A woman's place is in the oven.")

Lately, we have had a rash of "tell it like it is" movies—all with men as the central characters. These movies are about men who try the System and leave, or men who from the beginning have nothing to do with the System, or System men who somewhere toward the last reel begin to see the light. (Whether they really tell it like it is remains a question worth asking.) These men are at odds with society in one way or another and the story of each movie is the coming to terms with that conflict. Above all, the important characteristic these men share is their *awareness* that something is very wrong with the society as it reveals itself to them; they sense that the fault does not lie entirely within themselves, that it also lies in a society which forces them into dehumanizing, dead-end, and even unnatural roles.

To men watching these movies, it is relatively unimportant what a particular hero's problems are or what particular answers he finds, if any. The important thing is that the male audience has a chance to see a man, some man, trying to work out solutions and pursuing alternatives. Characters like Bobby in "Five Easy Pieces" and the driver in "Two-Lane Blacktop" give their male audience a model and a starting point. Depending on the degree of response and identification, men who see these movies are at least made aware that other men in other places are trying other possibilities. This almost subconscious transmission of abstract ideas is where the real power of any art form lies.

But where is the movie about a woman going through the same processes? Where is the movie that shows us what alternatives and possibilities are open to us as women? A script for that movie is probably lying right now on some female writer's desk—or more likely in her head, unwritten, because who would make it anyway?

For women, there are very few relevant models offered by movies or the rest of the culture that will help ease the fear and pain of liberation. Consider the movies just mentioned as useful to men. The girl in "Two-Lane Blacktop" screws her way around the country; if she didn't, it isn't likely the men in the movie would want her around for very long. At no time are we given a clue to who this girl is. She is not permitted to express a single desire, thought, or feeling. She is totally nonperson, without even the single emotion credited to the driver and the mechanic—love for the car, an inanimate object. In all fairness, it should be noted that *no one* in the movie is alive—it has a certain kind of austerity and super-coolness that is no more real in our time than college movies of the Thirties and Forties were in theirs.

In "Five Easy Pieces," Rayette, the waitress, is a typical dumb broad, great for shacking up with but you wouldn't want to introduce her to your family. She loves the lug even though he treats her mean. We've seen her many times before (Shirley MacLaine in "Some Came Running," for instance) and she's more than a bit dull. The second woman, the musician, is more interesting and for a while it looks as if she might have something original to say to us. On the surface, she is the new woman—active, purposeful, sure of herself. But, after all, she turns out to be what we know all women *really* are; turned on and conquered by brutality, she is a cold-hearted security seeker who denies our hero his one apparent chance of happiness.

Perhaps the most interesting female character in a recent movie is Olive, the wife in "Drive, He Said." Sister to Catherine in "Jules and Jim," she very clearly exemplifies the waste and confusion that make up the lives of most women. The fact that she must be described as the wife, while the men are the basketball player, the revolutionary, the professor, etc., is the sum of her problem. She is the victim of men's attitudes toward her. Indulged, placated, protected, she is partially forced and partially allowed to remain in a virtual state of childishness—irresponsible, unpredictable, without direction or purpose. Expected to do nothing, allowed to do noth-

ing, she slips into boredom and apathy, the central emotions of her
life.

This seeming contradiction is at the heart of the dilemma in
which women often find themselves—prized yet ignored, prized as
object, ignored as person. It is this that makes it extremely difficult
for many women to perceive the prison in which they live and com-
pels them to attribute their unhappiness to faults and neuroses
within themselves. Suffering from that particular despair which
comes from having nothing to do, unable to account for her condition or to see how she can change it, Olive can only alleviate it
through temporary distractions—adultery and, finally, pregnancy.
Of course she has contempt for the men around her; it is they who,
through unconscious conspiracy, keep her there.

By this time we can all cite the discrimination and the prejudices
with which we as women are confronted every day. But if we are to
go beyond this awakening, we must deal with the ways in which this
discrimination has damaged us. Above all, we must realize that it
has left us without any structures, traditions, or guidelines to support us in the search for freedom. Perhaps the bravest, the most
determined and the luckiest of us can make it on our own, but most
of us, in order even to start on the road to liberation, need some sort
of help. We need suggestions of possibilities. We need to know that
we are not alone and that we are not peculiar. We need to know
that others have tried, are trying, or want to try.

The fact is that almost nowhere in our culture and society are
women exposed to this knowledge. Women's Lib spokeswomen, as
presented by the media, are often the sort who alienate the average
woman, locked in as she is by concern for male reaction and appro-
bation—a concern only natural since in most cases she thinks her
very existence depends on a man. Indeed, so many women are so
afraid of the ideas of liberation that any direct approach is too
threatening. Never taught to function as total, independent beings,
these women don't believe they *can* assume full and total responsibility for their own lives. For them, it is safer to remain in a familiar
prison than to venture out into an unfamiliar freedom.

This is not cowardice. It is the understandable fear of, say, a
woman, married, out of the labor market or perhaps never in it,
totally dependent and totally defined by the man to whom she is
married. How is she to deal with the challenges thrown at her by

young women who have turned away from the ideas and values which she has been told make her life worthwhile? How is she to face the possibility that most of her life has been, if not exactly wasted, then at least a lot duller and emptier than it needed to have been? What is she to think of the women who tell her this? And how is she to prefer them to the men who tell her that she is right not to respond to these women who challenge her?

For these reasons we must realize that while a direct battle cry mobilizes some, it alienates others. We must make certain that the message is sent out in all sorts of ways, directly and indirectly, gently and stridently, subtly and outrageously.

Unfortunately, it is the subtle, gentle, and indirect voice that is completely smothered by the culture at large. Because the ideas of Women's Lib are so foreign and threatening to the people who control the dissemination of ideas in this society (men and some bamboozled women), and because they threaten very basic structures of the society, those ideas are rarely presented as a natural, completely integrated part of life. Rather, the process of liberation is always made to seem as if it requires special circumstances, special strength. We are made to think that any try at change and development will leave us isolated, irrevocably cut off from what has given us comfort and support in the past. No attempt is made to show how all of us can help each other, can support each other through shared experience with compassion and sympathy.

And yet it is this very idea of the necessity of shared experience and mutual aid that is at the heart of all aspects of Women's Lib— from equal pay for equal work to lesbian liberation. Only through mutual support and concerned action will all women, no matter what their political and social preferences, gain the right and *know* they have the right to live their lives in the way they choose. No one claims that all women must live in a certain way, but every woman must be free to select from all possibilities. All options must be open to her; it is she, and not society, who will close some of them. Women as a group will find liberation only through unity, but what we make of that liberation depends on who we are as individuals.

In the past, we were told that if we were good, quiet and didn't make any trouble, some of us would be allowed into the real world, the man's world. We were told that if we wanted to be among those few, we had better play by the rules and make the required adjustments. It was, for example, a woman who wrote "Five Easy Pieces," a fact which says a great deal about what women are forced to do in order to compete.

What we need now are women who speak, write, and act as women. There have always been women who have managed to "beat the system" and "make it in a man's world." But too often in the past, these women have jealously guarded their success and purposely disassociated themselves from other women. These are women whose identity and self-assurance comes precisely from viewing themselves as different from and better than other women. Tell them they think like a man and it is a compliment; tell them they are like a woman and it means weak and emotional. They would not wish to work for another woman, but are puzzled when they are not promoted or given jobs of real responsibility.

This must stop. Those of us who manage, despite all the odds, to achieve some influence and to speak where we can be heard, must learn to help each other. We must remember that we are only one of a larger group and that our strength as individuals is directly proportional to our strength as a group. We must learn to speak to each other, to make each other aware of our possibilities, capabilities, and alternatives. Our freedom will not be handed to us by society, but it will be taken when we as a group have the strength and force to demand it.

We must all do what we can, either by addressing ourselves directly to the issues of Women's Lib or by making sure that in all areas of our lives we don't bow to the demands and expectations of conventional male (and often female) thinking. No matter which road we follow, we all have two things to do: to liberate ourselves and to liberate each other. We can't do one without the other and we can't do either unless we do both.